A Pot of Paint

A Pot of Paint

Aesthetics on Trial in *Whistler v Ruskin*

Linda Merrill

Smithsonian Institution Press

Washington and London

in collaboration with The Freer Gallery of Art · Smithsonian Institution

Editor: Janet Pascal
Production editor: Jack Kirshbaum
Designer: Linda McKnight
Typesetter: Peter Strupp/Princeton Editorial Associates

Library of Congress Cataloging-in-Publication Data

Merrill, Linda, 1959–
A pot of paint : Aesthetics on trial in Whistler v. Ruskin / Linda Merrill.
p. cm.
Includes bibliographical references and index.
ISBN 1-56098-101-6
1. Whistler, James McNeill, 1834–1903—Trials, litigation, etc. 2. Ruskin, John, 1819–1900—Trials, litigation, etc. 3. Trials (Libel)—England—London. 4. Whistler, James McNeill, 1834–1903. Nocturne in black and gold, the falling rocket. 5. Whistler, James McNeill, 1834–1903—Criticism and interpretation. I. Title.
KD379.W47M47 1992
345.42′0256—dc20
[344.205256] 91-10802

British Library Cataloging-in-Publication data available

Color plates printed in Hong Kong by South China Printing Company. All other elements printed in the United States of America

96 95 94 93 92 5 4 3 2 1

∞ The paper used in this publication meets the minimum requirements of the American National Standard for Permanence of Paper for Printed Library Materials Z39.48-1948.

Jacket illustration: detail from James McNeill Whistler, *Nocturne in Black and Gold* (ca. 1875), oil on panel (later titled *Nocturne in Black and Gold: The Falling Rocket*). Detroit Institute of Arts, Michigan; gift of Dexter M. Ferry, Jr. © Detroit Institute of Arts.

Frontispiece: photograph of Whistler by the London Stereoscopic Company, signed and dated 1878. Charles Lang Freer Papers, Freer Gallery of Art/Arthur M. Sackler Gallery Archives. Courtesy of the Freer Gallery of Art, Smithsonian Institution, Washington, D.C.

Mr. Whistler is clever and original,
but he will never hit upon anything more original in art
than the device of settling abstruse artistic questions
by an appeal to an intelligent British jury.

The Spectator, 30 November 1878

CONTENTS

FOREWORD

Charles Lang Freer, the Detroit industrialist who founded the Freer Gallery of Art, never encountered the contentious side of Whistler's personality that made an art of making enemies. His association with the artist was entirely amicable, and after Whistler's death in 1903 Freer said that he had never known a truer, nobler man. If Whistler had been belligerent, Freer maintained, it was only because his contemporaries had been insensitive to genius.

In 1890, when Freer met Whistler, Freer's collecting was confined mainly to prints. As his fortunes rose, he began to acquire oil paintings, and in 1892 he purchased *Variations in Flesh Colour and Green: The Balcony,* the first major work by Whistler to come to America. A few years later, Whistler told Freer that he wanted to help him assemble a fine collection of Whistlers—perhaps, he said, *the* collection. Whistler's wish to have his most important works congregated in America emerged from his growing disaffection from the English. The French government's purchase of Whistler's *Mother* for the Musée du Luxembourg in 1891 had enhanced Whistler's international reputation and the monetary value of his works. Consequently, paintings bought for a few pounds in the days of *Whistler v. Ruskin*—when the question of the supposedly inflated price of the "falling rocket" nocturne had dominated the debate—were beginning to be sold for tremendous profits by their original owners. Although the change in the English climate afforded Whistler some "mischievous pleasure," he confided to Freer, the disloyalty of his compatriots rankled and, to prevent further speculation in England, Whistler determined to sell his works to appreciative collectors outside the country.

Whistler's decision to cultivate Freer as the premier collector of his art resulted in the extensive collection preserved at the Freer Gallery, which includes over twelve hundred paintings, prints, and drawings from every stage of the artist's career, as well as Whistler's only surviving interior decoration, the Peacock Room. Although Freer officially conveyed the title to his collection to the Smithsonian Institution in 1906, he reserved the right to add to his holdings and dedicated the rest of his life to refining the collection and designing a museum to house it. Freer also acquired an important collection of Asian art, partly at Whistler's instigation, and he envisioned a setting in which works by Whistler would be displayed together with "masterpieces of certain periods of high civilization," as he explained his intention, "harmonious in spiritual suggestion." In 1923, when the Freer Gallery of Art opened to the public, those who recognized the artist's influence considered the museum to be Freer's monument to Whistler.

In addition to a comprehensive collection of Whistler's art, Freer carefully assembled copies of books, letters, photographs, exhibition catalogues, and other reference materials relevant to the artist's life and works. These resources are preserved in the library and archives of the Freer Gallery of Art, and, combined with the vast Pennell-Whistler Collection at the Library of Congress, they make Washington, D.C., a center for Whistler scholarship. Linda Merrill, Associate Curator of American Art at the Freer Gallery, has studied the collections in both Washington and Glasgow (where even more of Whistler's papers are preserved) and has produced a lively and informative reconstruction and documentation of *Whistler v. Ruskin,* a critical episode in the artist's career. Dr. Merrill's extensive discussion of the background and aftermath of the lawsuit adds substantially to our understanding of Whistler's art and times, and her reconstruction of the trial is in itself a valuable reference work.

FOREWORD

Through its collections and archives, the Freer Gallery has long provided diverse materials for understanding an important period of artistic taste in America. Dr. Merrill's excellent study greatly extends our understanding of contextual matters, incorporating issues as interesting to the social or literary historian as to the scholar of art. The gallery presents her work with great pleasure.

MILO C. BEACH
DIRECTOR,
FREER GALLERY
OF ART

ACKNOWLEDGMENTS

Research for this book began ten years ago as part of my postgraduate course at the University of London, and I remain grateful to the Marshall Aid Commemoration Commission for the scholarship that allowed me to study art history in the incomparable libraries and collections of Great Britain. William Vaughan, who supervised my work at University College, saw potential in a subject that might easily have seemed already overworked; his insights into English aestheticism helped me frame a thesis in which the Whistler/Ruskin trial figured as a central event. Dr. Vaughan and Leonée Ormond, the readers of my dissertation, suggested that I turn the story of the trial into a book, and when a few years later I took up the topic again, it was because of their encouragement.

At the Freer Gallery of Art, former director Thomas Lawton supported my application to the Smithsonian Institution Regents' Publication Program, which granted me a leave of absence to rethink and rewrite my dissertation away from the distractions of curatorial responsibilities; the fellowship also underwrote many of the costs involved in preparing the manuscript for publication and provided much of my motivation to do so. Milo Beach, director of the Freer Gallery of Art and the Arthur M. Sackler Gallery, continued to uphold the museum's commitment to scholarship in American art, showing his support of this project in particular by allowing me the time and resources necessary to complete it.

To reconstruct the history of the Whistler/Ruskin trial, I depended on the expertise and patience of numerous librarians and archivists, especially those in charge of collections in the manuscripts division of the Library of Congress in Washington and the newspaper division of the British Library in London. I am indebted to Nigel Thorp, Deputy Keeper of Special Collections at the Glasgow University Library, and to Kevin Sharp of the Department of Prints and Drawings at the Art Institute of Chicago, whose perseverance on my behalf was courteous and constant. At the Freer Gallery library and archives, Lily Kecskes, Kathryn Phillips, Reiko Yoshimura, and Colleen Hennessey were unfailingly generous with their time and assistance.

For information and advice, virtually every student of Whistler's work consults Margaret F. MacDonald, Honorary Research Fellow at the Hunterian Art Gallery in Glasgow and a leading scholar in the field. I am grateful for the comments she made on the manuscript, and I look forward to the friendly disagreements on matters of opinion that I feel certain lie ahead. Representing the other side of the controversy, Kristine Ottesen Garrigan of DePaul University, an authority on Ruskin's art criticism, reviewed the text and offered cogent suggestions that strengthened the content of this book. Dr. Garrigan also called to my attention important sources I'd neglected, and her own distinguished publications enlarged my understanding of Ruskin's point of view.

At the Smithsonian Institution Press, acquisitions editor Amy Pastan and managing editor Ruth Spiegel ably oversaw the production of this book. Janet Pascal, the editor, approached the manuscript with extraordinary sensitivity, making what I had feared might be a painful process a pleasure; and Linda McKnight, the designer, transformed a complicated structure into a pleasing arrangement of words and pictures. During the final stages of the project, Mary Jones efficiently attended to numerous details. I owe many thanks to the individuals and institutions that allowed me to publish as illustrations works in their collections; to the University Court of the University of Glasgow for granting me permission to quote from Whistler's correspondence; and to Rayner Unwin of Unwin Hyman Ltd., who graciously permitted me to reprint as an appendix Ruskin's previously unpublished instructions to counsel.

Several friends and colleagues have facilitated my research through the years. I would like to especially acknowledge the help of Martha Severens, who assisted my investigation of Whistler's *Portrait of Miss Florence Leyland* at the Portland Museum of Art; of John Siewert, who read an early draft of the manuscript while writing his own dissertation on Whistler and offered constructive comments and kind encouragement; and of Charles Merrill, who tracked down an obscure reference to *Whistler v. Ruskin* in a Barcelona periodical and provided a translation from the Catalan for his sister. My enduring gratitude goes to Alastair and Jacqueline Wardlaw, whose hospitality brightened my days in Glasgow, and to David and Marilyn Clark, who opened their home to me in London. Ed Davis, whose friendship sustained me through the production of both the dissertation and the book, not only untangled for me the complicated legal issues raised by the trial but greatly improved the text with his discerning editorial eye. Maggie Edson, as always, and in too many ways to mention, helped me eliminate muddle.

Finally, I wish to thank my father, John C. Merrill, whose eagerness to see this work in print hastened its completion. His professional dedication to journalistic ethics underlies my own interest in libel and probably induced me to pore over nineteenth-century newspapers in pursuit of the truth about *Whistler v. Ruskin,* which could only be recovered from the pages of the press.

The publication of this book was made possible
by an award from the Smithsonian Regents Publication Program

INTRODUCTION

THE OFFICIAL TRANSCRIPT of *Whistler v. Ruskin (1877. W. 818),* the most celebrated lawsuit in the history of art, was once considered insufficiently important to merit preservation. After the action was settled in 1878, when no appeal was made, the court record was destroyed as a matter of course, depriving posterity of the complete and unbiased account of that singular event. The particulars of the testimony, therefore, are for the most part irretrievable.

Nevertheless, the story of the trial is familiar from frequent retelling. In 1877, having seen several paintings by James McNeill Whistler at the new Grosvenor Gallery in London, John Ruskin condemned *Nocturne in Black and Gold: The Falling Rocket* (plate 1) in a periodical of limited circulation called *Fors Clavigera.* "I have seen, and heard, much of Cockney impudence before now," Ruskin wrote, "but never expected to hear a coxcomb ask two hundred guineas for flinging a pot of paint in the public's face."[1] Whistler sued the critic for libel, claiming substantial damages, and the case went to court in November 1878; Ruskin himself was ill and psychologically unfit to appear. After two days of evidence from the plaintiff and several witnesses, the jury declared a verdict in Whistler's favor, but awarded him only a farthing in damages.

Whistler v. Ruskin is an event that lends itself to fictionalization; it has been dramatized on radio more than once and reenacted on stages as far apart as Hampstead and Detroit.[2] Latter-day accounts have often relied on anecdotes of questionable authenticity passed down through the decades. Even in its own time, the trial inspired scores of stories, some made legendary by Whistler himself. Whistler's "The Action," first published in 1890, twelve years after the trial took place, introduces *The Gentle Art of Making Enemies,* a collection of the artist's letters to the press and other writings on art. Whistler used Ruskin's defamatory paragraph as the prologue for a "transcript" of the trial drawn primarily from contemporary newspaper reports. He annotated his quasifictional account like a scholarly treatise, embellishing the margins with quotations from Ruskin he found particularly absurd and with his own "reflections," sarcastic comments signed with barb-tailed butterflies. He pointedly omitted the testimony of the three witnesses who spoke on his behalf, so that the victory, such as it was, could be construed as his alone. He also took the opportunity to polish his performance, recasting his courtroom speeches with the grace and wit he had lost from time to time under pressure in the witness box. With no true transcript for comparison, the plaintiff's own rendition of *Whistler v. Ruskin* has largely shaped our understanding of the events.[3]

Were it not for the Victorian tendency to commit even things of passing importance to print, the true story of the trial might have been lost altogether. The popular press is as inappropriate a place for transmitting aesthetic theory as the courtroom is for expounding it; nevertheless, *Whistler v. Ruskin*—an occasion overwhelmed by its own publicity—was an early flowering of that twentieth-century phenomenon, the media event. At least a dozen English newspapers published substantial accounts in their legal pages. Although presumably composed from notes correspondents had taken down in court, these reports are often garbled and inaccurate, and always incomplete. The account in the inveterate *Times* is exceptionally brief (and apparently tempered with a Ruskinian bias), but a number of other London papers contain accounts that are useful in framing a picture of the proceedings; the *Evening Standard,* for example, published a relatively complete report—perhaps because the case was of special interest to Londoners, for whom the paper was particularly intended.

The fragmentary testimony preserved in the press forms the substance of the partial reconstruction of the trial in Part Two of this book, for which Appendix C outlines the method of redaction and lists sources and significant textual variants. This text is not a word-for-word transcription of extant Victorian newspaper reports, yet it remains close in style and content to the sources from which it derives, and it purports to present a rendition of *Whistler v. Ruskin* that is clear, correct, objective, and intelligible. The reconstructed transcript, with surviving pieces of testimony restored to their original positions, affords an illuminating reevaluation of the trial. The judge emerges as more judicious, the jury more perplexed, the attorney general more sarcastic, William Michael Rossetti more discerning, Albert Moore more modern, Edward Burne-Jones more equivocating, William Powell Frith more ridiculous, Serjeant Parry more persuasive, Tom Taylor more pedantic, and William Gorman Wills more confused, than in any previously published account of *Whistler v. Ruskin.*

Perhaps the most surprising discovery is the part played by Whistler himself. His own representation of the trial in *The Gentle Art of Making Enemies* creates the impression that the laughter punctuating the proceedings was invariably inspired by his own clever repartee. In fact, the attorney general endeavored to make Whistler look ridiculous, not only in order to corroborate Ruskin's characterization of the artist as a coxcomb but also to induce the jury to award contemptuous damages; as a result, Whistler's wit was often upstaged by the humor at his expense.

Unfortunately, no amount of research can conjure Ruskin to the scene. The evidence he might have given in court can be inferred, however, from the extensive memorandum of instruction he prepared for his counsel in hopes of influencing the defense strategy. A revised version of those instructions, entitled "My Own Article on Whistler," was published posthumously as an appendix to the Library Edition of Ruskin's complete works, but the original text survives only as a manuscript copy in the defendant's brief. Ruskin's memorandum appears in Appendix A as the defendant's testimony in absentia.

The circumstances surrounding the trial of *Whistler v. Ruskin* can be thoroughly documented through a wealth of papers assembled by Joseph and Elizabeth Robins Pennell, the artist's devoted friends and biographers. The Pennell-Whistler Collection in the Library of Congress contains nine boxes of material pertaining to the trial, including the correspondence of Whistler and his solicitor, J. Anderson Rose; legal briefs for both plaintiff and defendant; draft and fair copies of pleadings; subpoenas, motions, and answers to interrogatories; Rose's detailed bill of costs; copy extracts from newspaper articles and the writings of Ruskin; suggestions for witnesses' proofs; and manuscript notes on courtroom strategy.

Those letters and documents had not yet come into the Pennells' hands when their *Life of James McNeill Whistler* was first published in 1908. The authors' understanding of events therefore remained relatively uninformed, and their chapter on *Whistler v. Ruskin* heightens the glory of Whistler's performance and trivializes Ruskin's achievement.[4] The year after the *Life* was published, Edward A. Parry, a British barrister and the son of Whistler's legal advocate John H. Parry, wrote Joseph Pennell to inquire whether the legal documents relating to the lawsuit survived; he enclosed a copy of an important letter from Whistler to Rose that happened to be in his possession.[5] Ten years later the papers of Anderson Rose surfaced in New York, and the Pennells purchased them for their burgeoning collection of Whistleriana.[6]

Parry maintained an interest in *Whistler v. Ruskin,* and in 1921, motivated by a fortuitous encounter with the defendant's brief in the offices of Walker Martineau & Co., the firm of Ruskin's solicitors, published an article on the subject in which the contents of Ruskin's memorandum of instruction were first disclosed.[7] The Pennells saw the article in the *Cornhill Magazine* (their copy remains in their collected papers) and wrote immediately to inform Parry that since their last correspondence they had acquired Whistler's legal papers. Parry subsequently obtained the Ruskin documents on their behalf, making the Pennells' collection of papers relating to *Whistler v. Ruskin* virtually complete.

At the time that this important acquisition was made, the Pennells were preparing a compendium of notes and recollections about the artist called *The Whistler Journal,* published in 1921. In an illuminating but frequently overlooked appendix, they describe and begin to assess the documents recently added to their collection. The articles that occasioned the most surprise were Ruskin's memorandum, which the Pennells considered more outrageous than the libel itself, and the written opinion of the chief witness for the defense, Edward Burne-Jones, given for the benefit of Ruskin's counsel. Because that statement had never before been made public, the extensive extracts in *The Whistler Journal* revealed for the first time Burne-Jones's duplicity, although the Pennells discounted his obvious enmity toward Whistler with the observation that "his attitude was not exceptional among Whistler's contemporaries."[8] Burne-Jones's statement, reprinted in Appendix B, provides a sort of subtext to the testimony he presented, with alleged reluctance, in court.

The eight Grosvenor Gallery exhibits that provoked Ruskin to write his immortal critique would eventually enjoy the public's appreciation and respect, but until the turn of the century they continued to suffer various indignities. The unsold portraits were pawned or defaced in the financial turmoil that followed the trial, although the portrait of Thomas Carlyle (plate 2), often considered the exception to Whistler's usual style, was purchased by the city of Glasgow in 1891. Whistler's *Nocturne in Blue and Silver* (plate 3) was "received with hisses" when it appeared at auction in 1886, a demonstration signaling the audience's antipathy toward the artist, the painting, or both. Whistler apparently accepted the negative publicity with pleasure, writing a letter to the *Observer* to acknowledge that a distinguished, if unconscious, compliment had been paid him: "It is rare that recognition, so complete, is made during the lifetime of the painter, and I would wish to have recorded my full sense of this flattering exception in my favour." The nocturne eventually entered the collection of the Tate Gallery in London, where it is now regarded as one of the treasures of the museum.[9]

The notorious *Nocturne in Black and Gold,* the most abstract and abused of Whistler's paintings, remained unsold until 1892, when an American, Samuel Untermeyer, bought it for eight hundred guineas. Fourteen years had passed since the trial, but Whistler had not yet begun to forget the terms of Ruskin's critique. He was eager, therefore, for the news to be heard that "the Pot of paint flung into the face of the British Public for two hundred guineas has now sold for four pots of paint, and that Ruskin has lived to see it!" The sale of the nocturne was a "commercial slap" in Ruskin's face, Whistler said, "the only rebuff understood or appreciated in his country."[10]

In matters of art, a verdict is best left to posterity, and it is Whistler's point of view that has survived into the twentieth century. At the time of the trial, traditional artistic standards were already in decline, with subject pictures and "finished" pictures beginning to fall from their customary preeminence. In 1878 there was no word in the lexicon to signify nonrepresentational art: Whistler could not simply say that his nocturnes were nearly "abstract," although by suggesting that color conveyed meaning and that painting was analogous to music, he defined abstraction without naming it. When Whistler's contemporaries did not see his paintings as travesties, they considered them to be prophecies. Ruskin, with his idealistic devotion to the past, was called the Don Quixote of art, Whistler, the artist of the future. Indeed, from the modern perspective, Ruskin's libelous figure of speech evokes the literal paint-slinging of Pollock, and Whistler's explanation of art as an arrangement of color calls to mind the paintings of Mondrian. *Whistler v. Ruskin,* a story of trial and error, marks a critical hour in the evolution of modern art.

PART ONE

THE LIBEL

THE PALACE OF ART

IN THE SPRING OF 1877 an undergraduate on suspension from Oxford, Oscar Wilde, attended the inaugural exhibition of the Grosvenor Gallery, wearing a coat made to resemble a cello. His aesthetic sensibilities already unfolding under the influence of Walter Pater and John Ruskin, Wilde wrote a rhapsodic review of the exhibition for the *Dublin University Magazine,* his first foray into art criticism. "Taking a general view of the works exhibited here," he wrote, "we see that this dull land of England with its short summer, its dreary rains and fogs, its mining districts, and factories, and vile deification of machinery, has yet produced very great masters of art, men with a subtle sense and love of what is beautiful, original, and noble in imagination." Wilde regarded the founding of the Grosvenor Gallery as part of an English renaissance, a "revival of culture and love of beauty," born of the writings of Ruskin.[1]

Although Wilde's review would have attracted little attention from his contemporaries, it reveals the tendency to reconcile the philosophies of Ruskin and Pater—and thus the demands of conscience and imagination—that would characterize the English aesthetic movement. Britain's poet laureate, Alfred, Lord Tennyson, had confronted the ideological conflict in "The Palace of Art," an allegory of a soul who resides for years in splendid isolation, "a quiet king," before recognizing the error of living exclusively for art and rejoining the

Fig. 1. Photograph of Sir Coutts Lindsay by Julia Margaret Cameron, ca. 1865. National Portrait Gallery, London

natural world. That the Grosvenor Gallery was a veritable palace of art did not pass unnoticed: inspired by the inaugural exhibition, *Punch* published a pastiche of Tennyson's poem in which a "man of taste" happily inhabits a "lordly picture-place" until he, too, suffers the fate of the aesthetic soul and comes to despise beauty divorced from life. "Give me green leaves and flesh and blood," the connoisseur cries, "fresh air and light of day."[2]

The model for *Punch*'s man of taste was the proprietor of the Grosvenor Gallery, Coutts Lindsay of Balcarres (fig. 1), a baronet and banker renowned for his good looks. Sir Coutts was introduced to the society of London artists by C. E. Hallé, the painter who was appointed manager of the gallery; almost every week for over a year Sir Coutts and his wife, Lady Lindsay (whose fortune effectively funded the project), entertained two or three artists for dinner and discussion

Fig. 2. "The Grosvenor Gallery of Fine Art, New Bond-street," *Illustrated London News,* 5 May 1877

of the proposed exhibition. Unlike the illustrious Royal Academy of Arts, the Grosvenor Gallery was to have no selection committee—exhibition would be "solely on Sir Coutts Lindsay's invitation."[3] James McNeill Whistler, one of the chosen artists, was particularly enchanted with the exclusivity of the scheme, imagining that the gallery might open to the public with a single picture on display, presumably one of his own.[4]

The Grosvenor Gallery was intended to celebrate the achievements of modern British artists, many of whom looked to the past for inspiration. The building on New Bond Street was accordingly fashioned in Renaissance style, constructed around a Palladian doorway salvaged from the Venetian church of Santa Lucia. The interior was luxuriant, with crimson damask wall hangings, velvet couches, Persian carpets, marble tables, Minton china, fresh flowers, and rainbow glass globes; silver stars and moons shimmered from the coved ceiling of the main gallery (fig. 2), which was modeled on the studio of the Lindsays' house in Cromwell Place.[5] The glitter of the "upholstery," as Ruskin referred to the interior decoration, received mixed reactions from reviewers. Tom Taylor, art critic for *The Times,* supposed that English eyes might find the brilliance harsh or overwhelming; Oscar Wilde, who delighted in every detail, considered the resplendent setting entirely "in harmony with the surrounding works of art."[6]

The 209 paintings and sculptures chosen for the opening exhibition, tastefully displayed and grouped by artist, seemed to be shown in the private residence of an acquisitive connoisseur rather than in a conventional, commercial picture gallery.[7] The sensitive arrangement afforded "freedom from fatigue," and the relatively small size of the exhibition halls eliminated the "terrible weariness of mind and eye" that often afflicted dedicated art lovers.[8] The Royal Academy, in comparison, appeared "too large and too vulgar," as Lord Henry Wotton would proclaim in *The Picture of Dorian Gray.* "Whenever I have gone there, there have been either so many people that I have not been able to see the pictures, which was dreadful, or so many pictures that I have not been able to see the people, which was worse. The Grosvenor is really the only place."[9]

The Grosvenor directors would persistently maintain that the gallery had not been founded in opposition to the Royal Academy,[10] but competition was inevitable. Several independent galleries—the Dudley Gallery, the New British Institute, and the Fine Art Society—had been established earlier in the 1870s as exhibition venues for artists neglected by the public, specifically those whose works had been rejected by the Royal Academy committee. The Grosvenor Gallery served a similar purpose, as Sir Coutts explained to the guests at an inaugural banquet, stating that he had deliberately chosen artists "whose works have not been so much known . . . as I could have wished." But many established artists—including several academicians—had been invited to exhibit as well, and that fact alone should

Fig. 3. Edward Linley Sambourne, "Welcome, Little Stranger!" *Punch,* 12 May 1877

sufficiently prove, Sir Coutts announced to a cheering assembly, that he bore no hostility to the august institution in Piccadilly.[11]

Perhaps because G. F. Watts, John Everett Millais, Edward J. Poynter, and Lawrence Alma-Tadema were sending some of their works to the Grosvenor Gallery that season, the Royal Academy's 1877 summer exhibition at Burlington House was "decidedly below the average," *Vanity Fair* reported, and virtually empty of visitors. At the Grosvenor Gallery, on the other hand, seven thousand people came the first morning alone.[12] The Royal Academy's hauteur, however, was hardly disturbed by the new "emporium of high art." As Edward Linley Sambourne illustrated so precisely in *Punch* (fig. 3), its attitude toward the Grosvenor was a kind of noblesse oblige. Crowned with royal patronage and flaunting faces in its tail so famous they require no identification, the "R.A. Cock of the Walk" greets the "Bond Street Bird of (Art) Paradise," a faceless creature, newly hatched, that hovers above a Coutts & Co. check conspicuously signed by the gallery's founder: the peacock patronizing the parvenu.

Indeed, the glamorous Grosvenor could never completely overcome the unfortunate aura of new money. It attempted to transcend the taint of commercialism by advertising the few works offered for sale with tact and discretion. A note at the beginning of the catalogue informed visitors that works still in the artists' possession were generally available for purchase, and that their prices could be obtained upon application. Nevertheless, the insinuation that the proprietor had purchased the right to show paintings of his own—which, as many pointed out, were prominently displayed in the exhibition—cast an opprobrious shadow over the entire enterprise; the Grosvenor was bound to appear a haven for outcast artists who happened to know the right people.

When he estimated the vulgarity of a purchased gallery in terms of pounds, Sambourne neglected to account for the value of honorable intentions. Sir Coutts may have desired an appropriate venue for the exhibition (and sale) of his own and Lady Lindsay's works, but he also wished to cultivate good taste and encourage the fine arts, to assist what Ruskin called the "promulgation of Art-knowledge."[13] The importance the Grosvenor Gallery would assume in the history of the aesthetic movement is suggested by Dante Gabriel Rossetti's letter to *The Times* published a month before the opening. Rossetti, who declined to show his own works in the new art gallery, predicted that the venture would succeed, if only for its association with "a name representing the loveliest art we have," that of Edward Burne-Jones.[14]

Burne-Jones (fig. 4), who would come to play an important part in the fall of Whistler's fortunes, had been Rossetti's protégé and a founding member of the decorative arts firm Morris, Marshall, Faulkner & Company. Under the influence of certain Italian Renaissance artists—particularly Botticelli and Mantegna, whose works he had encountered on a trip to Italy with his friend Ruskin—Burne-Jones had modified his early medievalizing manner and developed a distinctive, and to some eyes eccentric, artistic style. The course of his career had changed abruptly in 1870, when he sent to an exhibition at the

Fig. 4. George Howard, *Edward Burne-Jones,* ca. 1875, pencil on paper. National Portrait Gallery, London

Old Water Colour Society an illustration to a tale from Ovid, *Phyllis and Demophöon,* which bore the epigraph, "Tell me, what have I done, except not wisely love?" Either because of Demophöon's nudity or a possible embarrassing allusion to the artist's personal affairs, the painting was declared indecent and removed from the walls.[15] Burne-Jones had subsequently resigned from the society, for reasons, he said, of artistic integrity. From then until the opening of the Grosvenor Gallery in 1877, his works were seldom publicly displayed.

Although the Victorian public remained unfamiliar with Burne-Jones's art, his paintings were "the object of enthusiastic admiration,"

Fig. 5. Edward Burne-Jones, *The Fifth Day of Creation,* 1870–76, watercolor, shell gold, and gouache on linen mounted on paper. Exhibited Grosvenor Gallery 1877, no. 60. Courtesy of the Fogg Art Museum, Harvard University, Cambridge, Mass.; bequest of Grenville L. Winthrop

Fig. 6. Edward Burne-Jones, *The Beguiling of Merlin*, 1870–74, oil on canvas. Exhibited Grosvenor Gallery 1877, no. 59. Courtesy of the Trustees of the National Museums and Galleries on Merseyside (Lady Lever Art Gallery, Port Sunlight), Liverpool, England

the artist Walter Crane observed, "by an inner circle of devoted admirers."[16] One of Burne-Jones's first and most supportive patrons was William Graham, a Liberal member of Parliament from Glasgow who began purchasing the artist's paintings in 1856; another was Frederick R. Leyland, a Liverpool shipping magnate who met Burne-Jones in the 1860s through their mutual friend Gabriel Rossetti. Sir Coutts Lindsay, although not a patron, appears to have been another devoted admirer of Burne-Jones, for at the opening exhibition of the Grosvenor Gallery the works of that little-known artist occupied a wall to themselves in the West Gallery opposite paintings by the eminent G. F. Watts.

At the center of Burne-Jones's display hung *The Days of Creation* (see fig. 5), six narrow panels in which the story from Genesis takes place in iridescent spheres that Botticellian angels hold like crystal balls. On one side was *The Mirror of Venus,* a painting of handmaidens peering into a pool, owned by F. S. Ellis, a collector and publisher of fine books who was also a friend of Ruskin's; on the other was *The Beguiling of Merlin* (fig. 6), a melancholy illustration of the French medieval tale of Merlin and Nimuë, painted for the drawing room of Leyland's London home. Arranged above those major works were three smaller allegorical paintings, *Temperantia, Fides,* and *Spes* (Temperance, Faith, and Hope), all commissioned by Ellis; and two others, *A Sibyl* and *Saint George,* designated in the catalogue as "unfinished," that remained in the artist's possession.[17]

In front of the paintings by Burne-Jones the crowd was perceptibly thicker than elsewhere, Henry James remarked in the *Nation,* alluding to the comparatively unpopular pictures by Whistler arrayed on another wall of the same exhibition gallery.[18] Whistler's fame and notoriety had been steadily increasing during the years that Burne-Jones had all but disappeared from sight. Even so, as the critic Joseph Comyns Carr observed, in 1877 Whistler's "claims as an artist were not seriously entertained beyond the limits of a very narrow circle."[19] To many Grosvenor visitors, Whistler's paintings appeared to be the empty canvases described by the author of the *Punch* "Palace of Art": "Fit for each vacuous mood of mind, The gray and gravelike, vague and void, were there Most dismally designed."[20]

WHISTLER'S WORK

WHISTLER CUSTOMARILY remarked that nationality was to him inconsequential and testified at the trial of *Whistler v. Ruskin* that he had been born in St. Petersburg, Russia. The artist's birthplace, in fact, was Lowell, Massachusetts. In 1843, at the age of nine, he had moved with his family to Russia, where his father oversaw construction of the Moscow–St. Petersburg railroad, and Whistler began a course in drawing at the Imperial Academy of Fine Arts; for several formative years he lived like a little prince on the banks of the Neva. When he was sixteen, Whistler became a cadet at the United States Military Academy, but he proved unsuited to discipline and after three years was discharged from West Point. Later, at the Coast and Geodetic Survey in Washington, he learned the rudiments of etching. But Whistler's life as an artist did not begin until he departed for Paris in 1855.

Intending to live the bohemian life, Whistler immediately adopted the attitude of a struggling artist and occupied at least nine addresses during the three years he spent in the Latin Quarter. Six months after his arrival he enrolled in the atelier of Charles-Gabriel Gleyre, an artist who followed the classical tradition of Ingres, and befriended a circle of English art students that included Poynter, L. M. Lamont, Thomas Armstrong, and George Du Maurier. None of them could later recall Whistler doing any work in Paris, and Du Maurier

Fig. 7. Spy [Leslie Ward], "A Symphony," 1878, chromolithograph. "Men of the Day, No. CLXX: Mr. James Abbott M'Neill Whistler," *Vanity Fair,* 12 January 1878

would characterize him in *Trilby,* a novel about their student days, as "the idle apprentice."[1] Eventually Whistler fell under the influence of Gustave Courbet and adopted his antiacademic position. The paintings and prints Whistler produced in France manifested his allegiance to what Baudelaire called the heroism of modern life.

Even after settling in England in 1859, Whistler migrated frequently between London and Paris, further confusing the question of

Fig. 8. James McNeill Whistler, *An Artist in His Studio,* ca. 1856, ink and pencil on paper. Inscribed by Whistler, "J. Whistler Au 5me No. 7 Rue Galeres, Quartier Latin/Fuseli." Courtesy of the Freer Gallery of Art, Smithsonian Institution, Washington, D.C., 06.104

his nationality; many of his contemporaries, including counsel for the defense in the Ruskin trial, regarded him as "partly American and partly French." Whistler began to establish a reputation in London, sending several etchings and an oil painting to the Royal Academy's annual exhibition in 1860. *At the Piano* (fig. 9) satisfied the realist demand for modern subjects but hinted through its musical theme at

Fig. 9. James McNeill Whistler, *At the Piano,* 1858–59, oil on canvas. Taft Museum, Cincinnati, Ohio; bequest of Mr. and Mrs. Charles Phelps Taft, 1962.7

Whistler's incipient aestheticism. The painting, which had been rejected the previous year by the Paris Salon, was accorded a place of honor at Burlington House, where it hung at eye level, "on the line." Among its admirers were the president of the Royal Academy, Sir Charles Eastlake; the Pre-Raphaelite painter Millais; and John Phillip, an academician, who purchased it from the exhibition.[2] Bolstered by this success, Whistler continued to submit works to the academy, and his paintings were shown in almost every summer exhibition of the 1860s.

Whistler grew increasingly dissatisfied with painting modern life and gradually replaced his realism with the aesthetic attitude—an

Fig. 10. James McNeill Whistler, *Symphony in White, No. 1: The White Girl,* 1862, oil on canvas. National Gallery of Art, Washington, D.C.; Harris Whittemore Collection

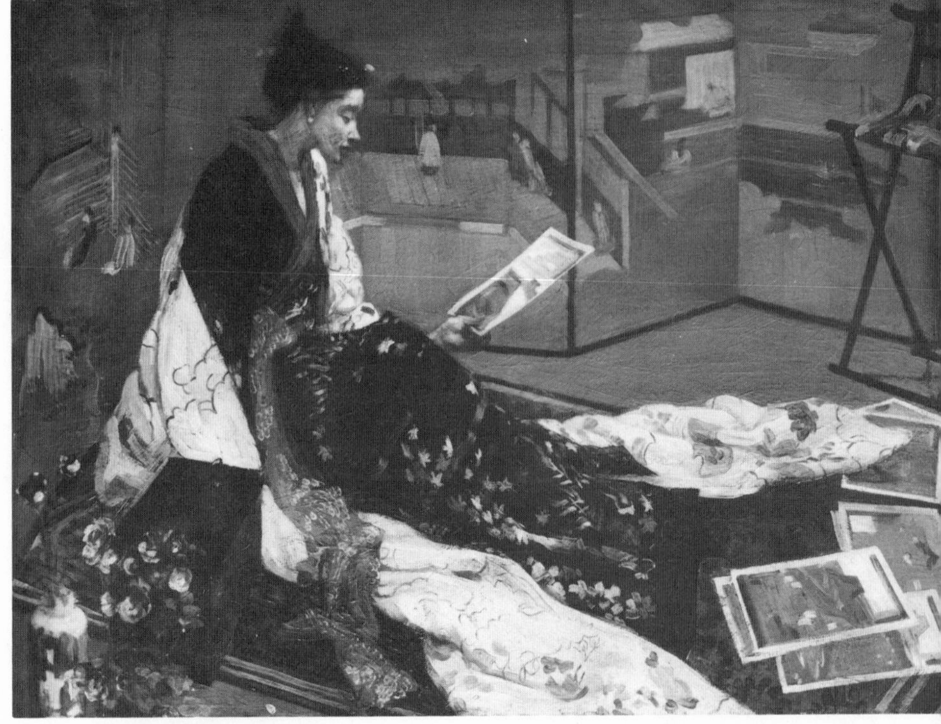

Fig. 11. James McNeill Whistler, *Caprice in Purple and Gold: The Golden Screen,* 1864, oil on panel. Courtesy of the Freer Gallery of Art, Smithsonian Institution, Washington, D.C., 04.75

interest in art for art's sake—displayed in works by certain Victorian painters. In subject and composition, Whistler's *White Girl* (fig. 10) suggests the influence of the Pre-Raphaelites, particularly Millais, although Whistler may have borrowed the device of white on white from *Ecce Ancilla Domini,* Rossetti's radical representation of the Annunciation. Whistler insisted that *The White Girl* was "a piece of pure painting," but to the literal-minded public the picture of a melancholy young woman in white standing on a bearskin rug strewn with fallen flowers appeared to involve something more than an exercise in color. To escape the story-telling tendency of Victorian pictures,

Fig. 12. James McNeill Whistler, *Symphony in White, No. 3,* 1867, oil on canvas. Barber Institute of Fine Arts, University of Birmingham, England

Whistler, like Rossetti, began to display a penchant for subjects remote from modern life. Paintings such as *Purple and Rose: The Lange Leizen of the Six Marks* and *Caprice in Purple and Gold: The Golden Screen* (fig. 11) suggest that Whistler had discovered an indispensable inspiration on the shelves of Paris import shops: free from literary and historical associations to the Victorian mind, the porcelains and prints that made their way from Asia exhibited an abstract elegance agreeably foreign to the prevailing pictorial style.

In another effort to eradicate Courbet's influence on his art and to foil the English habit of taking paintings literally, Whistler began to give his works names from another art. *Symphony in White, No. 3* (fig. 12), the first of Whistler's paintings to be given a musical name,

Fig. 13. Albert Joseph Moore, *The Marble Seat,* ca. 1865, oil on canvas. Present location unknown. From Alfred Lys Baldry, *Albert Moore: His Life and Works* (London, 1894)

has its title printed pointedly across the bottom of the canvas. Although the title was original, even radical for the time, the painting itself resembled works by Albert Joseph Moore such as *The Marble Seat* (fig. 13), which typically portrayed arrangements of women in classical drapery. Two years before *Symphony in White* was painted, Whistler had invited Moore to join the *Société des trois,* a mutual admiration society, as a replacement for Alphonse Legros; long after he and the third member, Henri Fantin-Latour, had drifted apart, Whistler sustained his friendship with Moore, which was rooted in a shared philosophy of art.

In *Notes on Some Pictures of 1868,* a review of the Royal Academy exhibition, Algernon Swinburne placed Albert Moore at the height of

Fig. 14. Albert Joseph Moore, *Azaleas*, ca. 1868, oil on canvas. Hugh Lane Municipal Gallery of Modern Art, Dublin, Ireland

aesthetic accomplishment by defining his art as "the faultless and secure expression of an exclusive worship of things formally beautiful." Swinburne's assessment of Moore's impassive pictures involved a formulation of the aesthetic creed composed, significantly, in musical terms: "The melody of colour, the symphony of form is complete: one more beautiful thing is achieved, one more delight is born into the world; and its meaning is beauty; and its reason for being is to be." Swinburne hinted at reciprocal influences between Moore and Whistler by couching a critique of Moore's *Azaleas* (fig. 14) in musical terms and by cultivating a horticultural metaphor to describe the "Six

Fig. 15. James McNeill Whistler, *The White Symphony: Three Girls,* one of the "Six Projects," ca. 1868, oil on millboard mounted on wood panel. Courtesy of the Freer Gallery of Art, Smithsonian Institution, Washington, D.C., 02.138

Projects," a group of oil sketches by Whistler (see fig. 15), of which he wrote: "They all have immediate beauty, they all give the direct delight of natural things. They seem to have grown as a flower grows, not in any forcing-house of ingenious and elaborate cunning."[3] Swinburne's praise has the ring of Ruskin, and his argument for naturalness against allegations of eccentricity ironically prefigures the elder critic's defense of Burne-Jones, ten years later, in an article libeling Whistler.

Variations in Flesh Colour and Green: The Balcony (fig. 16), a painting begun in 1864 and exhibited in 1870, summarizes the aesthetic experiments of the sixties, showing several of Whistler's prevailing interests: music, the contemporary scene, Asian accessories, and the harmonious disposition of figures. What sets it apart from previous

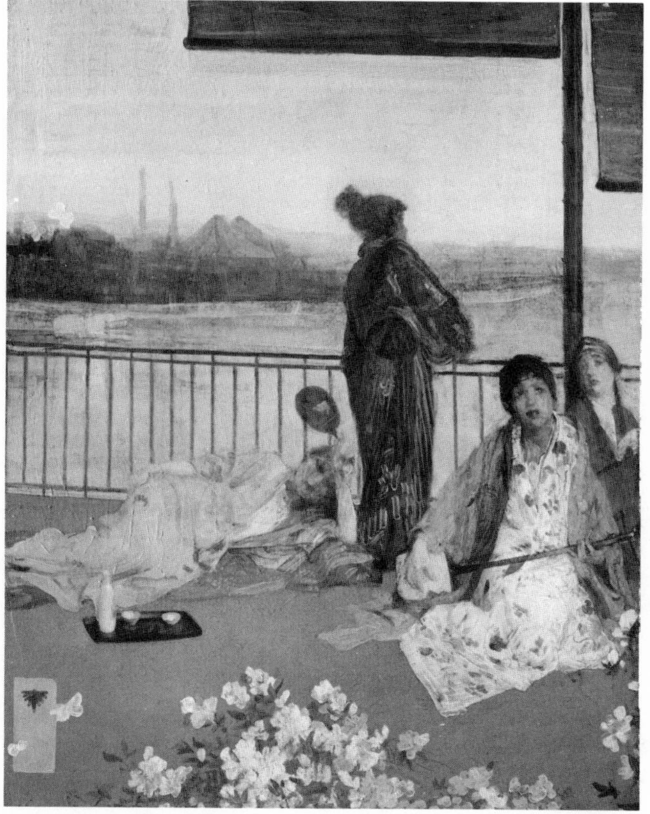

Fig. 16. James McNeill Whistler, *Variations in Flesh Colour and Green: The Balcony,* ca. 1864–70, oil on panel. Courtesy of the Freer Gallery of Art, Smithsonian Institution, Washington, D.C., 92.23

compositions is the setting—the balcony of Whistler's own home in Chelsea, overlooking Battersea on the opposite shore of the Thames. *The Balcony* documents Whistler's discovery of a subject, which brought about the discovery of a style; the colorful foreground harmonies set off by contrast the factories across the river, rendered in shades of gray. Whistler branded the cityscape with butterflies, emblems of his own metamorphosis; he would emerge from the decade an aesthete of striking originality.

Fig. 17. James McNeill Whistler, *Nocturne: Blue and Silver—Chelsea,* 1871, oil on canvas. Exhibited Dudley Gallery 1871, no. 265, as *Harmony in Blue-green—Moonlight.* Tate Gallery, London/Art Resource, New York

Although Whistler rarely lived out of sight of the river and throughout the sixties often etched and painted views of the Thames, it was in the early seventies that he began to see the riverside with eyes trained by Japanese prints and attuned to the poetry of the night. The atrocities of the industrial world faded in the limited light of evening, and Whistler portrayed the effect that a moonlit view cast upon his mind. It was his nocturnal practice to stroll along the riverbank or row on the water, committing a vision to memory. Paintings would be produced in the studio by the light of day, after he had prepared a palette in an appropriate key of color, and time had softened the impression.

The first of the London paintings that would come to be called nocturnes (fig. 17) was begun one summer evening in 1871, when

Whistler became entranced by the river "in a glow of rare transparency," as his mother described the scene, "an hour before sunset."[4] That work, then called *Harmony in Blue-green—Moonlight,* was shown at the Dudley Gallery in the autumn of 1871. An art critic for *The Times*, probably Tom Taylor, called Whistler's exhibits, "illustrations of the theory . . . that painting is so closely akin to music that the colours of the one may and should be used, like the ordered sounds of the other, as means and influences of vague emotion."[5] The following year Whistler exhibited "moonlights" for the first time as "nocturnes," a generic title suggested by his patron, Frederick Leyland, who happened to be an accomplished pianist. Whistler seems to have known little of the musical form, but he recognized immediately the value of the word. He wrote Leyland in gratitude: "You have no idea what an irritation it proves to the critics and consequent pleasure to me—besides it is really so charming and does so poetically say all I want to say and *no more* than I wish!"[6]

At the same time that Whistler was producing ephemeral paintings of London by moonlight, he was also practicing his art on portraiture. For the nocturnes, he could select sights to suit his fancy; for the portraits, he was compelled to impose his style upon the given subject, whether it lent itself to aesthetic arrangement or not. He began with a close relation. *Arrangement in Grey and Black: Portrait of the Painter's Mother* (fig. 18) depends, like the nocturnes, upon the careful disposition of color tones, drawn from an almost monochromatic palette. Portraiture freed Whistler from the management of complex groups of figures, yet the "arrangement" of a single person on canvas turned out to be as taxing as the orchestration of a symphony. He finished only about two dozen full-length portraits, because at every small dissatisfaction he would scrape a painting down and begin anew, covering his tracks so that the production appeared effortless. "Industry in Art is a necessity—not a virtue," he said. "Work alone will efface the footsteps of work."[7]

Although Whistler customarily sent his nocturnes to the Dudley Gallery, he chose to submit *Arrangement in Grey and Black* to the Royal Academy in 1872. According to legend, Whistler's *Mother* was ini-

Fig. 18. James McNeill Whistler, *Arrangement in Grey and Black: Portrait of the Painter's Mother,* 1871, oil on canvas. Musée d'Orsay, Paris

tially rejected by the selection committee, consigned to the cellars, and hung only after an eminent academician, Sir William Boxall, threatened to resign if it were not.[8] Whether Whistler harbored hostility toward the Royal Academy for that episode or not, he refused to enter works for the committee's consideration from that time forward, but continued to exhibit paintings elsewhere. In June 1874, he mounted his first one-man show, at the Flemish Gallery in Pall Mall.

"Mr. Whistler's Exhibition" allowed the artist to exercise complete control over the aesthetic conditions governing the reception of his work. Comprising prints, drawings, oil paintings, and a decorated screen, the exhibition was said to be a "harmony of colour agreeable to the eye."[9] The etchings and drypoints exhibited in Pall Mall drew the highest critical acclaim. As a printmaker, Whistler was frequently compared to Rembrandt, and even Ruskin's lawyers would later concede that he occupied an undisputed position "in the front rank of modern etchers."[10] The nocturnes were all but ignored by the press, but the portraits, although criticized for the eccentricity of their titles, were generally commended. Critics wishing to assess Whistler's style of portraiture often invoked the name of Velázquez.

During the months immediately preceding the Grosvenor Gallery's opening in the spring of 1877, Whistler's work in yet another form generated unprecedented publicity. Frederick Leyland invited the artist to paint a set of panels to line the staircase in the main hall of his new London home at 49 Prince's Gate. The architect Thomas Jeckyll had been commissioned to design a dining room to accommodate some of Leyland's prized possessions—embossed and gilded leather wall hangings, a collection of Chinese blue-and-white porcelain, and *La Princesse du pays de la porcelaine,* a Japanese-inspired portrait that Whistler had painted in 1864. Jeckyll had practically finished his decoration when he asked Whistler's advice about what color to paint the doors and shutters. Concerned that the colors of the room as they stood disturbed the delicate harmonies of the *Princesse,* Whistler obtained permission to make minor alterations.

After Leyland left the city late in the summer of 1876, Whistler's cautious experiments turned to extravagant feats of imagination. By

Fig. 19. James McNeill Whistler, *Harmony in Blue and Gold: The Peacock Room,* 1876–77, paint and metal leaf on leather, canvas, and wood; detail showing *La Princesse du pays de la porcelaine,* 1864, oil on canvas. Courtesy of the Freer Gallery of Art, Smithsonian Institution, Washington, D.C., 04.61

September he had painted golden peacocks on the shutters, gilded Jeckyll's shelving, and covered the ceiling with Dutch-metal leaf overlaid with a blue peacock-feather motif. Two months later the leather was painted blue, and two fighting peacocks shone in gold from the blue wall opposite the *Princesse.* As though it were an easel painting, the decoration was entitled *Harmony in Blue and Gold: The Peacock Room* (fig. 19) and signed in four places with Whistler's butterfly cipher. Mindless of his patron's privacy, the artist entertained visitors and the press, making the elaborate decorative scheme also a scheme of public relations, conveniently at Leyland's expense. Whistler's behavior, exacerbated by a dispute over payment for the project, provoked an acrimonious quarrel. Leyland ordered the artist out of the house and later threatened him with a horse whipping. But Whistler had gained a reputation as a gifted designer with an extraordinary eye for color, and by the time of the Grosvenor opening, he had become something of a celebrity.

Because of his preoccupation with the Peacock Room, Whistler had no new paintings to show at the Grosvenor Gallery, and the ones he had on hand remained unfinished. But Sir Coutts's invitation permitted him to send whatever he wished, freeing him from the strictures that might have been imposed by a conservative selection committee. The eight paintings he selected represented recent achievements in portraiture and landscape (if the nocturnes can be so classified), and four were exhibited for the first time at the Grosvenor. Some were works in progress, others belonged to prominent collectors, and one was for sale.

Arrangement in Grey and Black, No. 2: Portrait of Thomas Carlyle (plate 2) was, according to Oscar Wilde, the "one really good picture" among Whistler's exhibits. "The expression on the old man's face, the texture and colour of his grey hair, and the general sympathetic treatment," Wilde wrote, voicing the popular attitude, "shew Mr. Whistler to be an artist of very great power when he likes."[11] Similar in composition to the first *Arrangement in Grey and Black* (Whistler's *Mother*), the *Carlyle* had the comparative advantage of a famous sitter. Either because the subject seemed out of place in the glittering halls of the Grosvenor, or because the style of the portrait was not in keeping with the rest of his display, Whistler had hesitated to include the *Carlyle* and had entered it at the last minute, too late to be listed in the catalogue. Nevertheless, the portrait of the sage of Chelsea was given a privileged position in the vestibule, where it faced Massini's full-length statue of Cleopatra leaning on a sphinx.[12]

The other works by Whistler were grouped between paintings by Lady Lindsay and C. E. Hallé in the West Gallery. The arrangement began with *Nocturne in Black and Gold* (plate 1), listed in the catalogue as the property of the artist. This was the work that Whistler wanted to sell; its price of two hundred guineas was a reduction from the

£262 Whistler had asked at its premier exhibition in 1875. *Nocturne in Black and Gold* was the most abstract, and thus the most difficult to comprehend, of all Whistler's paintings. To many observers it looked like nothing but "a tract of mud," as *Punch* described it: "Above, all fog; below, all inky flood; For subject—it had none."[13]

To more discerning viewers, *Nocturne in Black and Gold* conveyed suggestions of the glitter and smoke of a falling rocket, a string of lights from a dance floor, and two of the four turrets that rose from the fireworks platform at Cremorne Gardens. A pleasure park situated at the west end of Chelsea between the river and the King's Road, Cremorne was the setting for several of Whistler's nocturnes before it was closed to the public in 1877, coincidentally the year of the Grosvenor exhibition.[14] The inspiration for Whistler's painting may have come from *Fireworks, Ryogoku,* a woodblock print by Hiroshige that Whistler is believed to have owned at the time, which shows a crowd on the Ryogoku bridge watching fireworks over the Sumida River.[15] Fireworks made an appropriate subject for a nocturne but proved an affront to conventional ideas of Victorian painting, which tended toward daylight depictions of clearly articulated narratives. Indeed, Whistler's falling rocket was a modern, urban, sensational, ephemeral, indescribable spectacle—a vision of beauty without a trace of moral meaning, a model of art for art's sake.

Two of the works Whistler sent to the Grosvenor bore the same title, *Nocturne in Blue and Silver*. The first (plate 4) showed the smokestacks and spires of Battersea Reach at dusk, from a point on the opposite shore of the river; its gilded frame was decorated with a blue wave pattern that completed the painting's design.[16] This *Nocturne in Blue and Silver* belonged to Frances Leyland; Whistler had presented it to her as a gift several years earlier. After the debacle of the Peacock Room, it is unlikely that Frederick Leyland would have cooperated with Whistler in any way, but Frances remained the artist's friend and probably lent the painting for exhibition without her husband's knowledge or consent.

The second *Nocturne in Blue and Silver* (plate 3) represented, in Wilde's words, a rocket "breaking in a pale blue sky, over a large dark blue bridge, and a blue and silver river"—fireworks, that is, flashing over Battersea Bridge. The theme is similar to that of *Nocturne in Black and Gold* although, as Wilde maintained, the *Blue and Silver* is "rather prettier."[17] The painting had been exhibited in Brighton in 1875[18] but was shown at the Grosvenor for the first time as the property of William Graham. Years earlier, Graham had requested a painting of Annabel Lee, the subject of a poem by Edgar Allan Poe, but Whistler had been unable to complete the commission: after repeatedly trying to finish the painting, he had "only by degrees brought about its destruction." In exchange for Graham's hundred-pound advance, Whistler sent *Nocturne in Blue and Silver*, assuring his patron that many were pleased with the painting and he himself prized it.[19]

The fourth in the series, *Nocturne in Blue and Gold* (plate 5), is an unusual depiction of the river at Westminster. Whistler generally painted scenes from the Embankment, farther down the Thames near his home in Chelsea, but had been inspired to paint *Nocturne in Blue and Gold* by a vision of the river on a warm summer night from the Houses of Parliament.[20] The painting had been shown with *Nocturne in Black and Gold* at the Dudley Gallery in 1875, and the critic William Michael Rossetti, reviewing the exhibition for the *Academy,* wrote that it would "be long remembered by visitors, and will always count as one of its author's chief masterpieces, and in its way never to be superseded and not often rivalled." Conceding that some did not credit Whistler with a serious command of color, structure, or sentiment, but "only with jumping at them, and falling on his feet now and again," he entreated the skeptical to consider *Nocturne in Blue and Gold* before settling their minds on the subject.[21]

At least one art critic failed to discern the special qualities that Rossetti extolled. Tom Taylor, the critic for *The Times* who had shown a rare understanding of the artist's intentions in 1871, accused Whistler of appraising his paintings above their worth, "as pictures instead of mere tone studies."

> Taken for what they are . . . what Mr. Whistler calls his nocturnes and symphonies have a real beauty and suggestiveness of their own.

> Only he must not attempt, with that happy half-humorous audacity which all his dealing with his own work suggests, to palm off his deficiencies upon us as manifestations of power, and try to make us believe that this sort of thing is the one best worth doing, because it is the only thing he can do, or, at all events, cares for doing, in colour.[22]

In spite of this unfavorable review, *Nocturne in Blue and Gold* sold for the listed price (£210) to a man Whistler had never met, the Honorable Percy Wyndham, who evidently bought the painting as a present for his wife. (Her portrait by G. F. Watts would later hang with the nocturne in the Grosvenor's West Gallery.) Whistler took particular pleasure in the sale of that "much blaguarded" picture, writing his friend Alan Cole in triumph: "So you see this vicious art of butterfly flippancy is, in spite of the honest efforts of Tom Taylor, doing its poisonous work and even attacking the heart of the aristocracy as well as undermining the working classes!"[23]

In addition to the four nocturnes, Whistler's display included three full-length portraits, all belonging to the artist. *Arrangement in Black* (plate 6) showed Henry Irving playing the part of Philip II in *Queen Mary,* an unsuccessful historical drama by Tennyson staged the previous spring at the Lyceum Theatre. The role had not been one of Irving's finest, and the play itself survived only twenty-three performances. But the actor, dressed in a monochrome costume and striking a pose from a painting by Velázquez, had appeared on stage like the personification of a Whistler painting. The artist's reasons for portraying Irving in that character were purely and obviously aesthetic.[24] Oscar Wilde recognized in Whistler's portrait the "queer stiff position that Mr. Irving often adopts preparatory to one of his long wolf-like strides across the stage," but the critic Harry Quilter could detect no likeness to the actor's familiar form in *Arrangement in Black,* and was moreover unable to understand the portrait when "viewed as a picture."[25] Alan Cole saw the work in progress in May 1876, when Whistler was "madly enthusiastic about his power of painting such full lengths in two sittings or so,"[26] but apparently the Irving portrait was not so easily accomplished: it was shown at the Grosvenor Gallery

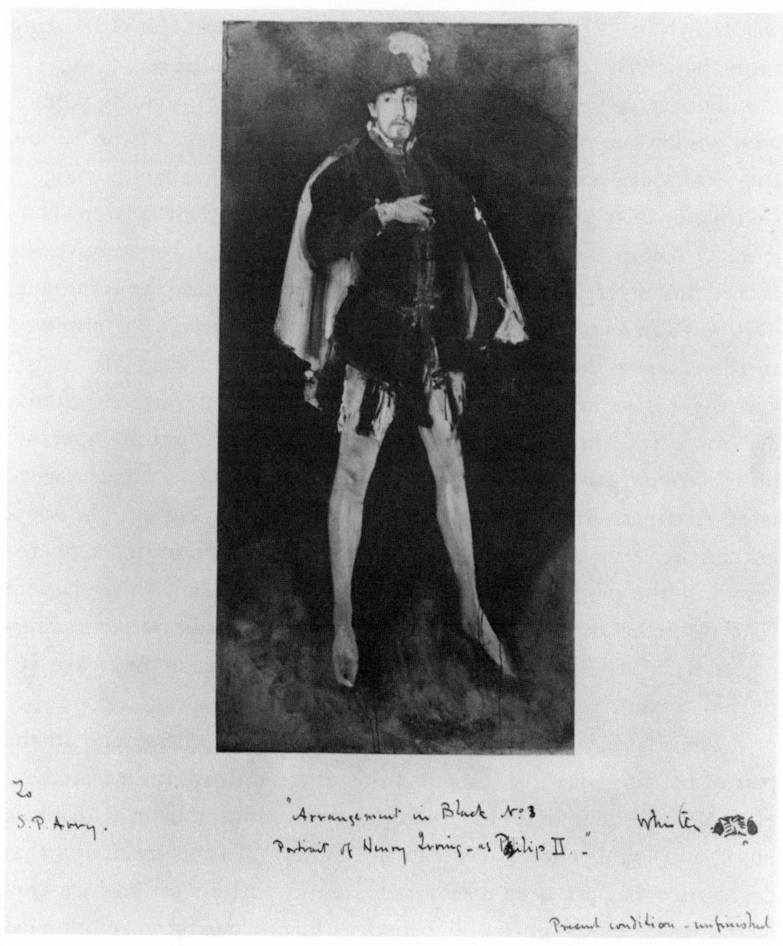

Fig. 20. Photograph of an early state of *Arrangement in Black No. 3* (plate 6), ca. 1876–77. Inscribed by Whistler, "To S. P. Avery, 'Arrangement in Black No. 3 Portrait of Henry Irving—as Philip II' / Whistler / Present condition—unfinished," and signed with a butterfly. S. P. Avery Collection, Miriam and Ira D. Wallach Division of Art, Prints, and Photographs, New York Public Library, Astor, Lenox, and Tilden Foundations

unfinished. Marie Spartali Stillman, one of the exhibitors, could recall seeing three distinct outlines of the figure when *Arrangement in Black* was shown in 1877, and a photograph of the portrait (fig. 20) dating from about that time is inscribed by Whistler "unfinished."[27]

The last two paintings were a pair of portraits of young women who somewhat resembled each other. According to Oscar Wilde, the sitters appeared like sisters "caught in a black London fog."[28] Confusion over the identity of the works, whose titles were *Harmony in Amber and Black* and *Arrangement in Brown,* began with the accidental inversion of their numbers in the Grosvenor catalogue. William Rossetti was the first to discover the mistake: he observed in the *Academy* that if the numbers were correct, "what Mr. Whistler regards as amber and black appears to the unpurged popular eye more like brown, and *vice versa*."[29] With the numbers transposed, *Arrangement in Brown* (plate 7) can be identified as the work later renamed *Arrangement in Black and Brown: The Fur Jacket,* a portrait of Whistler's model and mistress, Maud Franklin. A photograph of the painting in an early state (fig. 21), with the original title inscribed in Whistler's hand and signed with a butterfly characteristic of 1878, shows *Arrangement in Brown* as it may have appeared at the Grosvenor Gallery in 1877.[30]

The identity of *Harmony in Amber and Black,* the second in the pair of portraits, is more difficult to determine. Rossetti described the painting as a depiction of a "blonde lady in white muslin with black bows, and some yellow flowers in the corner." No picture fitting that description has yet been discovered,[31] but a portrait of Florence Leyland, one of the daughters of Whistler's former patron, matches most of the particulars of Rossetti's account and is likely to be the painting (plate 8). The young lady in the portrait is not blonde, but she is fair; her dress, which looks gray today, appears in an early photograph (fig. 22) to have originally been whitish and even then adorned with the black bow described by Rossetti; and she occupies an environment sufficiently vague and atmospheric to suggest fog to Oscar Wilde. The portrait of Florence Leyland lacks only the yellow flowers Rossetti mentioned—presumably the amber element of the harmony—but

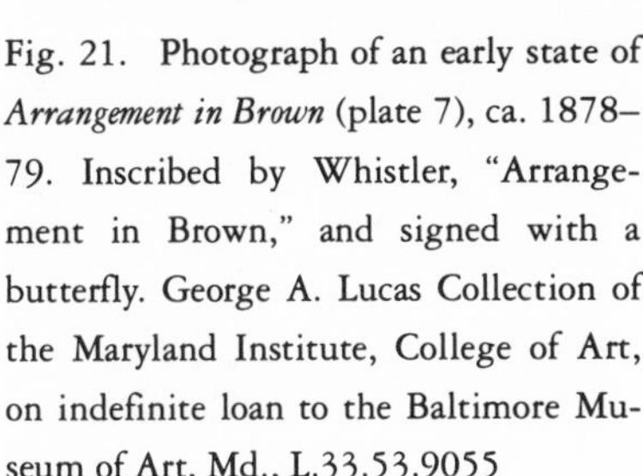

Fig. 21. Photograph of an early state of *Arrangement in Brown* (plate 7), ca. 1878–79. Inscribed by Whistler, "Arrangement in Brown," and signed with a butterfly. George A. Lucas Collection of the Maryland Institute, College of Art, on indefinite loan to the Baltimore Museum of Art, Md., L.33.53.9055

Fig. 22. Photograph of an early state of *Harmony in Amber and Black* (plate 8), ca. 1878–79. Inscribed by Whistler, "'Arrangement in Grey and Black,' No. 2," and signed with a butterfly. George A. Lucas Collection of the Maryland Institute, College of Art, on indefinite loan to the Baltimore Museum of Art, Md., L.33.53.9061

considering the major redecoration the controversial canvas underwent over the years, the detail must be seen as a minor omission.[32]

Whistler probably began the portrait of Florence Leyland in 1876, just before the painting of the Peacock Room absorbed all his attention and compelled him to abandon other projects; the subsequent dispute with Leyland precluded further sittings.[33] When it was shown in 1877 with the discreetly anonymous title *Harmony in Amber and Black,* the portrait of Florence was unfinished, like the portrait of Irving, and presumably for that reason identified in the catalogue as in Whistler's possession.[34] The artist explained to Theodore Watts-Dunton nearly a year later, when the painting was still in his hands, that it remained incomplete "simply because the young lady has not sufficiently sat for it—and as she is not likely to sit for it again I must do what I can to make it as worthy of me and of herself as possible."[35] To make it fit for exhibition, Whistler probably superimposed a different face on the figure, and it is likely that he used the familiar features of Maud Franklin. *Harmony in Amber and Black,* therefore, would have appeared with good reason a sister to *Arrangement in Brown,* the other portrait of Maud in the Grosvenor exhibition.

Because Whistler's assembled nocturnes, harmonies, and arrangements were shown in the same gallery as paintings by Burne-Jones, the artists suddenly became competitors for attention. They were, as the *Week* put it, the twin stars of the Grosvenor.[36] The public was intrigued and perplexed by the oddity and audacity of both artists' works. Indeed, it may be that the relative merits of red and gold walls generated unending debate on the floor of the Grosvenor Gallery and the pages of the press because the question of the comparative value of nocturnes and nymphs left the public all but speechless. "It may be all very well," the *Daily News* observed:

> and the pictures may please the learned, but they are not what the public is accustomed to. The spectator feels inclined to cry anxiously, "Where is the baby?" for babies and cradles are but inadequately represented in the Grosvenor Gallery. This is not as it should be; this is not in accordance with the practice of the Royal Academy and with the traditions of British art.

One critic feared being "laid up with a harmony in black, or an arrangement in blue, on the brain," and complained in *Vanity Fair* that no minds would ever be improved by admiring worn-out pictures refined of natural impulses. In the conclusion to the *Punch* "Palace of Art," the increasingly miserable man of taste eventually succumbs to a stupor induced by aesthetic indigestion.[37]

People who liked to be on the right side, the *Daily News* said, neither gushed nor sneered but reserved their judgment until the arbiter of English taste, John Ruskin, had issued his.[38]

RUSKIN'S REVIEW

WHEN THE GROSVENOR Gallery opened to the public on May Day 1877, John Ruskin was out of the country. The previous summer he had taken a leave of absence from his Oxford professorship to spend a year in Italy, intending to prepare a revised edition of *The Stones of Venice.* Ruskin also hoped to ease his ravaged mind, having strained throughout the decade to maintain its equilibrium. In June 1877, Ruskin returned to England and spent a month with his cousin Joan Severn and her husband Arthur at Herne Hill, their home in South London near Camberwell. It was from there that Ruskin attacked Whistler in one of a series of published letters bearing the recondite title *Fors Clavigera.*[1]

Ruskin had begun the publication in 1871, soon after assuming the Slade Professorship of Fine Art at Oxford, and he continued its production until his final resignation of the post in 1884. Because he considered the teaching of art a self-indulgence, Ruskin may have conceived *Fors Clavigera* to quiet his social conscience; the letters were addressed to the "workmen and labourers of Great Britain" and covered a wide range of topics—including, but not limited to, art and aesthetics. He underwrote the printing costs himself and established George Allen, his student and assistant, as publisher and agent.

Fig. 23. Adriano Cecioni, "The Realization of the Ideal," 1872, chromolithograph. "Men of the Day, No. XL: Mr. John Ruskin," *Vanity Fair,* 17 February 1872

Of Ruskin's numerous and varied publications, *Fors Clavigera* is the most difficult to describe. In its polemical tone, it is closest to *Time and Tide* (1867), Ruskin's letters to a literate cork-cutter interested in political economy; in its prescriptive spirit, as Joan Abse observes, *Fors* comes closer to the Epistles of the Apostles.[2] Its serial form and digressive style allowed Ruskin to write episodically at times when his hyperactive intelligence could not sustain protracted effort: fragments of autobiography, letters from readers, and newspaper extracts are interspersed in *Fors* with long, fluent paragraphs of fervid vituperation. One year he vowed that "one quite fixed plan" for the publication would be for it to be entirely free from abuse and controversy; but as George Bernard Shaw remarked, the commentary in its pages on social conditions exceeded even the writings of Karl Marx in invective force.[3] John Rosenberg concluded that the collected *Fors Clavigera* was less a book than "the diary of a nobly gifted mind, disturbed but not deceived by its sickness."[4]

Ruskin began writing letter 79, entitled "Life Guards of New Life," on Monday, 18 June 1877. The following Friday, when its composition would have been all but complete, he went with Arthur Severn to the Royal Academy and on Saturday to the new Grosvenor Gallery, dining afterward with Edward and Georgiana Burne-Jones.[5] His impressions of the exhibitions, which appear toward the end of the letter, are preceded by several complaints about the Grosvenor installation. Ruskin disliked the lavishness of the upholstery, which he considered "poor in itself; and very grievously injurious to the best pictures it contains, while its glitter as unjustly veils the vulgarity of the worst." He objected to grouping artists' works all together because, he said, "in general it is better that each painter should, in fitting places, take his occasional part in the pleasantness of the picture-concert, than at once run through all his pieces, and retire." And he disapproved of arranging paintings by artists who were only "scholars" indiscriminately beside the works by acknowledged "masters."[6]

Gathering momentum, Ruskin arrived at his opinion of the exhibited works of art. Beginning with Burne-Jones, the critic declared that his paintings were "simply the only art-work at present produced in England which will be received by the future as 'classic' in its kind,—the best that has been, or could be." Placing the artist securely in the pantheon of modern painters, Ruskin wrote of Burne-Jones's eight exhibits: "I *know* that these will be immortal, as the best things the mid-nineteenth century in England could do, in such true relations as it has, through all confusion, retained with the paternal and everlasting Art of the world." He explained away Burne-Jones's many mannerisms—melancholy faces, muted colors, claustrophobic compositions—as "natural to the painter, however strange to us," and forgave his faults as shadows of his virtues.[7] Style, Ruskin had said in *Modern Painters,* was "nothing but the best means of getting at the particular truth which the artist wanted; it is not a mode peculiar to himself of getting at the same truths as other men, but the *only* mode of getting the particular facts he desires."[8] Burne-Jones's idiosyncrasies appeared to Ruskin indisputably genuine, as habits of execution devised by necessity.

But other pictures of the "modern schools," Ruskin said, displayed eccentricities and imperfections that were "gratuitously, if not impertinently, indulged." Whistler's faults, in particular, appeared unredeemed by virtues:

> For Mr. Whistler's own sake, no less than for the protection of the purchaser, Sir Coutts Lindsay ought not to have admitted works into the gallery in which the ill-educated conceit of the artist so nearly approached the aspect of wilful imposture. I have seen, and heard, much of Cockney impudence before now; but never expected to hear a coxcomb ask two hundred guineas for flinging a pot of paint in the public's face.[9]

The comparison could not have been clearer. Beside Burne-Jones, a paragon among artists, Whistler was an impudent fool.

As a consequence of the legal action it engendered, that isolated paragraph would soon become notorious. Ruskin's remarks about the Grosvenor Gallery, and especially the image of the paint-flinging coxcomb, would be abstracted from *Fors Clavigera* and considered, out of context, an outrageous if articulate critique of the artist's work. The letter from which it came, originally entitled "The Social Monster," would be virtually forgotten.[10] Ruskin had discovered the theme for that letter on a scrap of paper that fell out of his pocket as he sat down to write. He quoted the sentences it bore as an introduction to letter 79:

> It is indeed a most blessed provision that men will not work without wages; if they did, society would be overthrown from its roots. A man who would give his labour for nothing would be a social monster.

These lines, Ruskin informed his readers, had been penned by an "extremely foolish, and altogether insignificant, person," whose folly he would reveal in subsequent paragraphs. The July issue of *Fors Clavigera,* therefore, set out to refute an anonymous author's unconscionable opinion that money, rather than labor, motivated the forces of a just society. The paragraphs concerning the Grosvenor were appended as a sort of postscript to the letter.[11]

An assessment of modern art would not in fact have figured in the original design, conceived before Ruskin had seen the latest London exhibitions. His condemnation of Whistler was but one detail in a sweeping castigation of the corrupt "modern system of accumulating wealth,"[12] but it made an appropriate conclusion to a call to the workmen of Sheffield to join the Guild of Saint George. Dedicated to "free-heartedness of unselfish toil," members of the guild labored "for the love of God and man," and in that utopian scheme, the "social monster" would be the worker motivated by Mammon alone. At the Grosvenor Gallery, Ruskin found a monitory example of a worker apparently obsessed with wealth. If the gallery had indeed been founded for the diffusion of "Art-knowledge," not as a commercial enterprise, then the presence there of an artist whose aims were inconsistent with that goal corrupted the purity of its purpose. Whistler's paintings appeared to Ruskin a monstrous intrusion; he registered his alarm with a graphic metaphor, which would become immortal.

Ruskin's reference to the sum Whistler demanded for flinging paint in the public's face led some contemporaries to believe that Ruskin was preoccupied with money. Elizabeth and Joseph Pennell, Whistler's biographers, perpetuated the idea by taking the two hundred guineas remark to mean that the "financial side of connoisseurship" was Ruskin's primary concern. They dismissed the critic with the curious conclusion that Ruskin exemplified the "new British patron of the arts."[13] It is true that Ruskin would have had to make some effort to learn the price of Whistler's painting, since that information was not included in the catalogue, but he ordinarily took little notice of market value, maintaining that worthy art would take care of itself. His interest was not in finance, as the Pennells maintained, but in economy, which he defined as "the wise management of labour" and established as the prevailing theme of *Fors Clavigera*.[14]

The commercial tone of the critique simply suggests that in *Fors Clavigera,* Ruskin was writing as something other than an art critic. Indeed, his concise analysis of Whistler's work fails to meet his own standards of criticism, outlined in the 1855 *Academy Notes:*

> No criticism is of any value which does not enable the spectator, in his own person, to understand, or to detect, the alleged merit or unworthiness of the picture; and the true work of a critic is not to make his hearer believe him, but agree with him.[15]

Composed in the spare, direct style of denunciation rather than the expository mode of explanation, Ruskin's words about Whistler are powerful, but hardly persuasive; and unless paint-slinging is taken as a valid description of the artist's technique, the sentences give the reader no key to comprehension. But in less than a paragraph Ruskin denounces the artist's production and distribution of goods and implicitly condemns their consumption as well. The issue of a nocturne's price falls outside the jurisdiction of the art critic and lands squarely in the domain of the art economist.

Ruskin would later remark that he looked forward to asserting "principles of art economy" in connection with Whistler,[16] principles he eventually proposed in a memorandum to his lawyers in which "honesties of Commerce" are linked with "veracities of Art" as the interdependent concerns of an art economist (App. A). Suspecting that his position might be misunderstood, he wrote Arthur Severn soon before the trial:

> I should like you to express to whichever of our Counsel listens best, the *one main* difference between me and other economists—that I say, all economy begins in requiring and teaching every craftsman to give as *much* work as he can for his money, and all modern economists say he must give as *little* as he can for his money.

Referring to himself as an economist—unqualified by the word "art"—Ruskin concluded his letter by casting Whistler as an ordinary wage-earner. "All sums spent on bad workmen," he said, "are so much lost to good ones."[17] His aesthetic complaint was subsumed, therefore, by the larger and more urgent issue of the integrity of the artist's labor.

But even as an "art economist," Ruskin continued to abide by the principles he had established in *Modern Painters* and other writings on art. Ruskin recognized a fixed criterion separating right art from wrong and believed that a negative assessment of a work of art necessarily entailed judging its creator negatively. Reflection on the artist's character was part of the critical process. As a critic, his responsibility was to recommend meritorious "authors" to the public and prevent unworthy ones from occupying its attention (App. A). Whistler's *Nocturne in Black and Gold*—exhibiting neither noble subject matter nor truthful beauty, neither sincerity nor invention—failed at every point Ruskin's test for greatness of style. And poverty of style, he would say, reflected poverty of spirit.[18]

The *Fors* critique was consistent with Ruskin's previous appraisal of Whistler's work, expounded in an Oxford lecture of October 1873. Possibly alluding to a painting exhibited in 1872 as *Harmony in Grey* (fig. 24), Ruskin declared that he had never seen

> anything so impudent on the walls of any exhibition, in any country, as last year in London. It was a daub professing to be a "harmony in pink and white" (or some such nonsense); absolute rubbish, and which had taken about a quarter of an hour to scrawl or daub—it had no pretence to be called painting. The price asked for it was two hundred and fifty guineas.[19]

In less memorable but equally scathing terms, Ruskin here asserted the charge he would repeat four years later in *Fors Clavigera*: Whistler's works were ill-conceived, poorly crafted, overpriced parodies of paintings.

To diminish the chance that the public would confuse such morally impoverished productions with great works of art, Ruskin's criti-

Fig. 24. James McNeill Whistler, *Symphony in Grey: Early Morning, Thames,* 1871, oil on canvas. Exhibited Society of French Artists 1872, no. 122, as *Harmony in Grey.* Courtesy of the Freer Gallery of Art, Smithsonian Institution, Washington, D.C., 04.50

cal method customarily proceeded by comparison. In the passages about Burne-Jones in *Fors Clavigera,* for instance, he places the modern painter in the company of Giotto, Masaccio, Bernardino Luini, Tintoretto, and even Turner, and mentions in passing Bellini, Botticelli, and Carpaccio. Reference to the Old Masters is conspicuously absent from the paragraph on Whistler, although the eccentricities and imperfections of his style are contrasted to the idiosyncrasies of Burne-Jones. But the peril of comparison lies in the possibility of imposture. Just as an inferior picture that vaguely resembled a great painting might be accepted by the public as adequate, a Whistler nocturne, which might appear to the average person a little like a Turner, might be mistaken for a masterpiece. Ruskin undoubtedly noticed the resemblance that has since struck every dilettante and scholar, and we may assume that the superficial similarities between Whistler's *Nocturne in Black and Gold* and the late works of Turner infuriated him at least as much as their profound differences. When he wrote his instructions to the lawyers, Ruskin was reminded of the critical lambastes that had initially "provoked" him to write in Turner's defense. One of the first of those critiques, published in 1842, said that the artist's works appeared to have been painted "by throwing handfuls of white, and blue, and red, at the canvas, letting what chanced to stick, stick,"[20] and the strikingly similar image in *Fors Clavigera* was probably not coincidental. Ruskin must have thought that Whistler uniquely deserved the words so unfairly flung at Turner more than three decades earlier.

Turner, then, appears to have been on Ruskin's mind when he wrote the Whistler critique, and his allegation that Whistler "nearly approached the aspect of wilful imposture" may convey a suspicion that Whistler's unfocused pictures were an unconscious, or perhaps impertinent, imitation of Turner's grand manner. Poor as the counterfeits might be, their simulative style could give them an unfortunate advantage in an environment favorable to Turner, largely conditioned by Ruskin himself. Never in the course of the controversy did Ruskin refer directly to Turner, perhaps out of fear that even to mention the master's name in connection with Whistler might bring about the dreaded comparison. Still, at least one contemporary commentator remarked that Ruskin had "exhausted reams of paper and floods of ink in praise of Turner's 'arrangements,' many of them less definite than Whistler's."[21] Several years later, in 1882, the notion of the nocturnes as travesties of Turner paintings was made explicit by Walter Hamilton in *The Aesthetic Movement in England:*

> Ruskin clearly demonstrated that Turner, in spite of his peculiarities, knew and painted more of nature than any other artist that ever lived, but at the same time he was not prepared to go to the

> length of praising the absurd parodies of Turner's style then being produced in almost any number, and dignified by such appellations as symphonies in black and yellow, or harmonies in green and gold.[22]

Ruskin, then, had sound and serious reasons for detesting Whistler's work, but his manner of expression was nonetheless extreme. Henry James explained to readers of the *Nation* that the Victorian public made allowances for even the most peevish of Ruskin's remarks: "His literary bad manners are recognized, and many of his contemporaries have suffered from them without complaining."[23] But the scurrilous tone of the *Fors* critique could appear calculated to attract attention to itself,[24] and even before the case against him went to court, Ruskin would have to speak in his own defense. He confessed in a letter written the month after the publication of the alleged libel that his thoughts sometimes got away from him, or took "their own way in form," when he began to commit them to paper.[25] Less personally, Ruskin accounted for his impulsive style, and perhaps by implication his fulmination against Whistler, in the September issue of *Fors Clavigera,* composed soon after word came that Whistler intended to sue. If his writing appeared unpracticed and unpolished, he said, it was because *Fors* was a letter, "written as a letter should be written, frankly, and as the mood, or topic, chances." Revising or polishing the text would turn it into a serious treatise, when in fact much of it was meant as "a kind of bitter play."[26] Like a fool in motley, Ruskin maintained that in the pages of *Fors* he was licensed to speak his mind.

Ruskin would also contend that the spontaneous style was balanced by an innate sense of truth. While he wrote what first came into his head or his heart, he invariably weighed his words, he said, "accurate to the estimation of a hair."

> The language which seems to you exaggerated, and which it may be, therefore, inexpedient that I should continue, nevertheless expresses, in its earnestness, facts which you will find to be irrefragably true, and which no other than such forceful expression could truly reach, whether you will hear, or whether you will forbear.[27]

Vituperation was his way of reaching facts, not of attracting readers, and those facts were as incontestably true, he argued, as his manner of speaking was genuine. This public explanation of his style anticipated Ruskin's plea of justification in *Whistler v. Ruskin.* Although his counsel would defend him on the theoretical ground of privileged communication, Ruskin himself answered Whistler's charge concretely: the allegation of libel could be easily refuted, he said, because the description of Whistler was "absolutely true" (App. A).

It was not literally true, of course, that the artist was a jester who pelted the public with paint, but through artful exaggeration, Ruskin had revealed what he regarded as truth. The caricature was calculated to produce a comic effect while making a studiously serious charge. Ruskin maintained that criticism was powerless to affect an artist's fortunes—"except so far as it concurs with general public opinion"—but acknowledged that ridicule could be fatal to a reputation. "I have seen more real mischief and definite injury to property done in ten minutes by an idle coxcomb amusing his party, than could possibly be done by all the malice in type that could be got into the journals of the season," he said. "The printed malice only makes people look at the picture; the fool's jest makes them pass it."[28] He might have shattered Whistler in a page, as one contemporary critic observed, but preferred to toss him over with an epigram.[29]

The substance of the *Fors* critique seems, therefore, to have been the articulation of a deliberate judgment. But its unbalanced tone must be attributed at least in part to the critic's state of mind. Ruskin was not well in the summer of 1877. After exhausting himself in Venice—he had made countless studies of Carpaccio's *Saint Ursula* and written *St. Mark's Rest* and *Guide to the Principal Pictures in the Academy at Venice,* as well as preparing regular editions of *Fors Clavigera*—Ruskin continued to feel dizzy and lightheaded upon his return to England;[30] the outburst in *Fors* probably portended mental collapse. As Quentin Bell points out, one symptom of Ruskin's incipient madness was his professed belief, after several inclement summers, that the natural world was darkening,[31] and *Nocturne in Black and Gold,* a picture of night, might well have incited his furious attack. Other scholars have observed that Ruskin's "morbid sensi-

Fig. 25. James McNeill Whistler, *Symphony in White, No. 2: The Little White Girl,* 1864, oil on canvas. Tate Gallery, London/Art Resource, New York

tivity to light," apparent in his sketches from that period, must have made Whistler's nocturne especially menacing; and that his documented fear of light glittering against darkness could certainly have provoked an "involuntary expression of automatic panic."[32]

But the implicit malice of the libel has led some to seek motives beyond psychological instability for Ruskin's "inconsequent personal venom." The Pennells, while offering no evidence to support the claim, were sure that Ruskin cherished some special reason for disliking Whistler.[33] James Anderson Rose, the artist's solicitor, believed that Whistler's "manliness" (probably an allusion to Ruskin's unconsummated marriage), or else his "independence of the patron and art critic" made him especially disagreeable to Ruskin. Modern scholars have suggested that Ruskin was offended by Whistler's "lack of homage" to him; that he despised the artist's various forms of self-advertisement, such as Sunday breakfasts written up in society papers; that he distrusted Whistler because he was an American; or that he felt threatened by his association with the indiscreet and unscrupulous Charles Augustus Howell, who had once been Ruskin's secretary and confidant.[34]

Ruskin had never met Whistler, although their mutual friend Algernon Swinburne had attempted to arrange an introduction in 1865. Swinburne sent Ruskin a copy of his poem "Before the Mirror," together with effusive praise for Whistler's painting *The Little White Girl* (fig. 25), which had been its inspiration. He also issued a provisional invitation. Unless he heard otherwise from Whistler, he said, he planned to take "Jones" (Burne-Jones had not yet begun to hyphenate his name) to visit the artist's studio, and wondered whether Ruskin would care to come along. "As any artist worthy of his rank must be," the poet wrote, Whistler was

> of course desirous to meet you, and to let you see his immediate work. As (I think) he has never met you, you will see that his desire to have it out with you face to face must spring simply from knowledge and appreciation of your own works.[35]

This letter was interpreted by W. G. Collingwood and E. T. Cook, two of Ruskin's first biographers, as Whistler's overture to Ruskin[36] and has been read that way ever since. But the idea of bringing Whistler and Ruskin together appears to have been entirely Swinburne's. The poet presumed that Whistler was anxious to meet Ruskin but apparently had not asked Whistler's opinion or even his permission to pay a call; and his suggestion that the artist and critic "have it out" carries the implication that theoretical disagreements between them were already well established. One or the other must have found Swinburne's arrangements inconvenient or otherwise undesirable, for the meeting never took place. And because they did not appear together in court, Whistler and Ruskin would never have the opportunity to settle their differences, as Swinburne thought they should, face to face.

BRINGING SUIT

SHORTLY AFTER THE publication of *Fors Clavigera* on 2 July 1877, Whistler was with the American artist George H. Boughton in the smoking room of the Arts Club, Hanover Square, when Boughton came across Ruskin's inflammatory review. He was not reading *Fors Clavigera* itself, but one of the London papers that brought the critique to the public's attention—probably the *Architect,* which published excerpts from *Fors* innocuously titled "Mr. Ruskin on the Grosvenor Gallery" on 14 July.[1] Knowing that his friend generally enjoyed critical lambasting, Boughton nevertheless hesitated to show the review to Whistler. "I shall never forget the peculiar look on his face as he read it," Boughton recalled years later, "and handed the paper back to me with never a word of comment, but thinking, furiously though sadly, all the time." After a few moments of reflection Whistler declared that Ruskin's was the "most debased *style* of criticism" he had ever encountered. Boughton suggested, tentatively, that the paragraph might be libelous. "Well," said Whistler, lighting a cigarette and taking his leave, "that I shall try to find out."[2]

According to Théodore Duret, the art critic, Whistler delayed initiating his suit until finally "the desire to obtain reparation, coupled with his pugnacious spirit, carried him away, and Ruskin was cited for libel."[3] The surviving documents suggest, however, that immediately after reading Ruskin's critique Whistler went to Salisbury

Fig. 26. Phil May, "On the Brain—Mr. Whistler." *Pick-Me-Up,* 9 January 1892. From A. E. Gallatin, *Portraits of Whistler: A Critical Study and an Iconography* (New York, 1918)

Street, just off the Strand, to meet with his solicitor, James Anderson Rose. Rose was an old friend of the Rossetti family who had probably been introduced to Whistler by Gabriel Rossetti in the early sixties, when the artists were neighbors in Chelsea. In 1866 Rose had been named executor of the will Whistler had made shortly before a mysterious journey to Valparaiso, and throughout the 1870s, when Whistler's personal and financial affairs were often in disarray, Rose consistently restored peace, if not always prosperity, to the artist's life.

Rose's participation in the artistic circles of London made him particularly well fitted to direct a lawsuit meant to save an artist's reputation. With Swinburne, Irving, and W. S. Gilbert, he was an active member of the Arundel Club, a meeting place for rising talent, and he had negotiated a number of legal settlements involving artists, such as the deed of partnership for Morris, Marshall, Faulkner & Company in 1862 and the bankruptcy of the painter Frederick Sandys in 1876.[4] Rose also collected works within his means by his clients and friends. He owned a few paintings by Rossetti and a prized collection of Whistler prints. He had lent to the Dudley Gallery all fourteen of the etchings and drypoints by Whistler shown in 1872 at an exhibition of "Works of Art in Black and White," and two years later he contributed a selection of Whistler prints to an exhibition at the Liverpool Art Club.[5] Rose was one of the first to recognize the beauty of *Arrangement in Grey and Black;* he told Whistler's mother, whom he adored as his own, that when her portrait went on view at the Royal Academy he planned to look in on it every day.[6] Whistler, who admired his attorney's taste and appreciated his talents, told E. W. Godwin in 1878 that Anderson Rose was "the brightest little lawyer in London."[7]

Whistler must have consulted Rose about Ruskin sometime before 21 July 1877, when the *Athenaeum* published the rumor that the artist intended to sue the critic for libel.[8] By 27 July, when three clerks in Rose's office each ordered copies of the allegedly libelous issue of *Fors,* work on Whistler's case had definitely begun; and the next day, just one week after the critique had been reprinted in several leading papers, *London* reported that Whistler had written "a rather rough letter to his critic, insinuating that if the accusation of impudence is only ungentlemanly, that of 'imposture' is absolutely actionable."[9] Ruskin had not received a letter, as it happened, but a writ of summons. Rose officially initiated the action by notifying Ruskin that Whistler claimed damages for libel and compelling him or his representative to appear in court within eight days to answer the charge. Service of this writ was first attempted at the Severns' house at Herne Hill and at Corpus Christi College in Oxford; eventually the writ found its way to Brantwood, Ruskin's home on Coniston Water, where it was served on 8 August, exactly one week after the inaugural exhibition of the Grosvenor Gallery closed to the public.[10]

Whistler's decision to bring action evidently surprised the press. "It is hard to understand," a writer for the *Referee* remarked:

> why a gentleman who is supposed to court criticism, and who, at the breakfasts he so freely gives to society journalists and promiscuous paragraphers, is notorious for the hard and bitter things he says about famous painters who are not present, should be so sensitive about the utterances of one who is as lunatic in literature as he himself is paralytic in painting.[11]

Certainly Ruskin's critique was trenchant and, as Whistler confided to Boughton, its style deeply offensive to him, but the artist had suffered censure before without resorting to the queen's courts for retribution. According to the Pennells, Ruskin's review seemed malevolent to Whistler, while the writings of other critics appeared merely stupid; and because the critique had appeared (or at least been reprinted) in a "widely read" paper, the offense could only be addressed in the correspondingly public forum of a court of law.[12] George W. Smalley, London correspondent for the New York *Tribune,* suggested that Whistler brought suit because he thought Ruskin an impostor (the very charge that the critic had leveled at Whistler) and felt that "the moment had come to state his own case." Arthur Jerome Eddy, an attorney and collector from Chicago, believed that Whistler behaved as he did because he had a pose to maintain in the public eye and thought bringing suit against a critic whom everyone believed to be infallible would prove amusing. Some commentators have suggested, with reason, that Whistler "felt himself unwarrantably persecuted" when treated insolently, even though he immensely enjoyed his own insolence, and that he relished the opportunity to attack a popular critic while securing a bit of notoriety for himself.[13]

Whistler's reasons for suing Ruskin were undoubtedly as complex and multifarious as Ruskin's reasons for attacking Whistler. But one of the most compelling of the artist's motivations must have been the hope of winning cash. Although Smalley did not think Whistler ever expected to win a "substantial verdict,"[14] it is hard to imagine the artist sustaining his interest in the case for so long, and spending so much of his own and his solicitor's time and effort, if he did not think he had a case that could convince a jury to award a large compensatory payment. After years of Whistler's living beyond his means, his finances had fallen into a perilous state by the summer of 1877. He had intended to regain solvency the previous year by producing a set of Venetian etchings, but his trip to Italy was repeatedly postponed because of his preoccupation with the Peacock Room. For that effort, which had occupied him for six months to the exclusion of virtually all other work, he had counted on being handsomely remunerated. Leyland, however, paid less than half of the two thousand guineas Whistler required, and he forwarded bills to the artist for materials used in the decoration.[15] Only days before Whistler read Ruskin's critique, his creditors had begun to take action—on 6 July, Whistler wrote in dismay to his attorney that the sheriff had sent a bailiff to collect payment and that his present situation was altogether "very dreadful."[16] The prospect of earning a small fortune in damages was promising. The thousand pounds Whistler demanded might have alleviated financial disaster.

Whistler must also have realized that a public hearing would give him the chance to present formally the aesthetic principles he had been formulating throughout the 1870s. He had discovered the value of publicity during the decoration of the Peacock Room, and he agreed with Rose that a trial would also afford a useful "advertisement" for his work.[17] In court, Whistler would defend his paintings not only to clear his name from disrepute but also to correct what he believed to be a popular misconception of the very nature of art, engendered by Ruskin himself. Intending to create a taste that would approve a style, Whistler hoped to recast art in his own terms—"to enlighten the Britishers," as one correspondent said, to "the Whistlerian idea."[18]

The news that Whistler intended to take legal action would have reached Edward Burne-Jones as he was still basking in the radiance of Ruskin's review. Overwhelmed with gratitude for the effusive praise in

Fors Clavigera (a debt the critic would refuse on principle in the opening paragraph of "My Own Article on Whistler"),[19] Burne-Jones wrote immediately to volunteer his own and William Morris's assistance. Evidently, his letter arrived at Brantwood even before Ruskin received Whistler's writ. The idea of taking part in the cause was Burne-Jones's own, therefore, entirely unsolicited by Ruskin. The artist may have been relieved to hear, however, that his assistance would probably not be required. Ruskin assured Burne-Jones that he considered the trial an opportunity to advocate those principles of art economy that he had been unable to impress upon the public through his own writing but might have "sent over all the world vividly in a newspaper report or two." At that stage in the proceedings, the prospect of appearing personally in court was to him like "nuts and nectar."[20] The day after the writ was delivered, Ruskin retained the services of Walker Martineau & Co., a prestigious London law firm with offices in Gray's Inn. The solicitor responsible for preparing the case, Robert Loveband Fulford, promptly entered an appearance at the Queen's Bench Division of the High Court of Justice and announced the defendant's intention of acting as his own counsel.

Whistler was eager to learn Ruskin's "views on the subject of his writ,"[21] but was occupied during the month of September with plans for a new house on Tite Street, at the newly fashionable east end of Chelsea. "It is not given to everyone," the *Architect* remarked, "to enjoy the double luxury of building a house and fighting an art critic at the same time."[22] In fact, Whistler saw the house as a necessity. He had never had a proper studio or sufficient space for students, and as early as 1873 he had begun making plans for a more commodious home.[23] E. W. Godwin's designs for Whistler's "White House" (fig. 27) accordingly included a large atelier on the top floor. As much as he needed it, the house was an expensive enterprise that Whistler was ill prepared, in 1877, to undertake. To earn money quickly to finance the project, he acted on Howell's suggestion to produce prints from previously etched plates.[24]

In November, his debts mounting all the time, Whistler published his statement of claim (fig. 28), a pleading that declared him

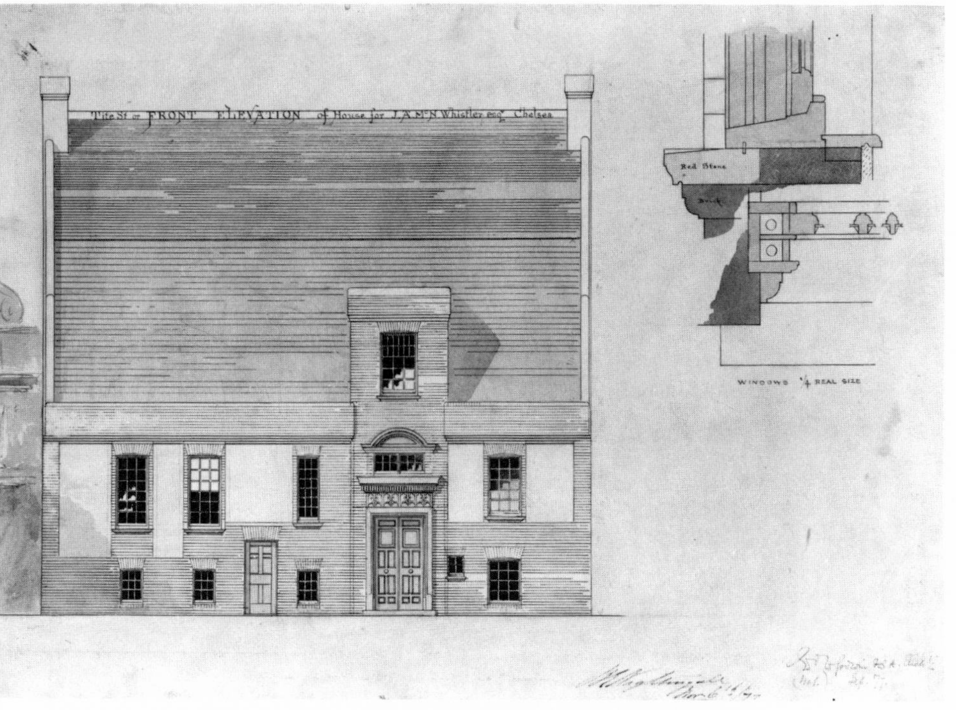

Fig. 27. Edward W. Godwin, front elevation of the White House, Tite Street, September 1877. Victoria and Albert Museum, London

entitled to payment for damages sustained as a result of Ruskin's critique. The statement established his right to bring suit: Whistler, it said, was an artist who sold his works, exhibited paintings at the Grosvenor Gallery (open to the public on payment of an entrance fee), and was the object of Ruskin's critique. And it detailed the nature of his injury: the criticism had been "falsely and maliciously printed and published," and as a consequence of its appearance in print Whistler's reputation had been substantially damaged.[25] The most pernicious part of Ruskin's critique was the allegation that Whistler's work approached the aspect of willful imposture, but the entire paragraph implied that Whistler lacked the qualifications necessary to produce a

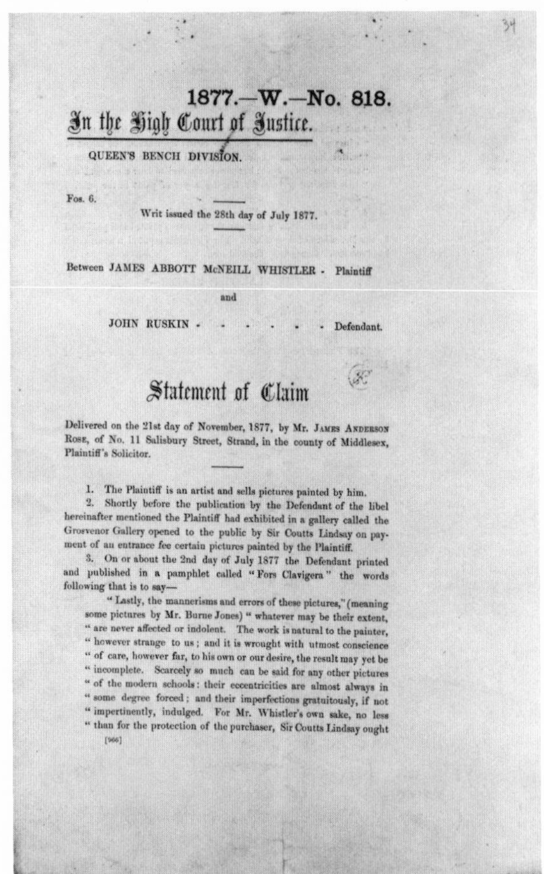

34

1877.—W.—No. 818.

In the High Court of Justice.

QUEEN'S BENCH DIVISION.

Fos. 6.

Writ issued the 28th day of July 1877.

Between JAMES ABBOTT McNEILL WHISTLER - Plaintiff

and

JOHN RUSKIN - - - - - - Defendant.

Statement of Claim

Delivered on the 21st day of November, 1877, by Mr. JAMES ANDERSON ROSE, of No. 11 Salisbury Street, Strand, in the county of Middlesex, Plaintiff's Solicitor.

1. The Plaintiff is an artist and sells pictures painted by him.

2. Shortly before the publication by the Defendant of the libel hereinafter mentioned the Plaintiff had exhibited in a gallery called the Grosvenor Gallery opened to the public by Sir Coutts Lindsay on payment of an entrance fee certain pictures painted by the Plaintiff.

3. On or about the 2nd day of July 1877 the Defendant printed and published in a pamphlet called "Fors Clavigera" the words following that is to say—

"Lastly, the mannerisms and errors of these pictures," (meaning some pictures by Mr. Burne Jones) "whatever may be their extent, "are never affected or indolent. The work is natural to the painter, "however strange to us; and it is wrought with utmost conscience "of care, however far, to his own or our desire, the result may yet be "incomplete. Scarcely so much can be said for any other pictures "of the modern schools: their eccentricities are almost always in "some degree forced; and their imperfections gratuitously, if not "impertinently, indulged. For Mr. Whistler's own sake, no less "than for the protection of the purchaser, Sir Coutts Lindsay ought

[966]

Fig. 28. Statement of Claim, 1877. Pennell-Whistler Collection, Manuscripts Division, Library of Congress, Washington, D.C.

valid work of art and seemed calculated to degrade him in public estimation—to expose him to hatred, ridicule, and contempt. It may be true, as the Pennells maintain, that Ruskin's review brought about an immediate decrease in custom,[26] but it would have been difficult for the plaintiff to prove that *Fors* was entirely to blame for nocturnes that would not sell. No special instances of injury were given in the statement of claim, only a demand for general damages of one thousand pounds, plus the costs of the action.

Ruskin's attorney responded to Whistler's claim with a request for additional time to deliver his client's answer.[27] This would have been the first in the sequence of postponements that would eventually delay the trial for twelve months, but the court denied the request, and Ruskin's statement of defense was delivered on 6 December 1877. The defendant's pleading denied Whistler's allegation that Ruskin's critique had been falsely and maliciously printed and set forth the defensive argument of fair comment on a matter of public interest: the alleged libel was privileged, since it was a "fair and bonâ fide criticism upon a painting which the Plaintiff had exposed for public view." Within a week, Rose had submitted Whistler's reply, in which the plaintiff took issue with the defendant's claim that the criticism had been fair and in good faith. With that, the pleadings—statements of the facts constituting the plaintiff's cause and the defendant's defense—came to a close.[28] The course of the action was set, and the disagreement between Whistler and Ruskin, as one reporter remarked late in December, was unlikely to be settled over teacups in Venice.[29]

But hopeful rumors that the action had been dropped continued to circulate in London. During the first month of the new year, the *Architect* published a report that Whistler, having consulted with his lawyers, had decided not to arraign Ruskin after all: "It is hard, no doubt, to be accused of throwing one's paint-pot at the public, of impudence, and even, if we remember right, of imposture; but, hard though it be, it must be meekly borne."[30] A few days after the article appeared, Whistler assured Godwin that "all the yarn about Ruskin" was untrue, which suggests that he fully intended to proceed with the action.[31] Ruskin's counsel had in fact been notified that a trial by jury was scheduled to take place on the second of February, 1878.[32] At the end of January, however, all proceedings stopped abruptly, not to begin again until spring. The defendant's sanity was slipping away.

The mental breakdown that Ruskin's critique apparently presaged finally occurred at the end of February.[33] Ruskin later confided to his American friend Charles Eliot Norton that he had lost his mind over Saint Ursula and others ("chiefly young-lady saints"), suffering from "strayed wits" and delirium caused, he believed, by temporary inflammation of the brain.[34] In March, as he himself wrote Thomas Carlyle, Ruskin went "heartily & headily mad," becoming terrified of specters raised by the reflection of firelight flickering on his mahogany bedpost,[35] an effect probably not unlike the one produced by Whistler's *Nocturne in Black and Gold.* News of Ruskin's illness, if not his insanity, appeared in the papers, but early in April, Anderson Rose read that Ruskin was improving and suggested to Ruskin's solicitor that the trial be postponed for no more than another month. In the belief that *Whistler v. Ruskin* would be tried later that spring, counsel for both sides began preparing for court.[36] Although an action for libel could be tried by a judge alone, Whistler requested a trial by jury in the hope that a panel of his peers would award greater damages. Because the intricacies of libel law could render the judgment of ordinary, reasonable men inadequate, nineteenth-century libel suits were typically tried before a panel of men who possessed some stature in society; both parties agreed in April to a "special jury" composed of educated property-holders who might better understand the legal issues under discussion.[37]

But Ruskin's recovery was not complete. On 29 April, his solicitor informed Rose that Ruskin would be too ill to attend court for several months, and upon his application the trial of *Whistler v. Ruskin* was postponed until the Trinity sittings of the court, which would begin in late July. One month later Fulford wrote to Rose that although he had not heard for sure, he doubted that Ruskin would be able to appear even then and so had applied for another adjournment. George Parsons, the Hawkshead physician who had seen Ruskin through his mental illness, prepared a statement certifying that Ruskin was, and probably would be for some time, "in a totally unfit state of health" to prepare for or take part in the pending action. Rose, against his inclination, decided to comply with Fulford's request to adjourn the trial further. That measure of cooperation, he wrote Whistler, would preclude the possibility of a grievance by the defense that Whistler had forced the trial on, knowing Ruskin to be unwell.[38]

By the middle of June, then, Walker Martineau & Co. had succeeded in delaying the trial for several more months, at least until the court's Michaelmas sittings, which would commence in November.[39] The repeated postponements caused the controversy to evaporate from public consciousness, and in some cases reinforced rumors that the matter had been entirely abandoned. The *New York Times* published the unlikely news that Whistler and Ruskin had met and parted "sworn friends," having resolved their differences out of court: "Whistler must have been glad of such an ending to an art quarrel when Ruskin soon afterward lay at death's door, and the doctors accounted for many of his latter day vagaries by the morbid working of an over-taxed brain."[40]

Perhaps Whistler did welcome the delay, for he had other projects under way during the spring and summer of 1878, when he would otherwise have been spending his time preparing for trial. At the end of April, a catalogue of Sir Henry Thompson's collection of blue-and-white porcelain, largely illustrated by Whistler, was published in a limited edition of 220 copies and exhibited together with the porcelain and the original watercolors at Murray Marks's shop in Oxford Street.[41] At the same time, Whistler wrote Rose, he was "working every minute of the day" to finish pictures, presumably the works he intended to show at the second summer exhibition of the Grosvenor Gallery, which would open on the first of May.[42]

Both Whistler and Burne-Jones would again be well represented in that showing although, as one reviewer remarked, "apart from the fact that the novelty of their styles has been somewhat worn off by last year's exhibition, they are not so preponderatingly the 'features' of the exhibition as they were before."[43] The critics offered the customary interpretations of Whistler's exhibits, commenting on the obscurity of the nocturnes and the eccentricity of their titles. William Michael Rossetti again voiced his admiration for Whistler's "remarkable gifts," but wished for "a little less of personal whim, and more willingness to take the world on the same terms on which other people take it."[44] A writer for the *Daily News* attempted to justify the peculiarities of Whistler's style with the statement that he "leaves off where other artists begin," and asserted an opinion that Burne-Jones would reiterate in court: "He shirks all the difficulties ahead, and asks the spectator to complete the picture himself."[45]

Apparently, Ruskin's critique from the previous year was not altogether forgotten. The art critic for the *Examiner,* explaining that the appreciation of Whistler's paintings depended on their being seen from a distance, made a particularly telling remark. "When the spectator goes so near that what appears a few feet off to be the light of a lamp or a squib is seen to be only a smear of paint, he has no right to complain that the artist has flung his paint-pot in his face; the truth is that he has put his nose into the paint-pot."[46]

If nothing else, the provocative exhibits at the second Grosvenor exhibition enhanced the notoriety Whistler had achieved as a result of the Peacock Room and the Ruskin critique. The *World* selected the artist as the subject for "Celebrities at Home," a series of articles on the domestic lives of prominent Englishmen; a profile of Ruskin had been published the previous summer.[47] Whistler's interview with the *World,* faithfully transcribed and published the third week of May, was not intended as an essay on art, but it constituted a stylistic manifesto and would be reprinted years later in *The Gentle Art of Making Enemies* as "The Red Rag," a treatise inviting attack.[48] In the pages of the *World,* Whistler gave the first public explanation of his style, expounding principles he would afterward use to defend himself against Ruskin. The interviewer explained that "the cornerstone of Mr. Whistler's art-philosophy" was that a picture "should have its own merit, and never depend upon dramatic or legendary or local interest." That essential idea, developed in various ways, formed the foundation for the article. It was recounted that Whistler condemned the English for refusing to "consider a picture as a picture, apart from any story which it may be supposed to tell." Art, the painter said, should be free from "clap-trap"—emotions unrelated to arrangements of color—and entirely independent of imitation, which was properly the province of the photographer.[49] Painting could be called the poetry of sight, just as music was the poetry of sound, because subject matter had nothing whatever to do with either painted or musical arrangements.

But readers of the *World* tended to take more interest in the lifestyles of celebrities than in their philosophies, and Whistler's observations on art were quoted amid chatty biographical notes and detailed descriptions of the decoration of his Chelsea home. Although its tone was generally complimentary, "Celebrities at Home" propagated tales of Whistler's many eccentricities: his penchant for Japanese design, his tendency to perceive people as color harmonies, his custom of drying works outdoors, his taste for buckwheat cakes, his oversize paintbrushes and table-top palette, his practice of painting without sketches and completing portraits in a matter of minutes. The serious aesthetic intentions the artist professed in the *World* were undermined, or perhaps simply overwhelmed, by trivial and amusing details of his peculiar way of life.

The celebrity's new home was standing by mid April, and Whistler hoped to assume occupancy in June. But the Metropolitan Board of Works, from whom the land was leased, objected to the design of the house as too simple to conform to the Tite Street style. The White House, as the *British Architect* reported, was "unhappily of white brick and is covered with green slates—two heresies in the last modern faith, that believes only in red brick and red tile."[50] The Board of Works demanded a number of changes, including ornamental moldings (see fig. 29), which were produced by Whistler's friend, the sculptor Joseph Edgar Boehm. The cost of the additions would exceed nine hundred pounds, and Whistler's move would be delayed until autumn.

Desperate for funds to finance the completion of the White House, Whistler began pawning paintings. His friend Charles Howell, ever industrious, deposited several of Whistler's works with Jane Noseda, a printseller in the Strand, as security for small loans. Howell clearly took advantage of Whistler's misfortune—he bought the unfinished portrait of Irving, for example, for ten pounds and a sealskin coat.[51] Whistler was vulnerable to exploitation and probably assented unhesitatingly to Howell's schemes, since Howell alone offered solutions to an increasingly dire situation.

For eight pounds and the promise of six proofs, Howell purchased the copyright to *Arrangement in Grey and Black, No. 2,* Whistler's portrait of Carlyle, and arranged with Henry Graves, the head of a printselling firm in Pall Mall, to have the painting reproduced in mezzotint by an engraver named Richard Josey.[52] That project was ill-

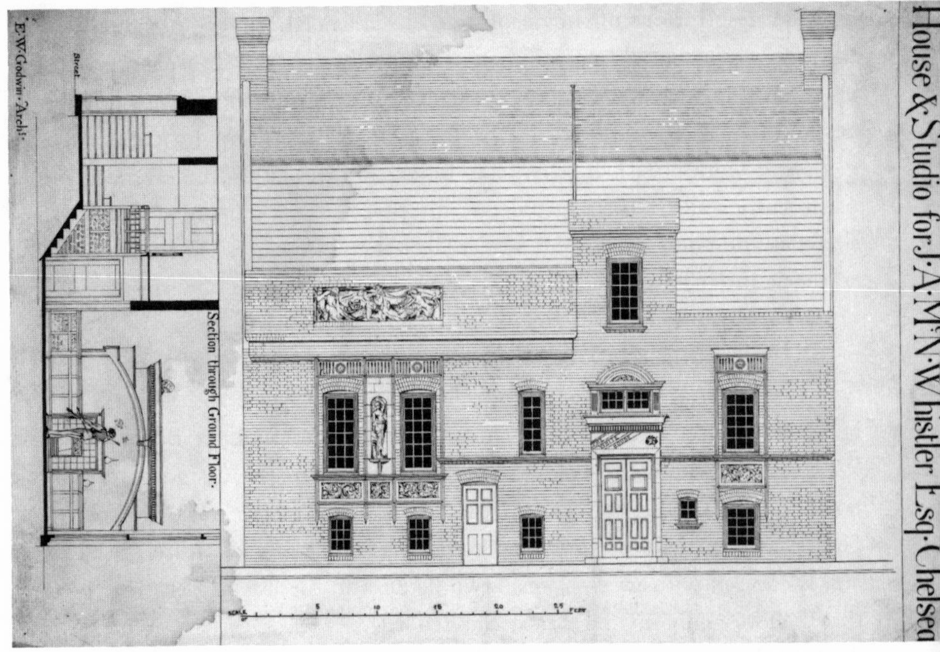

Fig. 29. Edward W. Godwin, front elevation of the White House, Tite Street, 29 November [1878]. Victoria and Albert Museum, London

fated from the start: Josey was to produce three hundred proofs of the first state, but the copper plate could not sustain so large a run, and an attempt at steel-plating was a dismal failure. When efforts to remove the steel ruined the ground, Josey had partially to re-engrave the plate, which had to be repaired again after only seventy more impressions.[53] Nevertheless, Graves decided to commission Whistler to paint a portrait of the prime minister, Benjamin Disraeli, from which mezzotint engravings could also be made for popular distribution; but Disraeli icily refused to oblige.[54]

As the months wore on Whistler sank ever deeper into debt, with an award of damages his only hope for regaining solvency and self-esteem. In mid October, when Whistler paid a visit to his friend Alan Cole, he appeared plainly depressed—"very hard up," Cole observed, "and fearful of getting old."[55]

Sometime around the middle of September a solution appeared in the form of an overture from someone representing Ruskin's interests—a proposition that the action be settled out of court by payment of costs and an apology. The suggestion, which was not conveyed in writing and seems not to have issued from Ruskin himself, may have been made by a well-meaning but meddlesome friend, or by a member of Walker Martineau & Co. who wanted to save the firm the time and expense involved in a trial it felt liable to lose. Charles Bowen, the respected junior counsel for the defense, had given the opinion early in the proceedings that Ruskin was unlikely to win—his trenchant words were clearly contemptuous, and an English jury was better equipped to criticize language than art.[56] Rose and Whistler spent four hours one evening in October discussing the form the apology might take, and Rose subsequently wrote Robert Fulford on the pretense of inquiring about Ruskin's health, so that, as he wrote Whistler (reminding him to keep the matter confidential), "if there be anything in the suggestion made to you—the door may be open for discussing the proposal."[57] But nothing came of Rose's letter. Perhaps the proposal had been only innuendo that Whistler seized upon in desperation. In any event, it is doubtful that Ruskin, even in a state of extremity, would have agreed to retract his words about Whistler.

By the third week in October, both sides were again preparing for the trial, then on the list for Monday, 18 November.

PLAINTIFF'S STRATEGY

ROSE'S FIRST STEP IN formulating Whistler's case had been to order three copies of Ruskin's miscellany, at tenpence apiece, direct from the publisher. Like Whistler, Rose had probably never before seen an issue of *Fors Clavigera.* Upon receiving the first copy, he discovered that it was a modest publication, consisting of twenty-four widely spaced pages of text and nine pages of notes and correspondence—a "very small modicum," as he defined it in the plaintiff's brief, "of the scandal and twaddle of the day." The Pennells presume that Rose, in pointing out that *Fors* was poor value for money, was acting on Whistler's suggestion that it was Ruskin (rather than Whistler) who was guilty of overcharging for his work.[1] In fact, the solicitor was simply identifying the readership of the publication: he doubted that the working men of England—to whom the letters were purportedly addressed—could afford to pay the "preposterous" price of tenpence for a pamphlet of so little substance. Had the audience of *Fors* comprised only members of the working classes, its distribution would have posed little threat to Whistler.

Rose was more concerned about the effect Ruskin's words might have upon potential patrons, those "masters and princes" to whom tenpence was a trifle. He would therefore instruct the plaintiff—"or some person who can speak from personal knowledge"—to testify that *Fors Clavigera* was commonly circulated among people who took

Fig. 30. Photograph of Whistler by H. S. Mendelssohn, London, ca. 1888. George A. Lucas Collection of the Maryland Institute, College of Art, on indefinite loan to the Baltimore Museum of Art, Md., L.33.53.9092

"an interest in art matters."[2] There is nothing to suggest that Whistler knew this to be a fact; his dubious statement in court that he had seen the publication in his friends' houses would cause the *Weekly Dispatch,* a paper intended for working-class readers, to comment that the artist's acquaintance was clearly peculiar, and "more limited than would have been imagined."[3] The prohibitive price of *Fors* did imply a certain exclusivity, and Rose wanted to suggest that Ruskin had deliberately adopted an outrageous style "to sell the muck he writes."[4]

To dismantle the defense that Ruskin had penned his critique for the public good, plaintiff's counsel would have to prove that Ruskin had prospered at Whistler's expense. It would have been difficult to prove, however, that *Fors Clavigera* was sold for profit. Because the author wished to retain complete control over its distribution, copies of *Fors* were relatively difficult to obtain. They were not available in the usual places, bookstores or railway-station bookstalls, and few news vendors had even heard of the publication.[5] Circulation depended almost entirely upon subscriptions, and Rose later subpoenaed the publisher, George Allen, to provide the court with the number of subscribers and their names. Allen, however, was not called to the stand, presumably because his figures would not have supported the plaintiff's premise.[6] Considering the restrictions on its sale, *Fors Clavigera* was remarkably successful, yet its annual circulation was smaller than that of a single edition of the *Echo,* a halfpenny evening newspaper with a limited London readership.[7]

If *Fors Clavigera* was a poor vehicle for disseminating Ruskin's views, the popular press was extrememly efficient. The *Saturday Review,* announcing the inaugural issue of Ruskin's publication in 1871, had pointed out that although the author did not advertise, copies of *Fors* were sent "to each of the principal journals and periodicals, to be noticed or not, at their pleasure."[8] By 1874, Ruskin had abandoned even that minimal publicity. Yet the infamous July number of *Fors Clavigera,* as Rose stated in the plaintiff's brief, was "more noticed and extracted from by the press than any other number . . . and solely because it contained this libel on Mr. Whistler." The plaintiff himself had first seen the libel reprinted in a London paper. Rose was advised that only the newspapers and journals that had copied Ruskin's paragraph word for word could be admitted as evidence in aggravation of damages; yet he argued that even those articles that condemned Ruskin's style of criticism (notably the leading article in the *Daily News*) had injured his client by attracting attention to Ruskin's review.[9] Ruskin could not be held accountable for the actions of the press, however, and that argument also could have been only feebly supported in court.

To demonstrate that Ruskin's censure had caused substantial pecuniary injury, Whistler's counsel would also have to demonstrate the defendant's formidable authority. Ruskin's position as an "art censor" was widely acknowledged,[10] and there would have been no difficulty in convincing a jury that Ruskin's popular prestige was sufficient to persuade the public to adopt his point of view. Artists and patrons alike accepted his opinions on art as gospel, Rose said. Ruskin, moreover, was "the ram of art criticism," whom other writers followed like sheep. But emphasizing Ruskin's power over the art community—indeed, over Victorian society—would only illuminate the defendant's achievements and affirm his right to speak freely about matters of public interest. Ruskin, the more eminent Victorian, appeared entitled to certain privileges. Accusing Whistler of making a "cheap and nasty attack on Mr. Ruskin," the *Referee* remarked that society had not yet bestowed upon the artist "the right to be insolent to its most respected member."[11]

Indeed, Ruskin's allegedly libelous passage in *Fors Clavigera,* a comment on a work of art that had been publicly exhibited, was prima facie privileged, or automatically immune from the consequences of the law, unless the plaintiff could find evidence of malicious intent. Rose argued that the intemperance of Ruskin's language, which betrayed his malevolent turn of mind, should be sufficient to prove that the defendant had transgressed the bounds of fair criticism. But as any reader will discover upon reviewing the text of *Fors,* the paragraph relating to Whistler is consistent with the publication's polemical style elsewhere. Rose himself observed in the brief that "without the slightest apparent connection the name of someone is unexpectedly dragged in and covered with abuse of insult or filth," and cited as examples the abuse flung at Henry Cole, the founder of the South Kensington Museum (now the Victoria and Albert Museum); the journalist Harriet Martineau; and the historian Goldwin Smith. If the insults riddling the pages of *Fors* supported the plaintiff's contention that Ruskin's language was often extreme, they also proved that the words about Whistler

Fig. 31. Spy [Leslie Ward], "A Lawyer," 1873, chromolithograph. "Men of the Day, No. LXXIII: Serjeant Parry," *Vanity Fair,* 13 December 1873

had been written in Ruskin's "usual style of comment." Ultimately, Rose was persuaded that any mention of other "libels" would only defeat Whistler's accusation of malice.[12]

The barrister Rose retained to represent Whistler in court was John Humffreys Parry (fig. 31), serjeant-at-law, the highest rank a barrister could attain, since 1856. Serjeant Parry was well acquainted with notoriety, having been involved in a number of celebrated causes, including the sensational trials of Arthur Orton, the

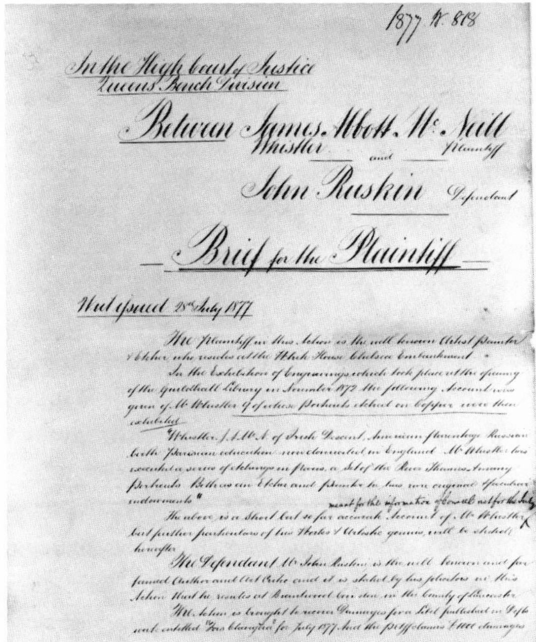
1877 W. 818

In the High Court of Justice
Queens Bench Division

Between James Abbott McNeill Whistler Plaintiff
and
John Ruskin Defendant

Brief for the Plaintiff

Writ issued 28th July 1877

The Plaintiff in this Action is the well known Artist Painter & Etcher who resides at the White House Chelsea Embankment.

In the Exhibition of Engravings which took place at the opening of the Guildhall Library in November 1872 the following Account was given of Mr Whistler 9 of whose Portraits etched on Copper were then exhibited

"Whistler, J. A. McN. of Irish Descent, American parentage, Russian birth, Parisian education, now domiciled in England. Mr Whistler has executed a series of etchings in [illegible], a Set of the River Thames, & many Portraits. Both as an Etcher and Painter he has very original & peculiar endowments"

meant for the information of Counsel not for the Jury

The above is a short but so far accurate Account of Mr Whistler but further particulars of his Works & Artistic genius will be stated hereafter

The Defendant Mr John Ruskin is the well known and far famed Author and Art Critic and it is stated by his solicitors in this Action that he resides at Brantwood Coniston in the County of Lancashire

This Action is brought to recover Damages for a Libel published in [illegible] work entitled "Fors Clavigera" for July 1877. And the Plff claims £1000 damages

1

Fig. 32. Brief for the Plaintiff, 1877–78. Pennell-Whistler Collection, Manuscripts Division, Library of Congress, Washington, D.C.

Tichborne claimant.[13] Parry's theatrical, even melodramatic, style made him a successful advocate who was especially gifted in making appeals on the part of starving widows and orphans. He was said to hold the jury's attention with perorations so impassioned that his wig would flop on his forehead.[14] Parry, Rose assured Whistler, was "acknowledged to be a man of great eloquence, but especially of sound judgment, discretion, and prudence." His junior, William Comer Petheram, came with sterling credentials as well: he was an excellent, experienced, and popular lawyer, with a large practice and good presence. Moreover, Rose told Whistler, Petheram was a gentleman.[15]

Parry chose not to employ many of the arguments that Rose proposed in the brief (fig. 32), leading the Pennells to propose the idea that he had ignored the document altogether.[16] The marginalia of the final copy suggest otherwise: Parry obviously read the brief, but must have found the strategy it outlined harmless to the defendant and inadequate to protect the plaintiff. Indeed, the plaintiff's brief is neither cogent nor entirely coherent, although multiple manuscript drafts testify to the pains Rose took in its preparation. This document, composed for the benefit of the barristers, is a compilation of the opinions of several consulting attorneys, interwoven with Rose's own views, which can be recognized by the emotional intensity of their expression. In one passage, for example, Rose relates that Whistler's intimate friends (of whom, we assume, he is one) find the author of *Fors* contemptible, "and but for Mr. Ruskin's age and known infirmities, a man . . . might be tempted to avenge himself personally."[17] Rose betrays his devotion to Whistler in the brief's introduction, where an unattributed quotation concluding with the assertion that Whistler's endowments were "rare, original, and peculiar" is given as a succinct and presumably disinterested account of the plaintiff's professional life. The quotation, published years earlier in an exhibition catalogue, had in fact been written by Rose himself.[18]

Anderson Rose was so convinced of his client's talents that he failed to anticipate the criticism that was bound to arise in court. Serjeant Parry did not share that blind admiration. Parry conferred with Rose about effective means of defending Whistler's peculiarities, but he confided to his son that he feared the plaintiff's eccentricity would make the verdict difficult to win.[19] Whistler's image was indeed an issue. Whistler himself advised Rose (who was told to tell Parry) that to represent him as anything other than "the well known Whistler," a persona he had carefully cultivated over the years, would be "bad policy," and that more could be gained "by sticking to this character." By maintaining in court the role of the butterfly, Whistler hoped to "explain away the appearance of Academicians" who might be called to testify against him. Having heard that Henry Stacy Marks, R.A., would come prepared to paint a nocturne in five minutes, Whistler fully expected an "Academic demonstration."[20]

As much as Ruskin himself, the Royal Academy would be Whistler's unseen adversary in court. Whistler had never been elected an associate and had not shown a painting at Burlington House since the exhibition of *Arrangement in Grey and Black* in 1872. Parry prudently requested a list of works Whistler had exhibited there in the past to add credence to the claim that he was a frequent, if not habitual, exhibitor at the Royal Academy.[21] Counsel for the defense were under the impression that Whistler had become "so eccentric in his work that his pictures were rejected year after year." To counter that assertion, Whistler proposed the argument that he was known to have held "an independent position in Art" and to have endured, as a result, the academy's opposition.[22]

But the establishment of Whistler's reputation would have to depend primarily on the testimony of expert witnesses. Whistler suggested Prince Teck, the husband of Queen Victoria's daughter Mary, who had visited the Peacock Room and could testify that it was "a great piece of Art," and the Reverend Hugh Reginald Haweis, who had the previous year in St. James's Hall delivered a "perfect poem of praise" on the subject of the Peacock Room and could swear "to what he had preached." He also recommended George William Reid, keeper of prints and drawings at the British Museum, and Richard R. Holmes of the Royal Library at Windsor, to testify that the collections under their care included Whistler etchings.[23] But these witnesses could not provide appropriate testimony. Whistler's counsel may have thought it wise to leave the Peacock Room—another topic of dissension—out of the courtroom, and the whereabouts of the etchings was not a matter of debate. Rose was advised to find "as many witnesses as possible of position and of known taste" who would be prepared to state that Whistler was a well-known artist, and that his paintings ("though they may not please some critics") were "of great and *recognized* merit." For that purpose, Petheram recommended art dealers, art critics, and artists.[24]

The dealers would stand as authorities on the market value of Whistler's paintings—a subject that Ruskin, as an art critic, had been unqualified to address. Charles Howell, who had been recruited early in November to help devise Whistler's battle plan,[25] gave Rose suggestions on evidence that he and other art dealers could present in court; but perhaps because he was busy with preparations for a trial of his own that would go to court the day after the end of *Whistler v. Ruskin,* Howell's name came last on the list of witnesses.[26] Another London picture dealer, Oswald Colnaghi, volunteered to testify that he was "well acquainted technically and practically with pictures of all schools foreign and British," which qualified him to state that Whistler's *Nocturne in Blue and Gold* (plate 5), in particular, was an "almost extraordinary and wonderful picture," indeed a "transcript of nature." Colnaghi further agreed to say that Whistler was highly educated and enthusiastic and that Ruskin's written opinion, which appeared calculated to damage the plaintiff's reputation, would depreciate the value of the paintings, if it did not stop their sale altogether.[27] The print dealer Algernon Graves also agreed to testify, primarily about the success of the Carlyle print. Graves was served with a subpoena, but his "proofs" do not appear in the plaintiff's brief. In the end, none of the art dealers would be called to the stand.[28]

The art critic chosen to speak on Whistler's behalf was William Michael Rossetti (fig. 33), identified in the margin of the plaintiff's brief as "the brother of Dante Gabriel Rossetti the celebrated painter." The distinguished man of letters always stood in the shadow of his more celebrated siblings.[29] Although not an artist himself, William Rossetti was one of the founding members of the Pre-Raphaelite Brotherhood and editor of its journal, *The Germ.* Among his literary achievements in later years were the publication of poems by Walt Whitman, which introduced the American poet to Britain; two editions of Shelley's poetical works; an eloquent defense of Swinburne's *Poems and Ballads;* a prose translation of Dante's *Inferno;* and a biography of William Blake, produced with the assistance of Dante Gabriel Rossetti and Anne Gilchrist, Blake's widow. Rossetti was also the editor of Moxon's "popular poets" series and the author of art reviews for countless journals, including the *Spectator, Edinburgh Weekly Review, Saturday Review, Fraser's Magazine,* and *Pall Mall Gazette.* From 1873, Rossetti was principal art critic for the *Academy,* a weekly journal of arts and letters.

Because his personality was less engaging than his brother's, William Rossetti was sometimes perceived by his contemporaries as a man

Fig. 33. Photograph of William Michael Rossetti, ca. 1865. Bancroft Archives, Delaware Art Museum, Wilmington; Samuel and Mary Bancroft Memorial

of mediocre intelligence.[30] Edward Burne-Jones took particular delight in telling about the time that Gabriel Rossetti, who did not share William Morris's enthusiasm for the Scandinavian story of Fafnar, professed himself unable to take "interest in a man who has a dragon for a brother," to which Morris is supposed to have replied that he would rather have a dragon for a brother than a fool.[31] Alluding to that often repeated anecdote, William Rothenstein maintained that Rossetti was a fool by no means, but a critic who "kept his faith in the power of art bright and clean; and his outlook on life was broad and humane."[32] Indeed, William Rossetti is an unacknowledged champion of the late nineteenth-century English avant-garde. Having begun his career as an apologist of the Pre-Raphaelites, he remained fearless in defense of artists outside the British art establishment, frequently dismissing enormously popular works, such as William Powell Frith's *Derby Day,* as "commonplace."[33] Remarkably ahead of his time, Rossetti held that the critic, in judging a work of art, should be mindful of the artist's intentions. He answered detractors of Burne-Jones's Grosvenor exhibits, for example, by asserting that each work was "justified to itself by adequately and exquisitely fulfilling its own conditions, and that these are essentially aesthetic conditions."[34]

From his first sight of a Whistler painting, Rossetti recognized that the artist was "destined for renown."[35] He remained an astute critic of Whistler's work, predicting in an 1863 review of etchings that "the fogs, beauties, and oddities" of the river Thames "bid fair to become Mr. Whistler's *specialité.*" In 1865 he summarized Whistler's aesthetic achievements with the statement that the artist possessed "a veritable intuition for a certain system of colour and handling, which, with him, produces the exact result he aims at."[36] One of Rossetti's critiques most favorable to Whistler, an *Academy* review of the Dudley Gallery's 1875 winter exhibition, convinced Anderson Rose that Rossetti was the critic to lend credibility to Whistler's reputation. Rose determined to subpoena Rossetti to testify that he had written in the *Academy* "what he believed to be true," and that he continued to hold a high opinion of Whistler as an artist.

William Rossetti had known Whistler since 1862, when he and his brother became Whistler's neighbors in Chelsea. During the first years of the seventies the Rossettis saw Whistler frequently and, according to William, "on the most intimate footing." Later, after Gabriel became a recluse in Tudor House and William, as a result of his marriage in 1874, spent less time "among old bachelor friends," Whistler and the Rossetti brothers met less often. William Rossetti claimed in his reminiscences the rare distinction of never having quarreled with Whistler. Indeed, when Whistler was unjustly expelled from the Burlington Fine Arts Club in 1867, Rossetti had resigned in protest.[37] And in 1878, when Whistler came to blows with Ruskin, Rossetti sided with him once again.

There was, however, a complication affecting Rossetti's participation in *Whistler v. Ruskin.* "The fact is," he wrote Anderson Rose after receiving a subpoena,

> Ruskin is an old and valued friend of mine (little tho' I have seen of him in late years); and, tho' I don't either agree in his ill-opinion of Wh[istler]'s pictures or approve the phrases he uses, still I sh[ould] be very sorry to take a personal part in getting him mulcted in damages.[38]

That friendship dated to the early 1850s, when Ruskin had come to the aid of the Pre-Raphaelite Brotherhood. Since 1860, however, Rossetti had seen the critic infrequently.[39] Rossetti inevitably found himself in conflict with Ruskin as he began to formulate standards of his own, and Ruskin brought about an irreparable breach in the friendship when in 1867 he asserted arrogantly and erroneously that he and Gabriel Rossetti had taught William everything he knew about art.[40]

Nevertheless, Rossetti was loath to testify against Ruskin. Rose understood the difficulty of his position, but considering his testimony vital to Whistler's cause, he wrote at length to Rossetti to explain the circumstances under which he had been subpoenaed. To remind Rossetti of his position, he appended extracts from the laudatory *Academy* review. Rose followed his letter with a personal visit to Rossetti at work at Somerset House, where Rossetti persisted in his protests but eventually agreed to attend court if absolutely necessary to give his "sincerely felt witness to the excellences" of Whistler's *Nocturne in Blue and Gold* (plate 5); he had criticized *Nocturne in Black and Gold* in the same notice, but the "Falling Rocket" seems to have made no lasting impression, for he denied in the *Reminiscences* ever having written anything about it.[41] Rossetti regretted, however, having been "coerced into so delicate, and in some sense so false, a position," and out of deference to Ruskin wrote him a letter "explaining the exact facts." However, Rossetti always believed that Ruskin had been "substantially wrong" in his critique of Whistler's *Nocturne in Black and Gold.* Decades after the trial he reconfirmed his conviction that Ruskin's "estimate, so far as one particular picture was concerned, may perhaps have been not very far from the mark: but there is such a thing as courtesy in criticism; and a critic of so much potency as Ruskin, in the wielding of his pen and in his influence over the public, ought not to have lost sight of that."[42]

It appears that Rossetti was the only art critic Whistler cared to subpoena. As witnesses, practicing painters would be more influential. Rose would instruct them to affirm that Whistler's works were "of the highest character of art" and that Ruskin, whose opinion they knew to be influential with patrons, had calculated his critique to prevent the sale of those works. Whistler at first assumed his fellow artists would rally to "drive the false prophet out of the temple,"[43] but he would be sorely disappointed. To his solicitor, he offered the explanation that the esoteric style of his work, "quite apart from the usual stuff furnished in the mass," accounted for the paucity of witnesses willing to testify on his behalf. "I don't stand in the position of the *popular* picture maker," he said, "with herds of admirers."[44] "Popular" was probably meant to modify "picture," but the implications of the word are cast upon "picture maker," or painter, as well—a syntactic ambiguity that may reflect Whistler's own uncertainty about whether his isolated stance was attributable to his paintings or his personality.

Having been abandoned by the "timid herd," as Harper Pennington recounted, Whistler felt "stung to the quick and thoroughly disgusted with the whole fraternity, who left him to battle single-handed for the honor of the profession." He never trusted any of them again.[45] After the trial, Whistler's disappointment would turn to bitterness, as he came to believe that the artists of England had conspired to bring about his defeat. "They all hoped they could drive me out of the country, or kill me!" he told the Pennells. "And if I hadn't had the constitution of a Government mule, they would."[46] It is telling that *The Gentle Art of Making Enemies* opens with an account of the trial.

Among the "witness-painters" Whistler proposed to subpoena was Charles Keene, a painter and etcher best known for his drawings in *Punch.*[47] Keene agreed to attest to his opinion of Whistler's work if necessary, but implored Whistler to do without his testimony, even though the trial promised to be "the greatest 'lark' that has been known for a long time in the courts."[48] Whistler could not afford to call reluctant witnesses, so Keene was not required to testify. Proofs—written statements of facts that witnesses would be asked to affirm in court—were also prepared for William Eden Nesfield, an architect who shared Whistler's interest in Japanese design; and Matthew Elden, a Wandsworth artist, probably the "mysterious man named Eldon" who according to T. R. Way was for a time constantly in Whistler's company.[49] Richard Josey, the engraver of the Carlyle mezzotint, was also proposed as a witness, to testify that through translating paintings into black and white he had become qualified to judge Whistler's works, which he believed to be "of the highest order of artistic merit."[50] It is probable that E. W. Godwin was also proposed as a witness, although as he was architect of the White House, his testimony might have been considered biased. Godwin attended court both days of the trial, however, making sketches and notes from his seat behind Whistler, where he may have been awaiting a call to the stand.[51]

Whistler founded his hopes for a favorable verdict on several letters "speaking highly of the moonlight pictures" written by some of the most celebrated artists of the day: Frederic Leighton, president of the Royal Academy; Frederick Burton, director of the National Gallery; and Edward John Poynter, director for art and principal of the South Kensington Museum. The only one of those letters that has come to light is Poynter's, regarding Whistler's exhibits at the Dudley Gallery in 1871. Referring to *Nocturne: Blue and Silver—Chelsea* (fig. 17), Poynter wrote that it rendered "the poetical side of the scene better than any moonlight picture" he had ever seen.[52] Whistler discussed the letters with Thomas Armstrong, an artist he had known since his student days in Paris, when they met at the Arts Club shortly before the trial. The assurance that Whistler held such influential evidence allayed Armstrong's fear that an English jury would be incapable of recognizing the beauty of a nocturne,[53] but the letters could not be admitted as evidence in court without the supporting testimony of their authors. On 11 November, Whistler thought all three artists would testify, but by the twentieth he had removed Poynter from the list. Two days before the trial he learned that Burton also refused to appear, leaving only Leighton, whose recent ascendancy at the Royal Academy would have made him the star witness. But unhappily for Whistler, Leighton was called to Windsor to be knighted by the queen on the day set for trial, a summons that superseded all others.[54] Armstrong himself was providentially out of town.

One artist Whistler assumed would be an eager ally was Jacques (James) Joseph Tissot, his friend since the 1850s. As students in Paris they had together painted copies of Ingres's *Angélique* in the Louvre, and their friendship remained cordial throughout the sixties and seventies as Tissot established a reputation in London. He was a frequent dinner guest at Whistler's house in Chelsea, and one memorable evening in 1875, at a "capital small dinner" served on blue-and-white china, the conversation centered on "ideas on art unfettered by principles"—the topic of art for art's sake that would inform Whistler's courtroom apologia.[55] Tissot's paintings of modern life were often shown at the Royal Academy to great acclaim, but many of his ten Grosvenor exhibits had been dismissed by Ruskin in *Fors Clavigera* as "mere coloured photographs of vulgar society."[56]

Whistler had every reason to believe Tissot would stand up for him in court and confidently recommended him to Rose as a witness. But Tissot also proved reluctant to appear on Whistler's behalf. He apparently offered to write down his views for the jury, but because the tentativeness of his opinion was transparent, Whistler advised Tissot to keep his letter to himself.[57] A subpoena was served on 23 November, but Whistler assured Tissot that he would not be called to the stand, as he would be useless to the cause in a state of anguished reluctance. The letter Whistler drafted 24 November advising his friend to appear in court only to comply with the law is among the saddest of the surviving documents relating to the trial. "I explained that I was wrong to suppose that Tissot would have been proud to proclaim himself the friend of Whistler," the artist wrote. "Useless,

Fig. 34. Joseph Edgar Boehm, *James A. McNeill Whistler,* ca. 1877, terracotta with ebonized wood plinth. Exhibited Grosvenor Gallery 1877, no. 5. Toledo Museum of Art, Ohio; gift of Florence Scott Libbey

my dear!—and I repay my last debt of friendship in helping you avoid prison."[58]

The sculptor Joseph Edgar Boehm, Godwin's collaborator on the White House, was a better ally. Whistler had known him at least since 1869, when he had written George Lucas that Boehm was a "very charming friend" and "one of the most distinguished sculptors of London."[59] Boehm had sculpted the portrait bust of Whistler (fig. 34) that had been shown in 1877 at the Grosvenor Gallery—"a mere sketch," as it was described in *The Times,* "but so instinct with vitality and character that no one who knows the original would wish it carried further"[60]—and in October 1878 affirmed his friendship by sending Whistler money, to be repaid, he said, whenever the artist was ready, with whatever work he chose. This was clearly an act of charity motivated by an "interesting conversation," presumably about the lawsuit, which must have touched on Whistler's straitened circumstances. "As I had always a fervent wish to have some specimen of your genius," Boehm had written, "I am mean enough to utilize the right moment . . . and take you at your word."[61]

As an associate of the Royal Academy, Boehm would have made an especially valuable witness, and Whistler counted on his testimony. A few days before the trial, he wrote Boehm a letter asking him to attest in court to his "scientific opinion" of the nocturnes. "This is a chance that will not occur again," Whistler said, "and that, were the tables turned, and you were in my place, I should only be too eager to seize upon for your sake! Indeed the cause of us doers and workers is at stake with the writers and praters."[62] The sculptor was duly subpoenaed, and Whistler felt so confident of his cooperation that he told Anderson Rose he wanted only Boehm and Albert Moore to testify. But Boehm unaccountably disappointed Whistler as well. Two days before trial Rose wrote dejectedly, "it now finally appeared that Mr. Albert Moore was the only witness who could be relied on to attend and give evidence."[63]

Albert Moore (fig. 35), unlike Boehm, lacked the credential of Royal Academy affiliation, but his paintings were regularly exhibited at Burlington House and generally well received. Ruskin, who might have detected in Moore some of the contrivance he disliked in Whistler, had praised Moore's 1875 exhibits as "consummately artistic and scientific work" and placed the artist, as a colorist, above even the accomplished academician Alma-Tadema.[64] Moore, however, disliked the praise as well as the blame of art critics. Like Whistler, he believed that their accounts were often misconceived, being based on a misunderstanding of his intentions.[65] He was especially outraged by Ruskin's remarks in *Fors Clavigera,* offended "as much by their injustice," he said, "as by the coarseness of the language."[66]

Moore was shy, retiring, and polite—the opposite in every way of Whistler. But according to Moore's pupil, Graham Robertson, Whistler was "always at his best and gentlest" with Moore. The friendship must have been extraordinary, since Moore overcame his temperamental aversion to public spectacle and his legendary dislike of being

Fig. 35. Photograph of Albert Joseph Moore. From Alfred Lys Baldry, *Albert Moore: His Life and Works* (London, 1894)

questioned for the sake of supporting Whistler in court. "I shall always have a pleasure in taking up the cudgels on y[ou]r behalf," Moore later wrote Whistler, adding that he would not ordinarily do as much for himself.[67]

By coming to Whistler's aid, however, Moore was also defending his own principles. Whistler appealed to their common aesthetic standards in a letter written shortly before the trial, addressed to "my dear brother professor."[68] At the Grosvenor Gallery in 1877, Moore had exhibited three artfully arranged paintings of diaphanously draped females, cool and remote as still lifes (see figs. 36 and 37); the most compelling was *Sapphires,* a nearly life-size painting of a woman in a blue turban and robe wearing strands of pearls and holding an

orange.[69] Despite the difference in the subjects depicted by Whistler and Albert Moore, their aesthetic affinity was clear. Like Whistler, Moore "deliberately excluded from his art all reference to emotion and passion," J. Comyns Carr observed, "and sought, within rigorous limitations, for a grace that owed nothing to any art but his own."[70] On the eve of the trial, Albert Moore presented Rose with several written suggestions of testimony he was prepared to offer, including the statement that Whistler was more than a competent painter: "some of his qualifications," he said, "amount to absolute genius." At the end of his written opinion, Moore expressed the wish that the plaintiff should "long continue to distribute his pots of paint,"[71] and Whistler signaled his intention to do precisely that in *Whistler v. Ruskin: Art and Art Critics,* a pamphlet dedicated to Moore, his most loyal friend.

An eccentric Irishman, William Gorman Wills (fig. 38), from whom Oscar Wilde had inherited one of his middle names, was the only other artist Whistler was able to recruit.[72] In England, Wills was known as a pastel portraitist with a special talent for depicting children, whom Queen Victoria once summoned to Osborne to paint the royal family (see fig. 39). (Wills first replied that he regretted a previous engagement but was compelled to obey the subsequent command.)[73] His greater ambition was to paint in oil. Wills's portrait of the Marchioness of Bute and his most famous subject picture, *Ophelia and Laertes,* had been exhibited at the Royal Academy, and eight of his paintings would eventually be shown at the Grosvenor; the artist Louise Jopling specifically recalled having seen a "Japanese subject" there.[74] But he never sold a single oil, and from necessity became a

Fig. 36. Albert Joseph Moore, *Sapphires,* ca. 1877, oil on canvas. Exhibited Grosvenor Gallery 1877, no. 50. Birmingham Museums and Art Gallery, England

Fig. 37. Albert Joseph Moore, *The End of the Story,* ca. 1877, oil on canvas. Exhibited Grosvenor Gallery 1877, no. 52. Collection of Joey and Toby Tanenbaum, Toronto, Canada

Fig. 38. Photograph of William Gorman Wills. From Ellen Terry, *The Story of My Life* (London, 1908)

playwright. For one success as a painter, Wills said, he would have sacrificed all his literary laurels.[75]

A painter who produced plays as potboilers, Wills disliked the drama and had to be dragged to the theater. His plays, however, were popular with the public. Henry Irving acted in and produced many of Wills's works and Ruskin reportedly revered one of the romances, *Claudian.*[76] But because he abhorred publicity, Wills was little known even at the height of his career; indeed, *Whistler v. Ruskin* went to trial at a time when he might, if he had wished, have been famous as the author of *Olivia,* a theatrical adaptation of Goldsmith's *Vicar of Wakefield* that launched its leading lady Ellen Terry into fame.[77] Terry remembered Wills as a curious combination of sloven and aristocrat,

Fig. 39. William Gorman Wills, *HRH Princess Louise,* 1870, pastel on paper. Royal Collection at Osborne House. Windsor Castle, Royal Library. © 1991 Her Majesty Queen Elizabeth II

who could eat raw onions every night like a peasant, although his ideas were "magnificent and instinct with refinement," and Louise Jopling recalled that the untidy bohemian wrote all his plays in bed. Paint and charcoal usually besmirched his face, but he nevertheless possessed the "unmistakable air of a gentleman."[78] Wills's aversion to soap and water was legendary—a writer for the *New York Times* observed in 1878 that only a genius would dare "go about unwashed and in old clothes"—and his Fulham Road studio, a converted brewery store, was said to be animated with stray cats and monkeys and unsavory characters who helped themselves to the money Wills stashed in a tobacco jar kept on his mantel.[79]

In view of this reputation, it is difficult to imagine the fastidious Whistler choosing Wills of his own accord. Yet he may have been considered as a possible sympathetic witness as early as August 1878, when Whistler mentioned Wills's name together with William Rossetti's in a letter to Rose.[80] There is nothing to suggest, however, that the artists had more than a passing acquaintance. Like Rossetti, Wills was an old and trusted friend of Anderson Rose, a long-time companion from the Arundel Club. According to Wills's brother and biographer, Rose had supported Wills in many times of trouble and there was no favor Wills would not have performed in return.[81] During the weeks immediately preceding *Whistler v. Ruskin,* Wills had been in Paris, practicing his painting in a rented artist's studio. Two days before the case went to court he returned to London, and Rose, then desperate to secure dependable witnesses, promptly had him served with a subpoena.[82] Out of devotion to Anderson Rose more than sympathy with the plaintiff himself, Wills agreed to testify on Whistler's behalf.

THE DEFENSE

RUSKIN'S ENTHUSIASM FOR professing principles of art economy in court diminished, then disappeared, as the day set for trial approached. He initially maintained a "facade of jauntiness about the action," according to Arthur Severn's biographer, refusing to consider Whistler "a serious antagonist"; but as the trial drew near, the matter began to prey upon his mind and as eagerness turned to anxiety his physician, Dr. Parsons, had to be called in several times.[1]

The traditional story—first told by Ruskin's counsel, and later reinforced by his biographers—is that the defendant's doctors resolutely forbade him to attend court, fearing that the excitement of the trial would imperil his mental health.[2] Putting Ruskin on the witness stand might well have disturbed his sanity, but there is reason to suspect that by November 1878, the month of the trial, Ruskin was not as ill as his lawyers would have had Whistler—and future historians—believe. The previous April, Ruskin had returned to work, completing a descriptive catalogue for an exhibition of Turner drawings at the Fine Art Society in London, and by July he was at the National Gallery cataloging works in the Turner bequest; he also toured Yorkshire with Arthur Severn that summer and visited William Graham in Perthshire. By autumn, Georgiana Burne-Jones related, Ruskin "had quite recovered from his illness."[3]

Fig. 40. John Ruskin, *Self Portrait,* watercolor on paper. Inscribed by Joan Severn, verso, "Di Pa by himself." Pierpont Morgan Library, New York, 1959.23

Arthur Severn, who was in a position to know the truth, indicated in his memoirs that Ruskin, rather than his doctors, made the decision that he would not attend the trial. "Ruskin," Severn said simply, "wouldn't go."[4] The critic recognized the risk to his health and reputation that a courtroom appearance would entail: he wrote H. G. Liddell on 18 November, the day Dr. Parsons testified to his patient's poor health, that owing to his condition any public appearance might bring "danger to myself and anxiety to others."[5] This concern was eventually supplanted, however, by the conviction that a confrontation with Whistler would offend his dignity. "The Professor of Medicine might just as well be brought into court for denouncing an apothecary who watered his drugs," Ruskin wrote Severn shortly before the trial, "as the Professor of Art for denouncing an ill finished picture."[6] Ruskin would later say that the "principal annoyance" of the affair had been the way that his "best friends"—presumably Burne-Jones, among others—had acted as though "Mr. W. was really something of a dangerous match and antagonist—and their expecting me to answer or debate with him."[7] Ruskin's refusal to participate in the trial was, then, at least partly a matter of principle.

In spite of Ruskin's reluctance, defense counsel continued to insist that he come to court, if he were well enough, because "in certain contingencies" it could become necessary to call him to the stand. Whistler also counted on Ruskin's appearance; to assure it, he planned to subpoena the defendant as a material witness. Early in November, Robert Fulford proposed to Anderson Rose that Whistler should attend trial voluntarily, without subpoena. Rose agreed only on the condition that Ruskin likewise appear in court prepared to testify. Fulford declined to speak for Ruskin—he was, Fulford said, "unwell and a peculiar man"—but later the same day, 9 November, posted a letter stating definitively that defense counsel would not call the defendant to court. Whistler demanded that Ruskin be subpoenaed or the case be postponed, and Rose, referring to the defendant's "alleged illness," informed defense counsel that if Ruskin were still unable to appear, the trial would have to be adjourned yet again. Fulford refused to consent to postponing the trial, but obligingly forwarded Ruskin's address so that the plaintiff could serve him with a subpoena. That information, however, was not received in Rose's offices until Friday, 15 November, with the trial scheduled to begin the following Monday morning—a delay Rose perceived as "a piece of disreputable jockeying" calculated to reduce his preparation time to a single day.[8] Ultimately Rose was informed that Ruskin had instructed his counsel to proceed to trial without delay, as he was "anxious to have the matter disposed of," but on Rose's application the trial was adjourned for one more week, until 25 November. Whistler continued to foster the hope that Ruskin would appear on subpoena.[9]

As the condition of Ruskin's health repeatedly postponed the proceedings, Fulford must have realized that even if his client were

Fig. 41. Spy [Leslie Ward], "Attorney-General," 1878, chromolithograph. "Statesmen, No. CCLXV: Sir John Holker," *Vanity Fair,* 9 February 1878

able to attend court on the appointed day, he would not possess the presence of mind to act as his own counsel, as he had originally intended. Walker Martineau & Co. therefore retained Sir John Holker (fig. 41), chief counsel of the British Crown, to represent Ruskin in court. Prior to 1895, the attorney general of England was allowed to supplement his public duties with private practice, and Holker's practice was enormous: a lumbering Lancashireman who never distinguished himself through eloquence or wit, Holker nonetheless had a way of winning verdicts. According to J. Comyns Carr, who was a lawyer as well as an art critic, the attorney general's talent lay in persuading jurors "that he was a plain man like themselves, and that the cause of justice was likely to suffer by reason of the superior intellectual attainments of his opponents, unless he and they laid their heads together as plain men, and stood shoulder to shoulder in earnest endeavour to vindicate the right." To make a case against esoteric art, "sleepy Jack Holker," as he was known (Comyns Carr said that he produced the impression of a giant talking in his sleep),[10] was an inspired choice.

In rhetorical style and aesthetic sensibility, the attorney general could not have been farther from either the plaintiff or the defendant of *Whistler v. Ruskin.* Arthur Severn doubted that before the trial Holker had ever heard of a nocturne or perused half a dozen pages of Ruskin.[11] But the ignorance of art and culture that the attorney general professed in court was, like his ingenuous advocacy, mostly insincere. Holker was sufficiently alert to the movements of modern art to commission at least one work from Whistler's friend Thomas Armstrong. That painting, *Girl Holding an Embroidery Frame,* was among the 1877 Grosvenor Gallery exhibits. The chief advocate for the defense, then, may himself have been one of the art enthusiasts he would mercilessly lampoon in court. Indeed, when the attorney general asked Armstrong a fortnight after the trial why Whistler hadn't chosen him as barrister instead of Parry, and Armstrong replied that his fees were too high, Holker declared that he would have "done it for nothing for Jemmie."[12]

Holker's junior, Charles Synge Christopher Bowen, had in 1872 been appointed Standing Counsel to the Treasury, otherwise known as the attorney general's devil, a position considered a certain step toward professional advancement.[13] Like Serjeant Parry, Bowen had distinguished himself in the Tichborne case. He was said to be "a cultured man of vast information" capable of conversing "on all worthy subjects," who was nevertheless unassertive and shy. He would come to be regarded as the best lawyer in England.[14] Arthur Severn, remarking on the contrast between the attorney general and his junior, observed that Bowen was the more "aesthetic" of the two.[15]

Like their personalities, the tactics Bowen and Holker chose to employ in Ruskin's defense were opposite but complementary. Holker calculated his performance to confirm the terms of Ruskin's critique, focusing the court's attention on the apparent deficiencies of the plaintiff's style. Bowen, on the other hand, concentrated on the legal definition of libel and the connotations of "fair comment," aiming to prove that the critic's remarks had been made in the public interest. Any other strategy would be fruitless, he wrote in his pretrial opinion, because it would be impossible to convince the jury that Ruskin's view was accurate: "They never could or would be able to decide on that."

Those two approaches had, in fact, been suggested by the defendant himself in a memorandum of instruction (see Appendix A) delivered early in November to the offices of Walker Martineau & Co.[16] But for the most part, the defense disregarded the details of Ruskin's explanation of the allegedly libelous review. Indeed, the attorney general referred to Ruskin's statement so rarely in court that the judge remained unaware the defendant had ever expressed his views on paper.[17] The text of the memorandum is quoted in the defendant's brief, and some of its passages are starred and underscored, suggesting that defense counsel actually read the document. During the trial, the attorney general reiterated one or two of its points wildly out of context as a token concession to the defendant's point of view. But as Serjeant Parry's son later observed, Ruskin's attorneys "must have thanked their stars that their outspoken client was safe at Brantwood," giving them freedom to do as they pleased with his carefully composed memorandum.[18]

Ruskin's statement disproves the contention that the *Fors* critique was written in haste or a moment of psychosis, for it anatomizes the offending paragraph and justifies its every assertion. The critic, Ruskin explains, is bound to distinguish "the artist's work from the upholsterer's":

> although it would be unreasonable to expect from the hasty and electric enlightenment of the nineteenth century, any pictorial elucidations of the Dispute of the Sacrament, or the School of Athens, he may yet, without severity of exaction, require of a young painter that he should show the resources of his mind no less than the

> dexterity of his fingers and without libellous intention may recommend the spectator to value order in ideas above arrangement in tints, and to rank an attentive draughtsman's work above a speedy plasterer's (App. A).

While Ruskin himself, he said, had manifestly fulfilled his duty as a critic, Whistler had sorely neglected his artistic responsibility by failing to offer "good value for money and a fair day's work for a fair day's wages." The exorbitant price attached to *Nocturne in Black and Gold* betrayed the artist's lack of education; it was kinder to accuse him of coxcombry, Ruskin remarked, than dishonesty.

Although Ruskin professed ignorance of the legal meaning of libel, the defenses he offered in his instructions imply that he was well acquainted with the standard answers to a defamation charge. To begin with, he asserted that his description of Whistler's work and character was "accurately true so far as it reaches," and that the sentence "in which the plaintiff is spoken of as throwing the palette in the public's face" was but a succinct "definition of a manner which is calculated to draw attention chiefly by its impertinence." By asserting that truth was on his side, Ruskin was making a statement of justification, the absolute answer to the charge of libel, which is always difficult to prove, and in the subjective climate of aesthetic judgment, nearly impossible.

Ruskin's second answer to the charge was the assertion that his condemnatory paragraph had been a sincere attempt to protect a semi-ignorant public from paint pots attempting to pass as pictures. "The Bench of honourable Criticism is as truly a Seat of Judgment as that of Law itself," Ruskin wrote, using terms he trusted his lawyers would comprehend, "and its verdicts, though usually kinder, must sometimes be no less stern." As the acknowledged arbiter of British taste, Ruskin could easily claim the critic's privilege, although his counsel would have to prove that he sincerely believed what he had written and harbored no malicious motives.

Less exacting than the defense of justification or truth, the plea decided on in the statement of defense was that of fair comment.[19] But the attorney general's courtroom posture did not admit the clear reasoning and mental acuity necessary to uphold that plea. His rhetorical talents were better suited to the argument of justification. Apparently ignoring the determined course of action, Holker set out to prove that Whistler's eccentricities justified Ruskin's diatribe.[20] Taking his cue from the defendant's references to coxcombry, he resorted to ridicule in order to show the jury that Ruskin's low opinion of Whistler's work had been substantially correct. Instead of lecturing the jury on the privileges of art criticism, Holker presented himself as one of their own—an ordinary Englishman, perplexed and annoyed by Whistler's incomprehensible productions.

The attorney general's conduct was calculated. He would have understood the difficulty of actually disproving a libel charge and heeded Bowen's opinion that Ruskin would probably lose the verdict. With those considerations in mind, Holker undoubtedly decided to conduct the trial in such a way that the jury would be inclined to award the plaintiff minimal or contemptuous damages. He attempted to discredit Whistler in the witness box and to suggest that his motives were dubious—that the so-called artist sought from the trial only money and publicity, while the critic defended honorable principles. By intimating that charlatan painters did not deserve the jury's attention, Holker scorned the entire action.[21]

To that end the barrister consulted the defendant's brief (fig. 42), prepared by Ruskin's solicitor for his use in court. The document outlined several of the plaintiff's eccentricities and was composed in such a way that the descriptions of his paintings and practices, while technically accurate, were made to sound peculiar. Whistler's works—to which the artist was said to give "vild titles"—were defined as "gradations of blue and gray" under glass, with frames reportedly painted "with some of the color of the picture so that the whole thing became an impression of grey and gold or blue and gold." Whistler did often decorate his picture frames: he embellished the reeded gilt frame of *Nocturne in Blue and Silver,* for example, with a bamboo design and fishscale pattern, and signed it with his butterfly cipher (see plate 3).

Another of the customs mentioned in the brief, and bound to inspire the court's incredulity, was Whistler's habit of hanging wet

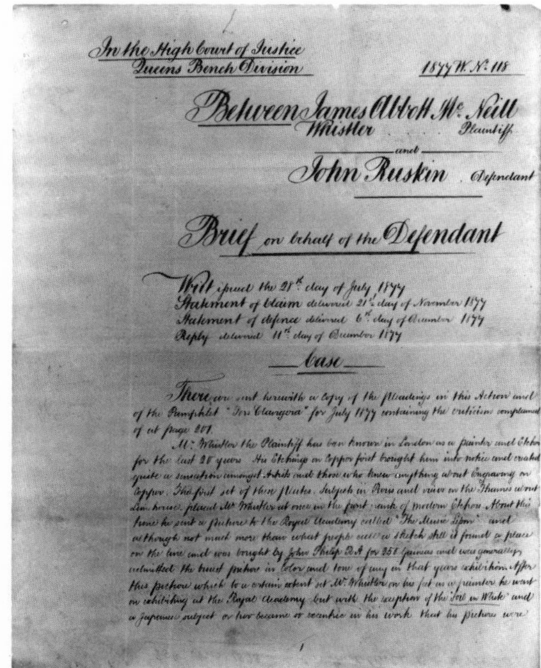

In the High Court of Justice
Queens Bench Division

1877 W. No. 118

Between James Abbott McNeill Whistler — Plaintiff
— and —
John Ruskin — Defendant

Brief on behalf of the Defendant

Writ issued the 28th day of July 1877
Statement of Claim delivered 21st day of November 1877
Statement of defence delivered 6th day of December 1877
Reply delivered 11th day of December 1877

Case

There are sent herewith a Copy of the Pleadings in this Action and of the Pamphlet "Fors Clavigera" for July 1877 containing the criticism complained of at page 201.

Mr. Whistler the Plaintiff has been known in London as a painter and Etcher for the last 20 years. His Etchings on Copper first brought him into notice and created quite a sensation amongst Artists and those who knew anything about Engraving on Copper. The first set of these plates, subjects in Paris and views on the Thames about Limehouse, placed Mr. Whistler at once in the first rank of modern Etchers. About this time he sent a picture to the Royal Academy called "The Music Lesson" and although not much more than what people call a sketch still it found a place on the line and was bought by John Philip R.A. for 25 Guineas and was generally admitted the finest picture in color and tone of any in that years exhibition. After this picture which to a certain extent set Mr. Whistler on his feet as a painter he went on exhibiting at the Royal Academy but with the exception of the "Girl in White" and a Japanese subject or two became so eccentric in his work that his pictures were

1

Fig. 42. Brief on behalf of the Defendant, 1877–78. Pennell-Whistler Collection, Manuscripts Division, Library of Congress, Washington, D.C.

pictures in his garden, "exposed to the weather . . . to give them a mellow tone." To Londoners, the notion of hanging anything outdoors sounded ridiculous, but Whistler had defended the practice in his interview with the *World* and reaffirmed its advantages in the witness box: dried by the sun and seasoned by the elements, the works would lose the glossiness that Whistler found objectionable in freshly painted pictures.[22] A writer for the *Week* would later remark that although ordinary pictures would suffer ill effects from the London atmosphere, a deposit of ash and soot might "save Mr. Whistler trouble in putting on colour."[23] *Funny Folks* pictured Whistler in the garden hanging out his nocturnes, with Ruskin, as a blackbird, hovering above the line (fig. 43).

The brief also brought up *The Grasshopper,* a comedy first performed at the Gaiety Theatre the previous December.[24] Alan Cole,

Fig. 43. "Funny Folk's Fairy Tales; Or, Old Friends with New Faces" (detail), *Funny Folks,* 28 December 1878

who attended a performance with Whistler early in January 1878, commented that the play was "not very good though a tremendous puff for Whistler."[25] The plot involves "an artist of the future" named Pygmalion Flippit who names Whistler his master and calls himself a "Harmonist in colours." A painting representative of his style, described as "a dual harmony in red and blue," depicted either the ocean at sunset or the desert beneath blue skies, depending on whether it was hung upside-down or rightside-up. Walter Hamilton would later remark that the laughter inspired by that picture "probably had more effect in discrediting these ridiculous travesties of art than all Mr. Ruskin's powerful articles."[26]

Fig. 44. Carlo Pellegrini, *Portrait of J. M. Whistler,* ca. 1878, oil on canvas. From A. E. Gallatin, *The Portraits and Caricatures of James McNeill Whistler: An Iconography* (London, 1913)

A portrait of the "Creator of Black and White in his own Manner" (fig. 44) also made a cameo appearance on stage during performances of *The Grasshopper.* Thomas Armstrong recalled that the figure was posed "according to the manner of the 'Whistlasquez' portraits" and the painting was framed in Whistler's distinctive style. Carlo Pellegrini, familiar to readers of *Vanity Fair* as "Ape," had produced the pastiche with Whistler's consent and cooperation. In the Gaiety Theatre this artful joke fell flat: few in the audience recognized Whistler as the object of the caricature when the "portrait" was unveiled.[27] In court, the attorney general attempted to recall those travesties of

Fig. 45. George Frederick Watts, *Portrait of E. Burne-Jones,* ca. 1877, oil on canvas. Exhibited Grosvenor Gallery 1877, no. 35. Birmingham Museums and Art Gallery, England

Whistler's style, hoping to further discredit the plaintiff, but found that none of the witnesses he questioned had even heard of *The Grasshopper,* much less seen a performance of the play.[28]

The primary source of information for Ruskin's attorneys was Edward Burne-Jones (fig. 45). On the second of November, well before the plaintiff had been notified that the defendant definitely would not appear in court, Ruskin decided to accept the offer Burne-Jones had made so many months earlier and invite his friend's aid in battle. The artist's name was given to Walker Martineau & Co. "as chief of men," Ruskin wrote Burne-Jones, "to whom they might refer for anything which in their wisdom they can't discern unaided concerning me."[29] Perhaps because of an inclination to associate artists with the images they portray, Burne-Jones managed to emerge from the Whistler/Ruskin controversy not only unscathed, but with his reputation enhanced by his courtroom appearance against a fellow artist. Recent biographical studies have shown, however, that at least in his personal affairs, Burne-Jones was no angel,[30] and a reexamination of his participation in the proceedings reveals that the part of honor he portrayed in court was nothing but excellent dissembling. It might be argued that by the time Ruskin called upon Burne-Jones—sixteen months after he had initially pledged support—the artist had undergone a change of heart and was tending toward Whistler's point of view; but the surviving evidence renders that reading improbable. Not a trace remains of the "considerable heart-searchings" that are supposed to have preceded Burne-Jones's "defection" to the other side.[31]

It appears that Burne-Jones's animosity toward Whistler, even more than the friendship he felt he owed Ruskin, impelled his participation in the trial. The artists' mutual dislike dates from at least 1867, when Whistler argued with his brother-in-law, Seymour Haden, over Haden's disrespectful handling of the death of a family friend in a brothel in Paris; in anger, Whistler pushed Haden through a plate-glass window, and when Alphonse Legros took Haden's side, Whistler struck him as well.[32] Although the disagreement concerned matters that were none of Burne-Jones's business, he told Howell (who may have communicated the confidence to Whistler) that out of loyalty to Legros, he wanted to take Whistler on.[33] Burne-Jones would never challenge Whistler directly, but the Ruskin trial provided an opportunity to settle the score—safe from the threat of physical injury—and Burne-Jones again displayed his penchant for taking sides in other people's disputes. After the trial he returned to his dream of a duel: sensing that Whistler would never let him have the last word, Burne-Jones wrote Joan Severn that Ruskin would have to be his second when he finally fought Whistler on the sands of

Calais: "The weapons I shall choose for I shall be the challenged party," he said, "the seconds must determine if the affair is to be to the utterance in which case we use pots of oil paint—in a slight affair—distemper— in either case I select prussian blue as the most effective weapon I know."[34]

It is probably not coincidental that the story (or part of the story) of Whistler's expulsion from the Burlington Fine Arts Club after the altercation with Haden appears in the defendant's brief among the facts provided for the defense. Most likely it came from Burne-Jones. A letter to Joan Severn written early in November appears to outline Burne-Jones's accessory role in preparing the brief, but strategic passages have been inked out by some censoring hand, leaving only the information that Burne-Jones would meet Arthur Severn in London after conferring with Ruskin's attorneys.[35] It is difficult to determine the exact extent of his assistance, therefore, but reasonable to assume that Burne-Jones provided much of the brief's ammunition, perhaps even the fantastic description of the dining-room decoration at Prince's Gate as "Devil Peacocks, being things with Devils' heads and peacocks' bodies" bearing sovereigns in their tails to represent the patron's wealth.[36]

Burne-Jones must have resented Whistler's intimacy with the Leyland family in the early 1870s—he is known to have preferred keeping his friends to himself[37]—and would have rejoiced when the Peacock Room episode brought about an irrevocable end to the relationship. He obliged Ruskin's counsel by asking Frederick Leyland for the loan of Frances Leyland's *Nocturne in Blue and Silver* (plate 4) to be used as evidence in the "rubbishy trial," and requesting details of several commissioned but undelivered family portraits.[38] Burne-Jones may also have helped to procure William Graham's *Nocturne in Blue and Silver* (plate 3), which Whistler had been led to believe would not be available for the trial. Graham and Leyland, two of Whistler's former devotees, thus became allies of his opponent. And Burne-Jones, who had the most to gain from their joint defection, stood conspicuously between them.

Burne-Jones gave himself away one evening at Prince's Gate shortly before the trial. Dinner was served in the Peacock Room, and when the conversation turned, inevitably, to Whistler, Burne-Jones adamantly refused to acknowledge the artist's talents. "He seemed to think," recalled Walter Crane, one of the other guests, "that there was only *one* right way of painting." Crane justified Burne-Jones's obstinacy as the necessary response of a man about to appear as a witness in court ("though much against the grain, and only under the strongest pressure from Ruskin"), who felt compelled to deny his opponent any credit.[39] But the enmity Burne-Jones disclosed in the Peacock Room is echoed in the statement he prepared for Ruskin's lawyers (Appendix B). That document, which is included in the defendant's brief, was first brought to light in 1921 by the Pennells, who were surprised at its hostility: "We knew that Burne-Jones was not in sympathy with Whistler's work, but we had not fancied him so blinded by narrow prejudice, and we wondered why he was so upset when we told him how his work interested Whistler."[40] Burne-Jones would not have been obliged to offer so extensive an opinion: Ruskin had specifically advised his lawyers to ask no more from him (or any other artist) "than may enable them to state the case in court with knowledge and distinctness."[41] But Burne-Jones seemed to think that Whistler, rather than Ruskin, was the one on trial, and told enough tales of the artist's vanities to convict him of assorted petty crimes.

Burne-Jones's statement begins with the assertion that "scarcely any body regards Whistler as a serious person" and proceeds to paint a portrait of the artist in shades of gall and green. Describing Whistler as lazy, immature, and insolent, Burne-Jones argues that any talent he might once have possessed had long been exhausted and that, being utterly bereft of principle, Whistler aimed to establish a "school of incapacity" to validate the meaningless scribbling he passed off as art. Obsessively, Burne-Jones attacks Whistler's arrogance, his self-professed superiority to all other artists, and his flagrant rejection of the qualities "that all mankind, ancients and modern, have striven for and demanded." Evidently, Burne-Jones took seriously Whistler's egotistical boasts: he seems to have believed that Whistler really did consider himself the only artist who ever lived, despite his obvious reverence for the old masters and his professed appreciation for certain modern painters.[42] At the heart of Burne-Jones's complaint lies an impression he found intolerable: that Whistler presumed to occupy the unrivaled position in art that Ruskin, in the pages of *Fors Clavigera,* had recently accorded Burne-Jones.

Burne-Jones assumed that other artists would be as happy as he to enlist in Ruskin's cause. Early in November he wrote Joan Severn, "he shall not be left alone in the matter—hundreds of us are eager to do something and only want to know what."[43] Ruskin's solicitor, bolstered by Burne-Jones's enthusiasm, expected a rally of support for the defendant and confidently set about gathering the names of several "artists of position" who had seen Whistler's paintings in the Grosvenor Gallery and would be willing "to justify Mr. Ruskin's criticism on them as well deserved." Whistler also believed in Ruskin's loyal legion, confiding to a friend that his opponent was rumored to have "an army of volunteers ready to come forward and swear that Whistler's work is sham and impudence."[44]

But the witnesses were not forthcoming. Word of the trouble seems to have reached Whistler, who wrote to Rose several days before trial that Ruskin's advocates were "not at all so cock sure as they pretend to be."[45] Although defense counsel had been given to believe that such eminent academicians as G. D. Leslie, George Richmond, and Henry Stacy Marks would testify on Ruskin's behalf, all were reluctant to appear in court. "This refusal does not we think arise in any way from the fact that they admire Mr. Whistler's paintings," Fulford explained in the brief, "but simply from a disinclination to appear and give evidence against an artist, however bad, and perhaps also from the fact that artists do not as a body like being criticised." Burne-Jones must have been mortified to learn that no one else would agree so eagerly to testify on Ruskin's behalf, and that his sole ally among artists would be William Powell Frith (fig. 46).[46]

Frith's animated illustrations of modern English life drew Victorians in droves. His extraordinary talent for calculating and producing precisely what the public would pay to see meant that his paintings, every inch crowded with anecdote and detail, invariably received the compliment of protection by a rail. As one critic remarked in 1879:

Fig. 46. Spy [Leslie Ward], "The Derby-Day," 1873, chromolithograph. "Men of the Day, No. LXIII: Mr. William Powell Frith, R.A.," *Vanity Fair,* 10 May 1873

> Whatever merits may exist in the various modern schools of art which are daily putting forth claims upon public attention, and however greatly they may differ from that in which Mr. Frith was educated and has worked, it will be many a long year, we take it, ere it will be necessary at a public exhibition to protect from admiring and interested crowds by a railing any specimen of the new aesthetic principles.[47]

Indeed, Frith's pictures represented, as the *Referee* observed, "the apotheosis of matter-of-fact," opposite in every respect to those "maniacal

À FORTIORI.

Philistine Father. "Why the dickens don't you paint something like Frith's 'Derby Day'—something Everybody can understand, and Somebody buy?"

Young Genius. "*Everybody understand*, indeed! Art is for the Few, Father, and the higher the Art, of course the fewer the Few. The highest Art of all is for *One*. That Art is mine. That *One* is—Myself!"

Fond Mamma. "There speaks my Own Brave Boy!"

Fig. 47. George Du Maurier, "À Fortiori." *Punch,* 31 May 1879 forms of art" represented by the inventions of Whistler and Burne-Jones (see fig. 47).[48] At the trial, Frith would speak for the bourgeoisie, vindicating the "usual stuff" that Whistler disparaged and herds of admirers adored.

Ruskin himself chose Frith to testify and enlisted Arthur Severn, who knew him better, to ask the artist to bear witness on his behalf.[49] As the Pennells were informed, Frith was probably selected because he would not have been considered biased in Ruskin's favor.[50] Unlike Burne-Jones, he owed none of his success to the critic. Ruskin had described *Derby Day* (fig. 48), on the occasion of its exhibition at the Royal Academy in 1858, as "a kind of cross between John Leech and Wilkie, with a dash of daguerreotype here and there, and some pretty seasoning with Dickens's sentiment," and offered a backhanded compliment: "of the entirely popular manner of painting, which, however, we must remember, is necessarily, because popular, stooping and restricted, I have never seen an abler example."[51] Frith was correspondingly critical of Ruskin, whose ardent support of Pre-Raphaelitism —which Frith classified among recent, ridiculous crazes in art—had convinced him that the critic's judgments were "often utterly mistaken and wrong."[52]

Having once recognized the "profound ignorance" of writers on art, Frith resolved never to read another word of criticism, asserting "very truly," his daughter said, "that as long as his pictures sold as they did, what people said about them mattered nothing at all."[53] Ironically, Frith concurred completely with Whistler's position on the incompetence of art critics: he too maintained that "printed opinion is but that of a gentleman or lady who can have no technical knowledge, and which, if expressed, *vivâ voce* in general society, would have little or no effect." Making this argument in his autobiography, Frith paraphrased Whistler's analogy of the National Gallery guard and the art critic, although he took care to refer to the author of *Whistler v. Ruskin: Art and Art Critics* as "a well-known pamphleteer," rather than an artist.[54]

But if Frith himself was impervious to criticism, his wife and family were driven "raving wild" by the adverse reviews regularly written by Ruskin and by F. G. Stephens of the *Athenaeum.* Frith may

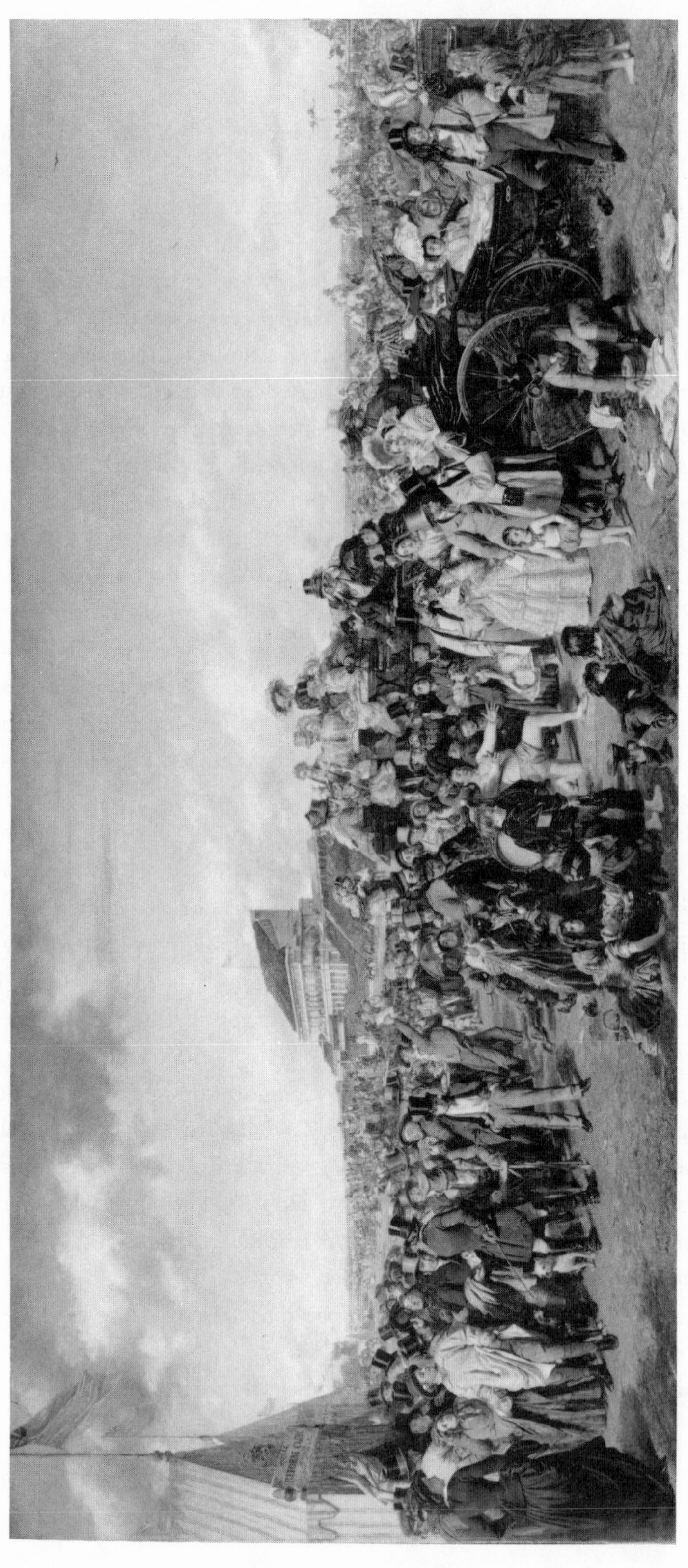

have recognized in Ruskin's allegedly libelous critique the same potential for damage as in these reviews, since he held that artists could not profit from criticism, although "much undeserved pain is often inflicted, and even injury caused by the virulent attacks that sometimes disgrace the press."[55] But unhappily for the plaintiff, Frith was subpoenaed by the defense. He would be called upon, not to profess his opinion of Ruskin's critical method, but to attest to the deficiencies of Whistler's style.

Frith's taste in art, as witnessed by his own productions, was conservative, patriotic, and rooted in the tradition of the Royal Academy. He advocated a distinctively British school of art, with Hogarth as its founding father, to challenge the preference of English patrons for foreign works.[56] He was, therefore, ideologically opposed to Whistler's unorthodox and evidently French style of painting. According to Frith, the school in which nocturnes and symphonies flourished—and of which Whistler was the chief, perhaps the only, exponent—abounded in examples of misdirected genius and endangered the future of British art, since impressionable young painters might be tempted to adopt its practices. In "Crazes in Art: 'Pre-Raphaelitism' and 'Impressionism,'" an article published in 1888, Frith defined the business of painting as "the power of thoroughly and completely representing—as the great masters did—the object before him, whether it be a human figure or any other model." He advised the aspiring artist: "Let him throw nocturnes and symphonies to the winds."[57]

Still, Frith testified for Ruskin only under subpoena. Nothing irritated him more, his daughter recalled, than being called to court as a witness.[58] Anderson Rose supposed that Frith agreed to participate from fear: Every Victorian painter was aware of Ruskin's prerogative to punish presumptuous artists—the *Fors* critique demonstrated his usual method of excoriation—and Frith probably imagined, Rose be-

Fig. 48. William Powell Frith, *The Derby Day,* 1856–58, oil on canvas. Courtesy of the Tate Gallery, London lieved, that "Apollo Ruskin" was preparing to flay Marsyas, and cooperated only to avoid the knife. But the prospect of Frith's appearance did not cause Rose much concern. Apparently assuming that his own taste would be shared by the jury, he felt sure that Frith's testimony would be canceled by every right-thinking man's abhorrence of his pictures, which displayed nothing more, Rose said, than "the commonplace of vulgarity and crime." Indeed, Rose hoped to discredit the witness during cross-examination on the basis of his pictures' subjects alone, arguing that Frith's most popular paintings betrayed his coarse and salacious frame of mind. *Derby Day,* for example, pictured "thimbleriggers," or swindlers, and prostitutes and "their keepers," and *The Railway Station* (fig. 49) represented a forger, two detectives, and a "big fat woman in imitation India shawl"—criminal, presumably, in their ignorance of either human decency or good taste.[59]

But Frith's most recent work, *The Road to Ruin,* exhibited the previous summer at the Royal Academy, seemed to Rose the best example of the artist's unhealthy attraction to Victorian scandal and vice. The series of paintings constituted a sort of "gambler's progress," as Frith later explained. A portrayal of the evils of gambling, the narrative followed a man's downfall from his college days to his death.[60] Frith claimed no pretensions to working along "Hogarthian lines" (he was unsuited, he said, to satire), yet *The Road to Ruin* was acknowledged to be an exemplary modern moral subject, and Frith was regarded by his contemporaries as a modern-day Hogarth. When *The Road to Ruin* was mentioned during the trial, almost every reporter made the same telling mistake of recording its title as "The Rake's Progress." Rose detected a grand hypocrisy in Frith's morality tale, and in the notes he made for Petheram repeated a rumor that Frith had led a young woman, his ward, down the road to ruin in his own house, "where lived his wife and his own numerous family."[61]

Fig. 49. William Powell Frith, *The Railway Station,* 1862, oil on canvas. Royal Holloway and Bedford New College, Egham, Surrey, England

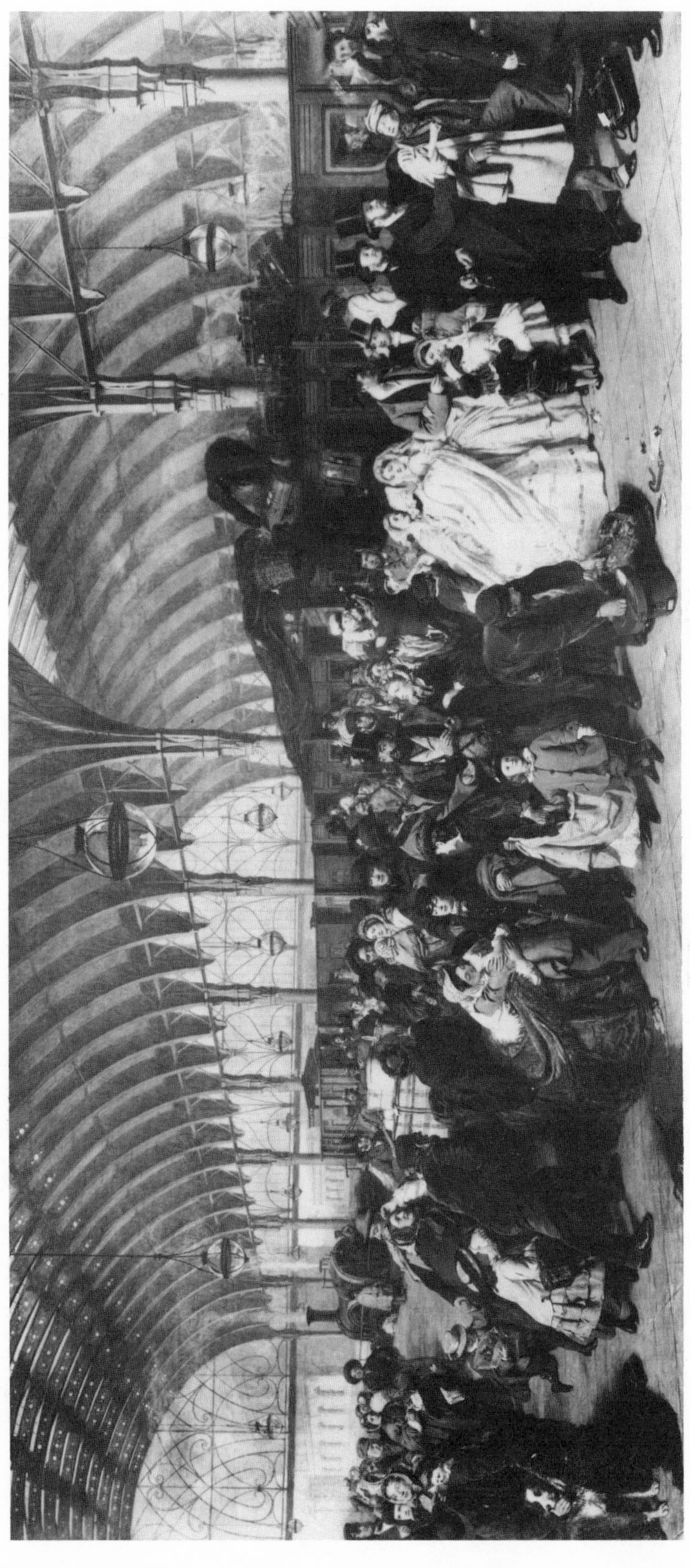

Apparently the morality of artists distracted Rose from the ethics of criticism. Petheram prudently neglected to introduce the information in court.

A more relevant moral problem, which Rose unaccountably failed to mention, concerned Frith's exploitation of the art-loving public for his own considerable profit. When a few of the 21,150 people who paid merely to look at *The Railway Station* in 1862 protested the admission charge, the London dealer Victor Flatow commissioned a pamphlet justifying the apparent commercialization of art. Its author was Tom Taylor (fig. 50), the dramatist and art critic, who like Frith understood the populace and always aimed to please. In defending Frith's lucrative practice, Taylor argued that art which could command a large price was art which appealed to the masses: "It must, as a rule, deal with some subject which all can understand, in a way all can enter into."[62] By that populist criterion, the works of Whistler deserved neglect.

Tom Taylor was the third and last witness Ruskin's counsel would call to court. He had led a varied and remarkably productive professional life, having been a barrister, a professor of English at London University, and secretary to the Board of Health at Whitehall; he was the author of two acclaimed artistic biographies, *The Life of Benjamin Robert Haydon* (in twenty-seven volumes) and *The Life and Times of Sir Joshua Reynolds,* begun by C. R. Leslie, and the editor of *Punch* from 1874 to 1880, a period said to be the worst in the history of the publication.[63] A prolific writer, Taylor produced leading articles for the *Daily News* and the *Morning Chronicle* and dramatic criticism and virtually all the art reviews for London's leading paper, *The Times*. He was also an amateur actor, who, according to Ellen Terry, once performed professionally in Manchester his favorite role of Adam in *As You Like It*,[64] and a poet of sorts—to illustrate a set of drawings by Birket Foster, he composed thirty little poems at a rate of four a week. But Taylor was best known as a playwright. In the thirty-five years of his career he produced more than seventy farces, comedies, and melodramas, which were performed on both sides of the Atlantic; from 1845 to 1870, he was the most popular dramatist in England.[65] Whis-

Fig. 50. Spy [Leslie Ward], "Punch," 1876, chromolithograph. "Men of the Day, No. CXXVI: Mr. Tom Taylor," *Vanity Fair*, 11 March 1876

tler would introduce Tom Taylor in *The Gentle Art of Making Enemies* as "Poor Law Commissioner, Editor of *Punch,* and so forth—and so forth," as a man whose responsibilities were disproportionate to his talents, which did not appear to include artistic ability.[66]

Tom Taylor, then, was only a part-time critic, but because his reviews appeared in *The Times,* his opinions were widely disseminated and accordingly influential. A contemporary critic argued in 1881 that Taylor had "played a more important part in the history of the English art and English artists of his time than did many contemporary painters of distinction."[67] The Victorian public undoubtedly enjoyed Taylor's narrative approach to pictures and approved his tastes, which tended toward unassuming narrative pictures. Taylor was tolerant of the more moderate Pre-Raphaelites, particularly Holman Hunt, but expressed a preference for the sentimental paintings of Charles Robert Leslie.[68] Among artists, Taylor was considered a well-meaning philistine. E. W. Godwin, noting that Taylor's reviews were often marred by unpardonable mistakes, nevertheless acknowledged that the critic was "always burning with the best intentions about everybody and everything."[69]

At one time Tom Taylor had shown an interest in Whistler. In two reviews of the 1865 Royal Academy exhibition, he had attempted to distinguish between instances of Whistler's "eccentricity, and, so to speak, defiance of the public" and indications of the "strange painter's genius." *Symphony in White, No. 2: The Little White Girl* (fig. 25) appeared to Taylor to belong to the latter category: "Before this picture," he wrote, "even those who resent most strongly what we take leave to call Mr. Whistler's freaks and impertinences—for his Japanese pictures, with all their delightfulness of colour and their cleverness in the expression of texture, *are* impertinences—must admit that he has power of the rarest kind."[70] Just after the publication of this rather mixed review, Taylor wrote the artist that most of the detailed notice he had given Whistler's paintings had been suppressed,[71] which suggests that the editorial position of *The Times* was markedly conservative.

A few years later, in 1871, Taylor wrote a surprisingly sympathetic review of Whistler's Dudley Gallery exhibits.[72] Whistler may have imagined that the critic was destined to be his champion, for the following spring he wrote that he had a painting ready to send to the Royal Academy, presumably *Arrangement in Grey and Black: Portrait of the Painter's Mother,* which he would "with pleasure" allow Taylor to preview. The resulting *Times* critique was not altogether favorable, but Taylor did remark that the "quiet harmony" of Whistler's *Mother* made

Fig. 51. James McNeill Whistler, *Harmony in Grey and Green: Miss Cicely Alexander,* 1872, oil on canvas. Tate Gallery, London/ Art Resource, New York

a welcome change from "the harsh, loud discords of the Exhibition."[73] From that time forward, however, Taylor's reviews of Whistler's works became increasingly critical. Like William Powell Frith, Taylor was a proponent of a modern, moral, British school of art, and Whistler's works were moving ever farther from the ideal of accessible pictures designed to edify the public.[74]

Tom Taylor's friendship with Whistler ended in 1873, when he was invited to the artist's studio to view *Harmony in Grey and Green: Miss Cicely Alexander* (fig. 51). Taylor made the fateful error of criticizing a vertical line that bisected the background wall, remarking that the picture would be better without it. "Of course," Taylor said to the artist, "it's a matter of taste." Whistler caustically replied, "I thought that perhaps for once, you were going to get away without having said anything foolish; but remember, so that you may not make the mistake again, it's not a matter of taste at all, it is a matter of knowledge."[75]

Had he been less affable, Taylor might have relished the opportunity the Ruskin trial afforded: he would be called to the stand to discourse upon Whistler's style from a position of professional expertise, rather than personal preference. But there is nothing to suggest that Taylor agreed to testify from vengeful motives. Though he was thought to possess no sense of humor, Taylor was known to be "kind-hearted and always ready to adapt himself to all men."[76] Among his many friends was Arthur Severn,[77] who at the last minute may have asked him the favor of appearing on Ruskin's behalf. Taylor obligingly came to court with an arsenal of newspaper clippings in his pocket, ready to reconfirm his previously published opinions.

FINAL ARRANGEMENTS

BEYOND THE TESTIMONY given by experts in art and art criticism, the most important and controversial evidence of the trial would be the paintings themselves. The eight nocturnes and portraits Whistler had shown and Ruskin presumably had seen at the Grosvenor Gallery in 1878 would visibly support or refute the critic's allegation that the works were ill-conceived, ill-executed, and worthless. Both sides, with opposite intentions, resolved to have the paintings available in court for the jury's inspection.

In preparing for trial, Ruskin's counsel determined to acquaint themselves with those of Whistler's works that had provoked Ruskin's attack. Robert Fulford sent Rose a list of the paintings he wished to see in advance and have produced in court, designating seven of Whistler's Grosvenor exhibits, including both portraits and nocturnes. He did not include the portrait of Carlyle, presumably because it was not listed in the catalogue. But Whistler was unwilling to cooperate. He argued that the defendant's lawyers were entitled to see only the works referred to in the libel: because the portraits had not been for sale at the time of the exhibition, they could not have been the object of Ruskin's criticism, which mentioned a price of two hundred guineas. Of the four nocturnes, only one remained in his possession, and he refused to produce the others for the convenience of the defense.[1]

Anticipating trouble, Rose suggested to Ruskin's counsel that they apply to inspect the paintings in the usual manner; this was a matter of law, he said, not a question of courtesy. Fulford indignantly entered a formal application, alluding to the plaintiff's contentiousness in the supporting affidavit, and the judge ruled that Ruskin's legal counsel "and others" should be allowed to inspect all of the Grosvenor exhibits by Whistler that were in the artist's possession. Whistler remained opposed, and urged Rose to obtain a counter order from the judge: "I am not going to allow any body to come here and discuss and criticize my pictures," he wrote, objecting that "the persons" were not necessarily "proper experts."[2]

But Ruskin's lawyers, having secured the court's permission to view the pictures, badgered Whistler's solicitor for an appointment and suggested that the exhibits be deposited in Rose's offices in the Strand to spare the lawyers the trouble of traveling to Chelsea. This request set off another explosion from Whistler. "Certainly not!" he wrote Rose. The judge's order did not stipulate that the pictures be "dealt with disadvantageously," and he would not have them exhibited in an "accidental and promiscuous manner." Maintaining that they must be shown to the lawyers as they had been seen by Ruskin, Whistler insisted on holding the inspection in his studio, "a fit place with proper light."[3] Indeed, as the progressive American art critic James Jackson Jarves would later explain, the condition essential to understanding the "new departure" in painting was its appropriate exhibition: "Unless the picture can be seen precisely in the light and situation for which it was designed by the artist, it seems to be as formless and void as the creative principle in a state of chaos."[4] A fit place with proper light was not, then, a punctilious demand, and Rose informed Walker Martineau & Co. that, as his office was "quite unfit for the exhibition of pictures," the commission would have to go to Chelsea. The lawyers settled on Saturday afternoon, 16 November, for the inspection of the four paintings that Whistler had been ordered to produce.

Because Ruskin's attorneys did not consider themselves "art experts," they requested the presence at the inspection of someone able to enlighten them "as to the points which in the eyes of competent judges constitute the artistic defects of the principal pictures," so that they would be prepared to cross-examine any "artistic witnesses" the plaintiff might call. The chosen authority was Ruskin's friend and relation by marriage Arthur Severn, who was also an accomplished watercolorist. Severn recorded in his memoirs that he met with Ruskin's counsel several days before the trial, and it was probably on this occasion that he explained the "artistic defects" of Whistler's paintings from Ruskin's point of view. Whistler noted in his own account that Severn "had been to his studio to inspect the paintings, on behalf of the defendant, for the purpose of passing his final judgment upon them and settling that question for ever."[5]

For compelling personal reasons Severn was obligated to assist Ruskin, but his loyalty was divided. He had known Whistler since 1864, when the artist painted *The Last of Old Westminster* from the window of Severn's flat,[6] and had always admired his work. Although he thought their prices absurd, he believed Whistler's paintings to be "carefully painted and generally very beautiful and true in colour," and considered Ruskin's criticism neither just nor instructive.[7] Severn's ambivalence may have excused him from testifying—Anderson Rose had fully expected him to be called as a witness—but during the trial he would sit beside Ruskin's counsel, looking up passages in the five-volume *Modern Painters* lent for the purpose by Edward Burne-Jones.[8]

The paintings Whistler intended to present as evidence in court, although not made available to Ruskin's commission, were gathered in the artist's new studio at the White House for the benefit of Serjeant Parry and Charles Petheram on the Friday afternoon following the defense's inspection. Dinner was served by the bailiffs, who had taken possession of the house pending payment of overdue bills.[9] On Sunday, 24 November, the day before the trial began, Whistler entertained a number of artists, including Albert Moore and Frederic Leighton, with breakfast and a private view.[10] Among the paintings he selected for the occasion were what he called the "dignified portrait" of his mother, the "fine sketch of Carlyle," and the "really beautiful picture of little Miss Alexander," *Harmony in Grey and Green.* All had recently been varnished by an Italian restorer named Buggiani, whom Whistler considered "greatly gifted in all understanding of pictures and their ways," so they could be seen "for the first time in their full richness of color." Whistler felt sure the display would convince his witnesses that truth was on their side.[11]

To vindicate his position as an established, accomplished artist, Whistler insisted on mounting a small retrospective for the jury, as well. Serjeant Parry was instructed to argue the plaintiff's right to hold an exhibition of works other than the Grosvenor exhibits, even though they had been the primary target of Ruskin's attack. As the location for the temporary display, Whistler suggested "the best room" in Petheram's club, which he thought might be "cleaned a little" in preparation; he volunteered personally to transport the paintings early Monday morning and arrange for Buggiani to have them properly hung while he went on to court. But the club evidently was not accommodating, for Anderson Rose roamed the streets of Westminster through the early hours of the first morning of the trial, searching for a place to rent. He finally settled on a room in the Westminster Palace Hotel on Victoria Street, convenient to Westminster Hall.[12]

A more important exhibition would take place in the courtroom itself. Counsel for the defense insisted that all Whistler's Grosvenor paintings should be seen by the jury; all but two would eventually be entered as exhibits in the trial.[13] The celebrated *Arrangement in Grey and Black, No. 2: Portrait of Thomas Carlyle* (plate 2), Whistler's greatest hope for reputability, would not be admitted because of a technicality: its title did not appear in the Grosvenor Gallery catalogue, so it was ruled outside the scope of the proceedings.[14] The other painting was *Nocturne in Blue and Gold* (plate 5). Its owner, Mrs. Wyndham, was out of town at the time of the trial, and although Whistler had arranged to borrow the painting in her absence, the loan apparently fell through at the last minute.[15] *Nocturne in Blue and Silver* (plate 4) was summoned from the Leylands' Liverpool home, Speke Hall; Mrs. Leyland was furious about the subpoena, reportedly because the painting was taken to court without its frame.[16] The other *Nocturne in Blue and Silver* (plate 3) was also admitted, apparently through the devices of the defense; Whistler had been informed that it was unavailable, since Graham, the painting's owner, was traveling abroad. The plaintiff himself was responsible for obtaining the four unsold works, which had been deposited with Mrs. Noseda by Charles Howell. Mrs. Noseda's husband, Urban, was served with a subpoena duces tecum, requiring him to produce *Arrangement in Brown* (plate 7), *Harmony in Amber and Black* (plate 8), *Arrangement in Black* (plate 6), and the most crucial exhibit of all, *Nocturne in Black and Gold* (plate 1).[17]

These works would endure a number of indignities in the courtroom. Arthur Severn told of a painting being passed through the audience that hit the head of a balding gentleman—much to the mirth of the crowd—on its way to the front of the room, and appeared liable to fall out of its frame by the time it reached the witness box. Whistler was asked whether the painting was his, and after inserting his monocle and pausing for dramatic effect replied: "Well, it was once. But it won't be much longer if it goes on in that way!"[18] Arthur Jerome Eddy recounted that Serjeant Parry himself held a nocturne upside down, prompting one of the lawyers for the defense to say that he had seen the painting at the Grosvenor Gallery the other way around; and according to Frances Graham, her father's *Nocturne in Blue and Silver,* Whistler's evocation of Battersea Bridge, was handed upside down to the judge, who proceeded to explain to the jury that the picture was a representation of Old Chelsea Church.[19] Some, and possibly all, of the anecdotes relating to the exhibition of the nocturnes in court may be apocryphal, but their variety and profusion suggest that the serious consideration Whistler sought for his art was not to be found in Westminster Hall.

The comedy of errors was completed by yet another work of art, whose introduction took Whistler and his counsel entirely by surprise. Perhaps at the bidding of Burne-Jones, Ruskin's counsel asked Arthur Severn to bring to court a painting attributed to Titian, which was placed on the bench beside Whistler's nocturnes for the purpose of comparison.[20] The portrait of the Venetian doge Andrea Gritti (plate 9) belonged to Ruskin; it usually hung in his rooms at Oxford, but must have been entrusted to the Severns during his sabbatical and illness. Believed to be the only work to have survived the fire that destroyed much of the ducal palace, the *Andrea Gritti* was only a fragment and badly damaged. Its attribution must have been disputed when Ruskin bought it for a thousand pounds in 1864, since he justified his purchase to Rawdon Brown: "It is my notion of Titian's work, and that is all I care about."[21] The portrait represented for Ruskin the virtues of Titian's Venice—"the breed of her race, their self-command, their subtlety, their courage, their refinement of sensitive faculty, and their noble methods of work."[22] As an eloquent, expressive work of art, it was meant to expose by contrast the vacuousness of Whistler's *Nocturne in Black and Gold.* But the lesson was lost on many observers as the courtroom confusion continued. When the portrait was brought into the dark chamber—upside down, according to Whistler—one of the jurors is said to have exclaimed, "Oh, come, we've had enough of these Whistlers!"[23]

On the morning of 25 November, as Severn mounted the valuable Titian atop a four-wheeled cab and Rose scurried about Westminster, Whistler shared a leisurely breakfast with W. S. Gilbert,[24] who probably accompanied him to court at ten o'clock. Ruskin, remote at Brantwood, wrote a letter to his American friend Charles Eliot Norton, enclosing a copy of his memorandum to counsel. He was unsure of the date, although he knew it was Monday—the day, he said, that "the comic Whistler law suit" went to trial.[25]

In 1878 the London law courts occupied a structure on St. Margaret Street adjacent to Westminster Hall, where the statue of Cromwell now stands (fig. 52); the building would be demolished a few years later, after the Royal Courts of Justice opened in the Strand in 1882. The chamber of the Court of Exchequer, where *Whistler v. Ruskin* was heard, was especially somber that day. A heavy fog prevailed outdoors, deepening the darkness of the candle-lit room. A correspondent for the Hartford *Courant* reported that the atmosphere caused the courtroom rather to resemble a nocturne: "the ensemble was dim, and ghastly, and indefinite."[26] Two of Whistler's works were prominently displayed on the bench; another hung on the wall behind the jury, all

Fig. 52. Photograph of the Palace of Westminster and the Courts of Justice. Royal Commission on the Historical Monuments of England, London. © B. E. C. Howarth-Loomes

but out of sight. Had the chamber been adequately lit, one observer remarked, those paintings might have been seen as well as talked about, but on that dreary, late November day, even the fireworks of Cremorne appeared dark and dismally obscure.[27]

The presiding judge of *Whistler v. Ruskin* was Sir John Walter Huddleston (fig. 53), who was described in *Vanity Fair* as "not over-educated yet with a great store of general knowledge, accounted a less profound lawyer than some yet ever ready to show that he had read Justinian." His success in society circles was usually ascribed to his

Fig. 53. Photograph of Sir John Walter Huddleston by Lock and Whitfeld. Prints and Photographs Division, Library of Congress, Washington, D.C.; gift of Joseph Verner Reed, 1955

brilliant conversation, yet he was famous for three other distinctions: "the tiniest feet, the best kept hands and the most popular wife in London."[28] Lady Diana De Vere Beauclerk, the daughter of the ninth Duke of St. Albans, undoubtedly elevated her husband's stature in society; she appears among the bevy of bridesmaids in *The Marriage of Their Royal Highnesses the Prince of Wales and the Princess Alexandra of Denmark,* a documentary painting produced in 1865 by William Powell Frith, a family friend who often visited the Huddlestons in Ascot. The beautiful Lady Di, as she was familiarly known, graced the courtroom with her presence, sitting on the bench beside her husband and Lady Holker.[29]

The aura of aristocracy was enhanced by the fact that the judge was a baron, indeed "the last of the barons," as he was proud to proclaim. The title recalls the time when barons of the realm heard

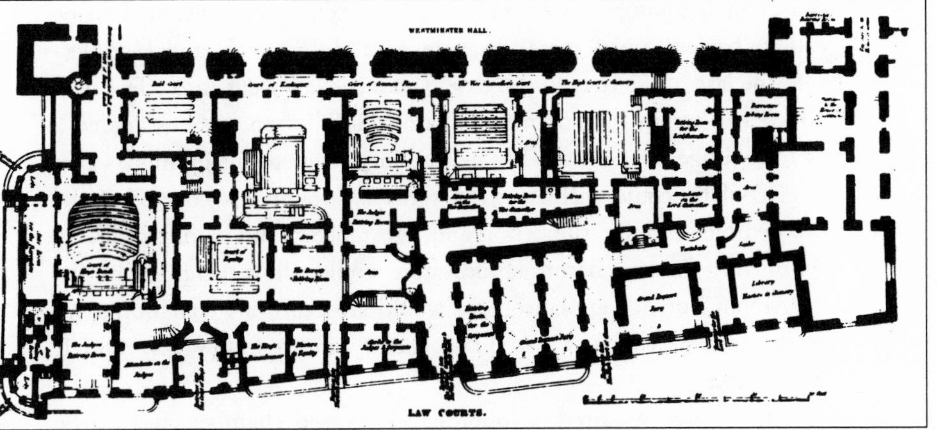

Fig. 54. Plan of the Old Royal Courts of Justice (Law Courts) at Westminster, 1866. The Exchequer Chamber is the second courtroom on the northwest side. Royal Commission on the Historical Monuments of England, London

Fig. 55. Whistler in the witness box. "A Contemptuous Verdict," *Mayfair,* 3 December 1878. Whistler press-cutting book 2, Glasgow University Library, Scotland

causes in the king's court; judges of the exchequer continued to be called "barons" until the Judicature Acts of 1873–75, and Huddleston, the last judge to earn the title before the law went into effect, was allowed to retain his honorific.[30] Baron Huddleston was considered a "strong judge" who invariably led the jury to adopt his opinion.[31] In a libel trial he could influence the verdict through his control of the proceedings and by the tenor and substance of his summation. In *Whistler v. Ruskin,* Baron Huddleston would allow laughter in the courtroom but not applause, and would structure his concluding remarks so that the jury had little choice but to follow his explicit instructions.

The judge required an oppressively heated chamber, and as the crowd overflowed the courtroom and blocked the passageways, air became as limited as light (see fig. 54).[32] That uncomfortable audience was understood to be highly educated and to include everyone of note in the London art community. Many of the artists in attendance were there on subpoena. The number of ladies in the gallery was also a matter of remark: they were made conspicuous by their green and brown beribboned hats, which obstructed the view but formed above the heads of the crowd an aesthetically harmonious pattern. The "girl-graduates of Oxford," *Mayfair* reflected, were typically attracted to Ruskin, and an illustrated lecture by him on the subject of Whistler's art would have rounded out the entertainment.[33] But the spectators would have to content themselves that day with a single speaker in the limelight, supported by a cast of somewhat lesser luminaries.

PART TWO

THE TRIAL

1877. W. NO. 818

IN THE HIGH COURT OF JUSTICE, QUEEN'S BENCH DIVISION

Between

JAMES ABBOTT McNEILL WHISTLER, PLAINTIFF

and

JOHN RUSKIN, DEFENDANT

Sittings at Nisi Prius

JUDGE	SIR JOHN WALTER HUDDLESTON
COUNSEL FOR THE PLAINTIFF	JOHN HUMFFREYS PARRY, *Serjeant-at-law*
	WILLIAM COMER PETHERAM
COUNSEL FOR THE DEFENDANT	SIR JOHN HOLKER, *Attorney General*
	CHARLES SYNGE CHRISTOPHER BOWEN
WITNESSES FOR THE PLAINTIFF	WILLIAM MICHAEL ROSSETTI
	ALBERT JOSEPH MOORE
	WILLIAM GORMAN WILLS
WITNESSES FOR THE DEFENDANT	EDWARD COLEY BURNE-JONES
	WILLIAM POWELL FRITH
	TOM TAYLOR

INTRODUCTION

Monday, 25 November 1878

[*Ellipsis points in the text suggest that an unrecorded question has been asked. Notes on the method of compilation, together with sources and textual variants, can be found in Appendix C.*]

This morning, in the Exchequer Chamber before Baron Huddleston and a special jury, an action of damages for alleged libel was brought by Mr. James Abbott McNeill Whistler, the well-known American artist, against Mr. John Ruskin, the eminent author and art critic.[1] The libel is said to consist in a criticism written by Mr. Ruskin upon the plaintiff's paintings at the Grosvenor Gallery, which appeared in a pamphlet entitled *Fors Clavigera* on the second of July 1877. That criticism was in the following terms:

> Lastly, the mannerisms and errors of these pictures [meaning some pictures by Mr. Burne-Jones],[2] whatever may be their extent, are never affected or indolent. The work is natural to the painter, however strange to us; and it is wrought with utmost conscience of care, however far, to his own or our desire, the result may yet be incomplete. Scarcely so much can be said for any other pictures of the modern schools: their eccentricities are almost always in some

> degree forced; and their imperfections gratuitously, if not impertinently, indulged. For Mr. Whistler's own sake, no less than for the protection of the purchaser, Sir Coutts Lindsay ought not to have admitted works into the gallery in which the ill-educated conceit of the artist so nearly approached the aspect of wilful imposture. I have seen, and heard, much of Cockney impudence before now; but never expected to hear a coxcomb ask two hundred guineas for flinging a pot of paint in the public's face.

The plaintiff alleged in his statement of claim that the libel was falsely and maliciously published and that it had much damaged his reputation as an artist; he claimed one thousand pounds in damages. The defendant pleaded that the publication was privileged, inasmuch as it was confined to a fair and bona fide criticism upon paintings that had been exhibited to the public view.

Mr. John H. Parry, serjeant-at-law, and Mr. William C. Petheram appeared for the plaintiff; and Sir John Holker, the attorney general, and Mr. Charles Bowen for the defendant.

The case appeared to excite great interest, the little court in which it was heard being most inconveniently crowded throughout the entire day, even the passages to the court being filled.

PLAINTIFF'S CASE

Opening Statement by Serjeant Parry

PARRY: The plaintiff, Mr. Whistler, has followed the profession of an artist for many years, both in this and other countries. He originally distinguished himself as an etcher, and is widely known by his later pictures as having taken an independent position in art. Mr. Ruskin, the defendant, is a gentleman well known to all of you. He holds perhaps the highest position in Europe or America as an art critic, and some of his works, I think I am not wrong in saying, are destined to immortality. He is, in fact, a gentleman of the highest reputation. It is the more surprising, therefore, that a gentleman holding such a position could traduce another in a way that would lead that other to come into a court of law to ask for damages. I think the jury, after hearing the case, will come to the conclusion that Mr. Ruskin has done Mr. Whistler a serious injustice.

Mr. Whistler was born in America, the son of an eminent military engineer, a citizen of the United States, who for many years was engaged in superintending the construction of the railway from St. Petersburg to Moscow for the Russian government. Having passed some years of his life in St. Petersburg, Mr. Whistler went to France and Holland, where he studied his profession. He also acquired a great reputation as a painter in America. Mr. Whistler is also an etcher, and has achieved considerable honor in that department of art. The gold medal was awarded to him at Amsterdam, and his works are exhibited in both the British Museum and the South Kensington Museum.[1] It might be said that Mr. Ruskin has not attacked Mr. Whistler's character as an etcher, but it must be remembered that no man can excel in any department of art if he has not the genius of the true artist.

Mr. Whistler has been exhibiting his works for many years in this country. He has also exhibited in France, where he was the pupil of a well-known painter. Mr. Whistler is, in fact, a gentleman who for years has devoted himself to art and endeavored to live by that profession. Whether or not these things ought or ought not to have been known to the defendant is not for me to say, but it is generally known that Mr. Whistler occupies a somewhat independent position in art. I will place the plaintiff in the witness box and he will state some of his theories. It might be that his theory of painting is, in the estimation of some, eccentric; but his great object is to produce the utmost effect which color will enable him to do, and to bring about a harmony in color and arrangement in his pictures. These might be eccentricities, but because a man has created a theory of his own and followed it out with earnestness, industry, and almost enthusiasm, is no reason he should be denounced or libeled.

In the summer of 1877 the plaintiff exhibited several of his pictures at the Grosvenor Gallery—which was opened, I understand, by Sir Coutts Lindsay for the purpose of exhibiting many pictures that were unable to obtain a place at the Royal Academy of Arts—and from year to year he exhibited many pictures at the Royal Academy, one of which was purchased by Mr. John Phillip.[2] Mr. Whistler also exhibited works in the Dudley Gallery.[3] Altogether he has been an unwearied worker in his profession, always deserving to succeed; even if he has formed an erroneous opinion, he should not have been treated with contempt and ridicule by Mr. Ruskin. He ought rather to have been treated with the highest respect by that gentleman, who without doubt is a sincere worker in his own profession.

Mr. Ruskin edits a publication called *Fors Clavigera,* which has a large circulation among artists and art patrons; the fact of its large circulation is of importance.[4] In the July number of 1877 there appeared a criticism of many matters besides art, but on the subject of art Mr. Ruskin first criticized in general terms what he called the "modern school." [After] speaking in complimentary terms of Sir Coutts Lindsay, Mr. Ruskin said: "Sir Coutts Lindsay is at present an amateur both in art and shopkeeping. He must take up either one or the other business, if he would prosper in either."[5] Then, referring to Mr. Burne-Jones:

> Lastly, the mannerisms and errors of these pictures [by Burne-Jones], whatever may be their extent, are never affected or indolent. The work is natural to the painter, however strange to us; and it is wrought with utmost conscience of care, however far, to his own or our desire, the result may yet be incomplete. Scarcely so much can be said for any other pictures of the modern schools: their eccentricities are almost always in some degree forced; and their imperfections gratuitously, if not impertinently, indulged.

Then follows the paragraph which is the defamatory matter complained of:

> For Mr. Whistler's own sake, no less than for the protection of the purchaser, Sir Coutts Lindsay ought not to have admitted works into the gallery in which the ill-educated conceit of the artist so nearly approached the aspect of wilful imposture. I have seen, and heard, much of Cockney impudence before now; but never expected to hear a coxcomb ask two hundred guineas for flinging a pot of paint in the public's face.[6]

In my opinion, there can be no doubt that these terms are injurious and hurtful to Mr. Whistler.

Mr. Ruskin says in his defense that the criticism I have just read is privileged, as being a fair and bona fide criticism upon a painting the plaintiff exposed for public view. I would ask you, however, whether you would speak of a man as an impostor and then ask the approval of the public. Mr. Ruskin has not only alleged that the plaintiff's paintings are worthless as works of art, but has actually said that Mr. Whistler is guilty of fraud in asking the price he has done,[7] though similar pictures of his have been sold for the same amount. I maintain that the terms in which Mr. Ruskin has spoken of Mr. Whistler are unfair and ungentlemanly, and coming as they have from so great an authority on art, were calculated to and have done Mr. Whistler considerable injury in his profession and in the public estimation. Those terms cannot, in any ordinary sense in which language is used, be considered privileged. To speak of a man as nearly approaching a willful impostor when criticizing a work the artist has publicly exhibited is to employ language that would not be tolerated in any sphere of life. Why should it be tolerated simply because it was used by a great art critic? That passage, no doubt, has been read by thousands, and so it has gone forth to the world that Mr. Whistler is an ill-educated man, an impostor, a cockney pretender, and an impudent coxcomb. Wherever that language is read, the plaintiff is condemned; and condemned by the pen of a very powerful man. It will be for the jury to say what damages the plaintiff is entitled to.

I do not know what course will be taken by the attorney general, but I hope no attempt will be made to judge Mr. Whistler's style by the exhibition of any single picture held up in court for purposes of ridicule. I would ask that a large number of Mr. Whistler's works be seen by the judge and jury so that an opportunity might be given for a full, fair, and proper criticism. Some of the paintings will be produced, but it would be impossible to exhibit the pictures properly in this court. A room has been engaged in the Westminster Palace Hotel, and all the plaintiff's pictures that could be procured have been arranged there, including a portrait of Mr. Carlyle and a sketch of Mr. Irving in the character of Philip II of Spain.

I trust that the case will be fairly tried and that no attempt will be made to ridicule Mr. Whistler. With this fairness to the plaintiff, which I have no doubt will be exhibited, I have no fear as to the consequences of the trial.

HUDDLESTON: I think it would be exceedingly desirable for Mr. Whistler's pictures to be seen by the jury, and I will consider any application that might be made for an inspection of the pictures. But I should think some place might be found for them within the precincts of Westminster Hall, instead of the jury being obliged to go to the Westminster Palace Hotel.

HOLKER: I will not deny that there are pictures of Mr. Whistler's that might be of great merit, but I think the jury should see only those that were exhibited at the Grosvenor Gallery.

PARRY: I would wish the jury to see two or three others as well.

HUDDLESTON: I saw the pictures at the Grosvenor, but my attention was not called to them. Probably the jury saw them also.

HOLKER: I think the proper course would be to show the jury the pictures Mr. Ruskin had in his mind when he wrote the alleged libel.

PARRY: We don't know what Mr. Ruskin had in his mind, and probably we never shall.

Direct Examination of James Abbott McNeill Whistler by Mr. Petheram

WHISTLER: . . . I am an artist of American parentage, and was born at St. Petersburg, where I lived until I was twelve or fourteen years of age.[8] My father was an engineer who constructed the railway between St. Petersburg and Moscow.

PETHERAM: After you left Russia you went to America?

WHISTLER: Yes, after remaining in England for about a year on my way back to America. I was educated at West Point.[9]

PETHERAM: When did you return to Europe?

WHISTLER: I came back to England in 1855 or 1856, and stayed in Paris a few years studying art. I was in the studio of M. Gleyre for two or three years. Among my fellow students were Messrs. Armstrong, Poynter, and Du Maurier.[10]

PETHERAM: After leaving Paris you came to London?

WHISTLER: Yes, and continued my art studies here.

PETHERAM: While in Paris did you do any independent work as an artist?

WHISTLER: Oh yes, certainly.

PETHERAM: You finally settled in London?

WHISTLER: Yes, I came to London to remain permanently when I exhibited my first picture at the Royal Academy. I cannot remember the year—I am a bad one for dates. I have continued my career here ever since.[11] . . . I have continually exhibited at the Royal Academy. The last picture I exhibited there was about three or four years ago, a portrait of my mother.[12] I have sent nothing to the academy since the Grosvenor Gallery opened.[13] . . . The first picture I exhibited in England, called *At the Piano,* I sold to Mr. Phillip, who was then a Royal Academician. Since then I have exhibited *La Mère Gérard, Wapping, Alone with the Tide, Taking Down Scaffolding at Old Westminster Bridge, Ships in the Ice on the Thames,* and *The Little White Girl.* There were a great many others. I have also exhibited in the Salon in Paris.[14] Those pictures were exhibited by me, as an artist, for sale. About five years ago I exhibited at the Dudley Gallery. . . . During the whole of my career I have been in the habit of etching a good deal, and I have published and exhibited a great many etchings both here and abroad. A number of my etchings were exhibited at The Hague in the year 1863 or 1864, and I received a gold medal for them; that was the first intimation I had that they were [on exhibition] there.[15] The authorities of the British Museum have collected a large number of my etchings, but they have not a complete set. Some are at Windsor Castle; the Windsor collection was made for Her Majesty's library. . . . I exhibited some pictures at the Grosvenor Gallery summer exhibition of 1877.

PETHERAM: Was that in consequence of any request?

WHISTLER: No pictures are exhibited there but on invitation; I was invited by Sir Coutts Lindsay. I exhibited eight pictures there. The first was *Nocturne in Black and Gold* [plate 1]; the second, *Nocturne in Blue and Silver* [plate 4]; the third, *Nocturne in Blue and Gold* [plate

5]; the fourth, another *Nocturne in Blue and Silver* [plate 3]; the fifth, *Arrangement in Black No. 3, Irving as Philip II of Spain* [plate 6]; the sixth, *Harmony in Amber and Black* [plate 8]; the seventh, *Arrangement in Brown* [plate 7]. In addition to these, there was a portrait of Mr. Carlyle [plate 2] painted from sittings he gave me. It has since been engraved, and the artist's proofs—or the mass of them—are all subscribed for. The portrait was an arrangement in green and gold. . . . Before the pictures went to the Grosvenor, all the nocturnes except one were disposed of. One of them, *Nocturne in Blue and Gold,* was sold to the Honorable Percy Wyndham.

PETHERAM: For what price?

WHISTLER: For two hundred guineas. . . . One [nocturne] I sent to Mr. [William] Graham in lieu of a former commission, the amount of which was 150 guineas. A third *Nocturne in Blue and Silver* I presented to Mrs. [Frederick R.] Leyland. The picture unsold was *Nocturne in Black and Gold,* and the price fixed for it was two hundred guineas.

PETHERAM: You know the publication called *Fors Clavigera?*

WHISTLER: Yes, and my impression is that it has an extensive sale. I see it on the tables of most persons I know.

PETHERAM: Since the publication of Mr. Ruskin's criticism, have you sold a nocturne?

WHISTLER: Not by any means at the same price as before.

PETHERAM: Which pictures of those that were in the Grosvenor Gallery have you been able to get for inspection today?

WHISTLER: The pictures of Irving as Philip II; *Nocturne in Black and Gold;* and *Thomas Carlyle.* I could obtain no more.

PETHERAM: Is the nocturne you sold to Mr. Wyndham here?

WHISTLER: I expected it, but a telegram came saying it could not be lent.

PETHERAM: Is the picture of Irving as Philip II a finished picture?

WHISTLER: It is a large impression, a sketch, but it was not intended as a finished picture[16] and was not exhibited for sale. There were no paintings exhibited for sale but *Nocturne in Black and Gold.*

PETHERAM: Will you tell us the meaning of the word "nocturne" as applied to your pictures?

WHISTLER: By using the word "nocturne" I wished to indicate an artistic interest alone, divesting the picture of any outside anecdotal interest which might have been otherwise attached to it. A nocturne is an arrangement of line, form, and color first. The picture is throughout a problem that I attempt to solve. I make use of any means, any incident or object in nature, that will bring about this symmetrical result.[17]

PETHERAM: What do you mean by "arrangement"?

WHISTLER: I mean an arrangement of line and form and color. Among my works are some night pieces, and I have chosen the word "nocturne" because it generalizes and simplifies the whole set of them; it is an accident that I happened upon terms used in music. Very often have I been misunderstood from this fact, it having been supposed that I intended some way or other to show a connection between the two arts, whereas I had no such intention.

Cross-examination of Whistler by Sir John Holker

WHISTLER: . . . I have done some etchings as well as paintings of scenes down the [Thames] river.[18]

HOLKER: You have sent pictures to the Royal Academy which have not been received?[19]

WHISTLER: Some of my pictures have been rejected by the academy committee. I believe that is the experience of all artists. *(Laughter)*

HOLKER: When did you last send to the academy a picture that was not hung?

WHISTLER: The last time I sent to the academy a picture that was refused was three or four years ago. The painting was called *Arrangement in Grey and Black: Portrait of the Painter's Mother* [fig. 18].

HOLKER: That was the same picture that was afterward hung?

WHISTLER: Yes.

HOLKER: Did you send to the academy any of the seven that were afterward exhibited in the Grosvenor Gallery?

WHISTLER: No.

HOLKER: What is the subject of the *Nocturne in Black and Gold* [plate 1]?[20]

WHISTLER: It is a night piece and represents the fireworks at Cremorne Gardens.

HOLKER: Not a view of Cremorne?

WHISTLER: If it were called "A View of Cremorne" it would certainly bring about nothing but disappointment on the part of the beholders. *(Laughter)* It is an artistic arrangement. That is why I call it a "nocturne."

HOLKER: You do not think any member of the public would go to Cremorne because he saw your picture? *(Laughter)*

WHISTLER: It wouldn't give the public a good idea of Cremorne. I do not know how to describe the picture. It is simply an arrangement of color that was for sale, and the price marked was two hundred guineas.

HOLKER: And two hundred guineas is the amount you thought a fit and proper price for it?

WHISTLER: Yes.

HOLKER: Is two hundred guineas a pretty good price for a picture of an artist of reputation?[21]

WHISTLER: Yes.

HOLKER: Is it not what we who are not artists would call a stiffish price?

WHISTLER: I think it very likely that may be so. *(Laughter)*

HOLKER: You know Mr. Ruskin as an art critic?

WHISTLER: I have never had the pleasure of meeting Mr. Ruskin. He has written some works on art. I have not read his *Stones of Venice,* but I know his other work, *Modern Painters.*

HOLKER: You know that Mr. Ruskin's view is that an artist should not allow a picture to leave his hands when, by any labor he can bestow upon it, he can improve it?

WHISTLER: No, but that is the correct view.

HOLKER: And that his view is that an artist should give good value for money and not endeavor to get the highest price?[22]

WHISTLER: Very likely.

HOLKER: Artists do not endeavor to get the highest price for their work irrespective of value?

WHISTLER: That is so; I am glad to see the principle so well established. *(Laughter)*

HUDDLESTON: Artists propose to give full value for their money?

WHISTLER: Yes.

PARRY: So does every honorable dealer, my lord.

WHISTLER: . . . *Nocturne in Black and Gold* is a finished picture. I did not intend to do anything more with it. It is not a picture of two colors only; there is every color on the palette in it, as there is in every painting. . . . *Nocturne in Blue and Gold,* Mr. Percy Wyndham's painting, was exhibited at the Dudley Gallery and bought on the walls. It is a scene on the river. *Nocturne in Blue and Silver* is a scene on the Thames in summertime, by moonlight. That nocturne is not here; I have not been able to procure it, the owner, Mr. Graham, being in Italy.[23] Another *Nocturne in Blue and Silver,* which I presented to Mrs. Leyland, is also a river scene. *Arrangement in Black No. 3, Irving as Philip II* I have not attempted to sell; it is intended to be Mr. Irving's.

HOLKER: Why do you call Mr. Irving an "arrangement in black"?[24] *(Laughter)*

HUDDLESTON: It is the picture, not Mr. Irving, who is the "arrangement." *(Laughter)*

HOLKER: Why did you arrange Mr. Irving in black?

WHISTLER: I thought it was appropriate.

HOLKER: No doubt. We often see Mr. Irving in black. What is the "Arrangement in Amber and Black"?

WHISTLER: *Harmony in Amber and Black* is a young lady in an amber dress with a black ground. I did not offer it for sale. *Arrangement in Brown* is similar. These are impressions of my own; I make them my study. I suppose them to appeal to none but those who may understand the technical matter. I did not intend to sell *Harmony in Amber and Black. Arrangement in Brown* was also the portrait of a lady; I believe it is here in court.[25] I have not got *Harmony in Amber and*

Black; it was used and painted over.[26] . . . I have made arrangements for the various pictures to be shown at the Westminster Palace Hotel.

HOLKER: The only picture you had in the Grosvenor Gallery for sale was the *Nocturne in Black and Gold?*

WHISTLER: Yes.

HOLKER: I suppose you are willing to admit that your pictures exhibit some eccentricities. You have been told that over and over again?

WHISTLER: Yes, very often. *(Laughter)*

HOLKER: You sent your pictures to the Grosvenor Gallery to invite the admiration of the public?

WHISTLER: That would have been such a vast absurdity on my part that I don't think I could have. *(Laughter)*

HOLKER: You don't expect your pictures not to be criticized?

WHISTLER: Oh, no, certainly—not unless they are altogether overlooked.

HOLKER: Did it take you much time to paint the *Nocturne in Black and Gold?* How soon did you knock it off? *(Laughter)*

WHISTLER: I beg your pardon?

HOLKER: I was using an expression which is rather more applicable to my own profession. *(Laughter)*

WHISTLER: Thank you for the compliment. *(Laughter)*

HOLKER: How long do you take to knock off one of your pictures?

WHISTLER: Oh, I "knock one off" possibly in a couple of days—*(Laughter)*—one day to do the work and another to finish it.[27]

HOLKER: After partly painting a picture, do you put it up to mellow? *(Laughter)*

WHISTLER: I do not understand.

HOLKER: Do you ever hang these pictures up on the garden wall?[28]

WHISTLER: Oh, I understand now. I did not put up *Nocturne in Black and Gold* or any other picture to "mellow." I should be grieved to see my paintings mellowed. *(Laughter)* I do put my paintings in the open air so that they may dry well as I go on with my work. I think this is a good thing to do—though I did not so treat *Nocturne in Black and Gold*—and if I were a professor I would recommend it to my pupils.

HOLKER: The labor of two days is that for which you ask two hundred guineas?[29]

WHISTLER: No. I ask it for the knowledge I have gained in the work of a lifetime.[30] *(Applause)*

HUDDLESTON: This is not an arena for applause. If this manifestation of feeling is repeated, I shall have to clear the court.[31]

HOLKER: You know that many critics entirely disagree with your views as to these pictures?

WHISTLER: It would be beyond me to agree with the critics. *(Laughter)*

HOLKER: You don't approve of criticism?

WHISTLER: It is not for me to criticize the critics. I should not disapprove in any way of technical criticism by a man whose life is passed in the practice of the science that he criticizes; but for the opinion of a man whose life is not so passed I would have as little respect as you would have if he expressed an opinion on the law. I hold that none but an artist can be a competent critic. It is not only when a criticism is unjust that I object to it, but when it is incompetent.[32]

HOLKER: You expect to be criticized?

WHISTLER: Yes, certainly; and I do not expect to be affected by it until it comes to a case of this kind.

The attorney general here proposed to produce Nocturne in Black and Gold. *Serjeant Parry objected.*

PARRY: It is unfair to show the jury only one of the plaintiff's productions. All of the pictures he exhibited at the Grosvenor Gallery should be seen by the jury. Besides, the light in the court is not fit for pictures.

HUDDLESTON: It would be scarcely fair to show an artist's pictures in a bad light. . . .

HOLKER: What is the subject of the *Nocturne in Blue and Silver* [plate 3] given to Mr. Graham?

WHISTLER: A moonlight effect near Old Battersea Bridge. The nocturne was exchanged with Mr. Graham for an old commission at 150 guineas.

HOLKER: What has become of the *Nocturne in Black and Gold?*

WHISTLER: I believe it is before you.

HOLKER: You have not sold it?

WHISTLER: No, but I have deposited it.

HOLKER: You can get it?

WHISTLER: It would be very difficult; I believe you have it.[33] *(Laughter)*

The attorney general proposed to show the jury Nocturne in Blue and Silver.

PARRY: It would be more convenient if a room could be obtained in the immediate neighborhood for the jury to see the collection of Mr. Whistler's pictures.

HOLKER: I decidedly object to an exhibition of Mr. Whistler's paintings. Mr. Ruskin dealt only with those which were exhibited at the Grosvenor Gallery. It is fair that the pictures to which Mr. Ruskin referred be seen by the jury.

PARRY: Inasmuch as the plaintiff's character was attacked, and as he has almost been charged with being an impostor, Mr. Whistler has a right to show the jury what his works have been.

HOLKER: No answer was given to a written application by the defendant's solicitors for leave to inspect the pictures that the plaintiff proposed to produce at the trial.[34]

WHISTLER: Mr. Arthur Severn has inspected the pictures on behalf of the defendant.[35]

HUDDLESTON: I think that in justice to Mr. Whistler it is only fair that the jury should have the benefit of seeing all the pictures that have been brought to the Westminster Palace Hotel for that purpose.

HOLKER: After your lordship's observation, the impression would be that I was dealing unfairly if the jury were not allowed to see the pictures. I do not wish it to be supposed that I am in any way acting ungenerously.

HUDDLESTON: As far as I am concerned, I have to tell the jury simply what the law of the case is, and I do not think I shall be much assisted in discharging that duty by going over to the Westminster Palace Hotel and seeing the pictures. Besides, I have already seen them in the Grosvenor Gallery.

The jury expressed its willingness to walk over to the Westminster Palace Hotel to see the pictures.

I think it would be inconvenient to proceed thither with a crowd following. *(Laughter)* Perhaps the pictures can be exhibited in the probate court; otherwise, the jury can go and see them after we have adjourned for luncheon.[36]

PARRY: The *Nocturne in Black and Gold,* with some others, has been deposited with Mr. Noseda, who has been summoned to produce four of the pictures. Those four are now, I believe, in court—two produced by the plaintiff and the other two by the defendant.[37]

HUDDLESTON: I would suggest that those four pictures be placed among the others in the Westminster Palace Hotel for the inspection of the jury.

After considerable discussion, Nocturne in Blue and Silver [plate 3] *was exhibited to the jury from the bench.*[38]

WHISTLER: . . . That is Mr. Graham's picture, *Nocturne in Blue and Silver.* It represents Battersea Bridge by moonlight.

HUDDLESTON: Which part of the picture is the bridge? *(Laughter)*

His lordship earnestly rebuked those who laughed, and the witness explained to his lordship the composition of the picture.

WHISTLER: Your lordship is too close at present to the picture to perceive the effect I intended to produce at a distance. The spectator is supposed to be looking down the river toward London. The picture gives a view of the bridge and, looking through the arch, Chelsea Church in the further distance.

HOLKER: Do you say that this is a correct representation of Battersea Bridge?

WHISTLER: It was not my intent simply to make a copy of Battersea Bridge. The pier in the center of the picture may not be like the piers of Battersea Bridge. I did not intend to paint a portrait of the bridge, but only a painting of a moonlight scene.[39] As to what the picture represents, that depends upon who looks at it. To some persons it may represent all that I intended; to others it may represent nothing.

HOLKER: What is that mark on the right of the picture, like a cascade? Is it a firework?

WHISTLER: Yes, the cascade of gold color is a firework.

HOLKER: What is that peculiar dark mark on the frame?

WHISTLER: The blue coloring on the gilt frame is part of the scheme of the picture. The blue spot on the right side of the frame is my monogram, which I place on the frame as well as the canvas; it balances the picture. The frame and the picture together are a work of art.[40]

HOLKER: The prevailing color is blue?[41]

WHISTLER: Yes.

HOLKER: Are those figures on the top of the bridge intended as people?

WHISTLER: They are just what you like.

HOLKER: That is a barge beneath?

WHISTLER: Yes, I am very much flattered at your seeing that. The thing is intended simply as a representation of moonlight. My whole scheme was only to bring about a certain harmony of color.

Another picture [plate 4] *was then produced.*

That is *Nocturne in Blue and Silver,* which was presented to Mrs. Leyland. It represents another moonlight scene on the Thames, looking up Battersea Reach.

HOLKER: How long did it take you to paint that picture?

WHISTLER: I completed the mass of the picture in one day, after having arranged the idea in my mind.

The examination of the other pictures was postponed.

Redirect Examination of Whistler by Serjeant Parry

WHISTLER: . . . I have several pictures which can be seen by the jury at the Westminster Palace Hotel. The collection includes Mr. Carlyle's portrait and a picture of a young lady that was not exhibited in the Grosvenor Gallery.[42] Besides those portraits, I have produced one other nocturne picture. . . . The picture of Philip II, also exhibited at the Grosvenor last year, is a mere sketch, unfinished. There is another picture [at the Westminster Palace Hotel], a balcony scene entitled *Variations in Flesh Colour and Green* [fig. 16], which was exhibited at the Grosvenor this year; and another representing the seaside and sand, called *Harmony in Blue and Yellow.*[43] . . . The *Carlyle* was not offered for sale. . . . *Nocturne in Black and Gold,* which has now been sent for, was the only picture at the Grosvenor for which I asked two hundred guineas and is therefore, I suppose, the picture referred to in the libel. . . . My system of harmony and arrangement, to whatever criticism it may be open, is the object of a life's study.

PARRY: Do you conscientiously form your idea and then conscientiously work it out?

WHISTLER: Certainly. I do not always sketch the subjects of my pictures, but I form the idea in my mind conscientiously and work it out to the best of my ability.

PARRY: And these pictures are published by you for the purpose of a livelihood?

WHISTLER: Yes.

PARRY: Your manual labor is rapid?

WHISTLER: Certainly. The proper execution of the idea depends greatly upon the instantaneous work of my hand. The pictures would not have the quality I desire to produce if I did not go on hammering away. I am a rapid etcher: I etch on the plate itself, not on the paper; that plan has been adopted by greater etchers than myself.

His lordship then adjourned the hearing for luncheon while the jury, accompanied by a gentleman representing each side, proceeded to the Westminster Palace Hotel to view the pictures exhibited there.[44]

Further Cross-examination of Whistler by Sir John Holker

The jury having returned into court, Nocturne in Black and Gold [plate 1], *which represented the fireworks at Cremorne, was produced and exhibited to the jury.*

HOLKER: This is Cremorne? *(Laughter)*

WHISTLER: It is a nocturne in black and gold. The picture represents a distant view of Cremorne, with a falling rocket and other fireworks.

HOLKER: How long did it take you to paint that?

WHISTLER: One whole day and part of another. It is a finished picture. . . . The frame is traced with black, and the black mark on the right side is my monogram, which was placed in its position so as not to put the balance of color out.[45]

HOLKER: You have made the study of art your study of a lifetime. What is the peculiar beauty of that picture?

WHISTLER: I daresay I could make it clear to any sympathetic painter, but I do not think I could to you, any more than a musician could explain the beauty of a harmony to a person who has no ear.[46]

HOLKER: Do you not think that anybody looking at that picture might fairly come to the conclusion that it has no peculiar beauty?

WHISTLER: I think there is distinct evidence that Mr. Ruskin did come to that conclusion.

HOLKER: Do you think it fair that Mr. Ruskin should come to that conclusion?

WHISTLER: What might be fair to Mr. Ruskin I can't answer. No artist of culture would come to that conclusion. I have known unbiased people to recognize that [the nocturne] represents fireworks in a night scene.

HOLKER: You offer that picture to the public as one of particular beauty as a work of art, and one which is fairly worth two hundred guineas?

WHISTLER: I offer it as a work that I have conscientiously executed and that I think worth the money. I would hold my reputation upon this, as I would upon any of my other works. I would not complain of any person who might simply take a different view.

Further Redirect Examination of Whistler by Serjeant Parry

WHISTLER: . . . *Nocturne in Black and Gold* was not painted to offer the portrait of a particular place, but as an artistic impression that had been carried away [from the scene]. . . . Many of my nocturnes are taken from the Thames; I reside near the Chelsea Embankment, and that induced me to take the Thames as a subject for most of them. I did live in Cheyne Walk, Chelsea, but I now reside in the White House, in Tite Street.[47]

Direct Examination of William Michael Rossetti by Serjeant Parry

ROSSETTI: . . . I have been connected with literature and art since 1850. During that period I have made art my special study, and have been extensively and frequently engaged in criticizing pictures. . . . I have known Mr. Whistler since 1862. I also know Mr. Ruskin. . . . I am an art critic.

PARRY: You have seen this *Nocturne in Black and Gold* before?

ROSSETTI: Yes. . . . I am well aware of the nomenclature of Mr. Whistler's pictures, and I appreciate its meaning.

PARRY: As regards this particular picture in black and gold, did you criticize it?

ROSSETTI: I criticized the pictures in the Grosvenor exhibition of

1877, and I suppose I must have said something about it. . . . I have seen the two [nocturnes] in blue and silver before.[48]

PARRY: Have you made yourself acquainted with Mr. Whistler's pictures generally?

ROSSETTI: Yes.

PARRY: What judgment have you formed upon them?

ROSSETTI: If I am to take that picture [plate 4]—the pale blue picture—

HUDDLESTON: That is the blue and silver nocturne, Mrs. Leyland's picture.

ROSSETTI: —I consider it an artistic and beautiful representation of a pale but bright moonlight.[49]

PARRY: Then take the other one, the other *Blue and Silver* [plate 3].

ROSSETTI: To that I apply nearly the same observation, except that it is darker. This painting of Battersea Bridge represents a general diffused moonlight, with a firework in the form of a cascade. . . . The first observation I should make as to *Nocturne in Black and Gold* [plate 1] is that it is an effort to produce something of an indefinite kind; being a representation of night, it must be indefinite. It represents the darkness of night mingled with and broken by the brightness of fireworks.[50]

PARRY: What is your opinion of Mr. Whistler as an artist?

HOLKER: [Objection.] Mr. Whistler has only been attacked in reference to the position of the works exhibited.

HUDDLESTON: [Objection sustained.] We are not discussing the merits of Mr. Whistler as an artist, but whether the criticism is a fair and bona fide one.[51]

PARRY: Have you seen the portrait of Carlyle [plate 2] that was exhibited in the Grosvenor Gallery?

ROSSETTI: [Yes.][52]

PARRY: What do you say to that as a work of art?

HOLKER: Objection![53]

HUDDLESTON: I say the question is admissible, as the portrait was one of the pictures exhibited at the gallery.

ROSSETTI: I think the portrait of Carlyle is a very fine portrait, treated with a certain degree of peculiarity and unlike the work of most artists. It is a very excellent likeness, to the best of my judgment.

PARRY: Taking the pictures exhibited by Mr. Whistler at the Grosvenor Gallery, what is your opinion of him as an artist?

HOLKER: Objection!

HUDDLESTON: [Sustained].

PARRY: What is your judgment of the works in the Grosvenor Gallery exhibited by Mr. Whistler?

ROSSETTI: Taking them all together, I admire them sincerely. They are very fine works, with one or two exceptions.[54]

PARRY: Do you, or do you not, consider them works of a conscientious artist desirous of working well in his profession?

ROSSETTI: I do, decidedly. I consider Mr. Whistler a sincere and good artist.

Cross-examination of Rossetti by Sir John Holker

ROSSETTI: . . . I do not paint myself, but I have been in the habit of criticizing works of art, sometimes with severity. I do not always praise. . . . My criticism of the Grosvenor exhibition appeared in the *Academy*. . . . I know Mr. Ruskin personally and consider him to be very much devoted to art. As we all know, he has written very much on the subject and has praised many pictures. He is the Slade Professor of Fine Arts at the University of Oxford.[55]

HOLKER: What is the peculiar beauty of the *Nocturne in Black and Gold* [plate 1], the representation of the fireworks at Cremorne? It seems very dark. Is it a gem? *(Laughter)*

ROSSETTI: No, I would not call the painting a gem.

HOLKER: Is it an exquisite painting?

ROSSETTI: No.

HOLKER: Is it very beautiful?

ROSSETTI: No.

HOLKER: Is it eccentric?

ROSSETTI: It is unlike the work of most other painters.

HOLKER: Is it a work of art?

ROSSETTI: Yes, in my opinion it is.

HOLKER: Is anything a work of art that produces a startling effect?

ROSSETTI: Yes, I think so. . . . I have not seen *The Grasshopper* at the Gaiety Theatre, or *La Cigale* in Paris.[56]

HOLKER: Why is the *Nocturne in Black and Gold* a work of art?

ROSSETTI: Because it represents what was intended. It is a picture painted with a considerable sense of the general effect of such a scene and finished with considerable artistic skill.

HOLKER: Has there been much labor bestowed upon the painting?

ROSSETTI: No, but I don't think it is at all necessary for a painting to show labor and finish. . . . I could not form an opinion with the light and shortsightedness.

HOLKER: Two hundred guineas is a stiffish price, is it not, for a picture of this kind?

ROSSETTI: I don't know that I am called upon to express any opinion on that point.

HOLKER: I call upon you to do so.

The witness appealed to the judge.

HUDDLESTON: I think the question ought to be answered.

HOLKER: Is two hundred guineas a stiffish price for a picture like this?

ROSSETTI: I would rather not express an opinion as to the value of the picture, but if I am pressed I should say two hundred guineas is the full value of it—*(Laughter)*—not a "stiffish price."

HOLKER: Do you think it is worth that money?

ROSSETTI: Yes.

HOLKER: And would you give that for it?

ROSSETTI: I am too poor a man to give two hundred guineas for any picture.

Redirect Examination of Rossetti by Serjeant Parry

ROSSETTI: . . . Mr. Ruskin has, I believe, severely criticized the works of other artists; he has abused as well as praised painters. . . . I adhere to my opinion as to the two lighter pictures [in blue and silver]. I do not look on the other, darker picture [*Nocturne in Black and Gold*] as an indifferent picture, but as the work of a conscientious artist. . . . There is no reason why fireworks should not be represented—I have seen them represented before in pictures—but I do not think it is a good subject.[57]

Direct Examination of Albert Joseph Moore by Mr. Petheram

MOORE: . . . I am an artist.[58] I have studied my profession all over Europe and have seen most of the picture galleries abroad. I studied in Rome and in England. For some years past I have carried on the profession of an artist in London. I have made my living by it for fifteen years. During that period I have exhibited at the Royal Academy and recently at the Grosvenor Gallery.[59] I continue to exhibit at the Royal Academy. I had two pictures in the Paris Exhibition.[60] . . . I know Mr. Whistler and his pictures well. I have known him for fourteen years.[61] I do not know Mr. Ruskin. . . . I have seen the pictures that have been produced here today.

PETHERAM: What is your opinion of the pictures produced?

MOORE: The pictures produced, in common with all Mr. Whistler's works, have a large aim not often followed. People abroad charge us with finishing our pictures too much. In the qualities aimed at, I say Mr. Whistler has succeeded, and no living painter, I believe, could succeed in the same way, in the same qualities. I consider the pictures beautiful works of art; I wish I could paint as well. There is one extraordinary thing about them, and that is that he has painted the air, which very few artists have attempted. I think the sensation of atmosphere in the bridge picture [*Nocturne in Blue and Silver*] very remarkable. As to the picture in black and gold, I think the atmospheric effects are simply marvelous. The peculiarity of the scene at Cremorne is, to my mind, wonderful.

PETHERAM: Would you call the *Nocturne in Black and Gold* a work of art?

MOORE: Certainly. Most consummate art.

PETHERAM: Is two hundred guineas a reasonable price?

MOORE: Looking at what pictures will now sell for, I should think a price of two hundred guineas is not too high for one of the paintings, any more than such a sum would be too high for one of the learned counsel to earn without working for days and days. *(Laughter)* The money is paid for the skill of the artist, not always for the amount of labor expended. If I were rich I would buy Mr. Whistler's pictures myself. . . . I have seen the picture of Carlyle. It is good as a portrait and excellent as a picture.

Cross-examination of Moore by Sir John Holker

MOORE: . . . I exhibited pictures myself at the Grosvenor in 1877.

HOLKER: Are you a member of a particular school of art?

MOORE: I belong to no confederation of artists, nor am I the leader of a school.[62]

HOLKER: Would you call Mr. Whistler a member or disciple of a particular school of art?

MOORE: Well, the practice of art as he follows it is not very common in England. I do not paint the same style of picture as Mr. Whistler; the father of that style is Velázquez.

HOLKER: Is the picture with the fireworks [*Nocturne in Black and Gold*] an exquisite work of art?

MOORE: There is a decided beauty in the painting of it. . . . If I were a purchaser of pictures, I should be glad to give two hundred guineas for the black and gold nocturne.

HOLKER: Is there any eccentricity in these pictures?

MOORE: I should call it "originality." What would you call "eccentricity" in a picture? *(Laughter)* . . . The frame may add to the beauty of the picture. I have seen the frames of old pictures colored.

HOLKER: Don't you know that Mr. Ruskin has devoted much time and consideration to art subjects?

MOORE: Yes. The wonder is that he should not have been a painter. I believe he has done something in watercolor.

Direct Examination of William Gorman Wills by Serjeant Parry

WILLS: . . . I am a dramatic author and have written several plays.[63] I have also studied as an artist and pursue the profession as a means of livelihood. . . . I know Mr. Whistler personally, and have known him for seven or eight years. I am a great admirer of his works and have often been in his studio. . . . I have seen the two moonlight pictures [the nocturnes in blue and silver, plates 3 and 4] before; I saw them at the Grosvenor Gallery exhibition of 1877. I think they show great consideration and knowledge. There is considerable charm about them. To my mind, they evince a great knowledge of art. Mr. Whistler looks at nature in a poetical light and has a native feeling for color. I think he must have studied much before painting the pictures. I look upon them as the work of a man of genius and a conscientious artist.

Cross-examination of Wills by Sir John Holker

WILLS: . . . I do not know Mr. Ruskin personally. . . . I wrote *Olivia*[64] and several other plays. . . . I have at times been severely criticized.[65]

HOLKER: Do you object [to being criticized]?

WILLS: No. . . . I have not seen *The Grasshopper* at the Gaiety.[66] . . . I consider the nocturnes in blue and silver original. I will not call them eccentric, nor do I call them gems. They are beautiful works of art in my opinion. They are perfect as far as they pretend to be. I do not quarrel with those who hold a different opinion, I only state my own. . . . I have never seen the *Nocturne in Black and Gold* before and it is too dark for me to see it now.[67] . . . I should call Mr. Whistler's works original.

Redirect Examination of Wills by Serjeant Parry

WILLS: . . . I exhibited a picture at the Grosvenor Gallery in 1877.[68] . . . I don't object to honorable and fair criticism.

. . .

PARRY: That is the case for the plaintiff.

HOLKER: I submit that my learned friend has made out no case whatever, as he has not shown malice. The defendant's criticism is fair and bona fide, without malignity.

HUDDLESTON: Surely this is a question for the jury. As it stands by itself, the criticism is calculated to hold Mr. Whistler up to ridicule and contempt, and so far it would be libelous. The question is whether it comes within the license of privileged communication, and that is a matter for the jury. A critic ought to be wise enough to form a right judgment and bold enough to express it. If it is an honest and fair criticism, it is privileged, and whether in this case the criticism is fair is a point to be decided. The lord chief justice of common pleas, Justice Erle,[69] pointed out in a similar case that the plaintiff would not be entitled to recover damages unless he could show that the defendant had been actuated by malice; he would have to show that the defamatory matter was published without any ground, legal or otherwise. Thus, in a case of literary criticism, considerable liberty is allowed. It is for the attorney general to make out that Mr. Ruskin's critique is fair and honest criticism, with that sort of allowance a critic is permitted to enjoy.[70]

DEFENDANT'S CASE

Opening Statement by Sir John Holker

HOLKER: I had hoped to spare the court the examination of any witnesses on Mr. Ruskin's behalf, but the course my learned friend Mr. Serjeant Parry has taken renders that impossible. It will now be my duty to put in the witness box gentlemen who are quite as well acquainted with art as those who have just been examined, to give their opinion on the plaintiff's pictures. The real question the jury will have to decide is not whether these pictures are pictures of great merit or no merit, but whether Mr. Ruskin has or has not criticized the plaintiff's productions in a fair, honest, and moderate spirit. I maintain that the criticism in question is of that description and that it was honestly believed in by the defendant when he wrote it.

A critic has a perfect liberty to indulge in ridicule if he likes, and to use strong language if he likes, without exposing himself to the charge of acting maliciously. The only question is whether Mr. Ruskin's criticism is a fair criticism, and whether it oversteps the reasonable bounds of moderation.

No doubt there are a good many people in the world who do not like criticism. No doubt a great many artists would like to do away with art critics altogether. There is more abuse of critics than of any other persons; but, after all, critics have their uses. I should like to know what would become of literature, of poetry, of oratory, of politics, of painting, if critics, competent and able men, were to be extinguished?[1] If there were to be nothing but praise, there would be no incentive to excel. If artists were to have everything praised only, what would be the reward any painter could obtain?

Every painter struggles to obtain fame. I would not like to see incompetency and gross eccentricity and exaggeration on the same footing as the greatest possible excellence. If art is to live and flourish, so must criticism, for no artist can obtain fame except through criticism. Actors are freely criticized, as also are authors. It might be said of a man's book that it is devoid of interest and shows ignorance; but he must submit. Take the advocate if you choose, or the politician: they are all criticized, but they never think of resenting it, provided personal matter is not got into.

It will, I suppose, be said of Mr. Ruskin that his criticism oversteps the bounds of moderation, but I will endeavor to show that this is not so. I regret that I will not be able to call Mr. Ruskin before you, as he is far too ill to attend the court. It is only for that reason that he will not be able to repeat the criticism by word of mouth in the witness box that he has already written in the publication [*Fors Clavigera*].

Mr. Ruskin, it is well known, has devoted himself for years to the study and criticism of art. From 1869 he has been Slade Professor of Fine Arts at the University of Oxford, and he has written many works on the subject of art.[2] Judging from the contents of those works, it is obvious that Mr. Ruskin is a man of the keenest appreciation of that which is beautiful. He has a great love and reverence for art and a special admiration for highly finished pictures. His love for art amounts almost to idolatry; and to the examination of the beautiful in art, he has devoted his life.

Rightly or wrongly, Mr. Ruskin has not a very high opinion of the days in which we live. He thinks too much consideration is given to money-making and that the nobility of simplicity is not sufficiently regarded. With regard to artists, he upholds a high standard and will not admire a picture because it contains a few flashes of genius. He requires a laborious and perfect devotion to art and holds that an artist ought to entertain a desire not simply to gain a large sum for his work, but that he should struggle to give the purchaser something worth the money paid. Mr. Ruskin holds, further, that it was the ancient code that no piece of work should leave the artist's hands that his diligence or further reflection could improve; and that the artist's fame should be built not upon what he received, but upon what he gave.[3]

Entertaining these views as to the duty of artists, it is not wonderful that Mr. Whistler's pictures should attract Mr. Ruskin's attention, and that he should subject those pictures, among others, to criticism. He did subject them to a severe and slashing criticism—or, if you choose, to ridicule and contempt. But in doing so he only expressed, as he was entitled to do, his honest opinion; and if he honestly believed what he wrote, he would have been neglecting his duty if he had hesitated to express the opinions he had honestly formed.[4]

You have seen the pictures for yourselves. I ask you whether, if they had been exhibited to you before the elaborate disquisitions that have been given by the witnesses who have been examined, you would not have come to the conclusion that those paintings were strange and extravagant productions.

Suppose I take you to the Grosvenor Gallery and pointing out one of Mr. Whistler's pictures say, "The value of that is two hundred guineas." Would any of you put your hand into your pocket and say, "Here is the money"? Or would you not rather say, "That price is extravagant and absurd"? Mr. Whistler takes you to the Grosvenor Gallery and says, "Here are beautiful works of art." Mr. Whistler might be right, but Mr. Ruskin is of a different opinion. I would ask you to find that Mr. Ruskin has not committed any misdemeanor or any breach of his duties and privileges as an Englishman because he has disputed Mr. Whistler's view of his own productions.

. . .

HUDDLESTON: The condition in which this court is now might be called "nocturne." As it is four o'clock, this court will adjourn until tomorrow morning at half past ten. The attorney general will continue his address, after which witnesses will be called for the defense.

The court then adjourned.

Tuesday, 26 November 1878

The interest manifested in the case continued unabated, and the little court, utterly inadequate for the purpose when a case exciting much public attention is heard, was again densely crowded.

HUDDLESTON *(upon the assembling of the court)*: There appears to be some misapprehension as to my remarks relative to privilege. What I said [yesterday] was that if a criticism comes within one of the well-known rules of privilege, the presumption is that it is justified; but the burden of proof that it is a bona fide criticism is with the defendant.[5]

. . .

HOLKER *(resuming his address on behalf of Mr. Ruskin)*: I hope to convince the gentlemen of the jury, after they have heard the evidence which I shall adduce, that Mr. Ruskin's criticism upon Mr. Whistler's picture [*Nocturne in Black and Gold* (plate 1)] is perfectly fair and bona fide; and that however severe it might be, there is nothing that can be reasonably complained of.

I do not know whether you have ever been to the Grosvenor Gallery. Yesterday I was asking you to accompany me thither in imagination. After partaking of an artistic chop served on a plate of ancient pattern and some claret in a Venetian glass, we would get into the gallery and be attracted by Mr. Whistler's pictures.[6] We would of course have some difficulty in getting near them, for there is an intense admiration of his pictures among those votaries of art who principally frequent the Grosvenor Gallery. We would find "nocturnes," "arrangements," and "symphonies" surrounded by groups of artistic ladies—beautiful ladies who endeavor to disguise their attractions in medieval millinery, but do not succeed in consequence of sheer force of nature[7]—*(Laughter)*—and I daresay we would hear those ladies admiring the pictures and commenting upon them.

For instance: A lady, gazing on the moonlight scene representing Battersea Bridge, would turn round and say to another, "How beautiful! It is a 'nocturne in blue and silver.' Do you know what 'a nocturne' means?" And the other would say, "No, but it is an exquisite idea. How I should like to see Mr. Whistler, to know what it means!" Well, having seen Mr. Whistler and heard him give his explanation of a nocturne in the witness box, I doubt whether the young lady would be any the wiser. *(Laughter)* Then another lady would say, "Oh, how delightful it is that Mr. Whistler should have discovered the affinity between the two arts of music and painting! For he has given us not only nocturnes, but symphonies, arrangements, and harmonies. Only fancy a 'Moonlight in E Minor' or a 'Chiaroscuro in Four Flats'!"[8] *(Laughter)*

And the ladies would admire and adore, and after they had all poured incense upon the altar of Mr. Whistler, other people would be able to get near the pictures. After the ladies had dispersed, you would perhaps feel inclined to look at those pictures for a minute and see what you think of them yourselves. Of course you should not criticize at all; but let yourselves be bold and approach the pictures for a minute or two.

Let us examine the *Nocturne in Blue and Silver* [plate 3], said to represent Battersea Bridge. I daresay you will see beauty in it as a sketch. As a sketch, perhaps, there may be a good deal in the picture. There is a good deal of color, it is true; but you will no doubt come to the conclusion that it would have been better, perhaps, if a great deal of the color had not escaped from the picture and wandered over the frame. *(Laughter)* But what in the world is that structure in the middle? Is it a telescope or a fire escape? Or is it the great tubular bridge brought from the Menai Straits to span the Thames?[9] *(Laughter)* Why, what likeness can be said to exist to

Battersea Bridge? If Mr. Whistler wanted to make a picture, why did he not make the bridge something like Battersea Bridge?

Then you will ask, What are these figures at the top? Are they men and women, or are they horses and cattle? And should you succeed in coming to the conclusion that the figures on the bridge are human beings and horses and carts, you will naturally inquire, How in the name of fortune did they get on, and how are they going to get off? *(Laughter)*

These are the kind of remarks we would be inclined to make; but if the plaintiff's argument prevails, we must not venture publicly to express an opinion. If we criticize the pictures, we must do so sotto voce. We must not speak openly in the Grosvenor Gallery, lest we have an action brought against us.

But a word about critics. A critic should be a person dreaded in some respects—respected, if not loved. You remember the words of Byron:

> At his nod
> Hushed Academe sighed in silent awe,
> Soprano, basso, even the contralto,
> Wished him five fathoms under the Rialto.[10]

(Laughter) The critic used to be feared and respected, but now it is not so, as he cannot express his opinion lest he have brought against him an action for damages. However, I will criticize these pictures.

Passing to the Cremorne nocturne [plate 1], I do not know what the ladies would say to that, because it has a subject they would not understand—I hope they have never been to Cremorne—*(Laughter)*—but men will know more about it. Mr. Albert Moore says the picture is a piece of art. Why? I see the blackness of night with a falling star or some fireworks coming down from the top, and a sort of blaze at the bottom, perhaps a bonfire. That is all. But Mr. Moore says it is very beautiful.

Mr. Whistler does not see things as other people do.[11] He sees things we cannot see and hears artistic voices we cannot hear. *(Laughter)* With him, a rocket falling in sparks is not a rocket, but some strange fantastic form he will depict for the entrancement of the British public. I do not deny that he has done exceedingly good things; but as to these pictures, I think the visitors who have accompanied me in imagination to the Grosvenor Gallery will leave it under the impression that these are fantasies and exaggerated conceits, having elements of beauty, some of them, and having some value, no doubt; but unworthy of the title of great works of art.

There is at present a mania for what is called Art. It has become a kind of fashion among some people to admire the incomprehensible and to say of something that cannot be understood, "It is exquisite." *(Laughter)* So too in painting. With respect to the Cremorne picture, though people have not the least idea what the artist intended to portray, they may feel bound to come to a conclusion that the picture has some mysterious beauty and to look upon Mr. Whistler's fantastic conceits—his nocturnes, symphonies, arrangements, and harmonies—with delight and admiration. This is not a mania that should be encouraged; and if that is the view of Mr. Ruskin, he has a right, as an art critic, to fearlessly express it to the public.

It is Mr. Ruskin's opinion that care and conscientious labor in a picture are matters to be appreciated, and that an artist ought not to present a picture to the public until he has brought it, as far as he is able, to a state of perfection.[12] That is also the opinion of the artists and art critics whom I am obliged I might almost say to drag before the jury. Those artists will say that whatever Mr. Whistler has done in the past, and there is no doubt that he has produced more beautiful etchings and pictures, these pictures are not works to be proud of, not works deserving admission into any art gallery in the country.

I come now to the alleged libel. The defendant has a right to criticize. It is his business to do so. But, says my learned friend [Serjeant Parry], Mr. Ruskin is not justified in interfering with a man's livelihood: He must not say anything that will prevent Mr.

Whistler from earning his living. But why not? In fulfilling the duty of a critic, was Mr. Ruskin upon that ground to be tender or not to criticize at all? But then it was said, "Oh, you have ridiculed Mr. Whistler's pictures." If Mr. Whistler disliked ridicule, he should not have subjected himself to it by publicly exhibiting such productions.

Mr. Ruskin is not a stern, hard, and unyielding critic who deals in nothing but severity. He blames when he thinks he is called upon to blame and praises highly when he thinks he is called upon to commend. While he aims his trenchant criticisms right and left, he ungrudgingly gives high praise where it is due, as is shown in his criticism in the same publication [*Fors Clavigera*] on the works of Mr. Burne-Jones and Mr. Millais.[13] The whole article complained of is a sweeping condemnation of the modern school. In criticizing the plaintiff's style, Mr. Ruskin said that the artist had a fervid imagination, but his fault consisted in his being led away from one imagination to another before the first had been finished in its entirety.[14] Mr. Ruskin did not think these paintings of Mr. Whistler's were works of art.

Mr. Rossetti saw no particular beauty in the *Nocturne in Black and Gold.* He said that the painting of Cremorne was not a gem, not an exquisite work of art, and not beautiful, but that it was a work of art. Well, there are degrees in art, as in anything else; but Mr. Ruskin has probably had much more experience than Mr. Rossetti. Mr. Ruskin said that the *Nocturne in Black and Gold* was a mere conceit, a piece of monstrous extravagance, and that it was an insult to the public to offer it as a work of art—especially if Mr. Whistler asked two hundred guineas for it. He has the same opinion of the *Nocturne in Blue and Silver,* the tubular bridge from the Menai Straits placed over the Thames. He called the picture a fantastic thing.[15] It is strong language, no doubt, to call an artist a "stick," but some artists are sticks, have been called so, and will be called so again.[16] It is not said that there is any harm in that language; it is hoped that it will do good to those to whom it is applied. It is, moreover, language that is applied to a great variety of persons in other walks of life. If a man thinks a picture is a daub,[17] he has a right to say so without subjecting himself to the risk of an action [for libel].

The defendant has a strong wish for the progress of art. How can art be made to flourish more successfully than by fair and bona fide criticism?—in which alone, I submit, the defendant has indulged on the present occasion. Mr. Ruskin went on to say [in *Fors Clavigera*] that for Mr. Whistler's own sake, these pictures should not have been admitted into the Grosvenor Gallery, and spoke of the ill-educated conceit of the artist so nearly approaching the aspect of imposture. If the pictures are mere extravagances, how can it redound to the credit of Mr. Whistler—who has done very good work—to exhibit these fantastic things as works of art? He was careless of his name and fame when he offered such things for sale. Some artistic gentleman from Manchester, Leeds, or Sheffield might perhaps be induced to buy one of the pictures because it was "a Whistler." What Mr. Ruskin meant was that the gentleman might better have remained in Manchester, Leeds, or Sheffield, with his money in his pocket.

My learned friend [Serjeant Parry] asked what right Mr. Ruskin had to speak of Mr. Whistler's ill-educated conceit when the plaintiff has devoted the whole of his life to educating himself in art. Mr. Whistler has educated himself, no doubt; but Mr. Ruskin's views as to his success do not accord with Mr. Whistler's. In Mr. Ruskin's view, Mr. Whistler has not educated himself in his art as an artist should.[18] I ask why it should be wrong to call another member of a profession ill-educated in reference to his work? Many times in my profession has a learned counsel been called ill-educated, yet never have I heard of an action for libel being brought in consequence. If that is Mr. Ruskin's opinion, judging from these productions, is it libelous to say so?

Then the article went on to say: "I have seen, and heard, much of Cockney impudence before now; but never expected to hear a coxcomb ask two hundred guineas for flinging a pot of paint in the public's face." I would remind you that Mr. Ruskin did not call Mr. Whistler a coxcomb as a man; he applied that epithet to him as an artist.

What, however, is the real meaning of "coxcomb"? While this case has been going on, I looked into the dictionary and found that the word comes from the old idea of the licensed jester who wore a cap with bells and a cock's comb on his head and went about making jests for the amusement of his master and family. If that is the true definition, then Mr. Whistler should not complain. Has he not performed such a part with his pictures? I do not know when so much amusement has been afforded to the British public as by Mr. Whistler's pictures.[19]

I say without fear of contradiction that if Mr. Whistler founds his reputation upon the pictures he has shown at the Grosvenor Gallery—the *Nocturne in Black and Gold,* the *Nocturne in Blue and Silver,* his "arrangement" of Mr. Irving in black, his representation of the ladies in brown, and his "symphonies" in gray and yellow[20]—he is a mere pretender to the art of painting, an accomplishment he does not possess, and is worthy of the name of coxcomb.[21]

I have now finished.

Mr. Ruskin has lived a long life without being attacked. No one has been able to say that he purchased Mr. Ruskin's praise, and no one has attempted to control Mr. Ruskin's pen through the medium of a jury.[22] The defendant requested me to say that he does not retract one syllable of what he said in the criticism: he believes he is right. For nearly all his life he has devoted himself to criticism for the sake of the art he loves. I ask the jury not to paralyze his hand now. If you give a verdict against Mr. Ruskin, he must cease to write. It would be an evil day for the art of this country if he were prevented from indulging in proper and legitimate criticism, and from pointing out what is beautiful and what is not, and if all critics were reduced to a dead level of forced and fulsome adulation.

The following evidence was then adduced for the defense.[23]

Direct Examination of Edward Coley Burne-Jones by Mr. Bowen

BURNE-JONES: . . . I am a painter and have been so for twenty years.

I have painted some works that have become known to the public within the last two or three years.[24] Among them are *The Days of Creation* [see fig. 5] and *Venus's Mirror,* both of which were exhibited at the Grosvenor Gallery in 1877. I also exhibited *Temperantia, Fides, Spes,* and two others, unfinished: *A Sibyl* and *Saint George.* I have exhibited several other pictures there since. I have one work, *Merlin and Vivien,* now being exhibited in Paris.[25]

BOWEN: In your opinion, what part do finish and completeness bear to the merit of a painting?

BURNE-JONES: I think complete finish ought to be the object of all artists, that they should not be content with anything that falls short of what for ages has been acknowledged as essential to perfect work.[26]

BOWEN: Have you had the opportunity of seeing the pictures by Mr. Whistler that have been produced in this court?

BURNE-JONES: I saw them yesterday.

Witness shown Nocturne in Blue and Silver [plate 4].

BOWEN: Take the *Nocturne in Blue and Silver,* Mrs. Leyland's picture, and tell us: What is your deliberate judgment of that picture as a work of art?

BURNE-JONES: I think it is a work of art, but very incomplete. It is an admirable beginning—a sketch, in short.

BOWEN: Does it in your opinion show the finish of a complete work of art?

BURNE-JONES: Not in any sense whatever.

BOWEN: What is there in the picture that leads you to that conclusion?

BURNE-JONES: I think the picture has many good qualities. It is masterly in some respects, especially in color. It is a beautiful sketch; but that is not alone sufficient to make it a good work of art. It is deficient in form, and form is as essential as color.

BOWEN: You have spoken of the color. Are composition and detail also of great importance in a picture?

BURNE-JONES: Yes.

BOWEN: What is your opinion as to the composition of this picture?

BURNE-JONES: I think it has no composition whatever—but it has distinct and high merit so far as color goes.

Witness shown Nocturne in Blue and Silver [plate 3].

BOWEN: Take the next picture—"Battersea Bridge," another *Nocturne in Blue and Silver*. What do you say to that?

BURNE-JONES: It is similar to the last, only I think the color is still better. It is really very beautiful in color, but more formless than the other. It is bewildering in its form.

BOWEN: And as to composition and detail?

BURNE-JONES: It has none whatever.

BOWEN: Mr. Whistler has told us that the picture was painted in a day or a day and a half.

BURNE-JONES: That seems a reasonable time for it.

BOWEN: Does this picture show any finish as a work of art?

BURNE-JONES: No. I should say the same of it as I did of the other [*Nocturne in Blue and Silver*]: It shows no finish. I should call it a sketch.[27] I do not think Mr. Whistler ever intended it to be regarded as a finished work.

BOWEN: Take, lastly, the *Nocturne in Black and Gold* [plate 1], representing fireworks at Cremorne. What is your judgment upon it?

BURNE-JONES: I don't think it has the merit of the other two at all.

BOWEN: Is it, in your opinion, a work of art?

BURNE-JONES: No, I cannot say that it is. It would be impossible to call it a serious work of art.[28]

BOWEN: Will you give your reasons?

BURNE-JONES: First, the subject itself. It is difficult to paint night: I have never seen one picture of night that was successful. This is only one of a thousand failures that artists have made in their efforts at painting night. The other two nocturnes look like night—they have a beautiful tone like night, especially the one of the bridge. I don't think [*Nocturne in Black and Gold*] is like night at all.[29]

BOWEN: Is the picture, in your judgment, worth two hundred guineas?

BURNE-JONES: No, I cannot say it is, seeing how much careful work men do for so much less.[30]

Mr. Bowen proposed to produce a portrait by Titian to show the jury what a finished work of art was like. Serjeant Parry objected.

HUDDLESTON: I think this is going a little too far. Counsel will first have to prove that the picture is one of Titian's.

BOWEN: My lord, I shall do that. *(Laughter)*

HUDDLESTON: That can only be done by repute. I do not want to raise a laugh, but there is a well-known case of an undoubted Titian that was purchased for the purpose of determining the secret of the master's wonderful coloring. On being rubbed down, a red surface was found, and the explorers said, "Oh! here's the secret!" But on going a little further in the process, it was discovered that the red substratum was a portrait of George III in a militia uniform.[31] *(Laughter)*

PARRY: My objection to the production of a work of Titian's is this: Mr. Whistler has never placed himself in the same position as that great artist and therefore it is unfair to institute any comparison between them. However, I will not press the objection.

The picture, a portrait of a doge of Venice [plate 9], *was then produced. The witness was asked to look at the picture.*

BURNE-JONES: . . . This is a beautiful example of Titian's work. It is a portrait of one of the doges, Andrea Gritti. I believe it is a real Titian. . . . I have seen the picture before. . . . It is a most perfect specimen of a highly finished work of ancient art. The flesh is perfect, the modeling of the face round and good; the color is in perfect tone, and the drawing sufficiently fine. This is an arrangement in flesh and blood.

BOWEN: Do you see in the three pictures by Mr. Whistler that you have spoken of any mark of labor?

BURNE-JONES: Yes, in Mr. Whistler's pictures I see marks of great labor and artistic skill.[32] Mr. Whistler gave infinite promise at first, but I do not think he has fulfilled it.[33] I think he has evaded the great difficulty of painting by not carrying his pictures far enough. The difficulties in painting increase daily as the work progresses;[34] that is the reason so many of us fail. We are none of us perfect. The danger to art by the plaintiff's want of finish is that men who come afterward will perform mere mechanical work, without the excellencies of color and unrivaled power of representing atmosphere which are displayed by the plaintiff, and so the art of the country will sink down to mere mechanical whitewashing.

Cross-examination of Burne-Jones by Serjeant Parry

A JUROR: What is the value of the picture by Titian?

BURNE-JONES: That is a mere accident of the sale room.

PARRY: Is it worth one thousand guineas?

BURNE-JONES: It would be worth many thousands to me, but it might be sold for forty.

PARRY: Do you mean to say that the picture could be bought now for forty guineas?

BURNE-JONES: Yes, it might. I do not know how much was given for it, but Lord Elcho has a beautiful Titian that he purchased for twenty guineas.[35]

PARRY: He was very lucky.

BURNE-JONES: . . . The picture produced I believe belongs to Mr. Ruskin.[36]

PARRY: You have said Mr. Whistler has an unrivaled sense of atmosphere.

BURNE-JONES: Yes, I certainly think so. I have already spoken of the merit and color of Mr. Whistler's pictures, and of their almost unrivaled appreciation of atmosphere; but that is all that can be said of them.

PARRY: How long have you known Mr. Whistler?

BURNE-JONES: For thirteen or fourteen years.[37]

PARRY: You have exhibited unfinished pictures yourself?

BURNE-JONES: Yes, I exhibited two unfinished sketches at the Grosvenor Gallery, *A Knight* and *A Sibyl.*[38]

PARRY: Is it a wicked thing to exhibit unfinished pictures?

BURNE-JONES: I do not think it is very desirable. . . . Mr. Whistler's color is beautiful, in his moonlight pieces especially. . . . I have known Mr. Albert Moore for many years; I thought many things he said yesterday were correct. . . . The pictures alluded to in this case I look upon as incomplete.

PARRY: You would not, however, look upon a man who exhibited such pictures as a willful impostor?

BOWEN: I object to that question.

PARRY: I will not press it.

Direct Examination of William Powell Frith by Mr. Bowen

FRITH: . . . I am a Royal Academician and have devoted my life to painting. I am a member of the academies of various countries[39] and am the author of *The Railway Station* [fig. 48], *Derby Day* [fig. 49], *The Road to Ruin,*[40] and other works.

BOWEN: You have seen the pictures of Mr. Whistler's that were presented yesterday?

FRITH: Yes.

BOWEN: What is your opinion as to the merit of those pictures; are they works of art?

FRITH: I should say not.

Nocturne in Black and Gold [plate 1] *is handed to the witness.*

BOWEN: Take the *Nocturne in Black and Gold,* representing the fireworks at Cremorne. Is this a serious work of art?

FRITH: Not to me.[41]

BOWEN: Take the two others.

Mr. Graham's Nocturne in Blue and Silver [plate 3] *handed to the witness.*

FRITH: There is a beautiful tone of color in the picture of Old Battersea Bridge, but the color does not represent any more than you could get from a bit of wallpaper or silk.[42] I cannot see anything of the true representation of water and atmosphere in it; there is a pretty color that pleases the eye, but nothing more. I should say exactly the same in regard to the other picture [plate 4]. I have heard it described as a good representation of moonlight, but it does not convey that impression to me in the slightest degree. To my thinking, the description of moonlight is not true. . . . The *Nocturne in Black and Gold* is not, in my opinion, worth two hundred guineas. I would not give two hundred guineas for one of the plaintiff's pictures; they are not serious works of art. . . . I have seen pictures without extreme finish that were extremely fine. . . . I do not trace any resemblance between Velázquez and Whistler.

BOWEN: Are composition and detail important elements in the merit of a picture?

FRITH: Very. Without them a picture cannot be called a work of art.

BOWEN: You attend here very much against your own will?

FRITH: Yes. I only attend upon subpoena. It is a very painful thing to be called on to give evidence against a brother artist. On Monday morning I received my subpoena. I had previously been asked to give evidence, but declined to come before.

Cross-examination of Frith by Serjeant Parry

FRITH: . . . I have seen the pictures previously, at the Grosvenor Gallery. . . . I agree with the last witness, Mr. Burne-Jones, that Mr. Whistler has very great powers as an artist, but I do not see those powers displayed in these "things."

PARRY: Do you agree that Mr. Whistler has unrivaled atmospheric power?

FRITH: No, I do not see that he has exceptional power in painting the atmosphere.

PARRY: I suppose in your profession men may honestly differ as to the merits of a picture?

FRITH: Yes, that constantly happens. Artistic opinions differ. One may blame while another praises a work. . . . I have not exhibited at the Grosvenor Gallery.[43]

PARRY: Have you read Mr. Ruskin's works?

FRITH: Yes.[44]

PARRY: We know that Turner is an idol of Mr. Ruskin.

FRITH: I believe Mr. Ruskin has a great estimate of Turner's works. I think Turner should be an idol of all painters.

PARRY: Do you know one of Turner's works at Marlborough House called *Snow Storm* [fig. 66]?

FRITH: Yes, I do. I don't know how long ago it was painted—about twenty years ago.

PARRY: Are you aware that it has been described by a critic as "a mass of soapsuds and whitewash"?[45] *(Laughter)*

FRITH: I am not.

PARRY: Would you call it a mass of soapsuds and whitewash?

FRITH: I think it very likely I should. *(Laughter)* When I say that Turner should be the idol of painters, I refer to his earlier works and not to the period when he was half crazy and produced works about as insane as the people who admire them.[46] *(Laughter)*

HUDDLESTON: Somebody described one of Turner's pictures as lobster salad. *(Laughter)*

FRITH: I have heard Turner himself speak of some of his productions as nothing better than salad and mustard.[47] *(Laughter)*

PARRY: Without the lobster.

Redirect examination of Frith by Mr. Bowen

FRITH: . . . The *Snow Storm* was not one of Turner's fine pictures.[48]

Direct Examination of Tom Taylor by Mr. Bowen

TAYLOR: . . . I am an art critic of long standing. I have acted in that capacity for *The Times* and other periodicals for more than twenty years.[49] I edited *The Life of Reynolds* and *Haydon*.[50] I have always studied art. . . . I saw the three pictures of Mr. Whistler's at the Grosvenor Gallery. I also saw them on a previous occasion when exhibited at the Dudley Gallery. . . . I think the names "nocturnes" and "harmonies" are admissible as applied to pictures; the names seem to me to indicate a connection between painting and music.[51] . . . I should not consider the *Nocturne in Black and Gold* a good picture; I do not think it a serious work of art.[52] . . . I have already expressed my opinion in the criticism I wrote for *The Times,* which I well considered and adhere to now.

The witness here read his criticism of the pictures.

> Close to the picture Mr. [J. D.] Watson christens, in commonplace fashion, "Moonlight," hang . . . two of Mr. Whistler's "colour symphonies"—a "Nocturne in blue and gold [plate 5]," and a "Nocturne in black and gold." If he did not exhibit these as pictures under peculiar and, what seem to most people, pretentious titles, they would be entitled to their due meed of admiration. But they only come one step nearer pictures than delicately graduated tints on a wall paper would do. Taken for what they are, and setting aside the evidence supplied by peculiar titles and unusual frames that the painter appraises them beyond their value, as pictures instead of mere tone studies, what Mr. Whistler calls his nocturnes and symphonies have a real beauty and suggestiveness of their own. Only he must not attempt, with that happy half-humorous audacity which all his dealing with his own work suggests, to palm off his deficiencies upon us as manifestations of power, and try to make us believe that this sort of thing is the one best worth doing, because it is the only thing he can do, or, at all events, cares for doing, in colour.[53]

Cross-examination of Taylor by Serjeant Parry

TAYLOR: . . . I saw the portrait of Carlyle and did not mention it in combination with the others. I said, "Mr. Whistler's full-length arrangements suggest to us a choice between materialized spirits and figures in a London fog." *(Laughter)* "The most substantial is the 'arrangement' in black and gray, which, off the canvas, is known as Thomas Carlyle."[54] I meant it as a compliment to say the *Carlyle* was substantial—against the insubstantial ones. . . . I thought the portrait of Mr. Whistler's mother was very feeling and a very admirable work within its limits. I am of the same opinion still. . . . All Mr. Whistler's work is unfinished. It is sketchy.

PARRY: Do you think Mr. Whistler possesses high artistic merit?

TAYLOR: Yes, he no doubt possesses high artistic qualities and the power of producing very delicate tones of color, but he is not complete. I would describe the plaintiff's works as being unfinished beginnings of pictures. All his works are in the nature of sketching.[55] Within those limits, I call it good work.

Redirect Examination of Taylor by Mr. Bowen

BOWEN: Do you still retain your opinion that these pictures only come one step nearer pictures than a delicately tinted wallpaper?

TAYLOR: Yes. I think if you bring art down to delicacy of tone, it is only like the tone of wallpaper.[56] I meant that on the canvas, [night] is a shadowy subject.

SUMMATIONS

Summation of Defendant's Case by Mr. Bowen

BOWEN: That is the whole of the defendant's evidence. I would have called Mr. Ruskin, but he is still unable to attend owing to illness.

We have been traveling over wide ground. I would like to recall you to the simple and short issue in this case. The issue is not what are the merits of Mr. Whistler's pictures, nor whether you think the *Nocturne in Black and Gold* worth two hundred guineas, nor whether the nocturnes in blue and silver are serious works of art or fantastic extravagances. The question is whether the comments of Mr. Ruskin are the fair and honest expressions of a critic. It was thought desirable for the jury to know that there are artists of distinction who agree with Mr. Ruskin in his estimation of Mr. Whistler's works. I have called before you artists of different schools of art, Mr. Burne-Jones and Mr. Frith, and one of the most famous critics of the present day [Tom Taylor], with a view to showing that persons who have a serious knowledge of art disapprove of the pictures, in order that you might see how an art critic might honestly have been led to express such an opinion as that given by Mr. Ruskin. It is sufficient for the defense that you should come to the conclusion that Mr. Ruskin's comments, strong as they may be and indignant as they may be, are the fair and honest expressions of the opinion of the critic.

Mr. Serjeant Parry has described Mr. Ruskin as one of the greatest writers on the subject of art in this country or America; he has done more than anybody else to reveal the beauties of the past and to add a new beauty to the English language. Mr. Whistler is a gentleman who has devoted some portion of his life to art. He has exhibited these pictures for criticism, and he ought not to complain when his performances are criticized.

The line the law draws with regard to libel is clear and sharp. The critic must not descend into a man's private life; he must not rake up dirt to cast at his name; he must not, if he criticizes a man's public performance, indulge in personal malice. But beyond that—whether the matter be literature, art, or politics—the critic is not bound to speak with bated breath. He may say what he likes and what he chooses, provided he does so honestly, without traveling out of the subject matter before him, and provided what he says is a fair and honest expression of opinion.

Of that nature, I maintain, Mr. Ruskin's criticism is. In this instance, there is not a suggestion that Mr. Ruskin has done what he ought not to have done in the interests of the public or of art. There is not a scintilla of evidence that Mr. Ruskin was actuated by any malignant motive. It has not been shown that he knew Mr. Whistler personally or that he did more than he conceived to be his duty to the public, or the art he loves, in his capacity as a public critic. All he did was express an opinion upon Mr. Whistler's pictures—an opinion to which, be he right or be he wrong, he adheres.

Ministers and statesmen are called charlatans, but they do not bring actions for libel. All persons who devote themselves to literature and art must be prepared to meet the keenest words of criticism. It is in the interests of artists themselves and for the general public that comments on art be free, provided they are honest. I hope it will be long before an English jury, whatever might be its sympathy for an individual, consents to forge one single link of a chain to fetter free criticism and thus do irreparable injury to the noble future of art in this country.

Summation of the Plaintiff's Case by Serjeant Parry

PARRY: I consider the tone of many of the attorney general's remarks exaggerated and out of place, and important only as showing the animus of the defendant toward Mr. Whistler. When the honorable and learned gentleman sneeringly conjured up an imaginary group of young ladies admiring Mr. Whistler's paintings, he must have forgotten that there are women's names in art that are entitled to the greatest consideration and respect. The course the attorney general has taken this morning has made the case even more serious than it first appeared to be. He has given the libel an additional sting.[1]

Mr. Ruskin's defense in this case comes practically to this: "I shall say what I please and nobody must interfere with me in uttering an opinion upon art." Mr. Ruskin, we have been told, will not withdraw a single word he has said, so it appears he desires to place himself on a throne from which he will threaten to do as he likes and say what he likes, whether it injures a man or not. It is to be hoped, however, that the jury in this case will tell Mr. Ruskin that he must not do anything of the kind. Whatever might be the demerits of Mr. Whistler, Mr. Ruskin has no right to use such language as has been the subject of this case. If this is the mode in which Mr. Ruskin is to carry on his criticism, he must be told that he cannot be allowed to continue: he must be kept within bounds. I am astonished that a gentleman in the defendant's position should have condescended to use the language he has done and that my learned friends, when they saw the libel, did not express some regret at its terms. They have not dared to ask whether, in painting these pictures, Mr. Whistler deserved to be stigmatized as a willful impostor. It is a matter of remark that no one has been brought forward who agrees for one moment with the statement that the exhibition of these pictures on Mr. Whistler's part is akin to willful imposture.

I know Mr. Ruskin is ill and cannot attend the court, but he might have been examined before a commission and asked if he knew Mr. Whistler's works generally and how long he had been in examining the pictures in question. Whatever the genius of Mr. Ruskin might be, there is no reason that he should exercise his great powers of criticism and bring down all the influence he has gained in order to crush, and ruin, a comparatively struggling man.[2]

In consequence of the course taken by the attorney general, I contend that the conduct of Mr. Ruskin has been greatly aggravated, while the evidence for the defense has not borne out the opinion expressed in the libel in any way. Witnesses have been called in support of the defendant's case, but though their opinions have been asked, it is important to recollect that the words of the libel have never been put into their hands and their opinion asked upon them; I would not hesitate to say that they would have expressed their decided disapproval.[3] The witnesses for the defendant proved no justification for the use of Mr. Ruskin's language. They spoke of Mr. Whistler as a gentleman possessing very high qualities as an artist, and the [chief] witness for the defense [Burne-Jones] did not speak of Mr. Whistler in the tone of disparagement that might have been expected of him.

As to the peculiarities in the titles selected by Mr. Whistler, it has been suggested that he was making an attempt to show an analogy between music and painting. There is some analogy, for music is the poetry of the ear, while painting is the poetry of the eye; and if Mr. Whistler has made that discovery, he is not to be condemned.[4] Taking the whole mass of the evidence, I think it would be impossible to say that Mr. Ruskin's was a fair criticism.

I will not say that Mr. Whistler's whole career is involved in the verdict of the jury, but this is for him a most serious business. Mr. Whistler has not been able to sell some of his pictures at the price he formerly did.[5] Mr. Ruskin's decree that Mr. Whistler's pictures are worthless went forth, but he has not supported it with evidence, as he might have done without leaving his own threshold. He has not condescended to give any reasons why he formed such opinions. No, he has treated us with all the contempt with which he treated Mr. Whistler and has declined to give any explanation of the grounds upon which he condemned Mr. Whistler's works. He said: "I, Mr. Ruskin, seated on my throne of art, say what I please upon it and expect all the world to agree with me." Mr. Ruskin cared not whether his decree injuriously affected others and loftily declined to discuss his judgment or to justify himself before a jury.

It is important, therefore, for you at all events to consider the character of the great writer who passed his opinion upon things around him in such a manner as appeared in *Fors Clavigera.* Mr. Ruskin is great as a writer, but not as a man. As a man, he has degraded himself. Mr. Ruskin has been represented as a very benevolent man who is wrapped up in art—in nothing else. But the fact is, the defendant deals with personalities. He likes them and mingles them with his writing. The tone of Mr. Ruskin's mind, as I shall show from passages in *Fors Clavigera,* is personal and malicious.[6]

Mr. Ruskin quoted the sentence, "A man who would give his labor for nothing would be a social monster." While he said the saying was worth preserving, he described its author as an utterly worthless and insignificant person.[7] In a small pamphlet of twenty-five pages, he twice described Professor Goldwin Smith, one of the most eminent men of the day, as a goose.[8] *(Laughter)* That proves how much Mr. Ruskin likes to deal in personalities and call people names. Speaking of Sir Henry Cole, Mr. Ruskin said, "The Professorship of Sir Henry Cole at Kensington has corrupted the system of art-teaching all over England into a state of abortion and falsehood from which it will take twenty years to recover."[9] That is pleasant talk about Sir Henry Cole. *(Laughter)* Mr. Ruskin also attacked Messrs. Agnew, the picture dealers of Manchester.[10] All his comments show that he is a man who exceeds the fair limits of criticism and allows personal feeling to carry him too far.

Mr. Ruskin's criticism upon Mr. Whistler's pictures is almost exclusively in the nature of a personal attack. While all fair criticism on art is allowable, a pretended criticism of art, which is really a criticism upon the man himself, which is calculated to injure the artist and is written recklessly and for the purpose of holding him up to ridicule and contempt, is not allowable.[11] Mr. Ruskin went out of his way to attack Mr. Whistler personally and must answer for the consequences of having written a defamatory attack. It has been said that Mr. Ruskin's motives were good, but a man must not be allowed to assail the character of another and do him wrong, even from good motives.

The words "wilful imposture" ought never to have been used. Is there any difference between telling a man that he nearly approaches willful imposture and that he is a willful impostor? If the jury finds in favor of Mr. Ruskin's criticism, it will go forth that Mr. Whistler, as a painter, is a willful impostor. Surely after the evidence of Mr. Burne-Jones, Mr. Frith, and Mr. Taylor, the jury cannot say that it thinks Mr. Whistler an impostor.

It was said that Mr. Ruskin had a right to call the plaintiff a cockney, though Mr. Whistler was not born within the sound of Bow Bells; but "cockney" means something dirty and disagreeable.[12] *(Laughter)* I hope the jury will tell Mr. Ruskin he cannot use such language with impunity. This is what is called pungent criticism, stinging criticism; but it is not criticism—it is defamation. This is the language of a libelous mind, utterly indifferent to others' feelings but gratifying its own vanity. Mr. Ruskin might delight in the reflection that he is a smart, a pungent, and a telling, writer; but he must not be allowed to trade in libel.

The attorney general has described one and the same object in the picture of Battersea Bridge [*Nocturne in Blue and Silver,* plate 3] as being like, first, Muhammad's coffin; then, Jacob's ladder; then, the Menai Straits tubular bridge; and lastly, a telescope. The jury can estimate the value of such criticism as that. *(Laughter)*

The works of Mr. Whistler are open to fair and honest criticism. He has not shrunk from any public investigation; but his detractor has.

In conclusion, I would remind you that whatever might be the plaintiff's views or the style of his art, there can be no doubt that

Mr. Whistler is a genuine artist. I do not suppose he estimates himself a man of genius; but he is a conscientious, hard-working, and industrious artist who has followed his profession for years and years—perhaps not so successfully as others, occupying an independent and somewhat isolated position, holding original or even eccentric views—but depending upon his profession entirely for his livelihood and position. Is he to be expelled from the realm of art by the man who sits there as a despot? I hope the jury will say by its verdict that Mr. Ruskin has no right to drive Mr. Whistler out by defamatory and libelous accusations.

The court then adjourned for lunch, and reassembled at quarter to two.[13]

JURY INSTRUCTIONS

HUDDLESTON: It is now the jury's duty to endeavor to settle the question of difference between the two gentlemen. You must do so upon certain well-known principles of law, which it will be my duty to describe to you.[1]

The claim is that the defendant, Mr. Ruskin, has libeled the plaintiff, Mr. Whistler. Now if any man commits to paper language disparaging to another and holding him up to hatred, contumely, and contempt, he is guilty of libel. Ordinarily speaking, a libel, to make it actionable, must be proved to be malicious; but the law infers malice if the statement made is libelous and untrue. The presumption of malice might be rebutted, however, if the criticism is a bona fide one. In this case, it has been proved that Mr. Ruskin wrote certain remarks about Mr. Whistler in a pamphlet that was published, and I should think no one would entertain a doubt that those words hold the plaintiff up to contempt and ridicule. That being so, the defendant must be said to have libeled the plaintiff.

But the defendant has pleaded that the passage amounted only to fair and bona fide criticism. That is the question you have to try. Once a libel is proved, the onus of proof shifts from the plaintiff to the defendant, [who must] show that the criticism is fair and bona fide. Formerly it was for the judge to say whether the words amounted to a libel or not. I cannot help thinking that the legislature of the country interfered in a most wholesome way when it transferred the duty from judge to jury. In this case, the defendant said in his plea that his criticism was fair and bona fide. You will have to say whether you consider that has been proved.[2]

In the course of this case a good deal has been said about what criticism is. I daresay the jury knows that for many years there has been a continual warfare going on among authors, artists, and critics. Authors and artists say of critics that they are failures in literature and art,[3] and that criticism is a study by which men grow formidable at little expense to themselves. On the other hand, the critics say they would not have those words applied to them if the authors and artists did not wince under the strictures that critics feel it their duty to make. You might, however, leave authors, artists, and critics to continue to quarrel among themselves while you consider the duty of the critic—though let me say this: It is of the very last importance that the critic, having mind enough to form his judgment, should have strength to express it. While the critic is to be allowed to use unsparing censure if he honestly thinks he ought to do so, he must be very careful to confine himself to criticism and not make his remarks a veil for personal censure, nor allow himself to run into reckless and unfair attacks upon the character of the author or artist merely from love of exercising his power of denunciation.

It has always been said by learned judges that it is of the utmost importance that a large and wide power should be given to a critic to express the views he honestly formed, and for that purpose there is no reason that he should not use even ridicule as a fair weapon. Authorities are not wanting to that effect, and although I take it upon myself to tell the gentlemen of the jury so, I cannot do better than refer them to greater authorities than myself. Lord Ellenborough said in one of his judgments that ridicule was often the fittest weapon for criticism: he said that a critic really must not be cramped in his observations upon authors, because authors' works should be liable to criticism and exposure; reflections of a personal character were, however, a different thing, and any attack upon character, unconnected with authorship, ought to be punished.[4] The critic, Lord Ellenborough said, did great service to the public, particularly one who wrote down a vapid or useless book or work; the critic checked the dissemination of abuses, as he prevented people from wasting their time and money upon trash. Other judges have held similar views. The lord chief justice [Ellenborough] and Lord Tenterden to a certain extent agreed with the view that the critic should be allowed large powers. It is to the advantage of all that this be so.[5] When artists send their pictures to an exhibition or authors publish a book, they covet and enjoy the praise that is given them. On the other hand, they must submit to the adverse criticism passed upon them, provided those strictures are honest and bona fide.

While those large powers are given to the critic, it is for the jury to say whether in this case they have been fairly and honestly used, or whether the critic's remarks were warped by a personal feeling of malignity and a desire to reflect beyond the mere work of the artist. If a critic honestly expresses an opinion, though he does so in strong language, he ought to be protected; but if his object is to use his powers of denunciation without regard to facts and feelings, and to reflect unjustly upon the individual whose picture he is criticizing, then his conduct is unjustified and he cannot claim the critic's privilege. The question in this case is whether Mr. Ruskin's criticism of Mr. Whistler's pictures is fair and bona fide. I agree that in discussing the works of a man, we have no right to go into his personal character or private life, and that we ought not to make use of personal malignity or to heap dirt upon anyone. If, however, a critic honestly feels he is dealing with a charlatan and an impostor and desires to expose him, he has a right to make use of strong expressions about that artist's works, though not about his personal character. If, therefore, you think Mr. Ruskin's language is honest and bona fide, even though it might be strong, you must find a verdict for the defendant. If, on the other hand, you think he used words that were not fair, honest, and bona fide, then the plaintiff is entitled to the verdict.

It is admitted on all hands that Mr. Ruskin is a distinguished critic and experienced in that capacity. Mr. Whistler, also, is entitled to the benefit of all his counsel has said respecting his being a man of genius. Mr. Ruskin does not appear to be a man who measures too carefully the language he uses when he feels that the subject he is dealing with deserves strong treatment; he does not speak, as has been said, with bated breath. It has been said that Mr. Ruskin has not condescended to place his views before the jury and certainly, while he could not attend personally, owing to ill health, there is no reason he should not have put his views in connection with this case on paper.[6] Yet he has stated his views through the medium of the witnesses he has called, who have not an unqualified admiration of the plaintiff.

Mr. Whistler, on the other hand, has his admirers, who have spoken of him as a man of genius. Mr. Whistler has his own views of art, which he endeavors to follow out. The witnesses of experience in art who were called on the plaintiff's behalf said that there was great beauty and a masterly style in Mr. Whistler's works; but then again, witnesses in support of the defendant expressed the opinion that Mr. Whistler's works were greatly wanting in finish and that although they evinced some skill, the pictures were not entitled to the epithet of "perfect" works of art.

The question then arose whether in the face of such evidence Mr. Ruskin's criticism of Mr. Whistler was fair and in good faith. You must judge for yourselves, as best you can, the value of the plaintiff's pictures according to his own intention and the result attained, and then ask yourselves whether those ideas justify the language used by Mr. Ruskin.[7]

The idea of producing a picture by Titian to contrast with the works of Mr. Whistler is scarcely fair. Nobody has ever equaled, and probably never will equal, Titian.

Mr. Whistler did not say he was painting Cremorne Gardens or Battersea Bridge. What he said was that he had an effect in his mind that he was attempting to produce on canvas.

The learned counsel for the plaintiff said that criticism may be pungent and stinging without being libelous. A writer no doubt might use pungent words when dealing with works of art, but he must not make his criticism the means either of not honestly dealing with the work he was discussing or of merely exhibiting his own powers. It is for you [the jury] to say whether the defendant has satisfied [you] that his language is in the nature of fair and bona fide criticism. On that, it is no part of my business to offer any opinion: the responsibility rests entirely with you yourselves. Give full latitude to the critic, but confine his labors within the four corners of the chamber of fair and bona fide criticism; you might remember it has been said that the fangs of the bear are not so strong as the stings of the goose quill.

Now the pamphlet in which this libel appeared [*Fors Clavigera*] is addressed to the working men of Sheffield. In it Mr. Ruskin deals with a variety of subjects. He starts with a reference to another pamphlet that had been given him in Venice and speaks in strong terms of the author of that publication. Mr. Ruskin then proceeds to use forcible language regarding Professor Goldwin Smith, whom he describes as a goose, and speaks of the School of [Art at] South Kensington as corrupting the "system of art-teaching . . . into a state of abortion and falsehood." The defendant proceeds to refer to Sir Coutts Lindsay in terms that are strong in kind: He says Sir Coutts is an amateur in art and shopkeeping and must give up one if he wishes to succeed in either. No doubt great as well as lesser painters are strongly dealt with, Mr. Ruskin severely criticizing Millais and being unsparing in his language regarding Tissot.[8] At the conclusion of the pamphlet, the defendant says he has no words bitter enough, or time sufficient enough, to deal with such matters any further.[9]

From this it is plain that Mr. Ruskin is a man who uses strong language. The question is whether he is justified in using it. A critic is entitled to apply strong language to a picture or a book if he does not go beyond the picture or book, but language that sinks to the level of personal matters should not be tolerated.[10] Mr. Ruskin is evidently a man accustomed to calling a spade a spade, and, indeed, he sometimes calls a spade something more. The question is whether he expressed honest convictions. His language might not be that which you yourselves would make use of; but if Mr. Ruskin honestly believed what he wrote, I would be very much inclined to give him full license.

The words of the libel complained of are [as follows]: "For Mr. Whistler's own sake, no less than for the protection of the purchaser, Sir Coutts Lindsay ought not to have admitted works into the gallery in which the ill-educated conceit of the artist so nearly approached the aspect of wilful imposture." The attorney general said that those words were not intended to apply to the previous education of Mr. Whistler: he asked us to treat the term "ill-educated" as meaning that the plaintiff had failed to grasp the features of art—composition and finish—and had been wrapped up in his conceit of color, that Mr. Whistler had a notion of his own, which was not an educated notion. Mr. Serjeant Parry, on the other hand, held that the words were directed against the man, rather than his works.

Mr. Ruskin went on to say: "I have seen, and heard, much of Cockney impudence before now; but never expected to hear a coxcomb ask two hundred guineas for flinging a pot of paint in the public's face." Mr. Serjeant Parry said that "cockney" means something dirty and disagreeable. *(Laughter)* Now I protest against that assumption, because there are plenty of cockneys who would not condescend to do an ungenerous or ungentlemanly act. I have looked into Johnson's dictionary to see what definition is given there, and I find a cockney described, in effect, as "a person born in London, a southerner as opposed to a northerner, a townsman as against a countryman, one ignorant of things known familiarly in the country." *(Laughter)* "Cockney," therefore, appears to mean a man who does not know much beyond his own sphere. Whether it was in Mr. Ruskin's mind that there is some connection between the words "cockney" and "coxcomb" I know not, but on turning to Johnson, I find that the attorney general has not given the whole definition of the word "cockney." Following the definition he gave, I found the words: "As the cockney did to the eels when she put them in the pastry alive, and rapped the coxcombs with the stick and said, 'Down, worms, down.'"[11]

As regards the use of the word "coxcomb": If the gentlemen of the jury think it is a mere figure of speech applied to the painter for his works, disassociated from his personal character, then I do not think much need be said about its use; you might say the word occurs in what is a fair criticism. On the other hand, if you think the language of the article is language that [applies] to Mr. Whistler as a man and was flung at him with the object of hitting his personal character rather than his work, then it would not be bona fide criticism.

The judge handed down to the jury the pamphlet, marked with various passages that had been alluded to in the course of the case.

Nothing has been said by the learned counsel on the subject of damages, but if you think this criticism is not fair and bona fide, then the plaintiff will be entitled to your verdict and you will have to consider that question. There are three views you might take on the question of damages. You must consider whether the insult offered, if insult there has been, is of such a gross character as to call for substantial damages; whether it is a case for merely contemptuous damages, to the extent of a farthing or something of that sort, indicating that the case is one which ought never to have been brought into court and in which no pecuniary damage has been sustained; or whether the case is one which calls for damages in some small sum, indicating your opinion that the defendant has gone beyond the strict letter of the law.

You will have to fairly take into consideration the degree of difference between the criticism to which the plaintiff was entitled and that which the defendant applied. You must say whether the defendant's criticism is honest, fair, and bona fide, remembering at the same time the great responsibility that has been placed upon you.

. . .

The jury was locked up at twenty minutes to three o'clock to consider its verdict. After an absence of a little over an hour and a half, the members of the jury sent an intimation to the learned judge that, being unable to agree, they desired to ask some questions, which his lordship directed should be communicated in written form. Shortly after four o'clock, the jury sent a communication into court.

HUDDLESTON: The jury has agreed that the defendant spoke his honest opinion, but that is not enough. The criticism must be fair and bona fide.

The jury was called again to the box, and returned into court about a quarter past four.

Your verdict does not go far enough. Is the defendant's language fair and bona fide criticism? That is the question you have to answer. If it is, there must be a verdict for the defendant; but if it is [not], the verdict must be for the plaintiff.[12]

FOREMAN OF THE JURY *(after a short consultation)*: The difficulty among us rests in the opinion of some of us that the words "approaching willful imposture" are meant to refer to the artist.

HUDDLESTON: You must look at the words and say whether they come within the meaning of the term "fair and bona fide criticism." It was for the defendant to show that the criticism was fair and bona fide.

A JUROR: The way the case is put by some of the jurors is that—

HUDDLESTON: I am afraid I must not be admitted into your secrets. [I will read the passage again:]

> For Mr. Whistler's own sake, no less than for the protection of the purchaser, Sir Coutts Lindsay ought not to have admitted works into the gallery in which the ill-educated conceit of the artist so nearly approached the aspect of wilful imposture. I have seen, and heard, much of Cockney impudence before now; but never expected to hear a coxcomb ask two hundred guineas for flinging a pot of paint in the public's face.

A JUROR: If there is no reflection upon the man, and the words apply simply to his works, would they come within bona fide criticism?

HUDDLESTON: [Yes.]

The jury again retired, and after an absence of ten minutes came into the court, at half past four, to deliver the verdict.

VERDICT

HUDDLESTON: Are you all agreed?

FOREMAN OF THE JURY: We find a verdict for the plaintiff, with one farthing damages.

Baron Huddleston, on the application of Mr. Petheram, entered judgment for the plaintiff.

BOWEN: I submit that the costs, which are within the discretion of your lordship, should not follow the event, considering the nature of the action and the small amount of damages the jury has awarded, which shows that the action is one which ought not to have been brought. The jury has further said that Mr. Ruskin's criticism was honest.

PETHERAM: I would ask that costs follow in the usual course, given for the plaintiff on the verdict of the jury.[1]

HUDDLESTON: I have fully explained to the gentlemen of the jury that damages should have been found if they considered that a substantial injury had been done to the plaintiff. Considering the view the jury has taken of the matter, I enter judgment for one farthing for the plaintiff, without costs.

PART THREE

THE VERDICT

CAUSE CÉLÈBRE

AFTER A TRIAL THAT HAD lasted little more than eight hours, the jury deliberated the famous, equivocal verdict of *Whistler v. Ruskin* for nearly two. A correspondent for the Hartford *Courant* overheard the jurors' voices arguing in the adjacent room; one loudly declared that he would stay sequestered all night, if necessary, but the plaintiff should have the verdict.[1] Candles were brought into the courtroom to dispel the gathering gloom of the late November afternoon, but the dreariness of the scene deepened as preparations involving ominous coils of rope began for the next trial. Whistler looked anxious, Arthur Severn recalled, while the jury was out.[2]

Although contemporary commentators enjoyed the idea of a dozen "butchers, and bakers, and candlestick makers posing as art critics,"[3] the special jury that rendered the verdict in *Whistler v. Ruskin* was in fact composed of educated property holders chosen for their ability to try questions of unusual intricacy, who were almost certainly addressing points of law, not opinions on art, during their deliberation. Following the attorney general's attempts to justify Ruskin's critique, Charles Bowen had effectively returned the jurors' attention to the defense of fair comment, and Baron Huddleston had instructed them at length on the legal meaning of libel. Their responsibility was to decide whether or not the defendant's comments could have been made by any honest person, not to agree or disagree with his opinion.[4]

Having debated for an hour and a half and failing to reach a consensus, the jury indicated that it had questions for the judge. Evidently its members had decided that the offending paragraph did indeed express the defendant's honest opinion and were almost prepared, on that ground, to conclude the case in his favor; a few of them, however, still harbored doubts. Huddleston's remarks had at times been so obtuse, repetitive, and contradictory that Anderson Rose surmised the judge had been drunk;[5] Huddleston seems, in any event, to have confounded the jurors' understanding of libel law, and he did little to alleviate the confusion by summoning them back to the box for further directions. Although he had previously suggested that a critic was entitled to full license as long as he honestly believed what he said, the judge revised his instructions upon the jury's return, saying that Ruskin's critique would have to be judged fair and bona fide, as well as honest, if it were to be legally sanctioned.

As Rose wrote Whistler after the trial, "It is a very nice question whether 'honest' does not mean 'fair,'" and, indeed, a less sympathetic judge might have taken that opportunity to encourage a verdict for the defendant, since the distinction between honesty and fairness can be difficult to discern.[6] The jury's foreman, hoping to clarify the issue, asked the judge to confirm his understanding that Ruskin's language could be considered fair only if the words "approaching willful imposture" referred to Whistler as an artist and cast no aspersions upon the man himself, a question that reveals a clue to the content of the jury's private deliberation. Huddleston, evading the problem of distinguishing between the personal and professional connotations of Ruskin's charge, reiterated the need to judge the critique fair and bona fide but failed to elucidate the meaning of those obviously troublesome terms. Finally, he dropped honesty from the list of qualities a criticism should uphold, and then reread the allegedly libelous passage from *Fors Clavigera,* presumably with feeling, possibly influencing the jury in a way prejudicial to the plaintiff.

In light of Baron Huddleston's remarks, the jury took only another ten minutes to decide that although the libel expressed the genuine beliefs of the author, it exceeded the bounds of the critic's privilege. Huddleston's emphasis on fairness seems to have helped the jury out of its deadlock: whether or not Ruskin believed it, Whistler was a legitimate artist—the testimony of witnesses on both sides had upheld that fact—and to call him an impostor was certainly unjust, even if it were not malicious. A hush fell over the crowd as the jury came back into the courtroom, at quarter past four, to return a verdict that condemned the tenor and terms of Ruskin's critique and gave a nominal victory to Whistler.[7]

The plaintiff's triumph was tarnished, however, by the assessment of damages at one farthing—a quarter of a penny—when the cost to Whistler of Ruskin's libel had been assessed in the statement of claim at one thousand pounds. Desperate for guidance, the jury had followed to the letter the detailed directions the judge had given for determining damages: the contemptuous award (which Huddleston had defined as "a farthing or something of that sort") demonstrated its conviction that although the plaintiff was technically entitled to the verdict, he had suffered no material injury from the libel. The farthing was also meant as a rebuke: it signified, as the judge had instructed, that Whistler's complaint had been insufficiently important to deserve the court's attention. The decision to give Whistler the verdict at no significant cost to Ruskin could also have been the compromise of a hung jury.[8] In any event, it was not the result, as has often been supposed, of a philistine appraisal of Whistler's artistic style.

According to George W. Smalley, an American correspondent who was present at the trial, the jury's declaration appeared at first to puzzle Whistler, who was not sure whether it meant that he had won his case or not. Once assured that the verdict was his, at least nominally, Whistler said, "Well, I suppose a verdict is a verdict," and told Smalley, "It's a great triumph; tell everybody it's a great triumph."[9] To make his victorious attitude immediately apparent, he celebrated the trial's conclusion late into the evening with Anderson Rose and Matthew Elden. If Whistler was disappointed in the award—and given

Fig. 56. A. Bryan, "Mr. J. Whistler: An Arrangement in Done-Brown." *The Entr'acte and Limelight Almanack,* 1879

his financial state, it is unlikely that he was not—he seems to have determined never to show it. The story that he wore his damages on his watch chain may be apocryphal,[10] but it suggests Whistler's refusal to consider the damages a disgrace. He would conclude his own account of the trial, published years later in *The Gentle Art of Making Enemies,* with a drawing of a butterfly seizing the coin in its elegantly barbed tail (fig. 57). Through the artist's formidable power of transformation, the ignominious farthing was turned into a trophy.

After a few days of reflection, Whistler sent his solicitor assurances that the trial's outcome had satisfied him completely. "Rose my dear old friend," he wrote:

Verdict for plaintiff. Damages one farthing.

Fig. 57. James McNeill Whistler, "Verdict for plaintiff. Damages one farthing." From *The Gentle Art of Making Enemies* (London, 1890)

> what shall I say to you that can at all prove my warmth of feeling and my sense of the splendid way in which you managed and fought my battle for me! Nothing could have been finer. Morally, and in the judgement of all the world—all the world with whom high tone has weight—it is a complete victory![11]

But the moral victory had been a Pyrrhic one, and Whistler admitted to his friend Lasenby Liberty that "to the minds of some"—including his attorneys, no doubt—it would have been better if Ruskin had been made to pay at least the expenses of the action.[12] Ordinarily, as William Petheram had pointed out in court, the successful party would be entitled to have costs paid by the losing side; but since the damages had been contemptuous, the judge had ruled that the plaintiff could not recover even that relatively small sum. The decision left Whistler deeper in debt than ever, yet the farthing award saved him from having to pay Ruskin's costs in addition to his own.[13] He could also take solace in knowing that because Ruskin had not had to surrender so much as a penny, he would not attract public "sympathy or rather pity," as Whistler wrote Rose, "for a poor old man whose money was drawn from him." Refusing to cast the conclusion in anything but positive terms, he boasted to Lasenby Liberty that he always won in the end.[14]

The only tangible rewards of the trial came in the mail. John P. Heseltine, a trustee of the National Gallery, sent him a check for twenty-five guineas in protest of what seemed to him "an illogical verdict," and day after day Whistler received congratulations, some from total strangers. His table, he told Rose, was strewn with letters; his home, he told Liberty, was covered with them.[15] Many of his correspondents placed blame on the jury, following the popular notion of "twelve lunkheads"—as a Mr. Johnston of New York City called the gentlemen of the jury—who misjudged the merits of Whistler's paintings. "What can you expect," George Smalley asked, "when a lot of cheesemongers & pastry cooks are allowed to sit in judgment on works of rare & delicate art?" Elizabeth Lewis, whose husband, George Lewis, would presently handle Whistler's bankruptcy, declared that the verdict "would abundantly prove, if proof were wanted, that there are really no limits to the ignorance & folly of a British Jury."[16]

Encouraged by those responses, Whistler forwarded a sample of the sympathetic letters to Rose, in support of his own conviction that the matter would eventually assume a "more proper standing" in public estimation. Yet he seems to have remained uncertain that the battle was actually over: around 30 November he wrote Liberty that he was delighted with "the fight" as far as it had gone.[17] His intimation that the verdict might not be final may have been inspired by the many journalists who wrote of a "threatened" appeal. Virtually unanimous in the opinion that *Whistler v. Ruskin* had ended unsatisfactorily, commentators presumed, sometimes regretfully, that more of the controversy was to come. *Figaro* especially lamented the rumored news that there would be an application for a new trial: "We should be glad if the friends of the artist and the critic intervened and adjusted the dispute."[18]

It is unlikely that the defense lawyers were considering an appeal, since from their point of view the trial had ended according to plan. Holker and Bowen had both been prepared for Ruskin to lose the verdict and had only tried to minimize the damages; in the offices of

Walker Martineau & Co., the jury's contemptuous award must have been seen as a sign of their success. Neither had Whistler undertaken any further action himself, although he asked Anderson Rose for an explanation of the rumors he had heard that one side or the other might try to overturn the verdict.[19] Rose, anxious to defeat any hopes Whistler might have had of another day in court, replied immediately that he had considered the possibility of an appeal and concluded there were no grounds for it. Even if there were, he said, he would for a number of reasons advise his client against reopening the case.[20]

First—and Rose took care to tell Whistler to keep this to himself—he believed that Ruskin might have better grounds than Whistler for appealing the verdict. It seemed to him that the judge had misled the jury in his instructions: if Ruskin's criticism was honest, as the jury believed, then it was not technically libelous and the verdict should have been his. Second, Rose explained in his next letter, Whistler could never again have his case presented so well.[21] Parry and Petheram had both proved able advocates, and the witnesses who appeared on Whistler's behalf had all been "first rate." William Rossetti, despite his initial reluctance, had testified with an assurance Rose had hardly dared hope for, demonstrating that Ruskin's view was not necessarily the one taken by art critics; Albert Moore, who, *Portfolio* acknowledged, had been Whistler's best witness,[22] had proclaimed his aesthetic beliefs with such conviction that he had confounded the attorney general's attempts at levity; and W. G. Wills, although he had not done much to further Whistler's cause, had certainly not done it any harm.

Moreover, two of Ruskin's witnesses had testified in such a way that Whistler might well have won the verdict on their evidence alone. The chief witness for the defense, Burne-Jones, had said enough in court about the excellencies of Whistler's work to prove Ruskin's language indefensible, and Tom Taylor had shown through his testimony and the *Times* review he read aloud "that he himself was an Art Critic (good or bad whichever you please) and not a Vulgar insolent denunciator of the personality of a Painter—like Ruskin." Had there been only these witnesses, Rose maintained, Whistler might have won substantial damages; but William Powell Frith had given evidence obviously adverse to Whistler's cause, "to the extent," as Rose phrased it, "of his ability." Especially after the tentative testimony of Burne-Jones, Frith's assertions would have sounded comfortably steady and solid to twelve reasonable jurors—"a fair, honest, common-sense middle-class opinion," as the *Referee* remarked, "upon Mr. Whistler's artistic aberrations."[23] (In his own account, Whistler reflected that Frith had appeared "a decidedly honest man" at the trial. "I have not heard of him since," he said.)[24]

Rose argued further that Parry's reply, the last word in the presentation of the case, was another advantage Whistler had enjoyed, and that the judge, who had occasionally intervened on his behalf, appeared to have been in Whistler's favor from the start. Finally, the defense's ploy of producing an Old Master painting for comparison with *Nocturne in Black and Gold* had been so patently ridiculous that it could not have damaged Whistler's case and might well have assisted the jury in deciding to return a verdict for the plaintiff. "If it was necessary to bring a Titian to compete with you," Rose said, "then indeed the libel must have been most unjustifiable."[25]

Rose's reasoning seems to have settled Whistler's mind on the matter, but rumors of an appeal persisted in the press. At the end of the second week of December, the *New York Times* reported that Whistler's counsel were still considering an application for a new trial, although "if Whistler is wise," the writer remarked, "he will rest satisfied with his first taste of English law, which, in matters of libel, is a very expensive and unsatisfactory business."[26] As it happened, Whistler's first taste of the law only whetted his appetite for courtroom drama—there would be more lawsuits to come—but in the aftermath of *Whistler v. Ruskin,* he would seek satisfaction in other ways. "I judge that you have not done with J. R.," the New York art dealer Samuel P. Avery wrote to Whistler, "and I would like to be kept advised of what next."[27]

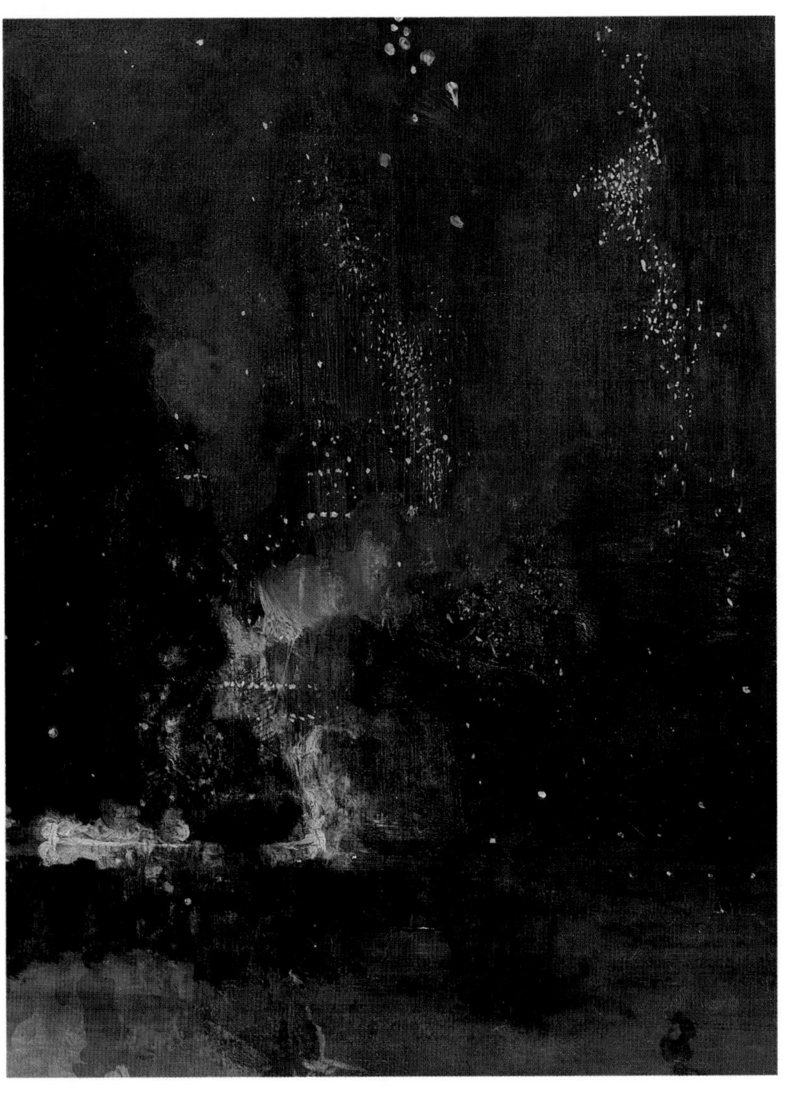

PLATE 1 *Nocturne in Black and Gold,* ca. 1875, oil on panel. Exhibited Grosvenor Gallery 1877, no. 4 (artist). Later titled *Nocturne in Black and Gold: The Falling Rocket.* Detroit Institute of Arts, Michigan; gift of Dexter M. Ferry, Jr. © Detroit Institute of Arts

PLATE 2 *Arrangement in Grey and Black, No. 2: Portrait of Thomas Carlyle,* 1872–73, oil on canvas. Exhibited Grosvenor Gallery 1877. Glasgow Art Gallery and Museum, Scotland

PLATE 3 *Nocturne in Blue and Silver,* ca. 1872–75, oil on canvas. Exhibited Grosvenor Gallery 1877, no. 6A (William Graham, Esq.). Later titled *Nocturne: Blue and Gold—Old Battersea Bridge.* Tate Gallery, London/Art Resource, New York

PLATE 4 *Nocturne in Blue and Silver,* ca. 1871, oil on panel. Exhibited Grosvenor Gallery 1877, no. 5 (Mrs. F. R. Leyland). Courtesy of the Fogg Art Museum, Harvard University, Cambridge, Massachusetts; bequest of Grenville L. Winthrop

PLATE 5 *Nocturne in Blue and Gold,* ca. 1871, oil on canvas. Exhibited Grosvenor Gallery 1877, no. 6 (Hon. Mrs. Percy Wyndham). Later titled *Nocturne: Grey and Gold—Westminster Bridge.* Burrell Collection, Glasgow Museums and Art Galleries

PLATE 6 *Arrangement in Black No. 3, Irving as Philip II of Spain,* 1876, oil on canvas. Exhibited Grosvenor Gallery 1877, no. 7 (artist). Later titled *Arrangement in Black, No. 3: Sir Henry Irving as Philip II of Spain.* The Metropolitan Museum of Art, New York; Rogers Fund, 1910 (10.86) © 1989 by the Metropolitan Museum of Art

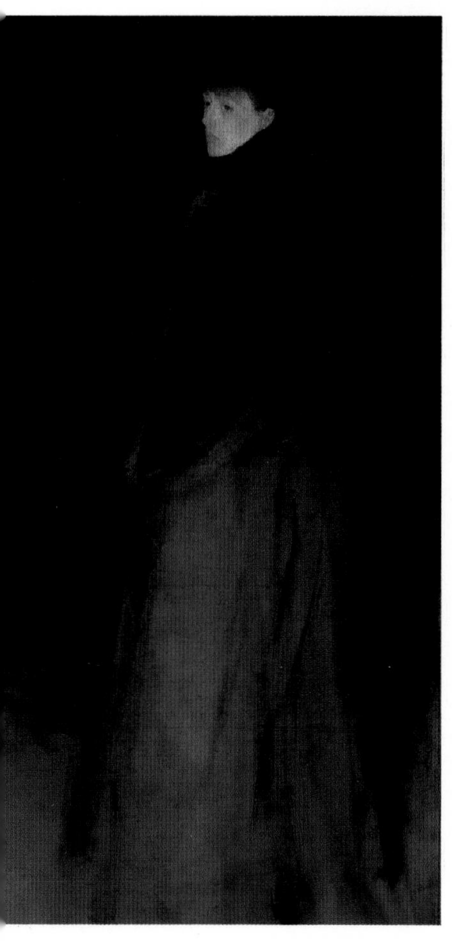

PLATE 7 *Arrangement in Brown,* 1876, oil on canvas. Exhibited Grosvenor Gallery 1877, no. 9 (artist). Later titled *Arrangement in Black and Brown: The Fur Jacket.* Worcester Art Museum, Massachusetts

PLATE 8 *Harmony in Amber and Black,* ca. 1876, oil on canvas. Exhibited Grosvenor Gallery 1877, no. 8 (artist). Later titled *Portrait of Miss Florence Leyland.* Portland Museum of Art, Maine; gift of Mr. and Mrs. Benjamin Strouse, 1968

PLATE 9 Vincenzo Catena (formerly attributed to Titian), *Portrait of the Doge Andrea Gritti,* ca. 1523, oil on canvas. Courtesy of the Trustees, National Gallery, London

THE LOSING SIDE

ARTHUR SEVERN HAD THE unhappy task of reporting the outcome of the trial to the losing party. He left London for the Lake District immediately after the verdict, arriving at Brantwood in a snowstorm. Severn recounted the events at Westminster to his wife, Joan, and to Ruskin, embellishing his story from time to time to entertain more fully his audience of two.[1]

But Ruskin was not amused. In a letter to George Allen written just after the event he did not disguise his anger: "Comic enough, the whole trial, the public may think—but I'll make them remember it, or my name's not mine."[2] Indeed, the farthing that was meant to confer disgrace on Whistler seems to have proved more deeply offensive to Ruskin. His memorandum of instruction had concluded with the statement that whatever the result of *Whistler v. Ruskin,*

> I cannot but hold it fortunate for myself that it should have been brought, since it justifies in my own mind the retirement from public life to which I was before sufficiently inclined by the languor of advancing age, without having been in all things (as my first written book clearly shewed) a *laudator temporis acti.*

But when he wrote those words, Ruskin must have expected to win the verdict. After the trial he revised the memorandum, presumably for publication, and substituted for that closing paragraph one that

Fig. 58. Hubert von Herkomer, *Portrait of John Ruskin,* 1879, oil on canvas. National Portrait Gallery, London

pointed out the abomination of the English law estimating the force of his "injurious opinion" at a farthing.[3] The verdict clearly rankled and began to assume disproportionate importance to Ruskin in his fragile frame of mind.

Shortly before the trial, Ruskin had written Dean H. G. Liddell of Oxford to announce informally his resignation from the Slade professorship. "You ought to know the fact," he said, "that I can't be Professor any more." Although he alluded to the lawsuit, Ruskin attributed his resignation entirely to illness.[4] Ten days later, on 28 November—the day he vowed to make the public remember the verdict's disgrace—Ruskin wrote another letter to Liddell, this time offering the "decisive intimation" that he planned to retire. Modifying the message of his previous correspondence, Ruskin explained that he had hoped to remain useful at Oxford "in some imperfect way," but the verdict of *Whistler v. Ruskin* had left him no choice but to relinquish the position: "I cannot hold a Chair from which I have no power of expressing judgment without being taxed for it by British Law."[5]

As John Dixon Hunt has pointed out, that was not quite fair of Ruskin, since the criticism judged libelous had been made in *Fors Clavigera,* not in his official capacity at Oxford.[6] The verdict, however, provided a timely excuse for retirement, and Ruskin eventually allowed his legal defeat to supersede illness as the principal reason for his decision. "It is much better that the resignation of the office should be distinctly referred to its real cause, which is virtually represented by this Whistler trial," he wrote Liddell:

> It is not owing to ill-health that I resign, but because the Professorship is a farce, if it has no right to condemn as well as to praise. It has long been my feeling that nobody really cared for anything that I *knew;* but only for more or less lively talk from me—or else drawing-master's work—and neither of these were my proper business.[7]

In Ruskin's mind, his resignation became the public's punishment for the verdict. He left them to fend for themselves and "appease the occasional qualms that may trouble the liberty of their conscience and the latitude of their taste," as he had concluded his memorandum, "with philosophy that does nobody any good, and criticism that does nobody any harm" (App. A).

Ruskin would become increasingly resentful. Two years after the trial, when a painting by Whistler called *Symphony in Blue and White* came up for sale, a Glaswegian who mistook it for *Nocturne in Black and Gold* wrote Ruskin to let him know that the work had inspired "languid interest" in Glasgow and brought only a few pounds on the market. Ruskin replied that the news pleased him more than his friends would think virtuous. Those who had urged him to confront

Whistler in court could not be expected "to sympathise with any dignities" of his, he wrote, "but they might expect me to express virtuous forgiveness and the like, of which there is no shadow (or light) whatsoever in my mind, but entire satisfaction in all that you tell me in all its bearings."[8]

Ruskin was never sorry for what he had said about Whistler. He never conceded to having committed any offense against morality or English law in his criticism of any painter, much less Whistler. The revised edition of *Modern Painters* was not, as the poet Richard Watson Dixon believed, penitential.[9]

Following Ruskin's resignation from Oxford, William Blake Richmond, the son of Ruskin's friend George Richmond, was appointed Slade Professor. Richmond obligingly resigned the chair in 1883 so that Ruskin could resume his teaching, and upon his return to the university Ruskin elected to conduct a course on modern English painting, the subject that had provoked the lawsuit. Subsequently published as *The Art of England,* his lectures pointedly excluded any mention of Whistler and began with praise of the artist who had faithfully stood by him in *Whistler v. Ruskin,* Edward Burne-Jones.[10]

The wholehearted support Burne-Jones had lent Ruskin's cause before the trial, confirmed by the unmitigated rancor against Whistler of his written remarks, would have assured Ruskin's counsel that his testimony alone could have secured the verdict for the defendant. But just before the battle began the chief witness for the defense seems to have lost his nerve; he did not possess the courage to face Whistler alone. On the eve of the trial, Burne-Jones's wife, Georgiana, attempted to calm his nerves by reading aloud from *The Pickwick Papers,* and on the day he was to testify—which Burne-Jones would remember as "Tuesday the Horrible-th"—his friend William Morris had to carry him "metaphorically in his arms to the door of the Court."[11] The ordeal terrified Burne-Jones out of all proportion. He was frightened of the wigs as well as the faces of the lawyers and "trembled a good deal," he wrote afterward to Joan Severn, "and wasnt very articulate and my tongue clave to the roof of my mouth (—no it was too hot &

dry to cleave to anything) . . . and I dare say I spluttered and was ridiculous."[12]

But the trouble with Burne-Jones's testimony had been less his nervous manner—though Whistler in his retelling would make much of his stammering—than his persistent qualification of every negative remark. The nocturnes were only sketches, Burne-Jones had said, but beautiful all the same; they showed an absence of composition, but a distinct mastery of color; they did not much resemble night, but that subject was impossible to paint; they were not worth two hundred guineas, but only because other artists did more for less. Burne-Jones confessed to Mrs. Severn that he had tempered the "harmful things" he said in court with all the praise he could think of, presumably to add credibility to his evidence;[13] but Ruskin's advocates, who had drawn their line of questioning from the vituperation of Burne-Jones's previously professed opinion, must have been mystified by his sudden change of tone. The witness had withdrawn from every opportunity to attack and even admitted on the stand that he agreed on many points with Albert Moore, who had testified eloquently the previous day to the originality and excellence of Whistler's work.

Burne-Jones's equivocating public performance seems to have convinced the court (as well as subsequent students of *Whistler v. Ruskin*) that he was loath to testify against Whistler, but in fact the "pang of mercy" that he said overcame him on the stand[14] might be better diagnosed as a symptom of acute embarrassment. Burne-Jones would subsequently complain that the lawyers had not only failed to ask the right questions but had even introduced the incriminating information that Ruskin had celebrated Burne-Jones's art in the very pages that contained the alleged libel of Whistler.[15] Indeed, that fact should have caused the court to reconsider the propriety of his appearance—to support Ruskin's position did, after all, imply advocating the Burne-Jones style—but fortunately for Burne-Jones, the suggestion of bias seems to have escaped notice.[16] At least one newspaper, however, did question the motives of an artist who had only recently emerged from obscurity, observing that Burne-Jones's conduct in court had failed to reflect the "supreme grace" that certain enthusiasts found in his pictures.[17]

Burne-Jones habitually avoided unhappy endings, and the trial, from his perspective, had not ended well. Afterward, he felt dejected and despondent, "ill & miserable over it all & . . . sleepless & sick of painting for a bit." His despair was deepened by the worry that G. F. Watts, Frederic Leighton, and other eminent artists would blame him for Ruskin's defeat and say that he need not have volunteered. He also fretted over the reaction of William Graham's daughter Frances, the beautiful young woman whose face had begun to appear in his pictures, fearful that she had come to court only to laugh when he stumbled.[18] In his anxiety, Burne-Jones told Gabriel Rossetti that the trial had been a "hateful affair" that he tried not to think about more than he could help,[19] a statement commonly quoted to help construct the myth of Burne-Jones's reluctance, even though, as has been shown, he had initially been eager to participate in the action. Burne-Jones may have remodeled his memory to accommodate the popular notion of his reluctance. He wrote George Howard that he had never disliked anything in his life more than appearing in that "abominable trial" and that he had "moved earth and hell to get out of it"; years later he told Frances Graham that nothing would have persuaded him to appear, "only he must stand by Ruskin and be on the side of the angels."[20] It is conceivable that upon reflection, Burne-Jones suffered some remorse.

Immediately after the verdict, however, Burne-Jones trembled in anticipation of Ruskin's response. Feeling, he said, like Nathaniel Winkle—the browbeaten witness in *Bardell v. Pickwick* who, reduced to a state of "nervous perplexity," had witlessly offered evidence adverse to his friend's case—Burne-Jones dispatched to Brantwood a quarter part of a halfpenny stamp in compensation for the damage his evidence might have done to the defendant's cause and waited, full of dread, for a reply.[21] Ruskin surprised Burne-Jones with compliments, based on Severn's report that his witness had spoken steadily under examination and appeared in the stand "serene and dignified." In light of Ruskin's pride in his performance, Burne-Jones revised his earlier

Fig. 59. Phil Burne-Jones, *Sir Edward Coley Burne-Jones,* 1898, oil on canvas. National Portrait Gallery, London

position, declaring that the trial had been "a triumph really"—even though, he wrote mendaciously to Ruskin, "I did feel it rather dreadful to say things against another painter, because I dont run them down much even in private do I."[22]

In spite of Ruskin's defeat, therefore, Burne-Jones secured the approbation he had hoped for all along. "I don't think you will be sorry hereafter that you stood by me," Ruskin assured him, "and I shall be evermore happier in my serene sense of your truth to me, and to good causes."[23] In the years after the trial, rewards Burne-Jones and Whistler might otherwise have shared were left to Burne-Jones alone. His works became immensely popular and correspondingly remunerative; at the sale of F. R. Leyland's estate in 1892, for example, when Whistler's *Princesse du pays de la porcelaine* (see fig. 19) sold for 420 guineas, Burne-Jones's *Beguiling of Merlin* (fig. 6) brought 3,600. His name, moreover, became so indelibly attached to the Grosvenor Gallery that by 1882 Henry James could say that "a Grosvenor without Mr. Burne-Jones is a *Hamlet* with Hamlet left out." Whistler was always there, James said, although he was "rather less a sign of the establishment."[24] Before the trial Burne-Jones and Whistler had been seen as the twin stars of the gallery; afterward, the artist in ascendancy shone alone. In deciding who, exactly, won *Whistler v. Ruskin,* one might conclude Burne-Jones.

Of course Whistler himself never betrayed a doubt that the triumph of the trial had been his, and posterity has subscribed to that point of view. The discomfited appearance of Edward Burne-Jones has dwindled to a detail in a story of more powerful personalities, just as Whistler, with his legendary arrogance, predicted that it would. "I personally owe Mr. Jones a friendly gratitude which I am pleased to acknowledge," he wrote in a letter to the *World* in 1892 that would be reprinted in the enlarged edition of *The Gentle Art of Making Enemies;* "for rare indeed is the courage with which, on the first public occasion, he sacrificed himself, in the face of all-astounded etiquette, and future possible ridicule, in order to help write the history of another."[25]

THE VALUE OF A NOCTURNE

IF WHISTLER HAD FAILED to win a thousand pounds in court, he had enjoyed a priceless opportunity to declare his right to paint and exhibit as he pleased, uncensored by uncomprehending critics; and Ruskin's quarter penny had purchased a public defense, albeit in absentia, of the critic's privilege to voice his opinion without stricture. The verdict, which did not appear to vindicate either position, was presented in art journals and the popular press as a judgment that remained open to interpretation—"a victory," as the *Examiner* put it, "which bears a very striking resemblance to a defeat."[1] Indeed, in the days and weeks following the trial it was not unusual for commentators to construe Whistler's verdict as Ruskin's success. A writer for the *Art Journal,* rejoicing in his understanding that the verdict had not gone against the defendant, remarked that *Whistler v. Ruskin* had been "a foolish action to bring: no intelligent or upright jury could have hesitated to consider that Mr. Ruskin had a right to say what he did of Mr. Whistler's picture."[2]

Contrary to Whistler's later assertion that newspaper correspondents had "seen nothing beyond the immediate case in law, viz., the difference between Mr. Ruskin and myself," the commentary published in the press during the days and weeks following the trial painstakingly examined many of the salient points of the controversy. If the debate of *Whistler v. Ruskin* had been unsatisfactorily resolved in court, it would be revived, and almost endlessly perpetuated, in print. One sympathizer drew Whistler's attention to the leading articles of 27 November published in the *Daily News* and the *Standard*, both of which made arguments for the plaintiff; and George Smalley assured Whistler that the journalists were exhibiting "the intelligence the jury lacked; on the whole in a way that could do you more good than the verdict does harm."[3]

One of the more important themes of contemporary commentary concerned Ruskin's apparent appraisal of Whistler's *Nocturne in Black and Gold.* As an art critic, Ruskin was entitled to assess paintings as works of art, but the public had not accorded him the right to comment on their prices—the legitimate concern, the *Saturday Review* observed, of art dealers.[4] Ruskin's impertinence might have been used to the plaintiff's advantage in court, but Whistler's advocate ignored that particular transgression of the bounds of art criticism, leaving William Rossetti to argue alone that art critics were unqualified to assign prices to paintings. Strenuously objecting to the attorney general's question of whether two hundred guineas was a "stiffish price" to pay for a nocturne, Rossetti stepped out of his professional role, when the judge insisted on an answer, and said that although he thought Whistler's painting worth the money, he himself was "too poor a man to give two hundred guineas for any picture." As an art critic, Rossetti claimed no authority in the matter of market value. He spoke as a potential, if improbable, purchaser of pictures.

William Rossetti's approval of a painting he could not afford probably puzzled those jurors and spectators who might have denounced *Nocturne in Black and Gold* on the basis of its price alone. Even Whistler conceded that two hundred guineas (£210) might sound "stiffish" to people who were not painters, although it was a "pretty good price," or a reasonable one, for the work of a reputable artist. In an effort to place the price of the nocturne in context, one of the jurors inquired of Burne-Jones the value of the *Portrait of the Doge Andrea Gritti* (plate 9), and the witness replied that the price of a work of art was "a mere accident of the sale room." To him, the painting would be worth thousands of pounds, he said, but it might be sold at auction for as little as forty. Perhaps to amplify the absurdity of Whistler's prices, Burne-Jones remarked that a Titian painting in the possession of Lord Elcho was said to have been purchased for only twenty guineas. The valuation of paintings, then, must have appeared to the court an entirely subjective process, for if a fixed relation did exist between a picture's price and its intrinsic value, Lord Elcho's fine Titian would be worth a trifling twenty pounds. Serjeant Parry could only comment upon the collector's good fortune; the art market was apparently ruled by chance.

A more objective and reliable measure of a painting's worth was thought to be the amount of labor expended in its production. Ruskin, whose authority as an "art economist," as opposed to an art appraiser, would go unchallenged, maintained that any product was valuable if the worker's efforts were sincere. "Do your work well, and kindly, and no enemy can harm you," he advised artists in the 1859 *Academy Notes:*

> If, indeed, you want to live by your art before you have learned it; or to sell what you know to be worthless, by catching the fancy of the purchaser; or to display your own dexterity, instead of truth in facts . . . you must take the chances of your speculation, or the penalty of your presumption.[5]

Whistler might have been exonerated from blame, therefore, by his declaration under oath that *Nocturne in Black and Gold* had been conscientiously executed; but Ruskin argued that even if the painter's motives were sincere, the unreasonably high price he had attached to a worthless piece of work could only be the mark of exaggerated self-esteem (App. A). Any unhappy consequences of an attack in *Fors Clavigera* would be the penalty of Whistler's own presumption.

The attorney general, attempting to represent the defendant's view, had insinuated during cross-examination that the plaintiff's motives had been mercenary: "Artists do not endeavor to get the highest price for their work irrespective of value?" Whistler, cleverly accepting the query as a statement of fact, announced his pleasure that the principle was so firmly established. His own advocate, Serjeant Parry, interjected that artists, like other honorable workers, proposed to give full value for money—a confirmation, unexpectedly from the plaintiff's side, of Ruskin's standard of vocational integrity, that an artist's dignity depended upon his giving "good value for money and a fair day's work for a fair day's wages" (App. A).

Whistler admitted that a nocturne could be painted in two days, and to anyone suspicious of his intentions, that rapid technique would appear to have been adopted in the interests of profit. "Keenly aware that Art is long and Life is short," the *Penny Illustrated Paper* surmised,

> Mr. Whistler has hit upon a happy expedient for extracting the coin from his believers. He has contrived to persuade a number of the aesthetic individuals who have more money than brains to pay high prices for a few hours' slapdash work with his brush.[6]

It was supposed that Whistler would supply whatever misguided patrons would purchase and that his unscrupulous profiteering threatened the system of remuneration that ordered the art world. "So long as 'a comparatively struggling young man' can 'knock off' a harmony in a day, and sell it for £200," said the *Examiner,* quoting both Parry and Holker, "it is scarcely to be expected that he will follow the example of such artists as Sir Frederic Leighton, M. Alma Tadema, and others, who spend many weeks of anxious thought and diligent labour over a picture."[7]

That Whistler asked so much money for so little work was presumptuous on his part; that he sometimes received the amount he asked was, to other painters, intolerable. Burne-Jones, who would claim to earn no more than five to seven pounds a day,[8] testified that although Whistler's pictures exhibited signs of labor and artistic skill, an excellent sense of color, and an unrivaled ability to represent atmosphere, *Nocturne in Black and Gold* could not be worth two hundred guineas, "seeing how much careful work men do for so much less."[9] In his statement to defense counsel, Burne-Jones had unleashed his irritation at Whistler's supposed prosperity: "There is often not so much appearance of labor in one of his pictures as there is in a rough sketch by another artist, and yet he asks and gets as much for one of these as most artists do for pictures skilfully and conscientiously finished" (App. B). He was obviously outraged that a fellow painter could manage to earn a hundred guineas a day—that nocturnes, in short, would sell.

To regard works of art as marketable commodities was to succumb to what Ruskin called in his memorandum "the confusion between art and manufacture . . . lately encouraged in the public mind by vulgar economists" (App. A). But Burne-Jones could not escape the inclination to consider the market value of paintings. With Frith, he maintained that the amount of money an artist earned should be commensurate with the number of hours spent at the easel, even though he was adamantly opposed to associating painters with ordinary craftsmen. Burne-Jones declared that there could be no greater degradation to English art than for it to become "mere mechanical work," a blue-collar occupation in which picture painters would be equal to house painters. Like Ruskin, Burne-Jones insisted that the artist's work be distinguished from the upholsterer's, yet his testimony implied that the artist should be paid by the clock.

Ironically, it was the plaintiff's advocate who supported Ruskin's maxim that an artist's reputation should rest on what he gave to his work rather than what he received for it; and while the witnesses for the defense appeared preoccupied with the money that Whistler earned (or asked) for his product, the witnesses for the plaintiff concentrated instead on the talents that Whistler brought to his endeavor. Albert Moore explained to the court that the price of a painting repaid the artist's skill, not necessarily the hours spent in its production, a point that the plaintiff himself had made in the most celebrated exchange of the trial: The attorney general had asked how quickly Whistler could "knock off" a nocturne; the plaintiff answered that the task usually occupied a day to begin the work, another to finish it. "The labor of two days," the attorney general declared, "is that for which you ask two hundred guineas," to which Whistler replied with decided brilliance, "No. I ask it for the knowledge I have gained in the work of a lifetime."[10]

From the plaintiff's point of view, the knowledge an artist acquired through years of experience superseded in importance the number of hours he devoted to the execution of a particular painting. If the nocturnes conveyed none of the great and just ideas upon which, Ruskin said, the "preciousness" of pictures depended, their creator nevertheless met Ruskin's demand that a painter "show the resources of his mind no less than the dexterity of his fingers" (App. A), or, as Ruskin emended the principle in "My Own Article on Whistler," that he "work a little with his head as well as with his fingers." Whistler testified that the nocturnes were painted after being mentally arranged: "I form the idea in my mind conscientiously and work it out to the best of my ability." With his statement that the "proper execution" of an idea depended upon the instantaneous work of his hand, Whistler turned conventional standards of wage-earning upside down. Suggesting that a prolonged period of production would not improve a painting and might even injure it, he said that his pictures would lack the quality he desired if he were to stop "hammering away" at them. His creative powers were best measured in the gestation of the idea: the "labor" of creation consisted in the delivery of an aesthetic conception, which emerged from the mind fully formed.

But Whistler's works often appeared to his contemporaries to be inchoate emanations of an unfinished mind. The poet Gerard Manley Hopkins, reflecting on the trial years later, remarked that the apparent deficiencies in Whistler's technique betrayed artistic immaturity:

> I agree to Whistler's striking genius—feeling for what I call *inscape* (the very soul of art); but then his execution is so negligent, unpardonably so sometimes (that was, I suppose, what Ruskin particularly meant by "throwing the pot of paint in the face of the public"): *his* genius certainly has not come to puberty.[11]

Tom Taylor attested to a similar belief in court. The nocturnes, he said, might possess "high artistic qualities," but Whistler as an artist was "not complete." Burne-Jones also suggested that Whistler had not satisfied his potential: "Mr. Whistler gave infinite promise at first, but I do not think he has fulfilled it." Before the trial, Burne-Jones had informed Ruskin's counsel that Whistler had exhausted in his youth any talents he might once have possessed. "The deficiency is insuperable," he wrote, "and he is clever enough to know it; and being notoriously without any principle or sentiment of the dignity of his art, he is perpetually eager to make the world believe that his own low standard of excellence is the standard that is alone desirable" (App. B).

Burne-Jones also believed that Whistler's technical failings, if left unchecked, would prove subversive to the art establishment: to support his own poor standards, Whistler intended to found a "school of incapacity" in which artists would succeed by virtue of their impoverished productions (App. B).[12] Following this direction, the attorney general tried to convince the court of the peril that would attend Whistler's ascendancy, envisioning eccentricity, incompetence, and exaggeration becoming equal to artistic excellence in the public estimation. Burne-Jones himself, ever more conciliatory on the stand than in private communication, testified that the danger occasioned by Whistler's "want of finish" was only that his followers might produce works lacking the best qualities of the master's art—"and so," he said, "the art of the country will sink down to mechanical whitewashing." Whistler seemed to Burne-Jones to be setting an English precedent for impressionism; and according to Georgiana Burne-Jones, that was "one of the most disheartening thoughts" of the artist's life.[13]

Another insinuation that threaded its way through *Whistler v. Ruskin* (and ultimately appeared in Du Maurier's *Trilby*) was that even if Whistler were capable of more, he would choose to do inferior work, that his problem was less incompetence than indolence. Because the nocturnes did not appear to satisfy the requirements of completed pictures, it was assumed that the artist had failed to move them through the requisite stages of the artistic process. Burne-Jones said in his statement that Whistler produced nothing but sketches, "more or less clever, often stupid, sometimes sheerly insolent, but sketches always"; never once, he said, had Whistler "committed himself to the peril of completing anything" (App. B). Concurring with that opinion, the *Illustrated London News* observed that Whistler's works were

> the merest artistic notes or memoranda of a few colour relations, such as every artist should, and many artists do often, "knock off," as Mr. Whistler said, "in a couple of days or a day and a half," by way of tentative experiment, and to serve modestly for after reference.[14]

Whistler's testimony that he worked directly from mind to canvas and rarely sketched on paper would have encouraged the notion that nocturnes were preliminary studies for paintings, or "commemorative sketches," as Ruskin called those works produced by painters "merely to put them in mind of motives of invention."[15]

The public's impression of Whistler as too lazy to complete his paintings may have been fixed by Burne-Jones's declaration that "the difficulties in painting increase daily as the work progresses," which made Whistler's two-day efforts seem facile and unfinished.[16] Perhaps to sound a note of humility, Burne-Jones added, "That is the reason so many of us fail. We are none of us perfect." The witness would presently confess to having shown two "unfinished sketches" at the 1877 Grosvenor exhibition, and although he would not call his action "wicked," he did confess it to be undesirable. Indeed, the exhibition of works not yet in final form contravened Ruskin's principle, as the attorney general conveyed it to the court, that "an artist ought not to present a picture to the public until he has brought it, as far as he is able, to a state of perfection." But the "ancient code of the Artist's honour" that the critic actually espoused was worded rather differently in his memorandum, where Ruskin said that no work should ever leave the artist's hands that "his diligence could further complete, or his reflection further improve" (App. A). Whistler, in fact, upheld that principle: like Burne-Jones, he occasionally presented to the public unfinished pictures, but he never allowed them to leave his hands—to be sold—until he had brought them to completion.

Whistler demonstrated the difference between completed pictures and sketches, or uncompleted pictures, with two of his Grosvenor exhibits, *Arrangement in Black No. 3, Portrait of Henry Irving as Philip II* (plate 6) and *Nocturne in Black and Gold* (plate 1), the notorious "Falling Rocket." During his testimony Whistler designated the Irving portrait "a mere sketch, unfinished" and "a large impression, a sketch," repeatedly pointing out that the work had not been for sale at the time of the exhibition. He defined *Nocturne in Black and Gold,* on the other hand, as "a finished picture": because he did not intend to do anything more with the nocturne, it had been priced for sale. Alone among the works listed in the catalogue as being in the artist's possession, *Nocturne in Black and Gold* could not have been further improved. It corresponded to Whistler's concept and possessed all its essential parts. "A picture is finished," Whistler would later declare, "when all trace of the means used to bring about the end has disappeared."[17]

Burne-Jones, however, refused to believe that Whistler recognized the distinction between finished and unfinished works of art. He maintained from the witness box that all of the nocturnes were deficient in form and called the Battersea Bridge nocturne (plate 3) incomplete, an admirable beginning of a picture, a sketch. Disregarding Whistler's testimony that the painting belonged to William Graham and that his pictures were never sold unfinished, Burne-Jones said he did not believe Whistler ever intended *Nocturne in Blue and Silver* to be considered a finished work. That remark, as an astute observer pointed out in a letter to *The Times* published a few days after the trial, had been presumptuous and ill informed:

> Mr. Burne Jones would admit, probably, that a picture is finished when its author has reached in the work that stage of realization which exactly embodies his intentions, together with qualities of execution which cannot receive after-painting without a marring of those technical values which it has been his special aim to secure.
>
> The pictures of Corôt, for instance, are as undefined as those of Whistler. Yet no one supposes that because Holbein and Van Eyck had other views of painting, Corôt's works would have gained by more labour, or ever thought them the "beginnings" of pictures only.[18]

Burne-Jones's understanding of Whistler's work was apparently impeded by his notion of a nocturne as an unfinished picture, a misconception that could present an insuperable obstacle to appreciation, as the attorney general's opening argument had shown. "I daresay you will see beauty in it as a sketch," Holker said of *Nocturne in Blue and*

Silver. "As a sketch, perhaps, there may be a good deal in the picture." Defined as a finished work of art, the nocturne appeared to lose all of its charm.

Tom Taylor, whose testimony was otherwise unremarkable, did offer one insightful description of Whistler's paintings. "All his works are in the nature of sketching," Taylor said. "Within those limits, I call it good work." Taylor's definition implied that works "in the nature of sketching" differed not only from commemorative sketches, but also from conventionally finished pictures, in the "limits" that a painter imposed upon them. Whistler's execution might have been governed by forbearance instead of indolence or incompetence, as even the defendant might have pointed out. In *Modern Painters,* Ruskin named the artist's ability to determine the limits he would not transgress ("even though here and there a painful sense of incompletion may exist") *reserve,* and numbered it among the "several characteristics of great treatment" of works of art. Indeed, the sense of incompleteness that so disturbed Burne-Jones may be the very quality that distinguishes the nocturnes as enduring works of art.[19]

The question that arose persistently from the defense, whether Whistler's works were finished pictures, seems therefore to have been the preoccupation of Burne-Jones. Ruskin's libel had not made that particular accusation. The attorney general, hazarding an explanation of Ruskin's complaint, had attempted to paraphrase a critical passage from *Fors Clavigera* in his opening statement to the court: "In criticizing the plaintiff's style, Mr. Ruskin said that the artist had a fervid imagination, but his fault consisted in his being led away from one imagination to another before the first had been finished in its entirety." The paragraph he alluded to, however, had not been a criticism of the plaintiff's style, but a defense of the faults that were but shadows of the virtues of Edward Burne-Jones: "With men of consummately powerful imagination, the question is always, between finishing one conception, or partly seizing and suggesting three or four." An apparent absence of finish, one of the "resulting conditions of execution," was not then to be condemned.[20] Ruskin did not consider unfinished pictures unconditionally culpable. He had explained in *Modern Painters,* on the contrary, that "perfectness" meant carrying a work of art "up to a degree determined upon," rather than "up to any constant and established degree of finish."[21] Nevertheless, in *Whistler v. Ruskin* "finish" not only became a primary subject of discourse but came to be seen as the principal object of art.

The defense's production of a portrait by Titian (plate 9) was ostensibly intended for the edification of the court, to illustrate the nature of finish. But as Albert Moore said in a letter to the *Echo* that was published just after the trial, the maneuver seemed "calculated to produce an erroneous impression." The *Portrait of the Doge Andrea Gritti* was an early work, Moore pointed out, that inadequately represented Titian's distinctive style:

> one obvious point of difference between this and his more mature work being the far greater amount of finish—I do not say completeness—exhibited in it. I do not anticipate that Mr. Ruskin's own witnesses will question the accuracy of this statement, and as the picture was brought forward with a view to inform the jury as to the nature of the work of the greatest painter, and more especially as to the high finish introduced in it, it is evident that it was calculated to produce an erroneous impression on their minds, if, indeed, anyone present at the inquiry can hold that those gentlemen were in any way fitted to understand the issues raised therein.[22]

Well aware that "finish" was open to more than one interpretation, Moore refuted two Victorian commonplaces at once: that finish was an indication of artistic maturity, and that the word itself was synonymous with "completeness."

The implication that a picture could be "a most perfect specimen of a highly finished work of ancient art," as Burne-Jones said of the Titian, yet still fall short of pictorial perfection, was a dictum adopted from Ruskin. "The imperative demand for finish is ruinous," he had declared in *Modern Painters,* "because it refuses better things than finish." Advising his readers to guard against the finish that might be measured by "number of touches," Ruskin maintained that finish as a kind of varnish, applied to a picture "for the sake of workmanship, neatness, or polish," was ignoble; noble finish consisted not in superficial smoothing, but in the "completeness of the expression of ideas."[23] What Ruskin termed "ignoble finish" was a deplorable fashion of the day, a stylistic element subject to historical variation.

"Finish" was also subject to national character, as Albert Moore suggested by testifying that "people abroad charge us with finishing our pictures too much." Ruskin, also, had pointed out that "one of the most remarkable points of difference between the English and Continental nations is the degree of finish given to their ordinary work." The greater finish of Victorian works of art could be attributed to a national "desire to do things as well as they can be done"—an inclination, he hastened to add, that was not necessarily a virtue.[24] Burne-Jones once again displayed his unfamiliarity with Ruskin's philosophy by suggesting that the taste for finish was a universal preference: when Charles Bowen asked him how important finish and completion were to the merit of a painting, Burne-Jones made one term modify the other, replying that "complete finish" should be every artist's aim; not stopping at personal opinion, he concluded broadly that artists should settle for nothing less than "what for ages has been acknowledged as essential to perfect work"—or, as another newspaper recorded his statement, "what the age acknowledges as essential to perfect work."[25] An artist, in other words, should comply with convention.

Clearly, Whistler's paintings "in the nature of sketching" failed to satisfy the requirement of finish, or other requirements of conventional Victorian pictures. Burne-Jones testified that composition and detail, the very elements Whistler's paintings appeared to lack, were of paramount importance to a great work of art, and Frith agreed that without those qualities, a picture could not be considered a work of art at all. The press perpetuated the notion that Whistler's nocturnes, whatever they might be, were not pictures. The *Times* said that the result of Whistler's labors "has charms of its own, but it can scarcely be called a picture in the sense in which that word is ordinarily used," and the *Referee* declared that "to many careful and painstaking students it is an insult to dignify any of Mr. Whistler's oddly-styled productions with the name of picture."[26] If *pictures* were by definition *finished,* Whistler's nocturnes could be summarily disqualified from competition.

FIGURES OF SPEECH

TO ENLARGE THE BOUNDARIES of Victorian art so they would encompass his unconventional productions, Whistler had to revise the meaning of the word *picture,* which carried connotations of representation. Ruskin had taught the public through precept and example that pictures were to be valued according to the "clearness and the justice of the ideas they contained and conveyed" (App. A), and his many disciples—those Victorian critics Whistler disdained—understood this theory to mean that pictures should be visual treatises, or figures of speech. Whistler's aim, as Serjeant Parry explained in his opening remarks, was "to produce the utmost effect which color will enable him to do, and to bring about a harmony in color and arrangement in his pictures." The idea of a work by Whistler was contained in and conveyed by its compositional constituents, rather than the objects those elements might incidentally depict. Unlike a picture, which indicated the external world, a nocturne was essentially self-referential.

Whistler required a label that emphasized paint more than image. The noun *painting* would have been an appropriate alternative to *picture,* but the words appear interchangeably in all accounts of the trial, and the plaintiff himself seems to have used them inconsistently. Whistler apparently recognized the impediment of a word conceptually opposed to his sensuous style, however, for he often avoided desig-

MODERN ÆSTHETICS.

(*Ineffable Youth goes into ecstacies over an extremely Old Master—say,* FRA PORCINELLO BABARAGIANNO, A.D. 1266—1281 ?)

Matter-of-Fact Party. "BUT IT'S SUCH A REPULSIVE *SUBJECT!*"
Ineffable Youth. "'SUBJECT' IN ART IS OF NO MOMENT! THE *PICKTCHAH* IS BEAUTIFUL!"
Matter-of-Fact Party. "BUT YOU'LL OWN THE *DRAWING'S* VILE, AND THE *COLOUR'S* BEASTLY!"
Ineffable Youth. "I'M CULLAH-BLIND, AND DON'T P'OFESS TO UNDERSTAND D'AWING! THE *PICKTCHAH* IS BEAUTIFUL!"
Matter-of-Fact Party (getting warm). "BUT IT'S ALL OUT OF *PERSPECTIVE,* HANG IT! AND SO ABOMINABLY *UNTRUE TO NATURE!*
Ineffable Youth. "I DON'T CARE ABOUT NAYTCHAH, AND HATE PERSPECTIVE! THE *PICKTCHAH* IS *MOST* BEAUTIFUL!"
Matter-of-Fact Party (losing all self-control). "BUT, DASH IT ALL, MAN! WHERE THE *DICKENS* IS THE *BEAUTY*, THEN?"
Ineffable Youth (quietly). "IN THE PICKTCHAH!" [*Total defeat of Matter-of-Fact P*

Fig. 60. George Du Maurier, "Modern Aesthetics." *Punch,* 10 February 1877

nating his paintings "pictures" by calling the works by name or referring to them generically as "nocturnes." The musical analogy itself was an ingenious way of counteracting the Victorian predilection for visual literature, since it exposed the confinements of a literal mind.

In "Modern Aesthetics" (fig. 60), a cartoon that appeared in *Punch* several months before the inauguration of the Grosvenor Gallery, George Du Maurier forecast some of the confusion that would result from Whistler's offering of paintings to a public prepared for pictures. An ineffable youth and a matter-of-fact gentleman pause before the work of an Old Master; the elder man, standing within inches of the painting and earnestly attempting to find something in its subject or composition to account for its acclaim, queries the younger one, who will only reply that the "picktchah" is beautiful. Their confrontation prefigures Whistler's courtroom contest with the attorney general, who during cross-examination asked, in effect, Where the dickens is the beauty? only to be chastened by the artist's implication that his inquisitor was simply insusceptible. The aesthete characteristically declines to anatomize a work of art, to assess its component parts. As the epithet Du Maurier gave his youth implies, the merits of paintings—as distinct from pictures—cannot be adequately expressed in words.

By giving both the philistine and the aesthete spectacles, Du Maurier suggested that each suffers from a perceptual disability; and by rendering one farsighted and the other nearsighted he implied that they will never attain a common point of view. The characters in "Modern Aesthetics," like the opposing parties of *Whistler v. Ruskin,* possess preconceptions that make their observations irreconcilable. William Powell Frith, who might have been the model for Du Maurier's matter-of-fact gentleman, betrayed his own myopia in an essay published in 1881, which defined painting as "the power of thoroughly and completely representing—as the great masters did—the object before [the painter], whether it be a human figure or any other model."[1] This statement reiterated the assertion he had made in the witness box that a picture without detail could not be a work of art. For Frith, details defined the subject the artist chose to portray; art, in his view, was invariably a matter of fact, and paintings were necessarily pictures.

Most people present at *Whistler v. Ruskin* would probably have agreed that painting, or picturing, meant describing. Because of a general preference for the written word, much visual art of the period aspired to the condition of literature. The subject picture, a genre well suited to literary tastes, was brought to perfection by artists eager to satisfy the unprecedented demand for works of art with engaging story lines; if legibly rendered, painted images could convey meaning as precisely as sentences printed plainly on a page. The single writer among Ruskin's witnesses, Tom Taylor, had demonstrated the ease with which a Victorian picture might be read like a book in his pamphlet on Frith's *Railway Station* (fig. 48): a virtual replica of the picture, Taylor's treatise examined the characters and incidents of the depicted scene, discovering anecdotes and intrigues a casual viewer might overlook. The author, by giving meticulous attention to the artist's details, turned figures into words.[2] The visual components that might inspire such a narrative excursion were notably absent from a nocturne, and before a work by Whistler even Taylor was at a loss for words.

The attorney general also found himself unable to read a nocturne because he could not recognize the scene it purported to portray. "If Mr. Whistler wanted to make a picture," Holker said of *Nocturne in Blue and Silver* (plate 3), "why did he not make the bridge something like Battersea Bridge?" He interrogated the plaintiff on the subjects of his paintings, but Whistler would only answer that *Nocturne in Black and Gold* (plate 1) was a "night piece" and *Nocturne in Blue and Silver* a "moonlight effect." He rarely conceded more than the vaguest indication of content—a scene on the river; a scene on the Thames in summertime, by moonlight; a river scene—so that the subjects of the paintings, all sounding the same, were made to seem inconsequential. Although Whistler admitted at last that many of his nocturnes were "taken from the Thames," he also mentioned that he lived near Chelsea Embankment, a circumstance that made his ostensible subject a matter of convenience, incidental to his aesthetic aim.

If for lack of a legible subject Whistler's nocturnes were usually considered unsuccessful, his portraits were often tolerated and sometimes widely praised, perhaps because a portrait—a representation of a particular person—is by definition a picture. A few of Whistler's "arrangements" had the look, as Taylor said in *The Times*, of "materialized spirits and figures in a London fog," but others nearly redeemed their maker in the popular regard. The portrait of Carlyle, *Arrangement in Grey and Black, No. 2,* demonstrated that Whistler had the ability to describe a physical subject. Taylor commented in court that in contrast to the nocturnes, the *Carlyle* was substantial (a remark, he added, intended as a compliment). William Rossetti, recognizing that Whistler had portrayed the sitter "with a certain degree of peculiarity," testified that the portrait was nonetheless "a very excellent likeness," and Albert Moore agreed that the *Carlyle* was "good as a portrait," adding that it was moreover "excellent as a picture." Perhaps only an artist on Whistler's side of the court could have seen past the sage of Chelsea to the beauty of the painting itself: Moore suggested that the qualities of color and composition that distinguished the portrait had nothing to do with the subject they happened to embody.[3]

Whistler's artistic ability may actually show to best advantage in the works dismissed by Taylor as insubstantial. Moore noted in his written "suggestions for his proof" that when looking at a nocturne he could almost feel the cool air rising from the water.[4] In court he pointed out that the nocturnes displayed Whistler's extraordinary talent for painting the atmosphere, something few artists dared to attempt. Rossetti, writing about the Leyland *Nocturne in Blue and Silver* (plate 4) in an 1877 review, also recognized Whistler's remarkable ability to render the most elusive effects of light and air: "A great reach and surface of water are conveyed to the eye by a sort of artistic divination, a curious power of intuition and suggestion working through means equally simple and subtle."[5] He did not look for likeness in the nocturnes, as he had with the *Carlyle,* but testified to the appropriateness of "a general diffused moonlight" and "a moonlight effect" as subjects for paintings. The judge, also, learned not to expect portraits from nocturnes: in instructing the jury, Baron Huddleston pointed out that "Mr. Whistler did not say he was painting Cremorne Gardens or Battersea Bridge. What he said was that he had an effect in his mind that he was attempting to produce on canvas." As the *Morning Advertiser* would attempt to explain, the subject of a Whistler nocturne was an "object of vision," the manifestation of the artist's mental picture.[6]

"The first condition requisite for seeing anything to admire in Mr. Whistler's most characteristic work," a critic for the *Examiner* observed, "is the admission that pictures may be painted in some other light than that of the broad and open day, that the painter may legitimately seek to represent objects as they appear in dim twilight or in moonlight."[7] That condition was evidently difficult for Whistler's audience to accept, since many of the alleged faults of his work were attributed to an injudicious choice of subject. Burne-Jones testified that *Nocturne in Black and Gold* was but one of thousands of failures made by artists who attempted to paint the night, and a writer for the *New York Times* concluded that "vague scenes, like a distant bridge over a dark river on a misty night, that baffle all effort at reproduction," would be better left unpainted. Because depictions of darkness could not contain illuminating ideas, the nocturnes seemed to prove, as *London* remarked, that Whistler "had rid himself utterly of all considerations of what might be intelligible to, or approved by, the public."[8]

Whistler's painting of a falling rocket, *Nocturne in Black and Gold,* appeared deliberately to negate the qualities of calmness, distinctness, luminousness, and positiveness that according to Ruskin characterized "high art."[9] In the Exchequer Chamber in the dark November afternoons, the nocturne would have appeared even more indecipherable than usual. Burne-Jones said after the trial that Whistler's works had appeared even "more abominable" than he remembered, and the plaintiff's own witness, William Gorman Wills, told Anderson Rose that he had not dared to speak of *Nocturne in Black and Gold,* "seeing it in the gloom of the court."[10] In efforts to shed light on the subject, Whistler had drawn attention to the flashes of color on the dark panel by describing the nocturne as "fireworks at Cremorne," and later to the park itself, "a distant view of Cremorne, with a falling rocket and other fireworks." William Rossetti also attempted to clarify the court's understanding of the nocturne, explaining that Whistler had depicted the "darkness of night mingled with and broken by the brightness of fireworks," an interpretation that shifted attention from the apparent motif, golden fireworks, to the black background. The obscurity of *Nocturne in Black and Gold* was intentional, Rossetti said: "Being a representation of night, it must be indefinite."

Previously, in an 1875 review, Rossetti had objected to the "artificial subject-matter" of *Nocturne in Black and Gold.*[11] When reexamined on the subject of the painting he betrayed a conservatism rooted in his Pre-Raphaelite past. "There is no reason why fireworks should not be represented," he said. "I have seen them represented before in pictures—but I do not think it is a good subject." The appropriateness of the nocturne's subject became a primary point of contention and a weapon the defense employed to invalidate the plaintiff's claim that he was a conscientious artist. The attorney general took the argument one step further, attempting to prove that Whistler's depiction of a falling rocket at Cremorne—an unappealing subject in itself—was so poorly painted as to be unrecognizable. In what must have been an artful attitude of bewilderment, Holker indicated the *Nocturne in Black and Gold* and asked Whistler to state its subject. "It is a night piece," Whistler replied, "and represents the fireworks at Cremorne Gardens." "Not a view of Cremorne?" The attorney general may have orally encased the phrase in quotation marks, for Whistler seems to have heard the pronunciation of a title. "If it were called 'A View of Cremorne,'" he answered, "it would certainly bring about nothing but disappointment on the part of the beholders." The audience laughed, and Whistler continued, "It is an artistic arrangement. That is why I call it a 'nocturne.'"

Recognizing that titles traditionally functioned as captions, with the images illustrating the words, Whistler acknowledged that the public would have been justified in comparing its recollection of the scene with the artist's depiction if the painting had been labeled "Cremorne." It was called "nocturne," therefore, precisely because that title held no associations for the painting to contradict. The attorney general, missing the point, continued his interrogation with the question, "You do not think that any member of the public would go to Cremorne because he saw your picture?" Amused at the idea of a nocturne advertising an amusement park, the audience again broke into laughter. "It wouldn't give the public a good idea of Cremorne," Whistler replied, ending wearily with the iteration that *Nocturne in Black and Gold* was an arrangement of color, nothing more.

Presumably that line of questioning was intended to establish evidence of a sort of pictorial perjury. Holker would have liked to have shown that *Nocturne in Black and Gold* not only withheld material facts but bore false witness. Burne-Jones declared that the nocturne was not "like night at all," and Frith was even more dismissive, failing to see "anything of the true representation of water and atmosphere" in any of Whistler's works. Comfortably attached to the conventions of pictures, Frith proclaimed that to his mind the "description of moonlight" was untrue. Yet as Ruskin himself had determined in *Modern Painters,* "the words true and false are only to be rightly used while the picture is considered as a statement of facts."[12] To those like Frith with literal minds, the distinction might have seemed oversubtle; but a nocturne, as an arrangement of color, could not reasonably be called dishonest.

Indeed, as the attorney general discovered in his interrogation, Whistler's musical nomenclature shielded him from charges of deceit. The word "nocturne," like the paintings it identified, was evocative and nondescriptive, and as the *Saturday Review* remarked, Whistler had been wise to choose a term that suggested his works were something other than pictures.[13] Titles conventionally provided subjects even for works that, like ill-constructed sentences, appeared to lack them; but Whistler's titles, as Oscar Wilde observed, did not convey much information.[14] The early works that Whistler named in court did bear traditional titles: *Alone with the Tide* suggests a single figure on a beach and *At the Piano* a domestic tableau; *The Little White Girl* and *La Mère Gérard* promise portraits of women; *Wapping* and *Ships in the Ice on the Thames* hint of river scenes; *Taking Down Scaffolding at Old Westminster Bridge* raises expectations of a pictorial record of a specific, historic event. Had those pictures been brought to Westminster, they could easily have been matched to their titles. But when Whistler came to enumerating the Grosvenor exhibits, he spoke in musical terms; and when the works themselves were set before the court, the audience could scarcely have called them by name. "By using the word 'nocturne,'" Whistler explained, "I wished to indicate an artistic interest alone, divesting the picture of any outside anecdotal interest which might have been otherwise attached to it."

Naming an object usually bestows upon it a specific identity, setting it apart from others of its class. But the names Whistler gave his paintings implied that one was rather like another. "Among my works are some night pieces," he said, "and I have chosen the word 'nocturne' because it generalizes and simplifies the whole set of them." Rather than designating differences, Whistler's titles affirmed the similarity of his works to one another and their separateness, as a set, from other pictures. Whistler's night pieces were not linked through narrative, like Frith's *Road to Ruin,* but through relation of form: "nocturne" was their family name. Less distinctive than the visual impressions they identified, the titles were a means of depreciating the importance of words relative to artistic effects. Two of the paintings Whistler exhibited at the Grosvenor Gallery and displayed in court bore exactly the same name, yet the nocturnes in blue and silver were unlikely to be confused on sight. Their singularity was independent of their verbal designation.

Although Whistler's titles were meant to direct attention to the qualities of painting, they tended rather to attract attention to themselves. Walter Hamilton supposed that Whistler's titles provoked as much ridicule as did the paintings; they seemed to him esoteric by design, an "eccentric affectation."[15] A *London* commentator theorized in 1877 that by using "foreign terms," Whistler hoped to "enhance the value of the simplest paintings; surround them with the glamour of another art, and the charm of sensations not hitherto produced by them." The *Examiner* alluded to Whistler's works in 1878 as "unadulterated nonsense in the garb of profundity," comparing the nocturnes to Walter Pater's prose, and concluded that a "musician is not elevated in his art by being called a tone-poet, nor is a picture improved in value when it is termed a 'Harmony in Blue,' a 'Symphony in Red,' or a 'Polka-Mazurka in Tartan Plaid.'" The musical metaphor would become hackneyed in the twentieth century, but in the 1870s it was still very much alive. As the *Standard* observed, people had "not yet grown accustomed to hearing pictures spoken of as 'harmonies,' 'arrangements,' 'symphonies,' and 'nocturnes.'"[16]

As early as 1863, when Whistler's *White Girl* had been exhibited at the Salon des Refusés in Paris, the critic Paul Mantz had designated the painting "la symphonie du blanc."[17] Not until the 1870s did Whistler himself adopt that nomenclature, and he testified in court that he had stumbled accidentally upon musical terms. "Very often have I been misunderstood from this fact," he said, "it having been supposed that I intended some way or other to show a connection between the two arts, whereas I had no such intention." Despite their musical overtones, therefore, Whistler's titles were meant to assert the primacy of painting, not to call another art to mind. To signify a connection between painting and music—as Tom Taylor presumed the titles were intended—would scarcely have improved upon the Victorian inclination to link painting with literature.

Even so, in hope of justifying the "peculiarities" of the titles Whistler assigned to his works, Serjeant Parry informed the jury that painting was poetry of the eye, just as music was poetry of the ear. This elegant equation, a variant of the explanation of Whistler's style that had previously appeared in the *World,*[18] shifted the emphasis of the analogy from music to poetry, thereby reinstating the customary correspondence between the sister arts. Whistler's nocturnes do have much in common with poems: their deviations from optical truth and pictorial syntax might be explained as poetic license, their unusual arrangement of form as a pattern of rhyme, their subdued color schemes as emotional tone. Had he chosen to employ the forms of poetry rather than music as titles for his paintings, Whistler's aesthetic intentions might have been more widely understood. A nocturne, defined by Whistler as an "artistic impression that had been carried away," was an expression of the painter's perceptions recollected in tranquillity.

A prose rendition of Battersea Bridge or the fireworks at Cremorne would have left little to a viewer's imagination, but Whistler's nocturnes, instinct with poetry, invited creative interpretation. Whistler attempted to explain to the attorney general that he intended the spectator to ascertain a painting's meaning: "To some persons it may represent all that I intended, to others it may represent nothing." Only enlightened appreciation, he implied, would reveal his original inspiration. When Holker inquired whether the figures on the bridge

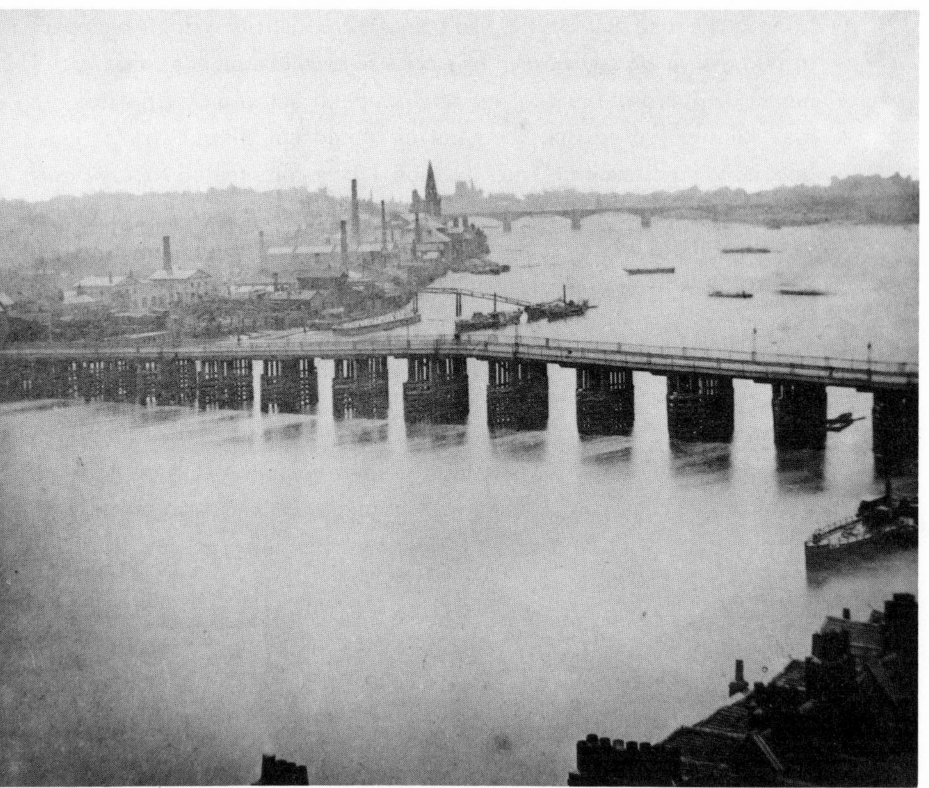

Fig. 61. Photograph of Old Battersea Bridge by James Hedderley, ca. 1870. Royal Commission on the Historical Monuments of England, London; Philip Norman Collection

of *Nocturne in Blue and Silver* were "intended as people," Whistler replied, "they are just what you like." Because the poetry would be lost in translation, the artist was unwilling to assign meaning to every stroke of paint. "Like the showman," the *Echo* remarked, "Mr. Whistler says, 'You have paid your money, you can have your choice.' If you think the object a barge, Mr. Whistler will not contradict you. If you think it is a whale, the artist may reply, 'Very like a whale.'"[19]

As it happened, the attorney general was gifted in the discovery of multiple meanings, and at the end of the trial Serjeant Parry reminded the jury that Holker had managed to identify a single element in *Nocturne in Blue and Silver* as Jacob's ladder, Mahomet's coffin, Britannia Bridge, a fire escape, and a telescope. If nothing else, his ridiculous reading proved that the painting would not submit to a single, invariable significance. James Jackson Jarves commented in the *New York Times* that Whistler's nocturnes provided "a sensuous impression of things more or less remote in themselves; dim visions of aesthetic phantoms, which suggest various interpretations to different minds, and operate on no two precisely alike."[20] Although it was generally imputed to Whistler's slapdash style, ambiguity should have been considered part of his work's poetic appeal; but the intellectual uncertainty arising from the interpretation of the nocturnes disturbed the Victorian frame of mind, which customarily sought communication from, rather than communion with, works of art. If ambiguity lent power to poetry, it deprived a picture of purpose by obscuring matters of fact.

Compared with the actual physical mass of Old Battersea Bridge (fig. 61), the vague impressionism of *Nocturne in Blue and Silver* suggests a basic tenet of aestheticism: reality, in art, is immaterial. Whistler deliberately neglected perspective and detail and strained the bounds of credibility with an unnaturally limited palette. Ironically, the type of ambiguity he categorically rejected was the one most common to the visual arts: optical illusion. Whistler's nocturnes neither deceive the eye nor disguise their artifice; they are ambiguous, not equivocal. Lacking objective titles and tangible motives, they do not profess to remedy the inhumanity of industrial society or elevate with moral messages the spirit of the age, but only to please the eyes, and possibly pacify the souls, of a few enlightened observers.

OBJETS D'ART

THE DETACHMENT OF THE nocturnes from the problems of humanity predictably annoyed those critics who affirmed Ruskin's belief that great art "compasses and calls forth the entire human spirit."[1] Henry James, in his review of the 1877 Grosvenor Gallery exhibition, confessed that Whistler's harmonies and arrangements failed to engage his attention: "It may be a narrow point of view, but to be interesting it seems to me that a picture should have some relation to life as well as to painting."[2] That most Victorians shared the critic's point of view is shown by the nearly unanimous approbation of Whistler's portrait of Carlyle—which Tom Taylor described in court as "very feeling"—and the corresponding disapproval of the nocturnes. Playing on the plaintiff's abstract nomenclature, Burne-Jones described the Titian portrait as "a splendid arrangement of flesh and blood," italicizing the inhumanity of Whistler's untenanted artistic arrangements.

Nocturne in Black and Gold, in particular, appeared bereft of human interest. Apart from "the blackness of night with a falling star or some fireworks coming down from the top, and a sort of blaze at the bottom, perhaps a bonfire," the attorney general could see nothing in it. His confession must have vindicated Whistler's belief, expounded in the *World,* that "the vast majority of English folk cannot and will not consider a picture as a picture, apart from any story which it may be supposed to tell."[3] Yet even in the absence of a story, Holker discovered the trace of a moral. The subject of the picture was Cremorne Gardens, he said, an amusement park offering pleasures not usually discussed in polite company; he assumed, therefore, that *Nocturne in Black and Gold* would be entirely incomprehensible to the ladies in court, who had never, he hoped, been to Cremorne. Hinting at depravity was the most Holker could do to bring the nocturne and its creator into disrepute on moral grounds, since Whistler had eliminated all vestiges of morality by obliterating anecdote in darkness.

It is telling that Frith, the author of the moralizing series *The Road to Ruin,* was the one to scorn the nocturnes as "things." The reification of paintings, their treatment as objects in themselves, was in fact Whistler's professed intention: the more abstract and objectified, the more material a work of art became, the more focused a spectator's attention would be on the essential elements of painting. As Ruskin had noted, Whistler conceived the "object of art to be ornament rather than edification" (App. A); or, as the leading article in the *Daily News* put it, Whistler had "chosen to give some pieces of canvas the sort of beauty which porcelain has, rather than the sort of beauty which pictures have."[4] If a picture was something with a subject, a nocturne was simply some thing—unobjectionable as an object, but inexcusably trivial as a work of art. Henry James conceded that Whistler's productions were "pleasant things to have about, so long as one regards them as simple objects—as incidents of furniture or decoration."[5]

Complying with Ruskin's command to "distinguish the artist's work from the upholsterer's," James suggested that the arrangement of colors on canvas was no more a fine art than the arrangement of flowers or furniture. The analogy of Whistler's paintings to household articles would soon be worn threadbare: the *Daily Telegraph* compared Whistler's recent works to "the pattern of a Turkey carpet," and Tom Taylor, in the *Times* review he read from the stand, had declared that the nocturnes came but "one step nearer pictures than delicately graduated tints on a wall paper would do."[6] The sentiment was echoed in court by William Powell Frith and subsequently employed as the

THE NEWEST THING IN WALL-PAPERS.

Fig. 62. "The Newest Thing in Wall-Papers." *Judy,* 11 December 1878

theme for a cartoon in the comic periodical *Judy* (fig. 62). A writer for the weekly *John Bull,* recalling Burne-Jones's professed concern that art under Whistler's influence might degenerate into whitewashing, said that "as a decorator of walls, Mr. Whistler is not without his merits; it is unfortunate, judging by such works as 'A nocturne in black and gold,' that he should aspire to be something more than a house painter."[7]

The artist himself did little to avert the suspicion that he was trivializing a noble enterprise. In fact, he encouraged the tendency to regard nocturnes as objets d'art by emphasizing their frames, where, as *Fun* explained, he placed "abstruse daubs of brown, of runic significance, without extra charge."[8] As constructions to support and protect paintings so that they could be moved about like pieces of furniture, picture frames were not normally noticed in art criticism. Like quotation marks, the elaborate cases surrounding Victorian pictures designated the borders of fiction by enclosing the artist's statement; they were irrelevant to the meaning of the work of art. Yet Whistler insisted in court that his works consisted of frames as well as paintings, and in response to the attorney general's doubts assigned a high aesthetic purpose to those abstruse daubs of paint. "The frame is traced with black," he said, "and the black mark on the right side is my monogram, which was placed in its position so as not to put the balance of color out." The figures on the frame were related to the painting's design, which made the form of the nocturnes as artful as their content.

Newspaper accounts of *Whistler v. Ruskin* document the movement away from art as subject toward art as object. Initially reporters identified Whistler's paintings by their subjects (Battersea Bridge, Battersea Reach), but eventually by their owners (Mr. Graham's nocturne, Mrs. Leyland's picture), suggesting that they found it easier in the end to think of nocturnes as things to be bought and sold than as portrayals of particular places. The plaintiff himself answered the attorney general's question of whether a picture represented Cremorne with the telling reply that the painting was a nocturne in black and gold (an object) for sale at two hundred guineas (a commodity). Ruskin, too, had approached Whistler's nocturnes as articles of trade: because to him art was innately valuable and *Nocturne in Black and Gold* appeared morally bankrupt, he implied that Whistler's picture should not be considered a work of art at all. William Rossetti's opposing opinion was discounted by the attorney general with the explanation that Ruskin's greater experience caused him to reject the nocturne; a well-trained eye, presumably, could spot fraudulence as readily as forgery. "If Mr. Whistler founds his reputation upon the pictures he has shown in the Grosvenor Gallery," Holker declared, "he is a mere pretender to the art of painting, an accomplishment he does not possess."

Summoning his defense, Whistler had said in a letter to J. E. Boehm, "It is necessary for me to bring men of my own craft to say that what I produce is Art—otherwise Ruskin's statement that it is *not* art remains."[9] Albert Moore would testify accordingly that *Nocturne in Black and Gold* was "most consummate art" and W. G. Wills that Whistler's nocturnes were "beautiful works of art." The artists who supported the defendant naturally assumed a different point of view: when asked whether the nocturnes were art, Frith answered "I should say not," a reply much admired by Burne-Jones, whose own condemnation of Whistler's work had been qualified, under oath, by compliments.[10]

There was, then, no consensus of opinion among men of Whistler's craft, although a number of prosperous patrons had demonstrated their faith in the artist's endeavor. "There are a good many persons who believe in him," the *Court Circular* said, "and are glad to purchase his 'pot of paint' whenever he offers it."[11] But believing in Whistler did not make him true. Like the paintings the attorney general characterized as "fantasies and exaggerated conceits," Whistler's delusions were in Ruskin's view the product of an unrestrained imagination. Ruskin imputed Whistler's behavior not to guile, but to overweening vanity: "I have given him the full credit of his candid conceit, and supposed him to imagine his pictures to be really worth what he asked for them" (App. A). The *Pall Mall Gazette* offered a cogent interpretation of the defendant's position:

> his expressed opinion of Mr. Whistler came to no more than this: that self-deception reaches to such a height in this artist's estimate of the value of his work as to produce results difficult to distinguish from those which would follow from a conscious design to pass off worthless pictures upon the public for good ones.[12]

Whistler's ill-educated conceit, in other words, which caused his failure to understand his position in relation to other artists, accounted for the unconscionable exaggeration of the value of *Nocturne in Black and Gold.* His grievous lack of judgment rendered him less an impostor, therefore, than a fool.

Burne-Jones's assertion that "scarcely any body regards Whistler as a serious person" (App. B) may well have been true, since Whistler cultivated the qualities of frivolity and even advised his attorney that he should not be presented in court as anything other than "the well known Whistler"—a charming public persona aptly emblematized by a butterfly.[13] It is not surprising that his motives were occasionally questioned. As one commentator remarked, Whistler might be "quite serious in his attitude towards Art, but the attitude is such an affected one that it is quite lawful not only to doubt of its seriousness, but even to say that one doubts."[14] The artist's antic disposition may have been in keeping with his style, but it created the impression, as Burne-Jones's written statement attests, that Whistler was not to be taken seriously. He would become "the buffoon of the Grosvenor," as Henry James said, "the laughing-stock of the critics."[15]

The casting of the artist as a clown had been encouraged by Ruskin's characterization of Whistler as a coxcomb. The attorney general professed himself unable to understand why the plaintiff objected to the appellation, since the dictionary he consulted showed that the word *coxcomb* meant a licensed jester whose occupation was to entertain. "Has he not performed such a part with his pictures?" the attorney general inquired. "I do not know when so much amusement has been afforded to the British public as by Mr. Whistler's pictures." Ruskin's derisive words had set the tone of the trial, and Holker, aiming to discredit the plaintiff's professional standing, attempted to keep the court amused. Although the judge once insisted that a legal action was not an entertainment, he succeeded only in suppressing the applause of the audience; he was helpless before its laughter. In his opening remarks, Serjeant Parry expressed concern that the most abstruse of Whistler's works, the notorious *Nocturne in Black and Gold,* might be held up in ridicule—as indeed it was, several times. At the close of the case, Parry reproached his opponent for his flights of forensic aspersion, arguing that Holker's ridicule had given the libel "an additional sting"; but by then the damage was done. Henry

James, acutely aware of the discrepancy between the serious issues under discussion and the comic face of the proceedings, found the trial's levity distinctly painful.[16]

Some of the laughter excited by *Whistler v. Ruskin* may have sprung from nervousness as much as mirth, since neither Holker's nor Whistler's wit was brilliant enough to provoke the many outbursts that punctuated the proceedings. The inscrutability of the nocturnes placed the unschooled spectator at a disadvantage, and in light of the artist's facetiousness it must have been difficult to know how to respond. If, as Whistler maintained, the pictures were not intended to be taken literally, were they then to be taken in jest? Or were the nocturnes parodies of pictures, as the *New York Times* surmised, "nothing more than clever satires on the very school of which it seems he was the chief apostle"?[17] To the jaundiced eye, Whistler's trifles must have appeared as strong confirmations of this doubt. The attorney general planted the suggestion that Whistler was banking on the public's credulity: to exhibit *Nocturne in Black and Gold* as a work of art, and to offer that "piece of monstrous extravagance" for sale at two hundred guineas, was, he said, an insult to the public.

The suspicion that Whistler's art was a kind of practical joke was not uncommon, as the *Examiner* pointed out a few days after the trial:

> The general notion has been that Mr. Whistler, cunningly perceiving how much a silly portion of the world nowadays is given to the worship of the Incomprehensible, and to profess enthusiastic admiration for aestheticism upside down, had taken advantage of the craze and produced a series of pictorial jokes—exceedingly bad ones from an artistic standpoint, but remunerative in inverse proportion to their merit.

Truth also contended that Whistler was as much a humorist as a painter, producing nocturnes "just to see what people will swallow in the shape of pictures. He *must* be a wag, and it was almost a pity to spoil his little game."[18] These interpretations recall Burne-Jones's written statement, in which Whistler's "vanities and eccentricities" were said to be a long-standing joke among artists, although the "semi-artistic part of the public" had occasionally fallen for the ruse (App. B).

It was this silly portion of the world, the "artistic" admirers of nocturnes, that the attorney general lampooned in a rhetorical visit to the Grosvenor Gallery, imagining devotees in medieval-looking millinery crowded around Whistler's paintings. The artist's admirers were invariably presented as female, either "gushing spinsters of fifty" or "pale, dishevelled beauties," society ladies whose "sole standard of beauty" was chic.[19] Whistler, it seems, was in style. Holker explained to the court that there was "a kind of fashion among some people to admire the incomprehensible and to say of something that cannot be understood, 'It is exquisite.'" The pitch of his voice probably rose at the end of the sentence to mimic the intonation of an imagined lady aesthete. The attorney general construed the taste for Whistler as emotional and irrational, which made it also feminine. The stigma of aesthetic mania, as seen at the Grosvenor Gallery, was taking Whistler seriously; laughing at a nocturne would manifest masculinity and mental health.

It was apparently inconceivable that the nocturnes could be appreciated for anything so simple as their beauty. "In truth," said the *London Express,* "Mr. Whistler's admirers are principally those who bow down before his shrine, not for the real talent he possesses, but for his oddities and eccentricities."[20] Ruskin had called Whistler's work impertinent; the defense called it eccentric. "I suppose," the attorney general said to Whistler, "you are willing to admit that your pictures exhibit some eccentricities. You have been told that over and over again?" Much to the audience's mirth the witness replied, "Yes, very often," ignoring Holker's supposition but acknowledging the public's preoccupation with the word indelibly attached to his reputation. "Yes," Whistler had admitted to the *World* the previous spring, "'eccentric' is the best adjective they find for me."[21]

But as the *Morning Advertiser* said, eccentricity was not necessarily to be maligned: "We have come to the petty in art in our day, as anybody may see for himself, and provided the eccentric took us to something of higher ground we could forgive the eccentric."[22] But eccentricity could be redemptive only if it were absolutely unaffected. Ruskin had written in reference to Burne-Jones, for example, that his works were "natural to the painter, however strange to us," suggesting that a good artist, like a devout Christian, would be absolved of the penalties of his transgressions so long as he kept his mind on the right side of the prescribed moral path and his eyes on that hallowed "higher ground" beyond. Whistler, on the other hand, appeared to have strayed too far, and Ruskin's defense of Burne-Jones concluded with an attack on those modern painters whose eccentricities were "almost always in some degree forced; and their imperfections gratuitously, if not impertinently, indulged."[23] Whistler's eccentricity appeared to Ruskin expedient. In declining to observe convention, he had also failed to respect the limits of artistic propriety.

The public, which was probably unaware of Ruskin's delicate distinctions, counted Whistler's work eccentric simply because it was different from, and thus inferior to, the accustomed pictorial fare. William Rossetti, who was identified in the press as the phraseologist of the school of eccentrics and exquisites,[24] appears to have recognized the derogatory connotations of the word: when asked by the attorney general whether a nocturne was eccentric, he replied that it was "unlike the work of most other painters." Rossetti had previously assigned that meaning to "peculiar," a word rarely tinctured in those days with its twentieth-century sense of "strange." *Peculiar* connoted singularity, as in Albert Moore's remark, "the peculiarity of the scene at Cremorne is, to my mind, wonderful." *Peculiar* implied that Whistler's art was sui generis, in a class by itself.

If Rossetti's euphemism for "eccentric" cast a more flattering light on the admitted oddity of Whistler's productions, it also aimed to correct the distorted understanding of the artist's intentions propounded by the defense. The attorney general repeatedly insinuated that Whistler had attempted to compete but fallen short, that he recognized a common and legitimate axis of artistic endeavor but only traveled around it in erratic circles. Admittedly, Whistler had nothing in common with his Victorian compatriots:

Frith, and even Burne-Jones, spoke for the art establishment, with which Whistler was obviously not aligned, and Moore acknowledged that Whistler's practices were uncommon in England. The *Standard* said that Whistler was "a disciple, or even an apostle, of a school of art perhaps more largely represented on the Continent than in London," and the *Illustrated London News* explained that his paintings carried "to the extreme the principles of the French *impressionnistes.*" *The Times,* with characteristic chauvinism, reported that Whistler was almost the only impressionist in England, "much outdoing in the qualities of this school those who are regarded as its leaders in France."[25]

Neither was the defense able to perceive any resemblance between Whistler and the masters of the past: although Moore maintained that Velázquez was the father of Whistler's style, Frith could not see the relation. The defense's misguided attempt to contrast Whistler with Titian turned out to be irrelevant and, as the judge finally declared, irreverent as well: "Nobody has ever equaled, and probably never will equal, Titian." As long as eccentricity was the issue, the public would continue to engage in the pointless exercise of determining the degree of Whistler's deviation from the norm.

It was left to Albert Moore, always astute in such matters, to relieve the discourse of its semantic obstacle. "I should call it 'originality.' What would you call 'eccentricity' in a picture?" he inquired of the attorney general. Wills, the last witness to speak on Whistler's behalf, followed Moore's example and testified, "I consider the nocturnes in blue and silver original. I will not call them 'eccentric.'" Although it may have sounded overprecise, the distinction was central to Whistler's cause. Although Parry had not articulated the concept clearly, his disquisition on eccentricity at the trial's beginning had in fact defined the meaning of originality:

> It is generally known that Mr. Whistler occupies a somewhat independent position in art. . . . It might be that his theory of painting is, in the estimation of some, eccentric; but his great object is to produce the utmost effect which color will enable him to do, and

to bring about a harmony in color and arrangement in his pictures. These might be eccentricities, but because a man has created a theory of his own and followed it out with earnestness, industry, and almost enthusiasm, is no reason he should be denounced or libeled.

To invent a theory unlike any other and create a work independent of all existing models is to originate: eccentric pictures go astray, but original ones strike out in new directions. Whistler's alienation from the Victorian art world was, as Parry attempted to suggest in his summation, the inevitable consequence of an advanced artistic sensibility:

> I do not suppose he estimates himself a man of genius; but he is a conscientious, hard-working and industrious artist, who has followed his profession for years and years—perhaps not so successfully as others, occupying an independent and somewhat isolated position, holding original or even eccentric views—but depending upon his profession entirely for his livelihood and position.

Genius, as the *Morning Advertiser* observed, could only escape destructive comment by sticking to the beaten path, the course most opposed to originality.[26] If aesthetic disobedience was a crime, it was punishable by art criticism.

ART AND ART CRITICS

WITHIN ONE WEEK OF THE verdict, Whistler had fired a shot at what he called the "Ruskin Camp."[1] His first target was Tom Taylor, whose homiletic testimony had proved particularly obnoxious to Whistler. The opportunity to embarrass Taylor publicly presented itself in the form of a letter from Linley Sambourne, who wrote on the first of December to advise Whistler that a "little bit of nonsense" relating to the trial would presently appear in the pages of *Punch.* The cartoon (fig. 63), which Sambourne defined as an attempt "pictorially to register the trial, without bias as a *fact* in art," pictured Baron Huddleston awarding a farthing to Whistler on the judgment of the jury, which was said to show "no symphony with the defendant"; the caption—"Naughty critic, to use bad language! Silly painter, to go to law about it!"—represented the common conclusion that the verdict had been a rebuke to both plaintiff and defendant. Sambourne hoped the illustration would not cause offense: "I have *every* sympathy with you in what must be a most trying & irritating time," he wrote, explaining to Whistler that he was compelled to illustrate any topic assigned by the editor of the journal, who happened to be Tom Taylor.[2]

Whistler penned a reply immediately and sent a copy to Edmund Yates, known as "Atlas," of the *World.* His letter, which was published on 11 December, not only recalled the spectacle of Tom Taylor self-

AN APPEAL TO THE LAW.

Naughty Critic, to use bad Language! Silly Painter, to go to Law about it!

Fig. 63. Edward Linley Sambourne, "An Appeal to the Law." *Punch,* 7 December 1878

righteously reading his own words aloud from newspaper clippings preserved in his pocket, but revealed through its tone the flippant attitude the plaintiff had assumed since the trial.

> Punch in person sat upon me in the box; why should not the most subtle of his staff have a shot? Moreover, whatever delicacy and refinement Tom Taylor may still have left in his pocket (from which, in court, he drew his ammunition), I doubt not he will urge

> you to use, that it may not be wasted. Meanwhile you must not throw away sentiment upon what you call "this trying time." To have brought about an "Arrangement in Frith, Jones, Punch and Ruskin, with a touch of Titian," is a joy, and in itself sufficient to satisfy even my craving for curious "combinations."

Years later Whistler's letter to Sambourne reappeared under the title "Professor Ruskin's Group" in *The Gentle Art of Making Enemies,* where a note in the margin indicated that the author considered it to be "a pleasant *résumé* of the situation." The reprinted letter forms a telling link between Whistler's partly apocryphal rendition of the trial, "The Action," and the text of his subsequent publication, *Whistler v. Ruskin: Art & Art Critics.*[3]

Whistler had wasted no time in preparing his own interpretation of the trial. The idea for *Whistler v. Ruskin: Art & Art Critics* may have been generated by the profusion of published commentary appearing the week after the verdict, for the pamphlet opens with Whistler's complaint about journalists who failed to recognize the "*fin mot* and spirit" of the matter. By 22 December the manuscript was complete; Whistler read it aloud to Alan Cole, who found it "pungent" and approved its "directness of purpose."[4] The pamphlet was published on Christmas Eve 1878, less than a month after the trial's conclusion. Whistler immediately visited the offices of Thomas Way, his lithographic printer, and read the text aloud with the dramatic flair he would later employ in the "Ten O'Clock" lecture.[5] The prompt appearance of *Whistler v. Ruskin: Art & Art Critics* may have caused Ruskin to withhold from publication his revised memorandum, "My Own Article on Whistler." Its title suggests that he, too, had been prompted by the proliferation of newspaper notices to state his own position in print. Once Whistler's article was published, however, Ruskin's might have seemed like a rejoinder.

Composed of seventeen "very prettily-printed small pages," as Henry James described it, *Whistler v. Ruskin: Art & Art Critics* was prominently displayed in several of the shop windows of London, where it sold for a shilling and enjoyed an immediate success.[6] The pamphlet was also available direct from the publisher, Chatto and

Windus in Piccadilly. Whistler directed his friend Harold Bird to go at once to Chatto's and ask for several copies and to send everyone he knew to do the same, "so that the run on the thing may keep up." Dr. Bird was asked particularly to send his sister, since ladies were "the ones to win the world with," Whistler said, "and especially they must eagerly cry out in full Piccadilly for Whistler's pamphlet!" The strategy seems to have succeeded. By 7 January 1879, *Art & Art Critics* was in its third edition, and one week later the fifth was in preparation; it would eventually go through seven identical editions.[7]

Whistler had originally planned to place a lithographic nocturne on the cover and in preparation had made a sketch showing the words "Whistler v. Ruskin" suspended above Battersea in a midnight sky, with a butterfly in the corner of what could be taken to be a conspicuously unfinished composition (fig. 64). The cost of that elaborate illustration proved prohibitive, however, and Whistler settled in the end for a simpler design on inexpensive, coarse brown paper (fig. 65). This solution struck some commentators as strange; it was supposed that the paper had been supplied by the artist's grocer.[8] Whistler himself considered the material both tasteful and practical and used it again in future publications, making brown-paper covers a trademark of his style.

The simplified cover design retained Whistler's butterfly from the preparatory sketch, positioned in approximately the same place on the page, and the artist's name and address and the date of publication again appeared in the lower left. But between the execution of the sketch and the production of the final cover, Whistler had appended the words "Art & Art Critics," which were printed prominently below the original title, *Whistler v. Ruskin*. The addition of the subtitle suggests that the author wished to clarify the point of the pamphlet: his objection to criticism exceeded a particular legal grievance. The shift in emphasis would have been necessary, in part, because the public had not entirely accepted the verdict as Whistler's victory; he sensibly stressed the cause and downplayed the effect of the libel trial. All too aware of his failure to win substantial damages, he attempted to effect through *Art & Art Critics* a more idealistic impulse for the legal ac-

Fig. 64. James McNeill Whistler, sketch of a proposed cover for *Whistler v. Ruskin: Art & Art Critics,* 1878. From Thomas R. Way, Memories of James McNeill Whistler (New York and London, 1912)

tion. "*I* shall have fought for the *principle* of the thing," he wrote Anderson Rose after the trial, as if willing could make it so.[9]

As Albert Moore would later remark, Whistler had a special talent for making victories of defeats.[10] Whistler must have realized immediately that the best way to celebrate contemptuous damages was to cast them as the cost of a righteous war. He had mentioned his altruistic motives before the trial in his letter to Boehm, in an effort to secure the sculptor's cooperation as a witness. Appealing for help on moral grounds, he had insisted that the lawsuit was an artists' cause, a

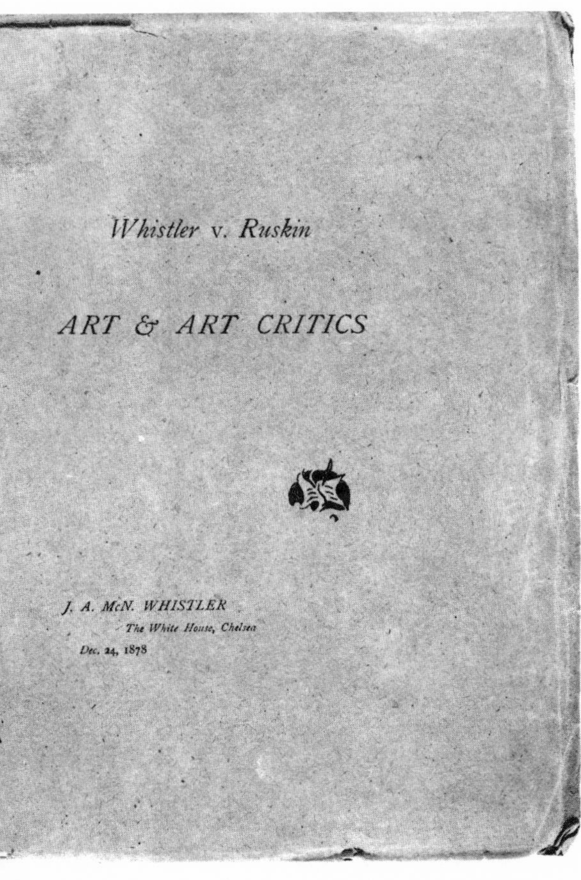

Fig. 65. James McNeill Whistler, cover of *Whistler v. Ruskin: Art & Art Critics* (London, 1878)

battle of "doers and workers" against "writers and praters."[11] After his qualified success in court, Whistler returned to the theme, writing Rose at the end of November that the libel suit itself had been but a pretext for addressing a more important purpose. "The question at issue has really been not merely a personal difference between Mr. Ruskin and myself, but a battle fought for the painters," he said, establishing the thesis of *Art & Art Critics,* in which the lines of battle would be drawn "between the Brush and the Pen." But if he entered the fray conscientiously, Whistler engaged in it vaingloriously, picturing himself the defender of Art and the champion of Right and exchanging the cap of the coxcomb for the helm of Mambrino. "For the moment," he said to Rose, "Whistler is the Quixote!"[12]

Whistler's belligerent attitude is obvious in the truculent tone of *Art & Art Critics.* There may have been a larger issue at stake, but the pamphlet undoubtedly served to vent its author's hostility toward the adversary he had not been able to criticize openly, or even confront, during the trial. "To have said that Mr. Ruskin's pose among intelligent men, as other than a *littérateur* is false and ridiculous," Whistler wrote, "would have been an invitation to the stake, and to be burnt alive, or stoned before the verdict was not what I came into court for."[13] After the verdict, when Whistler felt free to do as he pleased, he answered Ruskin in a pamphlet of his own. His motivation was plainly apparent to the critic Harry Quilter, who observed in the *Spectator,* "Mr. Ruskin's words, true or false, have sunk deeply, and produced all this bitter fruit; and surely no greater tribute to their power could have been shown than is found in the unreasoning virulence of Mr. Whistler against the author."[14]

As retaliation for Ruskin's graphic image of a coxcomb pelting the public with paint, Whistler described the critic's passive position before a painting in the National Gallery, standing beside his equal, an unschooled policeman:

> There they might remain till the end of time; the one decently silent, the other saying, in good English, many high-sounding empty things, like the cracking of thorns under a pot—undismayed by the presence of the Masters, with whose names he is sacrilegiously familiar; whose intentions he interprets, whose vices he discovers with the facility of the incapable, and whose virtues he descants upon with a verbosity and flow of language that would, could he hear it, give Titian the same shock of surprise that was Balaam's, when the first great critic proffered his opinion.[15]

The attempt to equate Ruskin with an ass through biblical allusion was ill conceived, as *Vanity Fair* pointed out, since it was the ass who saw the angel of the Lord and spoke the truth to Balaam. Whistler replied that Balaam's was the only ass who had ever seen an angel and, furthermore, that "we are past the age of miracles."[16] The analogy was meant only to punish Ruskin, who like Balaam's ass appeared to have made a fool of someone; Whistler wrote George Lucas that he had only kept from kicking his opponent "because he is an old man—but an old viper all the same."[17]

Although the sentences in *Art & Art Critics* sometimes run out of sense, their rhythms and alliterations faintly recall the writings of Ruskin. Indeed, Whistler's pamphlet is as polemical as *Fors Clavigera,* and often as vituperative. The *Examiner* noted that Whistler had shown himself able to equal Ruskin "on his own ground of fuliginous invective and ferocious epigram."[18] Had the defendant won the verdict, *Art & Art Critics* could be taken as an assertion of Whistler's right to make an attack as offensive as the one allowed by the court; but since the jury had ruled that Ruskin's critique was libelous indeed, the pamphlet's contentious tone can only mean that the lawsuit had taught Whistler nothing about courtesy in criticism. "Having elected to shut Mr. Ruskin's mouth with the help of a court of Justice," Harry Quilter observed in the *Spectator,* "he should surely be careful before he commits the offence which he has gone to law to punish." But Whistler seems to have been determined to offend as many people as possible, scorning the public "dragged from their beer to the British Museum" and gratuitously comparing the French with the English, concluding that "the Briton was badly begun by nature."[19] If ever Whistler flung a pot of paint in the public's face, it was in *Art & Art Critics.*

The publication of the pamphlet, a sort of sequel to the trial, effectively prolonged the publicity surrounding *Whistler v. Ruskin* and continued the debate of artists versus critics in the pages of the press. But this time the verdict of the press was unequivocal: there is scarcely a word of sympathy for Whistler in the numerous reviews of *Art & Art Critics* that appeared in the papers. The *Architect* conceded that the artist had been justified in presenting his own view of the trial and could not be blamed for writing "as a man with a grievance"; even so, the vitriolic prose of the pamphlet was bound to make people side, in the end, with Ruskin.[20]

Because the primary point of *Art & Art Critics* was that only the practitioners of an art could be capable critics, Whistler invited censure by submitting his writing to the review of professionals, who probably took uninhibited pleasure in finding fault with the artist's expository style. Several writers pointed out that while Ruskin was not (as Whistler maintained) altogether ignorant of artistic technique, having some proficiency as a draughtsman, Whistler had shown himself deplorably ignorant of the essayist's art. "As a literary production," the *Art Journal* said, "the brown-paper pamphlet is as poor, angry, inconclusive, and indescribably vulgar as we conceive anything can be."[21] The *Echo* observed that Whistler had "gone out of his way to prove that he can neither write good sense nor good English. Indeed, but for a little French he picked up during his stay in Paris, he would not have been able to express himself intelligibly at all."[22] His annoying habit of writing English "much besprinkled with French," as Henry James phrased it, was frequently condemned; and his "ponderous attempt at alliteration" in the parting blow at Ruskin—"as the Populariser of Pictures he remains the Peter Parley of Painting"—was considered so unforgivably awful that even the staunchest of admirers would be compelled to switch their allegiance.[23]

Yet Whistler seems to have welcomed even adverse reviews of *Art & Art Critics,* knowing the publicity would stimulate sales of his "belligerent Bravura in brown paper."[24] Newly impervious to criticism, he took pleasure in every sign of public indignation, forwarding newspaper clippings to Paris so that Lucas could see for himself the ire Whistler had aroused in London.[25] He was especially gratified when the pamphlet provoked a response from Tom Taylor, who had been singled out for abuse. Whistler's reference in *Art & Art Critics* to Taylor's appearance at the trial would have made it plain that his battle on behalf of the artists was also one of personal revenge, if the motive had not already been transparent. In an awkward and extended attempt to characterize critics in terms of the vehicles that conveyed them to work, Whistler made Taylor "Tough old Tom, the busy City 'Bus, with its heavy jolting and many halts; its steady, sturdy, stodgy continuance on the same old much-worn way." In another passage, Whistler used the writings of the critic (referred to only as "he of the *Times*") to exemplify "the crass idiocy and impertinence of those whose *dicta* are printed as law," extracting a quotation from *The Times* concerning his own idol Velázquez, whose work Taylor had reportedly described as "slovenly in execution, poor in colour—being little but a combination of neutral greys and ugly in its forms."[26] Ridiculing critics with their own words was one of Whistler's favorite practices: in 1892 he would compose the text of *Nocturnes, Marines, and Chevalet Pieces,* the catalogue for an exhibition at the Goupil Gallery, from contemporary criticism and the hostile testimony of witnesses in *Whistler v. Ruskin,* selecting extracts so absurd that they could stand alone as satire.

Whistler had the effrontery to send a copy of *Art & Art Critics* to Tom Taylor, inscribed "sans rancune." Taylor recognized that the pamphlet was in fact wholly rancorous, but that it was perhaps a natural outcome of Whistler's "late disagreeable legal experiences." In a letter of 6 January, he objected to the promiscuous quotation from the Velázquez critique. The extract Whistler had chosen, Taylor said, conveyed an impression opposite to the one presented by the article as a whole, which was a "fair and adequate" account of *Las Meninas.* "If the critics are not better qualified to deal with the painters than the painter in your pamphlet shows himself qualified to deal with the critics, it will be a bad day for art when the hands that have been trained to the brush lay it aside for the pen."[27]

Delighted that he had managed to draw Taylor into correspondence,[28] Whistler replied with a vindictive letter that began, "Dead for a ducat, dead! my dear Tom: and the rattle has reached me by post." The disputed quotation was accurate, he said, if admittedly taken out of context: "It is surely unimportant what more you may have written of the Master. That you should have written anything at all is your crime."[29] Taylor responded with an apology for having taken Whistler seriously—"I ought to have remembered that your penning, like your painting, belongs to the region of 'chaff'"—and Whistler, who always had to have the last word, replied by addressing

Taylor's ghost, on the pretense of having killed the critic "rather cursorily" in his last letter:

> Chaff, Tom, as in your present state you are beginning to perceive, was your fate here, and doubtless will be throughout the eternity before you. With ages at your disposal, this truth will dimly dawn upon you; and as you look back upon this life, perchance many situations that you took *au sérieux* (art-critic, who knows? expounder of Velasquez, and what not) will explain themselves sadly—chaff! Go back![30]

The letters were sent to "Atlas," presumably by Whistler, and the complete correspondence was published in the *World* on 15 January; Whistler urged Lucas to buy the paper and learn how he had left Tom Taylor "dead on the field." That single, symbolic casualty seems to have satisfied Whistler that the war was over. "I have thrashed the whole lot my dear Lucas," he wrote, "and the victory is most complete—hurrah! for our side."[31]

MATTERS OF OPINION

UNDERNEATH THE VIRULENCE of *Whistler v. Ruskin: Art & Art Critics* lie the seeds of a theory that would eventually grow, as Whistler predicted, into a philosophy of modernism. "Art is joyously received as a matter of opinion," Whistler proclaimed, "and that it should be based upon laws as rigid and defined as those of the known sciences, is a supposition no longer to be tolerated by modern cultivation."[1] With the trial behind him, the artist began to forge a new structure for art criticism that was free from the "fog of dilettantism" and respectful of the painter's province. As the title implied, the arguments of *Whistler v. Ruskin: Art & Art Critics* were inextricable from the disquisitions of the trial, and although references to the recent events at Westminster are few, the themes of *Whistler v. Ruskin* are felt as an undercurrent in every paragraph of the pamphlet.

The apparent motivation of the legal action, Whistler's animus toward art critics, is also the prevailing spirit of *Art & Art Critics.* "The cause that Mr. Whistler has at heart," said Henry James, "is the absolute suppression and extinction of the art-critic and his function."[2] Because it was undertaken with such zeal, Whistler's remedial enterprise assumed the character of a crusade: his mission was to drive intruders out of the aesthetic field. The usurpation had begun in the early decades of the nineteenth century ("the creature Critic," Whistler said, "is of comparatively modern growth"), when the critic's raison d'être had been to defend the arts against utilitarian protests. Having invaded the domain of art to endow it with morality, the critics seemed to have settled in to stay, and in efforts to preserve their purpose had continued to employ the methods of an outmoded practice.

Whistler conceded the reasonableness of writers destroying writing but maintained that the "merry game" became poor sport indeed when a pen was used to thwart a paintbrush.[3] He had previously professed his intention, as a "professor" (or practitioner) of painting, to "carry the day over ill-conditioned pendrivers whose ignorance is only equalled by their arrogance and conceit."[4] If critical ignorance originated from the writers' inexperience with paint, critical arrogance arose from their professional practice; their conceited appreciation of words confined the visual arts to the service of literature. As the popularity of Frith's works attests, narrative pictures could be enjoyed even by those with no feeling for visual images—the best-loved pictures of the Victorian age were those most readily turned to prose. Because the critic's professional achievement depended upon his power of discourse, he would naturally advocate those works that could be easily handled in words. Whistler argued in *Art & Art Critics* that the litterateur, who typically disregarded the nature of the painter's pursuit in order to advance his own, could hardly be an unbiased arbiter.

As *Whistler v. Ruskin* had shown, a reliance on words could often preclude appreciation of the "ineffable" qualities of aesthetic art. When Sir John Holker asked Whistler to identify the "peculiar beauty" of *Nocturne in Black and Gold,* the artist replied that although he could make it clear to a "sympathetic painter," he probably could not explain it to the attorney general "any more than a musician could explain the beauty of a harmony to a person who has no ear." Deprecating the aesthetic sensibilities of his interrogator, Whistler silenced other critics who might ask the same question. "Let work, then, be received in silence," he said in *Art & Art Critics,* "as it was in the days to which the penmen still point as an era when art was at its apogee."[5] Beauty, Whistler implied, was not open to discussion; art was a private province to which philistines were not admitted.

In an age permeated with suggestions of the occult, Whistler's implication that the appreciation of beauty required a special power of perception would have sounded vaguely supernatural, and the witnesses who could divine aesthetic qualities where others could discover nothing must have seemed to possess a sixth sense. The insights of Whistler's advocates arose, however, from the very sympathy the attorney general was said to lack—an awareness of the formal elements of art that compose a harmonious painting. Whistler stated in court that he expected his works to appeal only to those who understood the "technical matter"; with few exceptions, specialists in artistic technique were practicing artists. "I should not disapprove in any way of technical criticism by a man whose life is passed in the practice of the science that he criticizes," Whistler explained to the attorney general in the speech that launched the argument of *Art & Art Critics;* "but for the opinion of a man whose life is not so passed I would have as little respect as you would have if he expressed an opinion on the law. I hold that none but an artist can be a competent critic." Sympathy was not a painter's paranormal perception, but a critical qualification that grew from practical experience. Ruskin, who preached what Whistler presumed he could not perform, had become the "type of incompetence," Whistler declared in his pamphlet, "by talking for forty years of what he has never done."[6]

Yet the ability to paint proved to be an imperfect criterion of aesthetic judgment, since the painters who took the stand in *Whistler v. Ruskin* had as a group been no more laudatory than the critics of Whistler's works. As Frith avowed in the witness box, "artistic opinions differ. One may blame while another praises a work." Frith demonstrated the point himself when Serjeant Parry, apparently at Albert Moore's suggestion, introduced the name of Turner into the proceedings.[7] Parry established that Ruskin idolized the artist and Frith added that Turner should be the idol of all painters. Presumably to show that even acknowledged genius could be misunderstood, Parry mentioned the infamous "soapsuds and whitewash" remark that had once denigrated Turner's *Snow Storm—Steam-Boat off a Harbour's Mouth* (fig. 66); to everyone's astonishment, Frith concurred with the deroga-

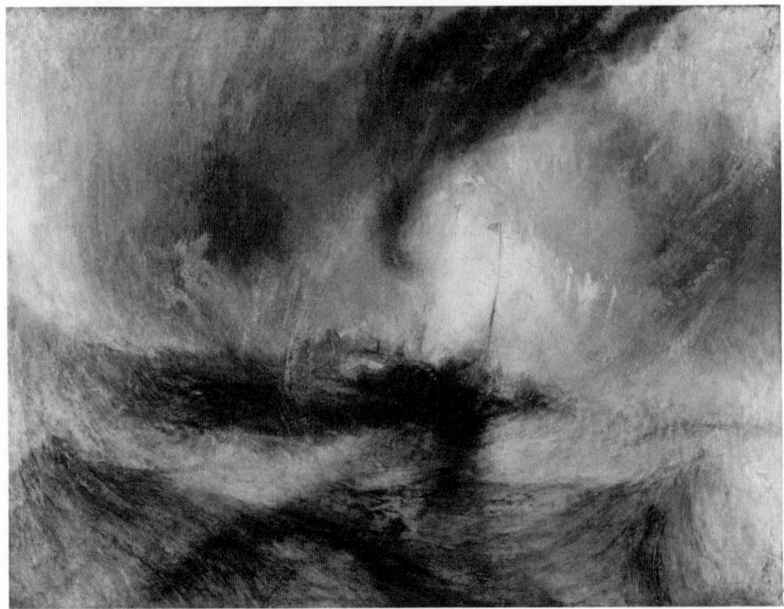

Fig. 66. J. M. W. Turner, *Snow Storm—Steam-Boat off a Harbour's Mouth,* 1842, oil on canvas. Tate Gallery, London/Art Resource, New York

tory critique and proceeded to qualify his previous approbation. Only Turner's early works deserved idolatry, he said, since the late ones were painted when the artist was "half crazy and produced works about as insane as the people who admire them." As Moore pointed out before trial to Whistler's counsel, Ruskin was especially effusive in his praise of Turner's late period. Parry would have liked to propose that the critic was capricious in his preferences, that the atmospheric imprecision of the nocturnes might have placed the plaintiff among the greatest artists of the age; if Frith's reply had not confounded his reason, Parry might also have remarked that the witness had, in effect, declared the defendant out of his mind. As it happened, the ensuing chatter about salad and mustard threw Parry too far from his course ever to arrive at an analogy of Whistler's style with Turner's.[8]

In any event, the fact that "artistic opinions differ," which has come to be a truism, was essential for Whistler to establish, since it defeated the Ruskinian notion that a work of art could be judged either right or wrong. *Whistler v. Ruskin* had been "especially edifying," the Hartford *Courant* observed, in demonstrating that there were differences of opinion regarding art works and art theories.[9] Charles Bowen alone prefaced his queries with the clause "in your opinion," but virtually every word uttered in court had to be considered in light of that important antecedent. W. G. Wills pointedly remarked that his statements were expressions of opinion and that he had no quarrel with those whose ideas differed from his own. Without an absolute truth to contradict, the dissenting views of the witnesses were not really in conflict. "Art is not bootmaking," as the *Saturday Review* remarked, "and the excellence of a work of art cannot be fixed by any amount of evidence, however eminent the source from which it proceeds."[10] Dispossessed of objective standards of judgment, art critics would lose their claim to authority; and without critical regulation, as the *Echo* observed, any artist could rise to the top of his profession: "There is evidently a good time coming for amateur painters."[11]

The old order of art criticism, chiefly comparative, had judged paintings according to the expectations of the critic; the new, more empathic system that Whistler proposed considered instead the aims of the artist. That approach was advocated in court when Baron Huddleston advised the jurors to judge for themselves "the value of the plaintiff's pictures according to his own intention and the result attained," the method apparently employed by Whistler's league of aesthetes. Rossetti testified that *Nocturne in Black and Gold* represented what was intended, Wills that the paintings were "perfect as far as they pretend to be," and Albert Moore, incontrovertibly, that Whistler had succeeded "in the qualities aimed at." Unless clairvoyant, the art critic could only surmise a painter's intentions. Whistler suggested in *Art & Art Critics* that the critic ask assistance from the artist, who too often remained unconsulted. "His work is explained and rectified without him, by the one who was never in it."[12]

If the best interpreter of a work of art was its producer, as Whistler seemed to suggest, artists would have to assume the awkward task of self-promotion. Although Whistler was particularly adept at publicizing himself and his work, several commentators recognized the irony in the limitation he proposed. The *Builder* remarked that without the attention of certain critics, Whistler's works "would never have obtained the notice and admiration they have (we say not here whether rightly or wrongly) obtained," and *Sketch* said simply that Whistler, if ignored, would surely die.[13] Defense counsel alluded to the widespread publicity that Whistler enjoyed by expressing concern for the unwary provincial who might succumb to the force of the artist's celebrity: "Some artistic gentleman from Manchester, Leeds, or Sheffield might, perhaps, be induced to buy one of the pictures because it was a 'Whistler.'"

Fame could quickly turn to notoriety, however, and a dishonorable signature could equally dispose a purchaser against a painting. The associations of a name entitled to contempt could blind a spectator to a painting. Arthur Severn recounts an anecdote, possibly apocryphal, about a juror who mistook the Titian for a Whistler and cried aloud, "Oh, horrid thing! I entirely agree with Ruskin!"[14] Had he been able to identify what he was looking at, the juror might have reacted with spontaneous approval. Years of unquestioning admiration had made Titian's works laudable by definition, as Burne-Jones demonstrated by showering the *Andrea Gritti* with superlatives, and the demand for paintings by the master's hand had created a flourishing market for forgeries. Baron Huddleston's request that the painting be proved authentic was a way of setting up a joke: a *Punch* cartoon (fig. 67) entitled "Sic Vos Non Vobis" (You do the work but another takes the credit) suggests that the number of reputed "Titians" in England had become a laughing matter. But the judge's stipulation was not entirely irrelevant, since a work by any other name would not have looked as great; an unsophisticated audience would never recognize the virtues of an unfamiliar hand. Indeed, without its glamorous label the portrait discloses its humbler self, a respectable but by no means "perfect"

SIC VOS NON VOBIS.

Auctioneer. "THIRTY GUINEAS—GOING AT THIRTY GUINEAS! ANY ADVANCE ON THIRTY GUINEAS FOR THIS FINE PORTRAIT BY TITIAN, PAINTED IN THAT GREAT MASTER'S BEST MANNER?" (*Hammer falls.*)

Brush (*to Badger*). "DOWNRIGHT DISHONEST, I CALL IT! OLD AARON'S GOT THIRTY FOR THAT TITIAN, AND HE ONLY GAVE THREE FOR PAINTING IT!"

Fig. 67. "Sic Vos Non Vobis," *Punch,* 18 November 1871

work of art, somewhat marred, as Albert Moore observed, by an over-ardent attention to finish.[15] The matter was settled in this century, when the portrait was reattributed to a lesser Venetian artist, Vincenzo Catena.

Recognizing that the name attached to a work of art could sometimes interfere with aesthetic experience, Whistler had reduced his signature, formerly painted inches high across a canvas, to a monogram that eventually emerged as a butterfly, making his name his attribute. The distinguishing mark of the artist's work was not the word "Whistler," but an element of design, an aesthetic motif. The script of the trial suggests that the emblem's significance was not common knowledge in 1878, for Whistler had to explain more than once that the "peculiar" dark marks on the frames of the nocturnes were monograms positioned to balance the color and compositions of the paintings. The butterfly was a sort of cipher whose meaning was apparent only to initiates of aestheticism. Philistines who didn't speak the language would be left to fend for themselves in Whistler's new regime, unassisted by signatures, titles, or subjects, and deprived of the counsel of critics.

Walter Hamilton, who considered himself an authority on art, wrote of Whistler's paintings, "these *may* be full of the deepest meaning and most exquisite beauty, but to the ordinary observer, it must be confessed, they convey no tangible idea whatever."[16] Identifying himself with the common man, the author betrayed his insecurity before Whistler's work; his status diminished, he took his place among the unenlightened majority. The indignation aroused by the nocturnes may suggest that the public was humiliated by what it could not comprehend, which perhaps accounts for Whistler's apparent pleasure in every critical review. If the paintings were generally misunderstood, Whistler's mission was achieved: art appreciation had been limited to those few individuals he called "artists of culture." To invite the public's admiration, Whistler proclaimed in court, would be absurd.

That the nocturnes were rendered meaningless to the masses ensured their exclusivity, but as Arnold Hauser has observed, an "ostensible lack of regard for the public" is often a cloak concealing the artist's actual wish for public approval.[17] Had Whistler been entirely indifferent to public regard, he would never have bothered to defend himself in a court of law, for the wish to air his views in public contradicted his professed elitism. His works demanded not only the sensitive response of an appreciative observer but this person's patronage as well, and *Whistler v. Ruskin* had provided an incomparable opportunity to publicize the paintings. Immediately after the trial, Algernon Graves proposed to hold a special exhibition of the *Carlyle* and the *Mother,* expecting tremendous public interest in works that had been discussed in court, and one week later the commissioner of the Grosvenor Gallery told Whistler that people were calling every day "to ask where the Whistler pictures can be seen."[18] Delighted that the populace now proclaimed his popularity, Whistler wrote his solicitor, "As you say look what an advertisement the whole affair has been—but my dear Rose the Philistines are upon me!"[19]

CONSEQUENCES AND COSTS

WHISTLER DISTRIBUTED *Art & Art Critics* as if it were a greeting card, which may account for the publication date of Christmas Eve, although the uncharitable spirit the pamphlet conveyed was sadly out of tune with the season. Inordinately proud of his production, Whistler posted copies to his few remaining friends in thanks for their support.[1] It seems not to have occurred to him that some of these artists and art critics might misconstrue his motives.

Dedicated to Albert Moore, *Art & Art Critics* was clearly intended as a gift to the artist who had proved to be Whistler's most loyal friend; yet Moore, known for avoiding unpleasantness of any kind, may have been more discomfited than flattered to find his name attached to the spiteful publication. William Michael Rossetti, whose testimony may have carried even more weight with the jury, since an art critic would not have been expected to side with an artist, must have been another of the first to receive a copy of *Art & Art Critics*. As a critic who was not a "professor," Rossetti was by Whistler's definition "a *littérateur*" and therefore subject to the artist's disdain. He might well have wondered whether the gift had been sent with Whistler's compliments and did not acknowledge the "piquant little pamphlet" until the end of January. Although his hesitation may be taken as a sign that he was uncertain how to respond, Rossetti himself blamed the delay on an attack of the gout and with customary good nature accepted *Art & Art Critics* as it was no doubt intended—in gratitude for his assistance in court. Rossetti assured Whistler that he had found in the pamphlet "not only plenty of point but plenty of reason":

> Tho' I have been figuring for so many years as a non-professional art-critic, I nevertheless agree to a very considerable extent in your thesis that the publishing of art critiques by non-professionals, whom the too easy-going public allow thus to assume a dominant authority over their own minds, is noxious and deserving of protest.[2]

Rossetti had addressed the theme himself in 1866, he reminded Whistler, in a notice in the *Fine Arts Quarterly Review.* The essay, "Mr. Palgrave and Unprofessional Criticisms on Art," had been reprinted in *Fine Art, Chiefly Contemporary,* a collection of Rossetti's writings that Whistler presumably would have known, since it contained a selection of reviews outlining his own artistic achievements. As part of his discussion of Francis Turner Palgrave's *Essays on Art,* Rossetti divided art critics into two categories, "the practical and the non-practical—or, as our business-like modern habit of speech might prefer to say, the professional and unprofessional," and with courtesy and reason that become especially apparent in comparison, made the same point as Whistler's *Art & Art Critics:*

> For our part—whatever may be the unfavourable inference as to our qualifications and performances which the reader may legitimately be pleased to draw—we suspect that the only criticism of much use in the long run is that by professional men; not only on the ground that they alone are qualified to pronounce upon technicalities, but that this knowledge of technicalities is a powerful sedative to the whole range of opinion upon art, and enables a man to say clearly and almost *ex cathedrâ* what attempts in art are desirable to be made, compatibly with the limits of technical attainment, as well as how far those limits have been reached in any particular attempt.

Rossetti himself engaged in art criticism, he explained in terms that Whistler's essay would echo, only "because the art-country is already, as it were, in a state of war, and one must take sides. . . . The golden age might include the silence of critics: but that is the golden age, and this the iron one."[3]

Rossetti seems to have mentioned his review only to underline his agreement with Whistler's position, not to allege plagiarism. He may have been wary of the pamphlet's vengeful overtones, since he explained that he had finally been prompted to write to Whistler by "an abusive little paragraph" about *Art & Art Critics* recently published in the *Academy,* which he feared might be ascribed to his hand. For the past six months, Rossetti informed Whistler, his place as reviewer of exhibitions had been taken by Joseph Comyns Carr.[4] Another "non-professional" art critic and one of the directors of the Grosvenor Gallery, Comyns Carr had been an admirer of Whistler. Immediately after the trial he had sent a sympathetic letter expressing disappointment in the verdict and complimenting Whistler on his dignified attitude in the witness box.[5] In return, Whistler sent him a copy of *Art & Art Critics,* presumably as a token of friendship. The pamphlet was forwarded to the critic in Brighton, where he was on holiday during the month of January, and received with displeasure.

Unlike Rossetti, Comyns Carr seems to have taken the message of *Art & Art Critics* personally, and he wrote a sardonic letter in reply that begins "Ave Whistler morituri te salutant" (Hail, Whistler, those about to die salute thee), a parody of the salutation of a gladiator to the Roman emperor.

> The expiring critic hails you as his deliverer; you have come to set us free from our bondage and drudgery; 'tis a noble mission. I only hope I may live (if any means of livelihood be left indeed) to witness the new regime and to note how painters like Christians love one another. From the scraps of private conversation I have chanced to hear I cannot but feel assured that the judgments of painters upon one another will be both loving and liberal.[6]

Indeed, if only because of his own belligerence, Whistler's proposed utopia in which artists would work in harmony and understanding—a "day-dream of a golden age," as Sidney Colvin called it—sounded more ironic than ideal.[7]

The mordant reply Whistler sent Comyns Carr suggests that he had taken irrevocable offense at his friend's defection. "Je m'en vant mon ami Jo," Whistler wrote, "and you can fancy the pride with which I fasten your scalp to my belt! You die hard though Joseph! and curse my future with your last cry . . . ungenerous Jo!" As Rossetti implied, Comyns Carr was probably the author of the unsigned *Academy* critique of *Art & Art Critics*, which Rossetti had reason to believe might cause offense: "We presume that this is its author's first literary production; for his own sake, we sincerely hope it may be the last, as, to tell the truth, we have seldom come across a more silly production."[8]

Comyns Carr had once been willing to contribute to a fund to pay Whistler's court costs, but true to predictions in the press, *Art & Art Critics* had alienated its author even from admirers and friends, who might otherwise have offered Whistler material assistance in his time of financial trouble;[9] for the expenses of the artist's righteous war remained to be paid. "Both plaintiff and defendant in this unhappy suit stand mulct at present in a sum of some six hundred pounds," G. A. Sala observed in the *Illustrated London News.* "Each has been presented with a very pretty oystershell, containing an 'arrangement in mother of pearl.' The fine fat oyster within falls to the share of the gentlemen of the long robe and the other legal benefactors concerned in the case."[10] Anderson Rose's account came to just over £260, a sum well beyond Whistler's crippled capacity to pay.

Ruskin's costs, largely due to the expense of having the Queen's counsel try the case, amounted to almost four hundred pounds. Burne-Jones had written Ruskin after the trial that he and William Morris were determined that the critic should not pay a penny of his legal costs. "People are longing to make a little demonstration about it," he said. A subscription to pay Ruskin's account was immediately opened at the Fine Art Society, apparently by Burne-Jones, whose five-guinea contribution headed the list and was followed by donations from his patron F. S. Ellis and from Marcus B. Huish, the society's managing director. Burne-Jones told Ruskin, however, that he did not know who had started the movement, although "they have only just anticipated other friends that I know and thousands for anything I know."[11]

On 29 November, three days after the verdict, an announcement of the campaign appeared on the front page of the *Daily News:*

> WHISTLER v. RUSKIN. MR. RUSKIN'S COSTS.
>
> A considerable opinion prevailing that a lifelong honest endeavour on the part of Mr. Ruskin to further the cause of art should not be crowned by his being cast in costs to the amount of several hundreds of pounds, the Fine Art Society have agreed to set on foot a subscription to defray his expenses arising out of the late action. Any one wishing to co-operate will oblige by communicating with the Society, 148, New Bond-street, London.

The subscription was advertised in most of the major newspapers, and within a few days the Society had published a simple circular (fig. 68) containing the text of the advertisement and an extract from the *Standard* of 30 November predicting that the requisite funds would be "speedily forthcoming":

> For admitting only for the sake of argument that Mr. Whistler's eccentric productions are the reverse of what Mr. Ruskin said of them, no one will for a moment believe that the Slade Professor did not most conscientiously believe every word he wrote; and it is to the last degree desirable that competent critics should be allowed boldly and fearlessly to express their opinion.[12]

Within ten days the campaign had raised £150 and a first list of subscriptions went on view at the society, making the names of the supporters public; by mid December the *Athenaeum* could report that the contributions amounted to £461, an amount already in excess of Ruskin's total costs.[13]

It was not until the end of April, however, that Huish wrote Ruskin to let him know that the law firm of Walker Martineau & Co. had been paid in full. Appending the list of the subscribers, Huish wrote, "I am sure that they will all join with me, in hoping that you

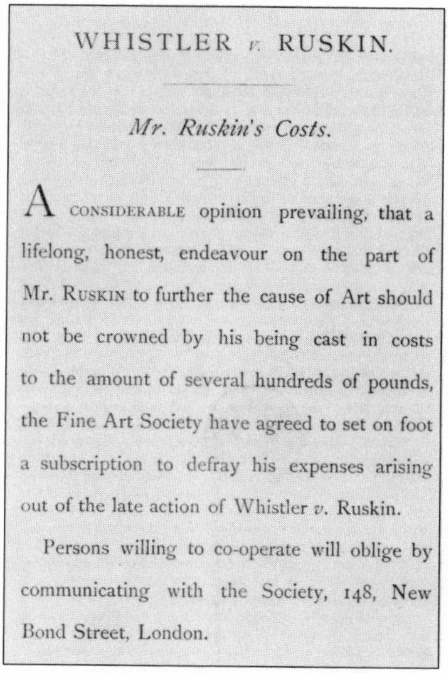

WHISTLER *v.* RUSKIN.

Mr. Ruskin's Costs.

A CONSIDERABLE opinion prevailing, that a lifelong, honest, endeavour on the part of Mr. RUSKIN to further the cause of Art should not be crowned by his being cast in costs to the amount of several hundreds of pounds, the Fine Art Society have agreed to set on foot a subscription to defray his expenses arising out of the late action of Whistler *v.* Ruskin.

Persons willing to co-operate will oblige by communicating with the Society, 148, New Bond Street, London.

Fig. 68. *Whistler v. Ruskin. Mr. Ruskin's Costs,* 1878, pamphlet published by the Fine Art Society. By permission of the British Library, London

may long be spared to disseminate by your writings the doctrine of honesty in art."[14] But Ruskin was ungrateful for the subscription, which repaid costs he felt should never have been incurred, and his reference to it in his article on Whistler seems to suggest a belief that law, rather than generosity, compelled his supporters to pay the legal fees. "The English law will . . . make my friends pay it four hundred pounds," he said, "for the expression of its own opinion to that effect"—that Whistler's work was deplorable. Illogically, Ruskin interpreted payment of costs as payment of damages and the verdict against him as symbolic approval of the substance of his remarks. In 1885, Ruskin belatedly, and grudgingly, thanked the 118 subscribers who had paid his costs six years earlier, but said that he would willingly have paid the price himself, "if only they would have helped me in the great public work which I have given certainly the most intense labour of my life to promote."[15]

Indeed, Ruskin could easily have afforded the expense of the ac-

Fig. 69. T. B. Witgman, *John Ruskin*, ca. 1886, pencil on paper. National Portrait Gallery, London

tion. Whistler, whose costs were much lower, had a greater burden to bear. As Gabriel Rossetti wrote soon after the trial:

> Alas for Jimmy Whistler! What harbour of refuge now, unless to turn Fire-King at Cremorne?—And Cremorne itself is no more! A nocturne Andante in the direction of the Sandwich Islands, or some country where tattooing pure and simple is the national School of Art, can now alone avert the long-impending Arrangement in Black on White.[16]

Well aware of Whistler's improvident ways, Rossetti recognized that bankruptcy was probably inevitable. Long before *Whistler v. Ruskin,*

Whistler had been falling into debt, and the situation had become serious by the summer of 1877, when he initiated the libel action against Ruskin. Whistler confessed to William Graham that he could not afford to repay a hundred-pound advance owing to the strain on his finances occasioned by the decoration of the Peacock Room, which had absorbed a year of his time and proved in the end "anything but remunerative," he said. "Indeed it has left me very ill off."[17] The thousand pounds Whistler claimed from Ruskin was precisely the sum Frederick Leyland had refused to pay.

The trial, then, was as much an effect of Whistler's financial trouble as it was one of its causes, although his failure to win substantial damages and recover the costs of the case did nothing to allay disaster. It may be true, as Whistler testified in court, that the sale of his works diminished after the publication of *Fors Clavigera* and, as others have maintained, that it diminished still further following the verdict of *Whistler v. Ruskin,*[18] but there is nothing to suggest that sales had been brisk since the summer of 1876, when he began work on the Peacock Room.

During the dreary winter months of 1879, as he fell ever deeper into debt, Whistler became desperate for solitude. He installed Maud Franklin, who was nearly eight months pregnant, in a London hotel and told her he was going abroad. To lend credence to the story he had letters sent to her through George Lucas, who obligingly posted them from Paris; the letters that Maud wrote Whistler, addressed to him in Paris, care of Lucas, were forwarded "under cover" to the White House. "I am sorry to give you all this trouble my dear Lucas," Whistler wrote, "but pray help us through this petite affaire and all will come right." The deception continued at least until the middle of January, when Lucas was notified that the "machinery of the whole affair" was finally working smoothly.[19]

Evidently, Whistler was spending his time alone at work in his studio, struggling to complete unfinished paintings and hoping to begin new commissions so that within a week or two, he wrote to Rose, he might be "out of the wood."[20] But fortune, Whistler said, was slapping him in the face. His creditors—wine merchants, cheesemongers, stationers, coal merchants, bootmakers, seed growers, picture liners, printsellers, theater agents, and photographers—were making demands and serving writs, which Whistler forwarded to his solicitor unopened, fearing the disturbance they would wreak on his creative energies. "Do contrive," he wrote his solicitor, "that I may not be called away from my work."[21] But the debt was too large. Coupled with the expenses incurred during the Peacock Room project and the costly construction of the White House, the accumulated costs of the legal action rendered Whistler's position practically hopeless.

Comyns Carr had suggested to Whistler that despite the judgment of the court, Ruskin ought to pay Whistler's costs in accordance with "his professed ideal of conduct."[22] Burne-Jones, suspecting that Ruskin might indeed feel some compunction, wrote Ruskin about a rumor he claimed to have heard that Whistler's solicitor had taken the case "on the principle of Dodson & Fogg" (the shady attorneys in *The Pickwick Papers* who took the case of *Bardell v. Pickwick* as a speculation, agreeing not to charge a fee unless they could procure the costs from Mr. Pickwick), "so you need not feel magnanimous ab[ou]t Whistler."[23] Anderson Rose was a devoted friend, but contrary to Burne-Jones's understanding, he did expect to be paid for his efforts on Whistler's behalf. No one knew better than he, however, that his client was incapable of producing a penny.[24]

As Ruskin's followers rallied to the cause at the Fine Art Society, it had occurred to Comyns Carr that the plaintiff's supporters might pay his legal fees, and Whistler, heartened by the idea, had suggested it to Rose:

> It is proposed that a subscription be made to pay the costs on our side—and it seems to me quite in keeping with our dignity that it should be so—Only this must be done openly with public announcement in the journals and publications of all names—so that there shall be no charitable sneaks—In short a *demonstration* on the part of all those concerned.[25]

But the demonstration Whistler expected scarcely got off the ground. The *New York Times* reported in mid December that although Whistler's friends were sympathetic, nothing was known about a subscription on his behalf.[26] The *Illustrated London News* did publish the rumor that an "influential committee" was arranging to pay Whistler's costs, and according to the Pennells, the London office of the French journal *L'Art* opened a fund; but subscribers, William Rossetti recalled, were not forthcoming.[27]

Anderson Rose, who had a particular interest in the venture's success, had planned an elaborate circular, regrettably never produced, which would open with a "quotation from Ruskin as to contradicting himself 3 times" and include salient points from evidence given by Rossetti, Wills, Moore, and "also particularly B. Jones," supplemented by extracts of published commentary (particularly the article in the *Daily News*) to show that "almost every newspaper after abusing Mr. Whistler proceeds to set upon Ruskin." Rose's draft for the text was written in the same spirit as the plaintiff's brief and similarly presupposes the existence of a loyal legion of Whistler devotees:

> The age of duelling has happily passed away and the physical condition and reported illness of one of the parties precludes the suggestion of the use of the horse whip but a British Jury have decided the following is a criticism of works of art (set out libel).
>
> The friends of Mr. Whistler believe that this is a personal and most injurious abuse of the man and a grievous wrong inflicted on Mr. Whistler for which justice is not to be obtained by law nor by the Code of Society. Many friends of Mr. Whistler deeply sympathize with him in the failure of his attempt to obtain justice and the knowledge of the fact that in making such attempt the result has been to entail upon him a very large liability for the costs of the legal proceedings. . . .
>
> Under the circumstances the admirers of Mr. Whistler's works and those who appreciate his manly courage in seeking redress for personal insult (not criticism which he courts) have determined to make this personal appeal for pecuniary assistance to enable Mr. Whistler to resume his artistic work as a painter and etcher freed from the legal claims and losses which have beset him in consequence of the violent personal attack made on him by Mr. Ruskin.[28]

But the image of a courageous yet deeply wounded Whistler would be falsified by the artist's sarcastic letter to Linley Sambourne in the *World.* Whistler seems to have decided to play a different part, and published his own, belligerent *Art & Art Critics* instead of the beseeching circular.

As part of his effort to garner sympathy for Whistler, Rose had intended to discredit the "so called Fine Art Society," which he understood had opened its subscription at Ruskin's request; until he searched the company records at the registry office, he was also under the mistaken impression that Ruskin was a shareholder.[29] The Fine Art Society had been established in 1876 by Longman, the publisher, primarily for the purpose of publishing reproductions of paintings by prominent Victorian painters, but also to exhibit works by contemporary artists; the company published original etchings from time to time, although its choice of artists to represent was generally conservative.[30] Rose informed Whistler that the society was an ordinary printseller's shop in Bond Street, smaller than the better-known establishments of Graves and Colnaghi, where Ruskin occasionally exhibited Turner paintings and works of his own in watercolor. Because the society traded as a limited company, which meant it would not be liable for its debts "if printselling turns out a bad speculation," it did not meet Rose's standards of respectability.[31]

The tactic of exposing the Fine Art Society was soon abandoned, however, presumably because the society became before long the source of Whistler's own salvation. Ernest Brown, who was responsible for organizing exhibitions and publishing etchings at the society, had become acquainted with Whistler the previous year, while working for Seeley, Jackson, and Halliday of Fleet Street, the publishers of Philip Gilbert Hamerton's "artistic periodical," *Portfolio;* a previously unpublished etching called *Billingsgate* executed by Whistler in 1859 was reproduced in the January 1878 number of the journal, and Seeley's issued an edition of one hundred artist's proofs on Japanese paper.[32] Probably on Brown's recommendation, the Fine Art Society came to Whistler's rescue in the early months of 1879 by purchasing the plates of the "Thames Set" and bringing out a second edition

Fig. 70. Photograph of Whistler by the London Stereoscopic Company. Inscribed by Whistler, "Paris in difficulty," signed and dated April 25, 1879. George A. Lucas Collection of the Maryland Institute, College of Art, on indefinite loan to the Baltimore Museum of Art, Md.

printed by Frederick Goulding, and also by continuing to buy copper plates from Whistler and impressions of newly executed etchings.[33] The society's patronage appeared to fulfill Whistler's wish, as he had expressed it to his mother, "to turn some copper into gold."[34]

As he came to see that his hope for solvency lay in prints, rather than paintings, Whistler revived his ambition to produce a set of Venetian etchings. Since the summer of 1876, when he had become diverted by the Peacock Room, Whistler had been hoping to make a trip to Italy. The Leyland project had been followed by other distractions, including the construction of the White House and preparations for *Whistler v. Ruskin,* but he may have intended to fund his travel

Fig. 71. James McNeill Whistler, *The Gold Scab,* 1879, oil on canvas. Fine Arts Museums of San Francisco; gift of Mrs. Alma de Bretteville Spreckels through the Patrons of Art and Music

with damages procured from Ruskin, since he wrote his mother in September 1878 that he hoped to leave for a six-week sojourn and return with enough prints to pay off his debts.[35] After the trial, he could not have afforded the cost of the trip, although he managed to find money for a brief visit to Paris in April. Maud Franklin went ahead, and George Lucas took her to the Louvre, the Museé du Luxembourg, the Panthéon, Notre Dame, and the races at the Bois de Boulogne before Whistler arrived at the end of the week,[36] bringing a photograph of himself inscribed "Paris in difficulty" (fig. 70).

By the next month, when papers were filed in the London Bankruptcy Court, Whistler's debts amounted to £4,500.[37] Bailiffs took possession of the White House and the sale of the artist's possessions was imminent, yet Whistler remained "in capital spirits," Maud Franklin assured Lucas, and took particular delight that year in the criticism of his Grosvenor Gallery exhibits. Still, the disagreeable prospect of liquidation strengthened his conviction that he should leave London as soon as possible. According to the *Academy,* by July he was preparing to produce a set of twenty Venetian etchings "at the urgent solicitation of some of his friends," to be followed, eventually, by a set produced in Holland and France.[38]

Nothing was said about funding for the travel such a project would entail, but when Whistler wrote Marcus Huish in August that he had "something to propose," it is likely that his proposition involved Venice. The Fine Art Society's board of directors, perhaps persuaded by Ernest Brown, voted to give Whistler the commission. The agreement, recorded on 9 September, stipulated the execution of a dozen Venetian etchings, to be published by the society in December.[39] As Whistler arranged his route to Italy he appeared in "great spirits," according to Alan Cole, undoubtedly delighted at having found a way to be out of London by the time his worldly possessions were put on the block, though he was "full of venom" for F. R. Leyland, whom he continued to blame for his fallen fortunes.[40] As a parting gesture, Whistler painted a cruel caricature of his former patron posed as a malevolent peacock, perched on the White House, and playing the piano (fig. 71).[41]

Within a fortnight of signing the contract with the Fine Art Society, Whistler, with Maud, was again in Paris, visiting his devoted friend George Lucas. And on the evening of the day that the White House was sold, ignominiously, to the art critic Harry Quilter, Whistler departed for Italy, where he would immortalize the stones of Venice.[42]

EPILOGUE

IN THE AFTERMATH OF the trial, when Whistler vanished to Venice and Ruskin to his home in the hills of Cumbria, the public's enthusiasm for art continued unrestrained, flourishing in the vacuum created by the antagonists' absence. The aesthetic movement was fundamentally an amateur production, performed in the spirit of the verdict's ambivalence; the actors, earnestly pronouncing Ruskinian doctrine in Whistlerian terms, fashioned a philosophy of art that attempted to reconcile two incompatible ideologies. In 1883 Ruskin reissued *Modern Painters,* primarily because, he said, it contained "so early and so decisive warning against the then incipient folly, which in recent days has made art at once the corruption, and the jest, of the vulgar world," but not even Ruskin could quell the clamor of popular aesthetics.[1] Whistler returned from abroad to find Oscar Wilde following in his footsteps and before long treading on his toes; he declared his disciple a dilettante, but Wilde's renown was already beyond recall. Whistler despised the vulgarity of the aesthetic movement; Ruskin deplored the frivolity. For once, they joined in lamentation: Art was on the town.

Whistler's "Ten O'Clock" lecture of 1885, delivered in evening dress at a fashionable hour, was meant to return art to the hands of "the few," who had lately been overtaken by the "intoxicated mob of mediocrity"—the public as pictured in *Art & Art Critics,* dragged from their beer to the British Museum. "And now from their midst the Dilettante stalks abroad," said Whistler, alluding to Wilde, "the amateur is loosed. The voice of the aesthete is heard in the land, and catastrophe is upon us." More seriously than did the art critics, "the many" threatened Whistler's imagined golden age, when art would be received in silence. Although he continued to argue that paintings could not be considered "from a literary point of view" and to assail Ruskin as a preacher who brought nothing but "powers of persuasion, and polish of language" to art, Whistler spoke in the "Ten O'Clock" of an even greater degradation, that art was becoming "a sort of common topic for the tea-table."[2]

Yet Whistler himself, by propelling ideas intended for the few into the courtroom and onto the pages of the periodical press, had publicized notions inherently unsuitable for general consumption; it is no wonder that aestheticism emerged from the fray in an altered, and often muddled, state. The "Ten O'Clock" lecture was the aesthetic movement's epilogue. Addressing an audience he professedly disdained, Whistler effectively provided a conclusion for the public's performance of art, bespeaking its future ill will.

APPENDIX A

RUSKIN'S INSTRUCTIONS TO DEFENSE COUNSEL

The original memorandum John Ruskin presented to his counsel to provide an "explanation of his criticism" was transcribed and included in the defendant's brief (PWC 26). The text is published here for the first time, by permission of the Ruskin Literary Trustees and Unwin Hyman Ltd. Because the only extant copy of the memorandum is itself a transcription, I have introduced punctuation marks and paragraph divisions to make the style of the text conform, whenever possible, to Ruskin's revisions as they appear in a later version of the essay, "My Own Article on Whistler," published in the Library Edition of The Works of John Ruskin *(29:585–87). Ruskin's article on Whistler begins with a paragraph written after the trial and ends, perhaps unfinished, after the eighth paragraph of the memorandum.*

The function of the critic, in his relation to contemporary art, is of course the same as that of the critic with respect to contemporary literature; namely, to recommend "authors" (the word is properly common to men of original power in both the arts) to recommend authors of merit to public attention, and to prevent authors of no merit from occupying it. All good critics delight in praising, as all bad ones in blaming (there is an interesting letter in Lockhart's *Life of Scott,* describing the vital difference between Scott and

Jeffrey in this respect);[1] and I am both proud and happy in being able to say of myself that the main strength of my life has been spent in the praise of artists who among the ancients had remained unappreciated, or among the moderns, maligned or unknown.

I use the word "maligned" deliberately and sorrowfully in thinking of the criticisms which first provoked me into literature; before I was old enough to learn with Horace and Turner, "*Malignum spernere vulgus.*"[2] If attacks such as those I refer to (in *Blackwood's Magazine,* anonymous,[3] and in recent periodicals by persons who even assert their ignorance for the pledge of their sincerity) could be repressed by the care and acumen of British Law, it would be well alike for the dignity of Literature and the interests of Art. But the Bench of honourable Criticism is as truly a Seat of Judgment as that of Law itself, and its verdicts, though usually kinder, must sometimes be no less stern. It has ordinarily been my privilege to extol, but occasionally my duty to condemn, the works of living painters. But no artist has ever yet been suspected of purchasing my praise, and this is the first attempt that has been made through the instrumentality of British Law to tax my blame. I do not know the sense attached, legally, to the word "libel"; but the sense rationally attaching to it is that of a false description of a man's person, character, or work, made wilfully with the purpose of injuring him.

And the only answers I think it necessary to make to the charge of libel brought against me by the plaintiff, are first, that the description given of his work and character is accurately true so far as it reaches; and secondly, that it was calculated, so far as it was accepted, to be extremely beneficial to himself

[1] John Gibson Lockhart in *Memoirs of the Life of Sir Walter Scott* (Edinburgh: R. Cadell, 1837–38) states: "It struck me that there was this great difference—[Francis, Lord] Jeffrey, for the most part, entertained us, when books were under discussion, with the detection of faults, blunders, absurdities, or plagiarisms; Scott took up the matter where he left it, recalled some compensating beauty or excellence for which no credit had been allowed, and by the recitation, perhaps, of one fine stanza, set the poor victim on his legs again" (quoted in *Works of Ruskin,* 29:585 n. 3). Lord Jeffrey (1773–1850) was a Scots critic and judge.

[2] "To scorn the noxious crowd" (Horace).

[3] "The Exhibitions," *Blackwood's Edinburgh Magazine* 40 (October 1836): 550–51. Ruskin's "Reply to 'Blackwood's Criticism of Turner'" is reprinted in *Works of Ruskin,* 3:635–40.

and still more to the public. In the first place, the description given of him is absolutely true. It is my constant habit, while I praise without scruple, to weigh my words of blame in every syllable. I have spoken of the plaintiff as ill-educated and conceited, because the very first meaning of education in an artist is that he should know his true position with respect to his fellow-workmen, and ask from the public only a just price for his work. Had the plaintiff known either what good artists gave, habitually, of labor to their pictures, or received, contentedly, of pay for them, the price he set on his own productions would not have been coxcombry but dishonesty.

I have given him the full credit of his candid conceit, and supposed him to imagine his pictures to be really worth what he asked for them. And I did this with the more confidence, because the titles he gave them showed a parallel want of education. All well-informed painters and musicians are aware that there is an analogy between painting and music. The public would at once recognize the coxcombry of a composer, who advertised a study in chiaroscuro for four voices, or a prismatic piece of color in four flats, and I am only courteous in supposing nothing worse than coxcombry in an artist who offers them a symphony in green and yellow for two hundred pounds.

Nor is the final sentence, in which the plaintiff is spoken of as throwing his palette in the public's face, other than an accurate, though a brief, definition of a manner which is calculated to draw attention chiefly by its impertinence. The standard which I gave, thirty years ago, for estimate of the relative value of pictures, namely, that their preciousness depended ultimately on the clearness and justice of the ideas they contained and conveyed,[4] has never been lost sight of by me since, and has been especially dwelt upon lately, in such resistance as I have been able to offer to the modern schools which conceive the object of art to be ornament rather than edification. It is true that there are many curious collectors of libraries, in whose eyes the binding of the volumes is of more importance than their contents; and there are many patrons of art who benevolently comply with the fashion of the day, without expecting to derive more benefit from the fronts of their pictures

[4] *Modern Painters,* vol. 1, in *Works of Ruskin,* 3:92: "But I say that the art is greatest which conveys to the mind of the spectator, by any means whatsoever, the greatest number of the greatest ideas; and I call an idea great in proportion as it is received by a higher faculty of the mind, and as it more fully occupies, and in occupying, exercises and exalts, the faculty by which it is received."

than from the backs of their books. But it is a critic's first duty in examining designs proposed in public exhibitions to distinguish the artist's work from the upholsterer's; and although it would be unreasonable to expect from the hasty and electric enlightenment of the nineteenth century, any pictorial elucidations of the Dispute of the Sacrament, or the School of Athens,[5] he may yet, without severity of exaction, require of a young painter that he should show the resources of his mind no less than the dexterity of his fingers and without libellous intention may recommend the spectator to value order in ideas above arrangement in tints, and to rank an attentive draughtsman's work above a speedy plasterer's.

And it gives me no little pain to be compelled to point out, as the essential ground of the present action, the confusion between art and manufacture, which, lately encouraged in the public mind by vulgar economists, has at last, in no small measure, degraded productions even of distinguished genius into hastily marketable commodities, with the sale of which it is thought as unwarrantable to interfere as with the convenient iniquities of popular trade.

This feeling has been still further fostered by the idea of many kindly persons that it is a delicate form of charity to purchase the feeble works of incompetent artists, and by the corresponding effort of large numbers of the middle classes under existing conditions of social pressure, to maintain themselves by painting and literature, without possessing the smallest natural faculties for either.

I will confine myself with reference to this (in my estimate) infinitely mischievous tendency of the public mind, to the simple statement that in flourishing periods, whether of trade or art, the dignity of operative merchant and artist was held alike to consist in giving, each in their several fashion, good value for money and a fair day's work for a fair day's wages. The nineteenth century may perhaps economically applaud itself on the adulteration of its products and the slackness of its industries; but it ought at least to instruct the pupils of its schools of Art, in the ancient code of the Artist's honour, that no piece of work should leave his hands, which his diligence

[5] Raphael, *Disputa* or *Disputation over the Sacrament* (1509) and *School of Athens* (1510–11), Stanza della Segnatura, Vatican, Rome. In 1872 Ruskin defined the *Disputa* ("Raphael's Theologia") as "the most perfect effort yet made by art to illustrate divine science" (*The Eagle's Nest,* in *Works of Ruskin,* 22:156).

could further complete, or his reflection further improve, and in the ancient decision of the Artist's pride, that his fame should be founded not on what he had received, but on what he had given.

I will only add, in conclusion, that whatever may be therefore of this action, I cannot but hold it fortunate for myself that it should have been brought, since it justifies in my own mind the retirement from public life to which I was before sufficiently inclined by the languor of advancing age, without having been in all things (as my first written book clearly shewed) a *laudator temporis acti.*[6] I have now long enough endeavoured, much to my own hindrance, to vindicate from the impatient modern some respect for the honesties of Commerce and veracities of Art which characterised the simplicity of his uncivilized forefathers. I contentedly henceforward leave the public of this brighter day to appease the occasional qualms that may trouble the liberty of their conscience and the latitude of their taste with philosophy that does nobody any good, and criticism that does nobody any harm.

[6] "A praiser of times past" (Horace).

APPENDIX B

BURNE-JONES'S STATEMENT TO DEFENSE COUNSEL

The statement Edward Burne-Jones made to Ruskin's attorneys was provided, according to the defendant's brief, "with a view to giving counsel the opinion of an artist on Mr. Whistler's work" (PWC 26). The copy included in the brief is a transcription of Burne-Jones's written statement, which has not survived. Because that transcription generally lacks punctuation marks and paragraph divisions, the form of the text has been edited to improve legibility.

The point and matter seems to me to be this, that scarcely any body regards Whistler as a serious person. For years past he has so worked the art of brag that he has succeeded in a measure amongst the semi-artistic part of the public, but amongst artists his vanities and eccentricities have been a matter of joke of long standing. Now when he first went before the public there was sufficient excellence in his work to make all artists look forward to his future with some interest, but the qualities he possessed appeared soon to be exhausted and it is long since there has been any expectation of further fulfillment. In fact, he lacks certain qualities *necessary* to the making of a *real* picture. It is clear by now that the deficiency is insuperable, and he is clever enough to know it; and being notoriously without any principle or sentiment of the dignity of his art, he is perpetually eager to make the world believe that his own low standard of excellence is the standard that is alone desirable.

It is a matter of jest, but a matter of fact, that he has been ceaseless in all company for years past in depreciating the work of all artists, living or dead, and without any shame at all proclaiming himself as the only painter who has lived. If he were asked if this were the case he would not care to deny it, for he has a perfect estimate of the value of this trumpeting, knowing that there will be always some to be staggered by it and some to believe it.

He has never yet produced anything but sketches, more or less clever, often stupid, sometimes sheerly insolent, but sketches always. Not once has he committed himself to the peril of completing anything. For all artists know that the difficulty of painting lies in the question of completion. Thousands can sketch cleverly, amateurs often as adroitly as artists. The test is finish. In finishing, the chance of failure increases in overwhelming proportion. To complete and not lose the first vigor, that is what all painters have always set before themselves, all without exception.

That Whistler should be an incomplete artist on such hard terms concerns himself alone, but that for years past he should have been proclaiming this incompleteness with all his power of speech to be the only thing worth attaining concerns art itself and all artists; and Ruskin's forty years of striving to rouse the ideal of his country's shell would have ended lamely if he could have quietly let pass such an exhibition as Mr. Whistler's theory and practice. His plan, in short, has been to found a school of incapacity, to declare loudly that no picture is of value for the qualities that all mankind, ancients and modern, have striven for and demanded; and it is no secret in London that he has often announced himself not merely as the only living artist, but the only artist that has been.

Meantime his work has the merit that one sees in the work of a clever amateur. I think this would be obvious to any unprejudiced person who could use his eyes; and if one of his later pictures were brought into court and the price named, I should think the whole matter would resolve itself into a jest. There is often not so much appearance of labor in one of his pictures as there is in a rough sketch by another artist, and yet he asks and gets as much for one of these as most artists do for pictures skillfully and conscientiously finished.

And I think Mr. Ruskin's language is justified on the grounds of the scandal that the violent puffing of what is at best a poor performance brings upon art. I am sure that an ordinary intelligent person would think that a bad joke was being put upon him if he were asked to admire as a serious work of art the sort of picture condemned by Mr. Ruskin.

It needs no length of explanation for the causes that should for a time give Mr. Whistler a little notoriety, but if any one caring as Mr. Ruskin does for the question of art, and looking with any reverence on the works handed down to us, could think this meaningless scribbling should be looked upon as real art, for admiration and reward I think he might lay his pen down and never write again, for art would be at an end.

APPENDIX C

SOURCE NOTES TO *WHISTLER v. RUSKIN*

The transcript of *Whistler v. Ruskin* in Part Two is a compilation of contemporary accounts that appeared in London newspapers. Only one unpublished source has been used—the notes taken in court by a clerk of J. Anderson Rose, which sometimes corroborate questionable press reports or contain material the reporters apparently ignored. Whistler's rendition of the trial in *The Gentle Art of Making Enemies* (1890), having already been subjected to extensive revision, was not used as a source; however, particularly telling differences and elaborations are signaled in the notes that accompany Part Two or quoted below as textual variants.

Constructing the transcript from various secondhand sources entailed a number of refittings and refinements. In some cases, a large block could be extracted from a single account, either because that testimony appeared only once or because the discrepancies among reports were minor or irrelevant. More often, one theme appears to have inspired several variations, and when two or more newspapers printed similar reports, the first published, or in some cases the more graceful or coherent version, was selected. In the redaction of the text, sentences were rearranged when the meaning was improved but the spirit unimpaired, and syntactical adjustments were made as necessary to preserve coherence. Third-person accounts were converted to first, verb tenses altered, conjunctions added or deleted, pronouns adapted, antecedents clarified, antiquated words (*amongst, anecdotical*) replaced with modern equivalents, and spelling, capitalization, and punctuation converted to modern American usage. The titles of paintings (given in italics) were edited for consistency. Titles of paintings by Whistler exhibited at the Grosvenor Gallery in 1877 were retained in their original form; the modern titles of other works referred to in the transcript by their former or colloquial titles are given in the notes to Part Two. Editorial insertions are bracketed, and quotations from published sources, such as *Fors Clavigera* and Tom Taylor's *Times* reviews, are reprinted in their original form.

Sources, significant textual variants, and important editorial emendations are noted below; except for spelling changes, the variants are direct quotations. A word followed by a square bracket signifies that the portion of the transcript preceding and including that word is taken from the cited source. When a word or phrase is isolated in brackets, the source note refers to differences surrounding only that passage.

The following abbreviations have been used; all newspapers were published in London.

DC	*Daily Chronicle,* 26 and 27 November 1878 (A.M.)
DT	*Daily Telegraph,* 26 and 27 November 1878 (A.M.)
DN	*Daily News,* 26 and 27 November 1878 (A.M.)
Echo	*Echo,* 25 and 26 November 1878 (P.M.)
ES	*Evening Standard,* 25 and 26 November 1878 (P.M.)
Globe	*Globe & Traveller,* 25 and 26 November 1878 (P.M.)
MP	*Morning Post,* 26 and 27 November 1878 (P.M.)
Notes	Plaintiff's counsel's manuscript trial notes, Pennell-Whistler Collection 27
PMG	*Pall Mall Gazette: An Evening Newspaper and Review,* 25 and 26 November 1878 (P.M.)
Times	*The Times,* 26 and 27 November 1878 (A.M.)
WD	*Weekly Dispatch,* 1 December 1878
WEN	*West End News and London Advertiser,* 30 November 1878
Whistler	J. M. Whistler, "The Action," in *The Gentle Art of Making Enemies* (1890), 1–19

INTRODUCTION

2 [special] PMG: common

3 McNeill Whistler,] ES

4 art critic.] Globe

23 public's face.] ES

26 in damages.] Globe / PMG: The plaintiff, in his statement of claim, alleged that the defendant had libeled him in a criticism upon one of his pictures exhibited at the Grosvenor Gallery, called a Nocturne in Black and Gold." The passage complained of appeared in *Fors Clavigera,* which is contributed to and edited by the defendant.

29 public view.] DT

34 crowded] ES

35 being filled.] DN

PLAINTIFF'S CASE

2 many years,] ES

other countries.] Echo

5 in art.] Globe

6 [. . . all of you.] DC: as would probably be known to the gentlemen of the jury

9 immortality.] DN

highest reputation.] DC

13 conclusion] ES

14 injustice.] Globe

15 in America,] ES

18 to Moscow] Times

Russian government.] ES

19 [. . . St. Petersburg,] ES: therefore resided in Russia

20 [studied] ES: followed

[acquired] ES: earned

21 America.] Times / ES: as a painter and an artist

Mr. Whistler] ES

an etcher,] Times / ES: was not merely an artist, but was an etcher or engraver

22 [. . . department of art.] Times: and in that capacity had likewise distinguished himself

35 Mr. Whistler] ES

36 in art.] Times

37 his theories.] ES

41 his pictures.] Times / ES: as to producing the greatest effect from colors

42 [. . . a theory] Times: adopted such a theory

his own] ES

46 Grosvenor Gallery] Times

I understand,] DT

48 Academy of Arts] Echo

55 highest respect] ES / Echo: held in great admiration

56 own profession.] Echo

63 Coutts Lindsay,] ES

65 in either.] Times

66 Burne-Jones:] ES / Times: and then, referring to Mr. Whistler, he wrote as follows

75 impertinently, indulged.] DN

76 the paragraph] Echo

complained of:] ES

84 public's face.] DN

87 his defense] ES

88 is privileged,] Echo

89 public view.] ES

91 the public.] Echo

95 same amount.] DC

96 ungentlemanly,] ES

97 on art] Times

98 injury] DN

99 estimation.] Times

103 [sphere of life] Echo: ordinary life

104 art critic?] ES

106 [. . . an impostor,] ES: that he exhibited works which were akin to willful imposture

107 impudent coxcomb.] DT

109 powerful man.] ES

110 entitled to.] DN

113 single picture] ES

116 proper criticism.] DT

117 be produced,] DC

118 this court.] Globe

119 Palace Hotel,] ES

120 be procured] Echo

122 of Spain.] ES

128 by the jury,] ES

131 Westminster Hall,] Globe

135 those that] ES

140 his mind] Globe

alleged libel.] ES

143 never shall.] Globe

146 St. Petersburg,] Globe

years of age.] Times / ES: I lived in that city for twelve or fourteen years / Globe: I left there as a lad.

an engineer] PMG

148 and Moscow.] Times / ES: the engineer of the St. Petersburg and Moscow Railway.

150 about a year] ES / Globe: a short time

151 to America.] Globe

152 return to Europe?] ES

153 1856,] DN

stayed] DN: resided

154 [Gleyre] *emended from* Gavie / ES: Glaird / PMG: Glayre / DT: Gavre / DN: Glare / Notes: Cleyer

155 three years.] DT / Echo: some time

156 Du Maurier.] Globe / Echo: well known artists

162 [You finally] MP: Your family

165 for dates.] DT

167 four years ago,] ES

168 my mother.] PMG

169 Grosvenor Gallery opened.] Globe / ES: I have sent no pictures since then. At that time the Grosvenor Gallery opened

170 Mr. Phillip,] DN, *emended from* Phillips / Times: the well-known artist of Spanish subjects.

Royal Academician.] Echo

173 *Little White Girl.*] DN / Echo: The White Girl / Notes: "The White Girl" not exhibited at the Royal Academy, at the Paris Salon.

174 I have] ES

also] Echo

175 Paris.] ES

[exhibited] ES / DN: painted

for sale.] DN

176 [About five years ago] Echo: Four or five years ago / Globe: subsequently

[exhibited] Echo: exhibited smaller pictures

178 great many] ES

179 here and abroad.] Globe

The Hague] DN / ES: Netherlands Exhibition

1864,] ES / Echo: in 1864 or 1865 / Globe: many years ago / DT: in 1865

182 there.] DN

184 Windsor Castle;] DT

186 [summer exhibition] DN: in the summer / Echo: in the winter

187 any request?] ES

189 Coutts Lindsay.] DN

196 gave me.] ES

198 subscribed for.] DN

and gold.] DT

200 were disposed of.] ES / Notes: 2 sold, 1 presented, and 1 for sale.

[One of them,] ES: two of them

Blue and Gold,] DN

201 [the Honorable] Echo: Sir

203 two hundred guineas.] ES

204 [in lieu of] Notes: in exchange for

[a former] ES: earlier

206 Leyland.] DN

207 [. . . *Black and Gold,*] DN: The one that was for sale was in black and gold.

210 extensive sale.] ES / PMG: I cannot say whether the "Fors Clavigera" has an extensive circulation / DN: I believe it has an extensive sale / Notes: It is my impression that "Fors Clavigera" has a large circulation.

211 I know.] PMG

214 [. . . as before.] Globe: Since Mr. Ruskin's criticism appeared I have not sold a picture at anything like that price / PMG: I have not been able to sell my pictures at the old price.

217 Philip II;] ES / Notes: The Arrangement in black

Black and Gold,] Notes

225 *Black and Gold.*] ES

228 [. . . to your pictures?] ES: What is your definition of a "nocturne"?

229 I wished] DT / ES: I have, perhaps, meant rather

230 the picture] DN / ES: pristine

anecdotal interest] DT / ES: sort of interest

232 color first.] DN

235 symmetrical result.] Globe / ES: I made use of any incident of it which shall bring about a symmetrical result. / PMG: with some incident or object of nature in illustration of my theory.

237 [line] Times: light

form and color.] DT

238 [pieces,] Times: views

239 [set] DT: lot

of them;] ES

243 such intention.] Globe

245 [. . . paintings] Notes: I devoted myself to etching, not absolutely, "Scenes on the River" and painted same.

248 been received?] ES

249 academy committee.] Globe

254 painting was called] ES

255 [*Grey*] ES: Green

Painter's Mother,] PMG

263 [night piece,] Notes: picture

at Cremorne] ES

268 artistic arrangement.] ES

269 a "nocturne."] PMG

271 picture? *(Laughter)*] ES

272 of Cremorne.] Notes, *followed by* supposed to consider it is at nighttime

278 Yes.] ES

282 [Is it not what] ES: It is what

284 may be so. *(Laughter)*] DN

285 art critic?] ES

286 [meeting] Notes: seeing

Ruskin.] PMG / Globe: I do not know Mr. Ruskin / ES: Yes.

287 works on art.] ES / Notes: I know him by reputation as having written works on Art / PMG: I have read some of his works.

288 *Modern Painters.*] PMG / Notes: I have not read his works / ES: I believe *Stones of Venice* is his; I know that *Modern Painters* is his.

291 can improve it?] ES / Globe: a picture shall only be exhibited when it is finished—when nothing can be done to improve it.

292 correct view.] Globe / ES: Very likely / Notes: I believe those are his opinions.

295 [Very likely.] Times: and that he should give value for what he received.

297 [. . . irrespective of value?] DN: Artists do not get as much as they can for their pictures, but are supposed to give the full value for their money? / Globe: But Artists always give good value for their money, don't they?

303 finished picture.] ES

304 more with it.] DN / Notes: I did not intend to bestow any more labor upon it.

306 every painting.] ES

308 [on the river.] Notes: I was paid 200 guineas for it. . . .

[*Nocturne*] ES: picture

309 on the Thames] DN

by moonlight.] Notes / ES: by summer night.

311 *Blue and Silver,*] DN

312 Mrs. Leyland,] Notes, *emended from* Mr. Leyland

[*Arrangement in Black*] DN: and Gold

313 to sell;] ES / Notes: I did not send it for sale, it was for myself, I did not say I ever intended to sell it.

314 Mr. Irving's,] Notes

317 the "arrangement." *(Laughter)*] ES / WEN: Mr. Irving was not in the arrangement.

319 in black.] Echo

322 [Arrangement] Notes: Harmony

324 black ground.] ES / Notes: This was not for sale, and it was in the Catalogue.

for sale.] Notes.

329 is here] ES

in court.] Notes

Amber and Black;] ES

330 painted over.] Notes / ES: I painted that one.

340 [invite] Whistler: incite

345 unless they are] ES

overlooked.] Echo

348 it off? *(Laughter)*] ES

349 your pardon?] Globe / Echo: I don't understand you.

351 profession. *(Laughter)*] Echo / Globe: Well, I am using a term that applies rather, perhaps, to my own work.

352 compliment. *(Laughter)*] Globe

353 of your pictures?] DT

354 of days—*(Laughter)*] Echo

355 [. . . to finish it.] Times: The "Nocturne in Black and Gold" he knocked off in a couple of days. He painted the picture one day and finished it off the next. / Notes: done in a day, completed on the second.

356 mellow? *(Laughter)*] ES / Echo: Do you allow your pictures to mellow? / Whistler: You put your pictures upon the garden wall, Mr. Whistler, or hang them on

the clothes line, don't you—to mellow?

358 not understand.] Echo

359 on the garden wall?] ES

361 understand now.] Echo

362 [grieved] Echo: sorry

364 on with my work.] ES

365 good thing] PMG

366 *Black and Gold)*] Notes

367 my pupils.] PMG

368 [. . . two hundred guineas?] ES: And that was the labor for which you asked 200 guineas?

371 a lifetime. *(Applause)*] Globe / ES: It was for the knowledge gained through a lifetime / Notes: It is the knowledge of 20 years which I ask the price for / PMG: I do not ask 200 guineas for a couple of days' work; the picture is the result of the studies of a lifetime.

372 arena for applause.] Globe

373 [. . . clear the court.] Notes: The Judge requested expressions of feeling would be suppressed.

377 approve of criticism?] ES

378 criticize the critics.] Globe

381 as little] ES

respect] WD / Whistler: regard / ES: opinion

382 on the law.] ES / Globe: I respect the opinion of those who are experienced in the art.

384 [unjust] Whistler: inimical

incompetent.] Globe

389 *Parry objected.*] ES

393 for pictures.] PMG

397 [given] Whistler: belonging

398 Battersea Bridge.] ES

400 150 guineas.] Globe

402 before you.] Whistler *adds* (Laughter.)

417 works have been.] ES

422 the defendant.] Globe

424 the jury should] DN

benefit of seeing] ES

425 for that purpose.] DN

435 Grosvenor Gallery.] ES

440 probate court;] Globe

441 for luncheon.] DN

443 deposited with] ES

Mr. Noseda,] Globe

449 of the jury.] ES

451 *the bench.*] PMG

453 by moonlight.] ES

454 [. . . is the bridge?] ES: Is this part of the picture at the top Old Battersea Bridge?

456 *of the picture.*] Globe

459 toward London.] ES

461 further distance.] Globe

462 Battersea Bridge?] Echo

464 Battersea Bridge.] Notes / Echo: I did not intend it to be a correct painting of the bridge.

466 of the bridge,] Globe

467 moonlight scene.] Echo

469 represent nothing.] Globe

473 Yes,] Echo

firework.] Globe

474 the frame?] Echo

477 monogram,] Globe

the canvas;] Times

479 of art.] Echo

486 [flattered] Whistler: encouraged

488 harmony of color.] ES

490 Mrs. Leyland.] DN

492 Battersea Reach.] Globe / ES: It is a picture of the Thames by moon-

light, looking up the river near Battersea.

493 that picture?] ES

494 [. . . of the picture] ES: the work of that

one day,] Echo

495 my mind.] ES

496 *was postponed.*] Echo / Notes: Cross-examination postponed till picture brought back

499 Palace Hotel.] PMG

Carlyle's portrait] Globe / DN: I have also painted the portrait of Mr. Carlyle / Notes: my mother

502 Philip II,] ES

503 last year,] Notes

504 another picture] ES

506 this year;] Globe

507 *Blue and Yellow.*] ES

508 offered for sale.] Notes

509 [been sent for)] Notes: about to be brought

511 the libel.] Globe

[. . . harmony and arrangement,] ES: This subject of the arrangement of colors

513 life study.] PMG / ES: has been a life study to my mind / Notes: It has been the study of my life as to the way the pictures are to be painted.

516 Certainly.] ES

518 ability.] Globe / ES: The pictures are painted off generally from my own thought and mind. Sketching on paper is very rare with me.

523 Certainly.] ES / Globe: All the hand work is done rapidly.

524 greatly upon] Globe

my hand.] Notes / Globe: rapidity

529 *hearing for*] Globe

luncheon] DN / Globe: a short time

531 *exhibited there.*] Globe / DT: The Court then adjourned for lunch, and during the interval, the jury visited the Probate Court, to view the pictures which had been collected at the Westminster Palace Hotel and brought over to Westminster Hall.

537 black and gold.] ES

538 other fireworks.] Globe

541 [. . . part of another.] Notes: One whole day it took me to paint, and finished it afterwards Globe: It occupied two days.

finished picture.] ES

543 monogram,] Globe

544 color out.] DN / Notes: The monogram is placed there not to present a proper balance.

546 of that picture?] ES

549 no ear.] Globe / Echo: It is impossible for me to explain to you the beauty of the picture, any more than for a musician to explain to you the beauty of harmony in a particular piece of music if you had no ear for music / ES: It would be impossible for me to explain to you, I am afraid, although I dare say I could to a sympathetic ear.

550 [anybody] ES: Mr. Ruskin

551 no peculiar beauty?] DN

552 distinct evidence] ES

556 [. . . I can't answer.] Globe: It is not for me to say that he could fairly do so.

557 conclusion.] DN / ES: I do not

think that any artist would come to that conclusion.

unbiased people] Echo / ES: uninfluenced people / Globe: persons comparatively ignorant of art

558 recognize] ES / Echo: express the opinion

559 night scene.] Echo

563 [executed] Globe: accomplished

564 [. . . worth the money.] Echo: as being worth £200 / Globe: and which I think worth 200 guineas / Notes: I think conscientiously that it is worth the money asked.

565 other works.] ES

566 different view.] Echo

569 [artistic impression] Notes: or arrangement, as a problem worked out

570 carried away] ES

571 the Thames;] Globe / ES: Many of my works are sketches of scenes on the Thames.

572 most of them.] Notes

574 in Tite Street.] Echo

577 special study,] ES

578 [and frequently] ES: from time to time

criticizing pictures.] Globe / DN: in art criticism

579 [since 1862] Globe: 1860 / Notes: 1863

Mr. Ruskin.] ES

580 art critic.] Echo

582 [well aware of] Globe: understand

583 Whistler's pictures,] ES

[its] ES: their

meaning.] DN

587 about it.] ES

588 silver before.] Globe

591 Yes.] ES

592 upon them?] Globe / ES: Have you formed any judgment as to the nocturne?

593 that picture] DN / Echo: the blue and silver painting of "Battersea from the River" / DC: The fine art silver painting of Battersea from the river / DN: the pale picture

597 [artistic and beautiful] Echo: very beautiful artistic

598 [pale but bright moonlight.] Times: pale bright moonlight / DT: bright but pale moonlight / Notes: the pale blue moonlight

600 observation,] DN

601 darker.] Globe / Notes: it is a dark blue moonlight.

602 cascade.] Echo

604 is that] Globe

[. . . indefinite kind;] Globe: The indefiniteness of it is part of the subject

606 [the darkness] Echo: indefiniteness

[the brightness] Echo: light / Notes: lightning

614 portrait of Carlyle] ES

616 Yes.] Echo

617 of art?] ES

618 Objection!] Globe

620 the gallery.] Notes

622 [treated] Echo: but painted

[degree] Echo: amount

[. . . peculiarity] Times: with a certain peculiarity.

623 most artists.] ES

[excellent] Echo: good

624 my judgment.] Globe

631 admire them] ES

sincerely.] Times, Notes / ES: "much" / Globe: very much

632 two exceptions.] Echo / ES: but not with exception.

635 decidedly.] ES

636 good artist.] Echo

639 [criticizing works of art,] DN: writing out criticisms / Notes: I have been a critic

severity.] ES / DN: I have occasionally written severe criticisms.

641 *Academy.*] Globe

personally] ES

642 devoted to art.] Globe / ES: gentleman who has a great love of art

643 the subject] ES

many pictures.] Globe / Echo: often praised artists for their works very much.

[He is] Notes: I believe he is

646 Cremorne?] ES

647 very dark.] Globe

648 No,] ES

gem.] Echo

654 [. . . other painters.] Echo: It was unlike most other paintings / Notes: It is unlike the painting of other artists.

656 Yes,] ES

658 think so.] Globe

659 Gaiety] DT / Echo: "The Grasshopper at the Gaiety."

Paris.] Notes

661 Because] Globe

was intended.] Echo

662 [general effect] Globe: appearance

such a scene,] ES

663 [finished] ES: "painted"

artistic skill.] Echo / ES: a considerable amount of manipulative skill / Globe: manipulative skill of an artist

665 No,] DN

667 shortsightedness.] Notes

675 like this?] ES

678 value of it] Globe

(Laughter)] ES

price."] Times / Globe: It is a stiffish price.

682 any picture.] ES / Notes: I am too poor to give it.

686 other artists;] DN

687 my opinion] ES

[. . . lighter pictures] ES: relative to the pictures produced

689 indifferent picture,] DN

conscientious artist.] Notes

690 be represented] Globe / Notes: no harm in representing fireworks

692 good subject.] ES / Globe: it is a very light subject.

694 [an artist] Echo and DT: and art critic.

695 [. . . galleries abroad.] Globe: the principal picture galleries in Europe.

698 [fifteen] Notes: five

years.] ES

that period] Globe

Academy and] ES

699 recently] Notes

Grosvenor Gallery.] ES

700 Royal Academy.] Notes

701 pictures well.] Globe

702 fourteen years.] DN

Mr. Ruskin,] Globe

703 here today.] DN

704 pictures produced?] Globe

708 [no living painter,] Globe: no other living man
709 [in the same way,] Globe: so well
710 [beautiful] Echo: real
works of art;] ES
paint as well.] Notes / Globe: do as good.
711 [. . . extraordinary thing] Globe: for one thing
712 the air,] ES
714 As to] Globe
black and gold,] ES / Globe: the Cremorne picture
atmospheric effects are] Globe
715 simply marvelous.] ES
716 mind, wonderful.] Echo
719 [consummate] ES: beautiful
consummate art.] DN
720 reasonable price?] ES
721 [. . . now sell for,] ES: I should say that as prices go
should think] Globe
722 [. . . too high] ES: Not an unreasonable price / Times: is not too large a price / Notes: a very reasonable price
724 and days.] Echo / Globe: you can't expect him to work very long for one hundred pounds, any more than you gentlemen would.
(Laughter)] Globe
726 labor expended.] Echo
727 pictures myself.] ES
of Carlyle.] Notes
728 a picture.] ES
730 in 1877.] Notes
732 of artists,] ES
733 of a school.] Globe / Notes: I am not the head of a particular school of art
737 in England.] ES
[same style of picture as] Notes: as well as was
738 Velázquez.] Globe / Notes: Velasquez and others were of a school.
741 painting of it.] ES / Echo: the witness could not say that the pictures in question were exquisite works of art, but they were good
743 gold nocturne.] Globe
745 [. . . "originality."] Globe: there is a great deal of originality in Mr. Whistler's works / Times: he thought there was great originality in the plaintiff's pictures. He could not call it eccentricity.
746 a picture? *(Laughter)*] ES
747 the picture.] Notes
pictures colored.] Globe
750 [Yes.] Globe: I know Mr. Ruskin as attached to art / Notes: I believe Mr. Ruskin has devoted a lifetime to criticism and art.
a painter.] ES / Globe: that he has not painted
751 watercolor.] Globe
753 dramatic author,] DN / ES: writer / DN: and art critic
several plays.] Notes
755 livelihood.] ES / Notes: I still continue the pursuit of art as a means of livelihood.
[personally,] ES: very well
757 his studio.] DN
[two moonlight pictures,] Notes: blue and silver
760 and knowledge.] ES
761 charm about them.] Notes
evince a] Globe
[great] Globe: trained

knowledge of art.] Notes

762 [poetical light] Globe: poetic fancy

763 feeling for color.] Times / ES: I consider the feeling for color native / Notes: nature, age, and feeling for color

[much] Notes: carefully

[painting the pictures.] Notes: before the finished pictures and the conception of it

764 man of genius] ES / Notes: a man of art and genius

765 conscientious artist.] Times

767 Ruskin personally.] ES

768 severely criticized.] ES

770 No.] Globe

772 gems.] Globe

773 my opinion.] Notes

774 [. . . different opinion,] Notes: I don't quarrel with other people's opinions

my own.] Globe

776 it now.] ES

777 works original.] Notes / ES: Mr. Whistler's pictures are original

780 fair criticism.] Notes

782 for the plaintiff.] DN

784 shown malice.] ES

785 without malignity.] Globe

787 ridicule] ES

788 be libelous.] DN

794 common pleas,] ES

Justice Erle,] DT / Notes: Ld. C. J. Erle

797 any ground,] ES

798 legal or otherwise.] DT

799 is allowed.] ES

801 enjoy.] DN / Echo: Baron Huddleston ruled otherwise.

DEFENDANT'S CASE

5 [. . . witness box gentlemen] Times: to call some witnesses

6 [. . . well acquainted with art] Times: well acquainted with the principles of art

7 examined,] ES

plaintiff's pictures.] Times

10 Ruskin has] ES

11 moderate spirit.] Times / ES: criticized them fairly, honestly, and bona fide / DT: in a fair, honest, and bona fide manner

14 [indulge in] Times: resort to

he likes,] ES

16 acting maliciously.] Times

18 [. . . bounds of moderation.] Echo: the real question to be tried was not simply whether the plaintiff had been held up to contempt and ridicule, but whether the defendant could come under the protection of having honestly and fairly criticized the plaintiff's pictures.

20 many artists] ES / Echo: many people / Times: perhaps some people

21 critics altogether.] Echo / ES: would be well pleased if critics did not exist / Times: would extinguish critics altogether.

22 [uses.] Times: value

24 [of painting,] Times: the fine arts

31 excellence.] ES

32 must criticism,] Times

40 is not so.] ES

regret that] Times

41 before you,] Echo

the court.] Times

42 word of mouth] Echo

43 witness box] ES
publication] Echo
46 the study] Times
of art.] ES
Professor] Times
48 [subject of art.] Times: much on art
50 [appreciation] Times: susceptibility
is beautiful.] ES
[a great love] ES: the greatest love
51 [special admiration] ES: the highest appreciation / Echo: peculiar and special fancy
[highly finished pictures.] ES: completed pictures / Echo: pictures which were well finished
57 [. . . sufficiently regarded.] Echo: had a strong opposition to the present days of money-making with the absence of noble simplicity
58 standard and] Times
59 of genius.] Echo
devotion to art] Times / ES: He required from an artist that he should be devoted to his profession
61 [. . . for his work,] Times: should not only struggle to get money
62 [. . . money paid.] Times: to give full value to the purchaser of his productions.
63 further,] ES
64 [. . . could improve,] ES: was capable of further labor—of being farther improved
65 [the artist's fame] Echo: the measure of the artist
67 these views] Times
duty of artists,] ES
69 those pictures,] Times / ES: determine to subject them
70 to criticism.] ES
slashing criticism] Times
71 contempt.] ES
72 honest opinion;] Times
80 extravagant productions.] ES / Times: pictures were marked by a strangeness of style and a fantastical extravagance which fully justified the language employed by Mr. Ruskin in regard to them.
85 and absurd?] DT
Mr. Whistler] ES
87 might] MP / ES: must
different opinion.] ES
90 has disputed] DT
own productions.] ES
93 four o'clock,] DT
94 tomorrow morning] ES
half past ten.] Notes
95 for the defense.] ES
97 *then adjourned.*] Echo
101 [*densely*] DN: most inconveniently
109 *on behalf of Mr. Ruskin)*:] ES
110 of the jury,] Echo
111 shall adduce,] DN
114 complained of.] DT / Times: objected to
115 Grosvenor Gallery.] DN
116 accompany me] DT
[. . . in imagination.] PMG: The attorney general entered into a satirical and amusing criticism of the eccentricities in the pictures of Mr. Whistler
117 artistic chop] DN
118 Venetian glass,] DT
119 Whistler's pictures.] DN
127 [commenting upon them.] ES: dis-

cussing the merits of the works before them.

131 a 'nocturne] DT

and silver.'] ES

132 means?"] DT / ES: I should like to know what a nocturne means. Where is Mr. Whistler?

would say,] DN

[. . . an exquisite idea.] DN: It is exquisite.

134 Well,] DT

Mr. Whistler] ES

135 doubt whether] DN

[the young lady] ES: they / DN: any of them

136 the wiser.] DT

(Laughter)] ES

137 [delightful] ES: beautiful

138 discovered] DN

[the affinity] DT: such a sympathy / DN: that there is harmony

two arts] ES

and painting!] DN

140 ['Moonlight in E Minor'] DN: Moonlight in C Minor / ES: Moonlight in a Mirror

141 ['Chiaroscuro in Four Flats'] DN: an arrangement in black in three flats

144 the pictures.] DT

146 them yourselves.] DN

148 minute or two.] Echo

150 Battersea Bridge.] DT

151 a sketch.] DN

the picture.] Echo

152 of color,] DN

155 frame. *(Laughter)*] ES

the world] Echo

156 [. . . in the middle] Echo: was the picture they had before them?

fire escape?] DT

157 tubular bridge] DN

[span the Thames?] Echo / DN: escaped and become Battersea Bridge

158 *(Laughter)*] ES

159 Battersea Bridge?] Echo

160 like Battersea Bridge?] ES

162 and cattle?] DN

165 of fortune] ES

167 to make,] DN

168 [prevails,] Whistler: avail

170 Grosvenor Gallery,] DT

171 [an action] DN: for libel / DT: for damages

against us.] ES

178 Rialto. *(Laughter)*] DT

181 for damages.] ES

these pictures.] DN

182 Cremorne nocturne] ES

185 not understand] DN / ES: he did not think that young ladies would be able to say much about it / DT: He did not know whether the young ladies would look at the blue and gold "nocturne" representing Cremorne.

Cremorne—*(Laughter)*] ES / DN: for of course they had never been to Cremorne / DT: they had not been there

186 [. . . more about it.] DT: The other sex might have been, and knew something about it.

187 of night] DN

191 people do.] DT / ES: Mr. Whistler did not see things which other people saw / DN: Mr. Whistler did not see things as they saw them.

192 cannot hear.] DN

193 *(Laughter)*] ES
194 [strange fantastic form] ES: fantastic and mysterious form
195 British public.] DN
196 these pictures,] DT
198 [exaggerated conceits] DT: strange, fantastical conceits
199 some of them,] DN
200 [value,] DT: merit
no doubt;] Echo
201 mania] ES
called Art.] DT / Times: In the present mania for art / ES: in literature, in art, and in the philosophy
202 [admire] ES: worship
incomprehensible] Times / DT: everything that was incomprehensible
203 [It is exquisite.] DT: How exquisite!
204 in painting.] ES
207 mysterious beauty,] DT
210 [. . . of Mr. Ruskin,] ES: this was certainly the view held by Mr. Ruskin
211 the public.] Times
215 the artists] DT
216 art critics] DN / PMG: art critics and other competent witnesses
220 the country.] DT
222 alleged libel.] DN
223 do so.] ES
learned friend,] DN
225 man's livelihood:] DT
226 his living.] DN
230 such productions.] DT / Times: rendered himself open to it.
232 [unyielding] DT: unbending
234 to commend.] ES / DN: spoke out as clearly and as loudly in his praise as in his blame / Echo: while he was loud in his praises of some whom he considered worthy of them, yet he did not forget to blame others whom he considered equally in need of rebuke.
236 is due,] Times
238 Millais.] DN / Times: quoting from *Fors Clavigera,* the attorney general showed that Mr. Ruskin was neither a partial nor a stern and hard critic.
239 modern school.] Times
242 its entirety.] Echo
244 works of art.] DN
245 *Black and Gold.*] ES
248 anything else;] Echo
249 Mr. Rossetti.] ES
251 [. . . monstrous extravagance,] Echo: an exaggerated conceit and a worthless fancy
255 fantastic thing.] DN
257 so again.] DT / ES: and yet they were often called sticks and would be called so again.
259 is applied.] ES
262 of an action] DT
266 present occasion.] Echo
268 Grosvenor Gallery,] DN
271 good work] ES
272 works of art?] DN
273 things for sale.] Times
278 his pocket.] ES
280 ill-educated conceit] DN
281 himself in art.] ES
282 no doubt;] DN
283 Whistler's:] ES
284 artist should.] DN
288 in consequence.] Echo / ES: Who ever heard of a lawyer bringing

an action because it was said that he was not a good lawyer?

290 to say so?] Times

293 public's face."] DN

remind you that] Echo

295 as an artist.] DN / Echo: applied to the plaintiff as an artist, and not to him in his ordinary position in life.

296 "coxcomb"?] Echo

297 [. . . the dictionary] ES: looked the word up / Times: looked out for the word

298 the word] DN

[licensed] Echo: court

299 [. . . making jests] Echo: with a special licence to jest

300 [. . . master and family.] Echo: for the benefit of the Royal Family

301 [true definition,] DN: the true idea of a coxcomb

not complain.] ES

302 his pictures?] Echo / DN: then Mr. Whistler's pictures were a jest, and in that sense the old meaning was well carried out / ES: his pictures had afforded a most amusing jest / Times: his pictures were capital jests.

304 Whistler's pictures.] ES

310 of painting,] DN / ES: accomplishment of painting

311 not possess,] DT

313 being attacked.] ES

315 [control] Times: restrain

316 a jury.] DT

317 the criticism.] DN

318 [. . . is right.] DN: He believed he had a right to criticize.

319 [. . . art he loves.] ES: from sincere love of art, to which he was devoted / DN: to criticism in the love and for the sake of art / Echo: for a long life given himself wholly to the worship of art

322 [legitimate] DN: liberal

324 fulsome adulation.] Times / DN: and when all criticism would be reduced to a dead level, and nothing was to be said of artists but what was couched in the language of fulsome admiration.

325 *the defense.*] ES

327 [twenty years.] Notes: twenty-five / PMG: about twenty years

329 *Days of Creation*] DN

330 [*Venus's Mirror,*] Notes: Venice Mirror

331 [*Temperantia,*] *emended from* Deferentia

332 [*A Sibyl,*] ES, *emended from* Sybil.

Saint George.] DN

333 there since.] PMG

334 in Paris] DT

337 of all artists,] ES / DN: I think that nothing short of perfect finish ought to be allowed by artist / Echo: There was nothing so essential in art as perfect finish / Globe: Complete finish ought to be the standard of painting / PMG: Complete finish is the necessary quality for a picture / Times: complete finish ought to be the standard of painting.

339 short of what] DN

[for ages has been acknowledged] DN: of what the age acknowledges

perfect work.] Globe / DT: complete finish.

343 them yesterday.] DN
345 *Blue and Silver,*] ES
347 work of art?] DN
349 in short.] Globe
355 good qualities.] DN
356 especially in color.] PMG
357 good work of art.] ES
358 as color.] DN
364 [. . . as color goes.] DN: Neither in composition, detail, nor form has the picture any quality whatever; but in color it has a very fine quality.
367 *Blue and Silver*] ES
to that?] DN
368 still better.] ES
369 in color,] PMG
370 bewildering] DN / PMG: but it is powerless
372 none whatever.] ES
375 time for it.] DN / ES: within which to paint it / PMG: for painting it / Times: for its production
377 No.] ES
other] DN
378 no finish.] DT
a sketch.] ES / PMG: It is not a finished picture; it is only a sketch / Times: It was, as he said, a mere sketch
380 finished work.] DN / Times: ever intended it should be finished.
383 at all.] ES
384 [a work of art?] ES: a finished work of art
385 it is.] DN / ES: It would be impossible for me to say so.
386 work of art.] DT
388 subject itself.] DN
paint night:] PMG
392 [tone like night,] Notes: tone of night light
the bridge.] DN
393 night at all.] Notes
397 much less.] ES / Notes: considering the finish other men do for less work / DT: for a much less sum / Whistler: when you think of the amount of earnest work done for a smaller sum
399 *was like.*] Globe / PMG: to show what was a finished picture
Parry objected.] ES
402 that. *(Laughter)*] Globe / ES: I shall be able to do that / PMG: I can do that
404 undoubted Titian] ES / Globe: you know the story of the "genuine Titian"
406 [. . . master's wonderful coloring.] ES: being purchased with a view to enabling students and others to find out how to produce his beautiful colors
409 uniform. *(Laughter)*] Globe / ES: full length portrait of George III in uniform
413 the objection.] DT
414 *then produced.*] DN / Echo: for purposes of comparison with the works of the plaintiff.
415 *the picture.*] DT
417 Gritti.] Globe, *emended from* Gretti / DN: That is a Titian.
real Titian.] DT
418 picture before.] DN
[most perfect specimen] DN: very perfect example / DT: sample
419 ancient art.] Times / DN: of the

highest finish that ancient artists aimed at

421 sufficiently fine.] DT

425 Yes,] DN

426 artistic skill.] DT / DN: There must have been great labor to produce such works and great skill / Globe: I consider that Mr. Whistler possesses great power / Times: He considered that Mr. Whistler possessed great power, but had not fulfilled his early promise.

427 [. . . has fulfilled it.] DT: I think he had great powers at first, which he has not since justified / Notes: Mr. Whistler gave infinite powers of promise of art at first

428 of painting] DN

far enough.] Globe / DN: Has not tested his powers by carrying it out / Echo: the artist showed signs of having evaded the great difficulty of painting / Times: He had evaded the difficulties of painting by not carrying his pictures far enough / DT: He has evaded the difficulties of his art

429 [. . . the work progresses.] DT: increases every day of his professional life / Echo: which increased day by day . . . as the picture approached a finished state.

430 us perfect.] ES

433 [atmosphere] Globe: sense of atmosphere

435 whitewashing.] DC / ES: The danger is this, that if unfinished pictures become common we shall arrive at a stage of mere manufacture, and the art of the country will be degraded.

437 A Juror:] ES

438 sale room.] DT / DC: the picture by Titian might be sold for 2000 guineas, but might in a sale room only fetch 20 guineas. He would give 1000 guineas for it himself.

444 it might.] ES

445 it, but] Notes

446 twenty guineas.] Times / ES: I know of a very fine Titian being bought by Lord Elcho for 20 guineas

447 lucky.] DT

448 [. . . to Mr. Ruskin.] Notes: I believe it has been sent up from London / Times: It now belonged to Mr. Ruskin.

452 think so.] ES

454 said of them.] Globe

457 [. . . or fourteen years.] Notes: I have known Mr. Whistler's paintings for 14 years.

459 Yes,] ES

Grosvenor Gallery,] DT

460 *A Sibyl.*] Notes

463 especially.] ES / DT: I think Mr. Whistler's color in moonlight pictures is extremely good.

465 were correct.] Notes

466 as incomplete.] DT

467 [look upon] ES: call

[who exhibited such pictures] ES: for exhibiting these pictures

470 not press it.] DT

475 [*The Road to Ruin,*] Echo, DC, DN, DT, Whistler: "Rake's Progress"

481 say not.] ES

482 *handed to the witness.*] Notes

486 two others.] ES
487 *the witness.*] Notes
490 or silk.] ES
491 [. . . water and atmosphere in it;] DT: It does not represent perfect atmosphere / Times: To him they did not represent either moonlight or water.
492 nothing more.] Echo
495 impression to me] ES
the slightest degree.] DN
496 not true.] DT
497 hundred guineas.] ES
499 works of art.] Echo
500 extremely fine.] ES / Notes: excellent work
501 Velázquez and Whistler.] Notes
506 Yes.] ES
upon subpoena.] Times
[thing] Globe: position
507 [give evidence against] Times: speak against
brother artist.] ES
508 my subpoena.] Notes / ES: I am here on subpoena.
509 but declined] ES
511 Grosvenor Gallery.] Notes
512 last witness,] Globe
Burne-Jones,] Notes
513 Whistler has] Globe
great powers] DT
artist,] ES
514 "things."] DT
517 No,] ES
518 atmosphere.] Globe
521 constantly happens.] ES / DT: In our profession men of equal merit differ as to the character of a picture.
differ.] Globe
526 Mr. Ruskin.] ES / DT: Is Turner an idol of Mr. Ruskin's?
527 Turner's works.] Notes
528 all painters.] ES / Echo: of everyone / DT: idol of everybody
529 [Do you know] ES: Have you seen
530 [. . . called *Snow Storm?*] ES: picture of the snow storm
531 Yes, I do.] DT
532 years ago.] Notes
533 [by a critic] Times: by Mr. Ruskin
535 [I am not.] ES: Yes; and I think it very likely that I should call it so myself.
537 should. *(Laughter)*] DT
539 [to the period] Times: his latest pictures / Globe: not in his later years / Echo: in the later ones
540 them. *(Laughter)*] ES
542 salad. *(Laughter)*] DT
544 mustard. *(Laughter)*] ES
545 lobster.] DT
547 fine pictures.] Notes
550 twenty years.] ES
552 studied art.] DT / Whistler: *always*
554 the Dudley] ES / Globe: saw Mr. Whistler's pictures at Bond Street, the Dudley, and the Grosvenor galleries.
555 to pictures.] Globe
558 good picture;] ES
work of art.] DT / Notes: I can't say that I consider it a work of art.
559 opinion in] Globe
560 adhere to now.] Echo / DT: to every word of which, he said, he still adhered
561 *the pictures:*] ES
579 in colour.] *fragments in* Echo, DN

582 the others.] DN / Notes: (read his criticism)

586 Thomas Carlyle."] *fragments in* Echo, DN

589 its limits.] Notes

opinion still.] Echo

590 sketchy.] DT

592 Yes,] ES

artistic qualities] DT

593 delicate tones] ES / DT: and he has got appreciation of qualities of tone

of color,] Notes

not complete.] DT

595 of pictures.] Echo

of sketching.] DT

596 good work.] DN / Echo: as such he valued very much.

600 Yes.] ES

602 shadowy subject.] Notes

SUMMATIONS

2 defendant's evidence.] Echo

3 called Mr. Ruskin,] DT

to illness.] Echo / Notes: Statement that Mr. Ruskin too ill was accepted by Pfts. Counsel.

4 recall you to the] Globe

5 [short] Globe: real

this case.] DT

6 Whistler's pictures,] ES

8 [fantastic] ES: mere

9 extravagances.] DN

10 of a critic.] DT

13 schools of art,] DN

20 Ruskin's comments,] ES

21 they may be] DN

[. . . of the critic.] DN: fair and honest criticism.

24 subject of art] ES

29 are criticized.] DT

33 [indulge in personal malice.] DN: speak with malignity

37 before him,] ES

38 expression of opinion.] DN

39 criticism is.] ES

41 or of art.] DT

43 malignant motive.] DN

44 personally,] DT

45 he loves,] ES / DN: that he had done more than he thought was due to art.

46 public critic.] DT

48 adheres.] ES

51 of criticism.] DT

52 [for the general public] DT: of the public and art

54 [hope] Globe: trust

English jury,] ES

56 chain] DT

57 this country.] Globe / Echo: it would be a serious matter for the noble future of art in this country if they should fetter the hands of critics in the manner in which they had been asked.

59 I consider] DT

tone of] ES

remarks] DT

60 of place,] ES

61 toward Mr. Whistler.] DT

62 learned gentleman] ES

group of] Globe

65 respect.] ES

66 appeared to be.] DN

67 additional sting.] Globe

70 upon art."] ES / Globe: Mr. Ruskin claimed the right to say anything he liked about an artist /

DN: the defense of Mr. Ruskin was that he had a right to say what he liked of artists
74 this case.] DT
79 to continue:] DN
within bounds.] Globe
81 has done,] ES
84 willful impostor.] DN
87 willful imposture.] ES
89 [. . . attend the court,] DT: It was said Mr. Ruskin was ill
91 works generally,] DN / ES: asked how long he had known Mr. Whistler's paintings
94 [. . . powers of criticism] DT: had used his great genius
95 [comparatively struggling man.] DT: a rising and talented young artist
99 in any way.] ES
103 upon them.] Echo
104 disapproval.] DC
105 [. . . Mr. Ruskin's language.] Globe: the libel had not been justified as a fair criticism.
107 an artist,] DT / ES: in the highest terms of the powers of Mr. Ruskin
116 fair criticism.] ES
118 jury, but] Globe
serious business.] ES
121 with evidence,] DN
122 threshold.] Globe
123 such opinions.] ES
125 treated Mr. Whistler,] DN
126 Mr. Whistler's works.] ES
128 agree with me."] DN
130 a jury.] Globe
133 appeared in] Echo
135 degraded himself.] DN
138 his writing.] ES
139 [personal] DT: unjust
and malicious.] DN
142 monster."] ES
144 insignificant person.] DN
twenty-five pages] Echo / ES: the same publication
145 Goldwin Smith,] DN
148 Henry Cole] ES: the presidency of Sir Henry Cole at Kensington
155 too far.] DT
163 defamatory attack.] ES
164 good, but] DT
166 good motives.] ES
167 been used.] Globe
169 willful impostor?] DN
178 impunity.] DT
179 stinging criticism.] DN
defamation.] DT
181 own vanity.] Globe
183 trade in libel.] ES
184 has described] DT
object in] Globe
187 telescope.] DT
188 criticism as that.] Globe / DT: This shows the attorney general knew very little of art.
189 honest criticism.] DT
190 [public investigation;] Globe: He had submitted himself to the fullest inquiry
191 detractor has.] ES
194 genuine artist.] DC
196 industrious artist] ES
197 as others,] DC
198 eccentric views] Globe
200 position.] DC
201 despot?] ES
202 that Mr. Ruskin] DC

203 accusations.] Globe / DC: sentiments

204 *to two.*] Notes

JURY INSTRUCTIONS

2 two gentlemen.] Echo

3 of law,] DT

5 the plaintiff] ES

commits to paper] DT

8 of libel.] Times

a libel,] DT

9 actionable,] ES

10 [. . . libelous and untrue.] Times: The law presumed malice

13 was published,] DT

15 those words] ES

18 to try.] Echo

20 bona fide.] ES

29 [. . . artists, and critics.] ES: as to this, there had been much diversity of opinion between authors, and artists, and critics

36 among themselves] DT

38 the critic,] ES

39 [to express it.] Echo: strength enough to stand by his opinion; but he must first have had the opportunity to express it / DT: full latitude to use language which would express the judgment he had formed.

42 nor allow] DT

43 unfair attacks] Times

44 author or artist] DT

45 denunciation.] Times / DT: his love of denunciation to run into a reckless attack / ES: lead him to use it for the purpose of showing his power

47 [wide power] ES: wide margin

48 [. . . honestly formed,] ES: judgment which he had honestly performed

52 than myself.] Times

54 weapon] DT

for criticism:] ES / DT: that could be employed to explain the judgment of the critic

56 [of a personal character] ES: upon personal character

57 [a different thing,] ES: is quite another thing

61 abuses,] DT

62 trash.] ES

63 similar views.] DT

66 this be so.] ES

72 honestly used,] DT

76 [. . . in strong language,] ES: a man honestly entertaining a judgment with reference to a work of art expresses himself strongly / Echo: the object of a critic was honestly to express his opinion upon a work of art

77 feelings] DT

78 is criticizing,] ES / Echo: if he was to indulge in personal invective

80 [critic's privilege.] Echo: he would not come under the privilege accorded by law / ES: he was not entitled to protection.

82 [discussing the works] Echo: if a critic ventured to deal with works of art

87 [expressions] ES: observations

personal character.] DT

88 Ruskin's language] Echo

89 [might be strong] Echo: and stronger than he would have used himself

91 bona fide,] DT
92 the verdict.] ES
93 distinguished critic] DT
94 capacity.] ES
97 he uses] DT
98 treatment;] ES
99 bated breath.] DT
103 on paper.] ES
104 has called,] DT
107 genius.] ES
of art,] DT
108 follow out.] ES
115 such evidence] Echo
116 good faith.] DT
119 yourselves whether] Echo
131 [exhibiting his own powers.] Echo: in order to gratify personal feeling.
135 yourselves.] ES
137 bona fide criticism;] Echo
146 goose,] DT
147 [system of art teaching] *from* school of art
149 in kind:] Echo
151 [lesser] *emended from* smaller
153 Tissot.] DT
156 any further.] Echo
158 in using it.] DT
159 or a book,] ES
161 tolerated.] Echo
163 something more.] Echo
167 license.] DT
172 wilful imposture."] Echo
174 Mr. Whistler:] ES
176 of color,] Echo
181 before now;] ES
183 public's face."] DN
192 sphere.] DT
199 down.'"] ES
203 about its use;] DT
222 the law.] ES
227 upon you.] Echo
229 *its verdict.*] Globe
238 *to the box,*] ES
239 *past four.*] Echo
242 answer.] Globe
245 among us] ES
246 to the artist.] Globe / ES: that the word imposture was supposed to refer to the artist
252 secrets.] ES / Globe: His lordship checked the foreman, who was relating in detail the differences among the jury
260 public's face.] Globe, *from* having again read the libel
262 [. . . to his works,] Globe: on the artist's personal character outside his works
264 [Yes.] ES, *from* Mr. Baron Huddleston replied in the affirmative.
265 *minutes*] ES

VERDICT

2 *the plaintiff.*] DT
6 costs,] Globe
8 awarded,] DT
12 usual course,] ES
13 the plaintiff] DT
the jury.] Globe
16 the plaintiff.] DT
18 without costs.] ES

NOTES

ABBREVIATIONS

BMA	Baltimore Museum of Art, Lucas Collection
Fors	*Fors Clavigera*
FGA	Freer Gallery of Art, Washington
GUL	Glasgow University Library, Whistler Collections
PWC	Pennell-Whistler Collection, Library of Congress

INTRODUCTION

1. The libelous paragraph appears in "Letter 79: Life Guards of New Life," *Fors Clavigera* 7 (July 1877), in *The Works of John Ruskin,* ed. E. T. Cook and Alexander Wedderburn, Library Edition, 39 vols. (London: George Allen, 1903–12), 29:146–69. Ruskin's critique of Whistler's work is in section 16, on page 160.

2. *The Amazing Trial of James McNeill Whistler* by Jon Palmer, Little Theater, Palace of the Legion of Honor, San Francisco, 1974; *Plague Wind* by Tamas McDonald, New End Theatre (Hampstead), London, 1983; and *Whistler's Play* by Howard Burman, The Hilberry Repertory Theatre, Wayne State University, Detroit, 1987.

3. James McNeill Whistler, "The Action," in *The Gentle Art of Making Enemies* (London: Heinemann, 1890), 1–19. The newspaper reports Whistler used for his transcript, which are preserved in press-cutting books in the

Glasgow University Library, include the *Daily Telegraph,* 26 November 1878; the *Evening Standard,* 25 and 26 November 1878; *The Globe,* 25 November 1878; the New York *Semi-Weekly Tribune,* 28 December 1878; and the *Weekly Dispatch,* 1 December 1878.

4. Elizabeth R. Pennell and Joseph Pennell, "The Trial: The Year Eighteen Seventy-eight," in *The Life of James McNeill Whistler,* 2 vols. (Philadelphia: Lippincott, 1908), 1:229–45; and in *The Life of James McNeill Whistler,* 5th ed., rev. (Philadelphia: Lippincott, 1911), 165–80.

5. Letters from E. A. Parry to J. Pennell, 21 and 28 January [1909], PWC 296. A typescript copy of the letter from Whistler to Rose, inscribed "sent to us by Edward A. Parry, son of Serjeant Parry," is in PWC 14; the original letter (received 21 November 1878), which is also quoted in the plaintiff's brief (PWC 26), is in GUL (R 128).

6. Presumably sold from the estate of J. Anderson Rose, the legal papers were offered for sale by E. Weyhe, a dealer in rare books and prints. The Pennells bought the collection in November 1919 (see letters from E. Weyhe, PWC 303). An abstract of the collection that was sent to the Chicago collector Walter S. Brewster in November 1919 is now in the Brewster Collection of Whistleriana, Art Institute of Chicago.

7. Edward A. Parry, "Whistler v. Ruskin," *Cornhill Magazine* 50 (January 1921): 21–33.

8. Elizabeth R. Pennell and Joseph Pennell, "Appendix III: The Papers in the Whistler v. Ruskin Action," in *The Whistler Journal* (Philadelphia: Lippincott, 1921), 316–27.

9. "Received with Hisses," *The Globe,* 12 April 1886, press cutting included in the Whistler autograph letters to Walter and C. M. Dowdeswell, vol. 2, Rosenwald Collection, Rare Books Division, Library of Congress; Whistler to the editor of the *Observer,* 11 April 1886, reprinted as "Early Laurels" in *Gentle Art* (1890), 176. The painting was auctioned at William Graham's estate sale, Christie's, London, 3 April 1886, as *A Nocturne in Blue and Silver,* no. 120. *The Globe* surmised that the nocturne might have been placed on the easel upside down "by a pardonable error," or that "the company conceived that it was upside down when it was really as its composer intended it to be." Robert H. C. Harrison of Liverpool bought the nocturne for sixty guineas and sold it in 1905 to the National Art Collections Fund for two thousand pounds. For a modern estimate of the painting, see Richard

Humphreys, *Tate Gallery Masterpiece Guide: A Short Introductory Tour* (London: Tate Gallery, 1990), 14.

10. Whistler to D. C. Thomson, director of the Goupil Gallery in London, postmarked 6 November 1892 and received 26 November 1892, typescripts, PWC 16.

PART ONE: THE LIBEL

THE PALACE OF ART

1. Oscar Wilde, "The Grosvenor Gallery," *Dublin University Magazine* 90 (July 1877): 126.

2. "The Palace of Art (New Version)," *Punch, or the London Charivari,* 7 July 1877, 305; 14 July 1877, 9.

3. C. E. Hallé, *Notes from a Painter's Life* (London: John Murray, 1909), 107, 104; *The Grosvenor Gallery,* exhibition catalogue (London: Wade Phoenix Printing, 1877), 3.

4. Alan Cole, typescript of diary extracts, 19 March 1876, PWC 281.

5. For descriptions of the Grosvenor Gallery interior, see "Fine Arts. The Grosvenor Gallery," *The World,* 2 May 1877, 10; Walter Crane, *An Artist's Reminiscences* (New York: Macmillan, 1907), 175; and Louise Jopling, *Twenty Years of My Life, 1867 to 1887* (New York: Dodd, Mead and Co., 1925), 114. Walter Crane thought that Whistler painted the frieze decoration (see his letter to E. Pennell, 12 August 1906, PWC 281), but I have found no evidence to support that belief.

6. [Tom Taylor], "The Grosvenor Gallery," *The Times,* 1 May 1877, 10; Wilde, "Grosvenor Gallery," 118.

7. "Fine Arts: The Grosvenor Gallery," *The World,* 2 May 1877, 10.

8. [Taylor], "Grosvenor Gallery," 10; Wilde, "Grosvenor Gallery," 118.

9. Oscar Wilde, *The Picture of Dorian Gray,* ed. Isobel Murray (1891; reprint, New York: Oxford University Press, 1981), 2.

10. Hallé, *Painter's Life,* 109.

11. "The Grosvenor Gallery," *The Times,* 10 May 1877, 6.

12. "The Grosvenor Gallery and Royal Academy," *Vanity Fair,* 5 May 1877, 281; Penelope Fitzgerald, *Edward Burne-Jones: A Biography* (London: Michael

Joseph, 1975), 168. For a discussion of the relative advantages of the Grosvenor Gallery and the Royal Academy, see "The Grosvenor Gallery: First Notice," *Magazine of Art* 1 (1877–78): 50.

13. "Fine Arts: The Grosvenor Gallery," *The World,* 2 May 1877, 10; *Fors* 79 (July 1877), in *The Works of John Ruskin,* ed. E. T. Cook and Alexander Wedderburn, 39 vols., Library Edition (London: George Allen, 1903–12), 29:157.

14. D. G. Rossetti to C. E. Hallé, 27 January 1877, published in *The Times,* 27 March 1877, 6.

15. The catalogue, *Exhibition of the Society of Painters in Water Colours, 1870: The Sixty-sixth,* lists only four paintings by Burne-Jones; *Phyllis and Demophöon* was apparently omitted from the list when it was removed from the exhibition. The incident is mentioned in Anderson Rose, notes for W. C. Petheram ([25 November 1878], PWC 27). Jan Marsh suggests that it was the painting's apparent allusion to Burne-Jones's affair with Maria Zambaco, as much as the nudity of Demophöon, that scandalized the members of the Society (*The Pre-Raphaelite Sisterhood* [New York: St. Martin's Press, 1985], 282).

16. Crane, *Reminiscences,* 161.

17. *The Mirror of Venus* (1873–77; Gulbenkian Foundation, Lisbon), listed in *Grosvenor Gallery* (1877) as "Venus' Mirror"; *Saint George* (1877; Wadsworth Atheneum, Hartford, Conn.).

18. Henry James, "The Picture Season in London, 1877," in *The Painter's Eye: Notes and Essays on the Pictorial Arts by Henry James,* ed. John L. Sweeney (1956; reprint, Madison: University of Wisconsin Press, 1989), 143; originally published in *Galaxy*, August 1877.

19. Joseph Comyns Carr, *Some Eminent Victorians: Personal Recollections in the World of Art and Letters* (London: Duckworth, 1908), 133.

20. "The Palace of Art (New Version)," *Punch,* 7 July 1877, 305.

WHISTLER'S WORK

1. George Du Maurier, *Trilby,* serialized in *Harper's New Monthly Magazine* 88 (January–July 1894).

2. The honor implied by Phillip's purchase was introduced at the Ruskin trial, but the *Echo* would report that "the amusing part of the story"—which was of course omitted from Whistler's testimony—was that Phillip had quickly tired of the painting and "sent it away" (Fresco, "Art Sayings and Doings," *Echo*, 6 December 1878). It does appear that *At the Piano* was sold soon after its purchase. Its title is not listed in the sale catalogue of Phillip's collection, which suggests that it left his hands sometime before 1867, and the circumstances of its subsequent acquisition by Seymour Haden (whose wife and daughter are depicted in the painting) are not known.

3. A. C. Swinburne, "Notes on Some Pictures of 1868," in *Essays and Studies* (London: Chatto and Windus, 1875), 359–61 and 374; originally published by Hotten in 1868. The oil sketches known as the "Six Projects" (ca. 1868; FGA) were not shown at the Royal Academy; Swinburne, who was a friend of Whistler's, must have seen them in the artist's studio.

4. Anna McNeill Whistler to Kate Palmer, 3–4 November 1871, PWC 34.

5. [Tom Taylor], "Dudley Gallery: Cabinet Pictures in Oil," *The Times,* 14 November 1871, 4. The article is reprinted in Robin Spencer, ed., *Whistler: A Retrospective* (New York: Lauter Levin, 1989), 101. The other work Whistler exhibited at the Dudley in 1871 was *Variations in Violet and Green* (1871; private collection).

6. Whistler to F. R. Leyland, [November 1872], PWC 6B. Whistler asks to borrow Mrs. Leyland's "little 'Nocturne'" for an exhibition; the quotation marks imply that the title remained unfamiliar. Leyland may have been inspired to suggest the title by the painting Whistler had presented to Frances Leyland the previous year, *Nocturne in Blue and Silver* (plate 4).

7. Whistler, "Propositions—No. 2," in *The Gentle Art of Making Enemies* (London: Heinemann, 1890), 115.

8. See, for example, Harry Quilter, "Mr. Whistler and the Royal Academy: To the Editor of The Times," 13 August 1903, 10; "Celebrities at Home, No. XCII: Mr. James Whistler at Cheyne-walk," *The World,* 22 May 1878, 4; and Elizabeth R. Pennell and Joseph Pennell, *The Life of James McNeill Whistler,* 2 vols. (Philadelphia: Lippincott, 1908), 1:157–58. Another, perhaps more credible, version of the story, related by George H. Boughton, who heard it from a member of the Royal Academy Council, claims that although the committee recognized the merits of the portrait and hung it from the start in an honorable place, someone suggested that it be hung higher on the wall so

that smaller pictures could be shown below, and Boxall, who had chosen the painting's position, had to insist that it remain where it was ("A Few of the Various Whistlers I Have Known," *International Studio* [New York] 21 [January 1904]: 215). According to the *Daily Telegraph,* "although not precisely on the 'line,'" Whistler's "unseemly eccentricity" occupied "a place of honour—and a most prominent one" ("Exhibition of the Royal Academy," 4 May 1872, 5).

9. Henry Blackburn, "'A Symphony' in Pall Mall," *Pictorial World,* 13 June 1874, 231. For further discussion of the exhibition, see David Park Curry, "Total Control: Whistler at an Exhibition," in Ruth E. Fine, ed., *James McNeill Whistler: A Reexamination,* Studies in the History of Art, vol. 19 (Washington: National Gallery of Art, 1987), 67–82; and Robin Spencer, "Whistler's First One-man Exhibition Reconstructed," in *The Documented Image: Visions in Art History,* ed. Gabriel P. Weisberg and Laurinda S. Dixon (Syracuse, N.Y.: Syracuse University Press, 1987), 27–49.

10. For an example of the critical view of Whistler's exhibition, see "Mr. Whistler's Paintings and Drawings," *Art Journal* 36 (August 1874): 230.

11. Wilde, "Grosvenor Gallery," 124–25.

12. Algernon Graves, "James Abbott McNeill Whistler," *Printseller and Print Collector* 1 (August 1903): 342; Frances Spalding, *Magnificent Dreams: Burne-Jones and the Late Victorians* (Oxford: Phaidon, 1987), 7; [Taylor], "Grosvenor Gallery." 10.

13. "The Palace of Art (New Version)," *Punch,* 7 July 1877, 305.

14. For a discussion of Cremorne and its place in Whistler's paintings, see David Park Curry, "Artist and Site," in *James McNeill Whistler at the Freer Gallery of Art* (New York: Norton, in association with the FGA, 1984), 71-87.

15. Whistler to Ernest Brown, 1890, cited in Katharine A. Lochnan, *The Etchings of James McNeill Whistler* (New Haven: Yale University Press, 1984), 179 n. 23. Another nocturne with fireworks (plate 3) owes its composition to a different night scene in the same series by Hiroshige, *The Bamboo Bank, Kyobashi.* Theodore Child may have been the first critic to remark on the similarity, although he considered the resemblance between *Fireworks, Ryogoku* and *Nocturne in Blue and Silver* coincidental ("American Artists at the Paris Exhibition," *Harper's New Monthly Magazine* [New York] 79 [September 1889], 496).

16. Elizabeth R. Pennell and Joseph Pennell, *The Whistler Journal* (Philadelphia: Lippincott, 1921), 103. The painting is no longer in its original frame.

17. Wilde, "Grosvenor Gallery," 124.

18. Second Annual Exhibition of Modern Pictures in Oil and Water Colour, Royal Pavilion Gallery, Brighton, from 9 September 1875. *Nocturne in Blue and Silver* was listed for sale at £315.

19. Whistler to William Graham, [after 23 July 1877], G 150, GUL.

20. Whistler to Alfred Chapman, [1874], PWC 1.

21. W. M. Rossetti, "The Dudley Gallery," *Academy,* 30 October 1875, 462. *Nocturne in Blue and Gold* was exhibited at the Dudley as no. 160, *Nocturne in Blue and Gold, No. 3.*

22. [Tom Taylor], "Winter Exhibitions. The Dudley," *The Times,* 2 December 1875, 4. Whistler quotes excerpts from Taylor's critique in *Nocturnes, Marines & Chevalet Pieces* (1892), an exhibition catalogue reprinted in *The Gentle Art of Making Enemies,* new ed. (London: Heinemann, 1892), 309; the quotations are misattributed to the *Daily Telegraph,* May 1877.

23. Whistler to Alan Cole, [December 1875], PWC 1.

24. *Ellen Terry's Memoirs,* ed. Edith Craig and Christopher St. John (1932; reprint, New York: Benjamin Blom, 1969), 101.

25. Wilde, "Grosvenor Gallery," 124; [Harry Quilter], "The Grosvenor Gallery (Concluding Notice)," *Spectator,* 2 June 1877, 696.

26. Alan Cole, diary extracts, 1 May 1876, PWC 281 (also quoted in Pennell and Pennell, *Life of Whistler* [1908], 1:199–200).

27. Elizabeth R. Pennell and Joseph Pennell, *The Life of James McNeill Whistler,* 5th ed., rev. (Philadelphia: Lippincott, 1911), 144. The butterfly drawn on the photograph is characteristic of Whistler's style in 1876 and 1877. A copy of the photograph in the Baltimore Museum of Art, virtually identical to the one reproduced as figure 20, caused the Pennells to wonder if there had been two portraits painted, since the difference between the early state and the final picture was so pronounced (*Life of Whistler* [1908], 1:200). Another photograph of the painting in a transitional state, owned by Ellen Terry's son Gordon Craig, was at one time determined to show a sketch for, or another version of, *Arrangement in Black* ("Museum Defends Irving Portrait," *Art News* [New York] 29 [4 October 1930], 25).

28. Wilde, "Grosvenor Gallery," 124.

29. W. M. Rossetti, "The Grosvenor Gallery. (Second Notice)," *Academy* 11 (26 May 1877): 467.

30. *Arrangement in Brown* is listed in the catalogue raisonné of Whistler oil paintings as no. 182, "whereabouts unknown" (Andrew McLaren Young et al., *The Paintings of James McNeill Whistler,* 2 vols. [New Haven: Yale University Press, 1980]. Another early photograph in the archives of the Freer Gallery of Art/Arthur M. Sackler Gallery, signed with a butterfly from around 1881, is inscribed by Whistler, "Arrangement in Brown and Black."

31. Young et al., *Paintings of Whistler,* proposes *Harmony in Grey and Peach Colour* (ca. 1872–74; Fogg Art Museum, Harvard University), no. 131, as the missing *Harmony in Amber and Black;* see also Margaret F. MacDonald, "Maud Franklin," in Fine, *Whistler,* 14. The subject of *Harmony in Grey and Peach Colour* does wear a white dress, and there are flowers in the composition, but the figure (who could never be taken for the sister of the subject of *Arrangement in Brown*) stands in a light-filled interior that would not have been mistaken for a London fog. Moreover, *Harmony in Grey and Peach Colour* had been exhibited in Whistler's one-man show in 1874, and Whistler considered it at that time "one of the important works" of the exhibition (quoted in Young et al., *Paintings of Whistler,* 80); it is unlikely that Whistler would have changed the title and altered the portrait's appearance so soon after a successful showing. "Grey and peach colour" is, in any event, a long way from "amber and black," even allowing for Whistler's capricious name changes and possible alterations to the picture's appearance. Finally, during preparations for the Ruskin trial, Whistler never indicated that *Harmony in Amber and Black* had been exhibited before, although there would have been every advantage in doing so.

32. The butterfly on the photograph (fig. 22) is characteristic of Whistler's style in 1878 and 1879. Another photograph of an early state of the painting in the archives of the Freer Gallery of Art/Arthur M. Sackler Gallery bears the same inscription, "'Arrangement in Grey & Black' No. 2." The portrait itself shows signs of having undergone at least one major change: at some point Whistler enlarged the canvas by folding out the upper tacking margin. This accounts for the noticeable difference in proportion between the photograph and the portrait. In answer to the interrogatories of the defense, Whistler said that *Harmony in Amber and Black* was in his possession, but that he had "painted over" it since the Grosvenor Gallery exhibition (PWC 26). In his instructions for those answers, Rose noted that although Whistler stated

the portrait had been destroyed, "in fact Mr. Whistler has painted over it to alter it and change its character as a picture. It is in a transition state" (PWC 27).

33. Florence Leyland, born in September 1859, remembered sitting for the portrait when she was seventeen or eighteen years old (Pennell and Pennell, *Whistler Journal,* 105).

34. The portrait of Florence was still in Whistler's possession in the summer of 1877, when Leyland wrote to demand that Whistler send him the portraits of himself, Mrs. Leyland, Florence, and another picture commissioned but never received, *Rose and Gray: Three Figures* (F. R. Leyland to Whistler, 27 July 1877, L 132, GUL).

35. Whistler to Theodore Watts-Dunton, 2 February [1878], *Nine Letters to Th. Watts-Dunton from J. McN. Whistler* (London: Privately printed, 1922), 17.

36. "Notes of the Week," *The Week,* 30 November 1878, 519.

37. "The Grosvenor Gallery," *Daily News,* 21 July 1877, 4; "The Grosvenor Gallery and Royal Academy," *Vanity Fair,* 5 May 1877, 281; "The Palace of Art (New Version)," *Punch,* 14 July 1877, 9.

38. "The Grosvenor Gallery," *Daily News,* 21 July 1877, 4.

RUSKIN'S REVIEW

1. The phrase *fors clavigera* signifies the Horatian figure of Fate the nail-bearer, a reference to the fixed power of necessity, but it bore multiple meanings for Ruskin. See John D. Rosenberg, *The Darkening Glass: A Portrait of Ruskin's Genius* (New York: Columbia University Press, 1986), 186 n. 3.

2. Joan Abse, *John Ruskin: The Passionate Moralist* (New York: Knopf, 1981), 234. Kristine Ottesen Garrigan points out that the *Academy Notes* of 1855 through 1859 and of 1875, Ruskin's commentary on Royal Academy exhibits, had a related purpose: see "Bearding the Competition: John Ruskin's *Academy Notes,*" *Victorian Periodicals Review* (Southern Illinois University) 22 (Winter 1989): 148–56.

3. Ruskin to Susan Beever, 13 November 1876, *Works of Ruskin,* 29:xxi; Shaw quoted in Horace Gregory, *The World of James McNeill Whistler* (New York: Thomas Nelson, 1959), 128.

4. Rosenberg, *Darkening Glass,* 186.

5. *The Diaries of John Ruskin,* 1874–1889, ed. Joan Evans and John Howard Whitehouse (Oxford: Clarendon Press, 1959), 963.

6. *Fors* 79 (July 1877), in *Works of Ruskin,* 29:158.

7. Ibid., 159–60.

8. *Modern Painters,* vol. 1, ibid., 3:193–94.

9. *Fors* 79 (July 1877), ibid., 29:160.

10. Ibid., 146 n. 1. Michael Beatty, the exception, reconsiders Ruskin's critique in the light of *Fors Clavigera* in "A Pot of Paint in the Public's Face: Ruskin's Censure of Whistler Reconsidered," *English Studies in Africa* 30 (1987): 27–41.

11. *Fors* 79 (July 1877), in *Works of Ruskin,* 29:146. Section 10 of the letter, which opens Ruskin's discussion of the Grosvenor Gallery, begins: "I must not close this letter without noting some of the deeper causes which may influence the success of an effort made this year in London, and in many respects on sound principles, for the promulgation of Art-knowledge; the opening, namely, of the Grosvenor Gallery" (157).

12. "The Guild of St. George: Master's Report, 1885," ibid., 30:96.

13. Pennell and Pennell, *Life of Whistler* (1911), 165.

14. Lecture on the political economy of art (Manchester, July 1857), published as *"A Joy for Ever"; (And its Price in the Market)* (1880), in *Works of Ruskin,* 16:19. For Ruskin's views on the sale of art, see, for example, *Academy Notes 1859,* in which he counsels aspiring artists, "So soon as your picture deserves to be bought, it will be bought" (ibid., 14:257).

15. Preface, *Academy Notes 1855,* ibid., 14:5.

16. Ruskin to Edward Burne-Jones, [before 8 August 1877], ibid., 37:225.

17. Ruskin to Arthur Severn, quoted in Sheila Birkenhead, *Illustrious Friends: The Story of Joseph Severn and His Son Arthur* (London: Hamish Hamilton, 1965), 274.

18. Preface, *Academy Notes 1875,* in *Works of Ruskin,* 14:262; "Of the Real Nature of Greatness of Style," in *Modern Painters,* vol. 3, ibid., 5:44–69.

19. "Shield and Apron," *Val d'Arno: Ten Lectures on the Tuscan Art* (1873), ibid., 23:49. News of this critique apparently never reached Whistler: the

plaintiff's brief indicates that other libels by Ruskin could be given in evidence to show malice, but this critique was not quoted in court.

The painting to which Ruskin refers has never been identified, though he seems to have been remembering something he had seen the previous year, 1872. Collingwood and Cook, in their annotation of the passage, propose that Ruskin was referring to one of the paintings shown at the Sixth Winter Exhibition of Cabinet Pictures in Oil at the Dudley Gallery: *Symphony in Grey and Green—the Ocean, Nocturne in Grey and Gold,* or *Nocturne, in Blue and Silver* (ibid., 49 n. 1). Of those, only *Nocturne in Grey and Gold*—probably *Nocturne: Blue and Gold—Southampton Water* (1871–72; Art Institute of Chicago) was priced for sale, at £316, frame included; none of the three is titled "harmony."

Symphony in Grey: Early Morning, Thames (fig. 24) was shown as no. 122, *Harmony in Grey,* at the Fifth Exhibition of the Society of French Artists, which opened at the Deschamps Gallery, New Bond Street on 4 November, 1872.

20. This criticism, published in the *Literary Gazette,* 14 May 1842, continues: ". . . and then shadowing in some forms to make the appearance of a picture. And yet there is a fine harmony in the highest range of color to please the sense of vision; we admire, and we lament to see such genius so employed" (quoted in *Works of Ruskin,* 3:xxiv).

21. "The Whistler-Ruskin Trial," unidentified press cutting, press-cutting book 3:3, GUL.

22. Walter Hamilton, *The Aesthetic Movement in England* (1882; reprint, New York: AMS Press, 1971), 17.

23. Henry James, "On Whistler and Ruskin, 1878," in *Painter's Eye,* 174; originally published as unsigned notes in the *Nation,* 19 December 1878.

24. See, for example, Walter Richard Sickert, *A Free House! or, The Artist as Craftsman,* ed. Osbert Sitwell (London: Macmillan, 1947), 4–5: "Ruskin, nourished on traditions totally opposed to those on which Whistler was based, failed to understand Whistler, and, as spoilt elderly ladies and gentlemen are liable to do, expressed his failure with violence and rudeness."

25. Ruskin to T. C. Hornsfall, 24 August 1877, *Works of Ruskin,* 29:591.

26. *Fors* 81 (September 1877), ibid., 197.

27. Ibid., 198.

28. *Academy Notes 1859,* ibid., 14:256.

29. "A Contemptuous Verdict," *Mayfair,* 3 December 1878, press-cutting book 2:25, GUL.

30. Ruskin wrote on 16 July 1877 "Fairly well myself, but anxious a little about giddiness or dizziness, scarcely perceptible, but not cured since my overwork at Venice" (quoted in E. T. Cook, *The Life of John Ruskin,* 2 vols. [London: George Allen, 1911], 2:392–93).

31. Quentin Bell, *Ruskin* (1963; reprint, New York: Braziller, 1978), 138.

32. Joan Evans, *John Ruskin* (New York: Oxford University Press, 1954), 372; R. W. Wilenski, *John Ruskin: An Introduction to Further Study of His Life and Work* (New York: Russell and Russell, 1967), 138–39. Beatty refutes the argument of Ruskin's psychological instability, first proposed by Wilenski, by showing that the *Fors Clavigera* critique is consistent with beliefs professed by Ruskin during times of mental health ("Pot of Paint").

33. Pennell and Pennell, *Life of Whistler* (1908), 1:230.

34. Tom Prideaux, *The World of Whistler, 1834–1903* (New York: Time-Life Books, 1970), 122; Derrick Leon, *Ruskin: The Great Victorian* (London: Routledge and Kegan Paul, 1949), 520; and Gregory, *World of Whistler,* 131–32. Alan Cole recorded in his diary that Howell had at one time related "various anecdotes about Ruskin" in Whistler's presence (9 October 1873, PWC 281). Edward A. Parry believed that the prominence of Whistler's works in the gallery where Ruskin's friend Burne-Jones's works were displayed excited Ruskin to anger ("Whistler v. Ruskin," *Cornhill Magazine* 50 [January 1921], 23). Ada Earland attributed Ruskin's wrath to the background of the nocturnes: "Imagine Ruskin, who would willingly have swept away every factory on the face of the earth, being called upon to admire a study of Price's Patent Candle Factory!" (*Ruskin and His Circle* [1910; reprint, New York: AMS Press, 1971], 257). E. T. Cook maintained that Ruskin's critique, "whether sound or mistaken, was at any rate disinterested" (*Life of Ruskin,* 2:430).

35. Algernon Swinburne to Ruskin, 11 August [1865], *Works of Ruskin,* 36:xlviii–xlix. "If I could get Whistler, Jones, and Howell to meet you," Swinburne wrote, "I think we might so far cozen the Supreme Powers as for once to realise a few not unpleasant hours." Cook maintains that if the

proposed meeting had taken place, Whistler and Ruskin "might have understood each other better, and a stormy episode of later years have been averted" (*Life of Ruskin,* 2:74). According to Robin Ironside, Burne-Jones had issued Ruskin the invitation to visit Whistler, who was "apparently prepared to be deferential" ("The Art Criticism of Ruskin," *Apollo* [March 1975]: 164). The Pennells simply say that Whistler, "knowing Ruskin's power in the Press, was willing to be written about by him" (*Life of Whistler* [1908], 1:231).

36. See *Works of Ruskin,* 29:xxii; Cook, *Life of Ruskin,* 2:74; and W. G. Collingwood, *The Life and Work of John Ruskin,* 2 vols. (Boston: Houghton, Mifflin, 1893), 2:479. According to the Pennells, "Ruskin was not taken seriously by the great artist" (*Life of Whistler* [1908], 1:231).

BRINGING SUIT

1. George Boughton remembered the criticism being in the *Spectator* ("Whistlers I Have Known," 212), but I have not found any reference to *Fors Clavigera* in that journal. A copy of the *Architect* article, with marks in the margin highlighting the paragraph about Whistler, is among the papers in the Pennell-Whistler Collection 27 and was one of the exhibits submitted by the plaintiff at the trial.

2. Boughton, "Whistlers I Have Known," 212–13 (also recounted in Pennell and Pennell, *Life of Whistler* [1908], 1:213).

3. Théodore Duret, *Whistler,* trans. Frank Rutter (Philadelphia: Lippincott, 1917), 50. The idea that Whistler hesitated to bring suit must arise from the long delay between the publication of *Fors Clavigera* and the trial, occasioned by Ruskin's ill health.

4. Anderson Rose's papers are contained in PWC 23.

5. Pennell and Pennell, *Life of Whistler* (1908), 1:198. Rose's collection of prints "illustrative of the history and practice of etchings," including several by Whistler, was also shown at the Corporation Art Gallery in Birmingham in 1874.

6. Anna McNeill Whistler to Kate Palmer, 3–4 November 1871, PWC 34.

7. Whistler to E. W. Godwin, 11 September [1878], PWC 4.

8. *Athenaeum,* 21 July 1877, 88. That report was among the copy extracts from newspapers that the plaintiff submitted as evidence (PWC 27). According to Rose's bill of costs, the instructions to sue were taken on the same day that the writ of summons was issued—28 July—but that seems unlikely, since Rose's clerks had ordered copies of *Fors Clavigera* the previous day. The date on the bill probably reflects Rose's vague recollection of beginning the action many months earlier. Rose and Whistler had their first "long conference on the Libel," according to the bill, on 31 July 1877 (PWC 26).

9. *London,* 28 July 1877, 613. That article, a copy of which is in the Pennell-Whistler Collection 27, refers to Ruskin's "outspoken criticism of Mr. Whistler's works" quoted the previous week (21 July 1877, 588). The *Fors Clavigera* critique was also published in *The World,* 18 July 1877, 12. *The Academy* refrained from quoting, but stated that "a single number of *Fors Clavigera* can, always, we believe, be got for tenpence" (21 July 1877, 76). Copies of those accounts are in PWC 25, and the copy extracts prepared for court are in PWC 27.

10. The writ of summons (PWC 26) is dated 28 July 1877. The porter of Corpus Christi provided Ruskin's Coniston address (John M. Davenport to Rose, 4 August 1877, PWC 27).

11. "The Value of a Reputation," *Referee,* 1 December 1878, press-cutting book 2:16, GUL.

12. Pennell and Pennell, *Life of Whistler* (1908), 1:213–14.

13. George W. Smalley, "Whistler: A Tribute from One of His Old Friends," New York *Tribune,* 19 August 1903, 10; Arthur Jerome Eddy, *Recollections and Impressions of James A. McNeill Whistler* (Philadelphia: Lippincott, 1903), 148; Leon, *Ruskin,* 522; Earland, *Ruskin,* 248–49.

14. Smalley, "Whistler," 10.

15. Whistler explained in a letter to Lasenby Liberty, whose bills remained unpaid, that all his financial "annoyance" had been caused by the lack of a "business contract" for his work on the Peacock Room ([1877], PWC 13).

16. Whistler to Rose, 6 [July 1877], PWC 4.

17. See Whistler to Rose, received 6 December 1878, PWC 4.

18. "Whistler: A Fantasia in Criticism," *London,* 18 August 1877, 63.

19. "My Own Article on Whistler," in *Works of Ruskin,* 29:585: "The sentiment that every expression of a man's opinions ought to help either himself,

his friends, or his party, is now so completely the first commandment of English morality that I have ceased to be surprised when, if I say anybody's picture is good—though I don't know the painter from Noah—he immediately writes to thank me for my unexpected kindness; and if I say it is bad, similarly writes to ask what he has done to offend me, or institutes an action for libel."

20. Ruskin to Edward Burne-Jones, [before 8 August 1877], ibid., 37:225.

21. Whistler to Rose, received 23 August 1877, PWC 2.

22. Untitled press cutting, *British Architect,* 21 December 1877, press-cutting book 3:23, GUL.

23. See Alan Cole, diary extracts, 20 September 1873, PWC 281. Whistler may have been influenced by the new home and studio of his friend George Lucas in Paris: see Whistler to Lucas, postmarked 18 January 1873, bound in *A Catalogue of Blue and White Nankin Porcelain Forming the Collection of Sir Henry Thompson,* formerly in Lucas's collection, now in the Rare Books Collection, Walters Art Gallery, Baltimore.

24. Pennell and Pennell, *Life of Whistler* (1908), 1:214. Howell probably realized he could profit from this project, but as W. M. Rossetti remarked in a memorandum to Joseph Pennell, Howell had a tendency to perform charitable acts—"more the sort of thing that one sees in lives of mediaeval devotees than what one expects in English middle-class society" (4 September 1906, PWC 298).

25. The plaintiff's statement of claim (PWC 26) was delivered on 21 November 1877. It had been prepared under Rose's direction by a consulting attorney, Warburton Pike, on 13 August and printed on 7 November 1877.

26. Pennell and Pennell, *Life of Whistler* (1908), 1:214.

27. Rose, bill of costs, 28 November 1877, PWC 26.

28. The statement of defense (PWC 26) was delivered on 6 December, the plaintiff's reply (PWC 27) on 11 December 1877.

29. Untitled press cutting, *British Architect,* 21 December 1877, press-cutting book 3:23, GUL.

30. "On the House-Top," *Architect,* 26 January 1878, 49.

31. Whistler to E. W. Godwin, 30 January 1878, G 101, GUL.

32. On 22 January 1878, the date of the trial was set for 2 February (PWC 27). *Whistler v. Ruskin* appears in the Additional List of Actions for Trial for the Hilary Sittings of the High Court of Justice (p. 4), which Rose purchased on 5 February 1878 (PWC 26). The date set for trial was subsequently changed to 13 April 1878.

33. Ruskin was well enough to write the introduction to *Notes . . . on his Drawings by the late J. M. W. Turner, R.A.*, the catalogue of an exhibition at the Fine Art Society, on February 12, 1878, although the final paragraph suggests that he was already losing his mental balance: "Oh, that some one had but told me, in my youth, when all my heart seemed to be set on these colours and clouds, that appear for a little while and then vanish away, how little my love of them would serve me, when the silence of lawn and wood in the dews of morning should be completed; and all my thoughts should be of those whom, by neither, I was to meet more!" (*Works of Ruskin,* 13:410). The first two editions of the catalogue included a notice inside the front cover that the latter part of the *Notes* was "presented in an incomplete state" and without an epilogue "in consequence of Mr. Ruskin's sudden and dangerous illness." The seventh, revised, edition included Ruskin's epilogue, dated "Brantwood, 10th May 1878" (see ibid., 394).

34. Ruskin to C. E. Norton, 23 July 1878, *The Correspondence of John Ruskin and Charles Eliot Norton,* ed. John Lewis Bradley and Ian Ousby (New York: Cambridge University Press, 1987), 412–13. See also "Mr. Ruskin's Illness Described by Himself," in *Works of Ruskin,* 38:172–73; originally published in the *British Medical Journal,* 27 January 1900.

35. Ruskin to T. Carlyle, 23 June 1878, *The Correspondence of Thomas Carlyle and John Ruskin,* ed. George Allen Cate (Stanford: Stanford University Press, 1982), 240.

36. Plaintiff's brief, PWC 26. On 12 April 1878 the parties consented to postponing the action (PWC 27) and the following day the judge ordered the action to be held on or after 15 May 1878. In preparation for trial, Rose retained a consulting attorney, G. M. Freeman, to advise on the plaintiff's evidence; that advice, which Rose incorporated into the plaintiff's brief, was submitted on 10 April 1878.

37. Upon the application of Walker Martineau & Co., 12 April 1877, PWC 26. The judge approved the defense's motion on 13 April 1878. For further discussion of the function and composition of special juries, see Francis L.

Fennell, "The Verdict in Whistler v. Ruskin," *Victorian Newsletter* (New York), no. 40 (Fall 1971), 18.

38. Rose to Whistler, 12 June 1878, R 126, GUL. Dr. Parsons had certified on 24 April 1878 that although Ruskin was "considerably better," he would not be sufficiently recovered to "take part in any serious business" for several months.

39. On 6 May 1878, Walker Martineau & Co. applied to have the trial postponed until the Michaelmas sittings, but the judge, on 8 May, postponed the trial only until the Trinity sittings, which began in September. On 5 June, Ruskin's solicitors informed Rose that although they had not heard for sure, they thought there was no chance that Ruskin would be able to attend trial during the Trinity sittings and on 8 June again proposed postponing the trial until Michaelmas. Dr. Parsons executed a second statement certifying that Ruskin was, and probably would be for some time, "in a totally unfit state of health to attend or take part" in the pending action. On 12 June, at Rose's insistence, Whistler complied with the defense's request, stating through his solicitor that he "would be very unwilling that the Action should be tried in the Defendant's absence." On 14 June, the judge ordered the trial postponed until Michaelmas.

40. "Americans and Londoners," *New York Times,* 3 June 1878, 3.

41. *A Catalogue of Blue and White Nankin Porcelain Forming the Collection of Sir Henry Thompson* (London: Ellis and White, 1878). Whistler had produced the drawings during the winter of 1876–77, the period he was working on the Peacock Room: see Margaret F. MacDonald, "Whistler's Designs for a Catalogue of Blue and White Nankin Porcelain," *Connoisseur* 198 (August 1978): 290–95.

42. Whistler to Rose, received 13 April 1878, PWC 4. On 19 April 1878, Henry James attended one of Whistler's famous Sunday breakfasts; Sir Coutts and Lady Lindsay, "who are very sociable (and Sir Coutts the handsomest man in England)," were among the invited guests (James to Henry James, Sr., *Henry James Letters,* vol. 2, *1875–1883* [Cambridge: Belknap Press, 1975], 167–68).

43. "The Grosvenor Gallery (First Notice)," *Examiner,* 4 May 1878, 569. Whistler showed *Harmony in Blue and Yellow, Variations in Flesh Colour and Green: The Balcony* (fig. 16), three nocturnes, and two portraits of Maud Franklin: *Arrangement in Blue and Green* (whereabouts unknown; see Young et

al., *Paintings of Whistler,* no. 193) and *Arrangement in White and Black* (1876; FGA).

44. W. M. Rossetti, "Fine Art: The Grosvenor Gallery (First Notice)," *Academy,* 18 May 1878, 447.

45. "The Grosvenor Gallery," *Daily News,* 1 May 1878, 6.

46. "The Grosvenor Gallery (Second Notice)," *Examiner,* 11 May 1878, 601. According to Arthur Severn, that is exactly how Ruskin approached a painting: "He never seemed able, or didn't care, to look at a picture first as a whole. He got no enjoyment out of it in that way. No, he must go near and see what it was all about. Quite a badly painted picture would interest him if there was a letter being pushed under a door or a pretty girl looking rather sorry or anything unusual. While on the other hand a picture with little or no subject but with tones and colours exquisitely true in relation and well painted, he might pass unnoticed" (*The Professor: Arthur Severn's "Memoir of John Ruskin,"* ed. James S. Dearden [London: Allen and Unwin, 1967], 108).

47. "Celebrities at Home, No. LIV: Professor Ruskin at Brantwood," *The World,* 29 August 1877, 4–5. There is a copy of the article among Rose's papers, PWC 27.

48. "Celebrities at Home, No. XCII: Mr. James Whistler at Cheyne-walk," *The World,* 22 May 1878, 4; partially reprinted in *Gentle Art* (1890), 126–28.

49. "Celebrities at Home . . . Whistler." Whistler's position on photography may have been influenced by Baudelaire, who had written in 1859 that if art were an "exact reproduction of Nature," it would be synonymous with photography (quoted in Lochnan, *Etchings of Whistler,* 90).

50. "Notes on Current Events," *British Architect,* 18 April 1878, 180.

51. Howell's diary, October 1878, quoted in Pennell and Pennell, *Life of Whistler* (1908), 1:200.

52. A subscription notice advertising the portrait of Carlyle, "Engraved in Pure Mezzotint by Richard Josey, under the immediate supervision of the Painter," is in the Pennell-Whistler Collection 25; Howell is named as the recipient of subscriptions. Rose became one of the first subscribers, ordering one signed artist's proof, at £3.30, on 3 July 1878.

53. Pennell and Pennell, *Life of Whistler* (1908), 1:227, and Graves, "Whistler," 341. Dissatisfied with the first proofs, Whistler insisted on inking the plate as though it were an etching, much to the amusement of the profes-

sional printers in the shop; the resulting mezzotint was so vague that he did not attempt a second impression.

54. Pennell and Pennell, *Life of Whistler* (1908), 1:227; and Cole, diary extracts, 19 September 1878, PWC 281. Whistler probably visited Disraeli at Hughenden, but according to Graham Robertson, he approached Disraeli in St. James's Park and was told, "after an icy pause . . . 'Go away, go away, little man'" (*Time Was: The Reminiscences of W. Graham Robertson* [1931; reprint, New York: Quartet Books, 1981], 198).

55. Alan Cole, diary extracts, 16 October 1878, PWC 281.

56. Bowen's opinion on the evidence, quoted in the defendant's brief, was delivered on 29 November 1877.

57. Rose to Walker Martineau & Co., 24 October 1878, copy enclosed in Rose to Whistler, 24 October 1878, R 127, GUL; and Rose to Whistler, 24 October 1878, R 127, GUL. The conference is described in Rose's bill of costs as having taken place at the White House on 16 September 1878, following the appearance on 13 September of a "paragraph in the newspaper about Mr. Ruskin" (PWC 26).

PLAINTIFF'S STRATEGY

1. Pennell and Pennell, *Whistler Journal,* 317.

2. G. M. Freeman, advice on evidence, 10 April 1878, PWC 27 (also quoted in the plaintiff's brief, PWC 26).

3. "Artists at War," *Weekly Dispatch,* 1 December 1878, 9. On 16 April 1878, Rose requested from the publisher the names and addresses of the subscribers to *Fors.*

4. Rose to Whistler, 30 November 1878 (morning), R 130, GUL.

5. Untitled article, *Citizen,* 6 November 1878, 4. For more about *Fors Clavigera,* see Brian Maidment, "Ruskin, *Fors Clavigera* and Ruskinism, 1870–1900," in *New Approaches to Ruskin,* ed. Robert Hewison (Boston: Routledge and Kegan Paul, 1981), 194–213.

6. Allen's subpoena prepared on 30 October and served on 21 November 1878.

7. Fresco, "Art Sayings and Doings," *Echo,* 29 November 1878, 4. As Quentin Bell pointed out, Ruskin's unadvertised publication "was sold in

such a way that it had the least possible chance of being widely disseminated" (*Ruskin,* 112). Two thousand copies of *Fors Clavigera* were printed in 1877, a decidedly limited run by contemporary standards; see *Works of Ruskin,* 29:xxix.

8. "Mr. Ruskin's *Fors Clavigera,*" *Saturday Review,* 7 January 1871, 13; Kristine Ottesen Garrigan, "'The Splendidest May Number of the *Graphic*': John Ruskin and the Royal Academy Exhibition of 1875," *Victorian Periodicals Review* 24 (Spring 1991): 22.

9. On 16 April 1877, Rose proposed to admit as evidence several newspaper articles, some of which had quoted or commented on the allegedly libelous passage in *Fors* (*Academy, Athenaeum,* and *Daily News* of 12 July 1877; *Architect* of 14 July 1877 and 26 January 1878; and *The World* of 29 August 1877).

10. See, for example, the leading article in the *Morning Advertiser,* 27 November 1878, 4.

11. Untitled press cutting, *Referee,* 12 January 1879, in press-cutting book 3:15, GUL.

12. G. M. Freeman, advice on evidence, 10 April 1878, PWC 27 (also quoted in the plaintiff's brief, PWC 26).

13. Arthur Orton had assumed the identity of Sir Roger Tichborne, Bart., who was presumed lost at sea. As a result of the series of controversial trials (1871–74), the claimant was found guilty of perjury and sentenced to fourteen years in prison. See Edward Abbott Parry, "Arthur Orton, the Claimant," in *Vagabonds All* (New York: Scribner's, 1926), 1–21.

Parry also served as leading counsel to *The World* and was elected Bencher of the Middle Temple just before the Whistler/Ruskin trial; his name is listed in the *Catalogue of Notable Middle Templars.* He was author of *Lord Campbell's Libel Act . . . with an Introduction on the Law of Oral Slander* (London, 1844); *A Letter on Feargus O'Connor, Esq. . . . on the Plan of Organization Issued by the Birmingham Conference* (London, 1843); and a book in Welsh, *Oriau hamddenol: Sef darnu difyrus ac addysgiadol* (Liverpool, 1866).

14. Jehu Junior [Thomas Gibson Bowles], "Men of the Day, No. LXXIII: Serjeant Parry," *Vanity Fair,* 13 December 1873, 199; and "Whistler v. Ruskin," *Spectator,* 30 November 1878, 1486. Rose retained Parry to represent Whistler on 6 December 1877.

15. Rose to Whistler, 30 November 1878 (evening), R 131, GUL. Petheram, later Sir William, Chief Justice of Bengal, was the author of *The Law and Practice Relating to Discovery by Interrogatories Under the Common Law Procedures Act, 1854* (London, 1864).

16. Pennell and Pennell, *Whistler Journal,* 317.

17. Rose returned to the idea in the manuscript draft for a circular intended to solicit contributions to pay Whistler's costs after the trial: "The age of duelling has happily passed away and the physical condition and reported illness of one of the parties precludes the suggestion of the use of the horse whip" (PWC 27).

18. J. Anderson Rose, *A Collection of Engraved Portraits; Catalogued and Exhibited by James Anderson Rose, at the Opening of the New Library and Museum* (London, 1872).

19. Edward A. Parry, "The Drama of the Law: Duel of Two Immortals," *Weekly Dispatch,* 17 June 1923, 6.

20. Whistler to Rose, received 21 November 1878, R 128, GUL (typescript in PWC 14); Whistler to J. Edgar Boehm ("Mac"), 20 November [1878], B 98, GUL; and Whistler to Albert Moore, 22 November 1878, M 437, GUL.

21. Whistler to Rose, [November 1878], PWC 4. Whistler crossed out the word "habitual"; his list included paintings that had been exhibited at the Royal Academy between 1860 and 1872 and works shown at the Dudley Gallery, at the 1878 Grosvenor Gallery exhibition, and in Paris.

22. Defendant's brief, PWC 26; Whistler to Rose, received 21 November 1878, R 128, GUL (typescript in PWC 14). The text of Whistler's letter is quoted in the plaintiff's brief, with Rose's note that it "contains Mr. Whistler's own view of his case and is worthy of the attention of Counsel on that account" (PWC 26).

23. Whistler to Rose, received 21 November 1878, R 128, GUL. "Money and Morals," Haweis's sermon, was delivered on 18 February 1877, at St. James's Hall, and later at Westminster Abbey and St. George's Hall, Marylebone. It was subsequently published as a pamphlet, *Money and Morals* (London: H.S. King & Co., 1877); part of the text is reprinted in Spencer, *Whistler,* 123. The author of *Music and Morals* and *Poets in the Pulpit,* Haweis was Whistler's neighbor in Cheyne Walk. G. P. Jacomb-Hood recalled an invitation to a luncheon party at Whistler's, with the added attraction of seeing the Haweises on tricycles (*With Brush and Pencil* [London: John Mur-

ray, 1925], 45). Richard Holmes had attempted to make as complete a collection as possible, and purchased many prints directly from Whistler (Holmes to Joseph Pennell, 1906, PWC 285). Petheram stated in his opinion on evidence that the appearance of Holmes and Reid would not be necessary (22 November 1878, quoted in the plaintiff's brief, PWC 26).

24. Petheram's opinion on evidence, 22 November 1878, quoted in the plaintiff's brief, PWC 26.

25. See Whistler to C. A. Howell, 12 November 1878, LB 11/28, GUL. Rose met with Whistler and Howell on 16 November and with Howell alone on 20 and 21 November 1878.

26. A subpoena was prepared for Howell on 16 November, but on 23 November, when Rose set out to serve it, Howell was nowhere to be found. For more on *Howell v. Metropolitan District Railway,* a case concerning the loss of Howell's Fulham home as a place of business, see Dudley Harbron, *The Conscious Stone: The Life of Edward William Godwin* (London: Latimer House, 1949), 132–34. Godwin was called as a witness for Howell and asked if a nocturne in black and gold could only be sold in a Queen Anne house. Howell testified that when he hung Whistler's pictures in his house, "I never laugh, I never even smile." Clearly the late trial was much on people's minds: when Whistler himself walked into the courtroom, Howell waved a welcome from the stand and shouted, "An arrangement in black and white!"

27. A subpoena was prepared for Oswald Colnaghi on 16 November and Rose met with him on 21 November to take down "very long particulars" of the evidence he would give in court; his subpoena was served on 23 November. Rose also intended to subpoena Colnaghi's father, the art dealer Martin Colnaghi (the document was prepared on 30 October), but his efforts to serve Colnaghi on 23 November 1878 failed.

28. A subpoena was prepared for Graves on 30 October and served on 23 November 1878. Graves's suggestions for proofs (PWC 27) were given on 18 November, the day Rose visited his shop to see Whistler's portrait of Carlyle. Graves was not called to the stand, perhaps (as he believed) because the *Carlyle* was disallowed as evidence (Graves, "Whistler," 342).

29. William Rossetti's obituary notice also identifies him as "brother of Dante Gabriel and Christina Rossetti" ("Death of Mr. W. M. Rossetti," *The Times,* 6 February 1919).

30. The novelist Vernon Lee, for instance, wrote in a letter to her mother dated 9 July 1881 that she considered Rossetti "pompous, shy, and dull" (*Vernon Lee's Letters* [London: privately printed, 1937], 74).

31. Robertson, *Time Was,* 88.

32. *Men and Memories: Recollections of William Rothenstein 1872–1900* (New York: Coward-McCann, 1931), 230.

33. W. M. Rossetti, *Fine Art, Chiefly Contemporary: Notices Reprinted, with Revisions* (London: Macmillan, 1867), 265.

34. W. M. Rossetti, "Fine Art. The Grosvenor Gallery," *Academy* 11 (5 May 1877): 396.

35. W. M. Rossetti, memorandum to Joseph Pennell, 19 November 1906, PWC 298.

36. W. M. Rossetti, *Fine Art,* 272; idem, "The Royal Academy Exhibition," *Fraser's Magazine* 71 (June 1865): 747.

37. W. M. Rossetti, memorandum to J. Pennell, 19 November 1906, PWC 298; *Some Reminiscences of William Michael Rossetti,* 2 vols. (New York: Scribner's, 1906), 2:318; William Michael Rossetti, comp., *Rossetti Papers, 1862–1870* (London: Sands and Co., 1903), 234–35, 245. In the memorandum to Pennell, Rossetti explained that when the motion was brought to expel Whistler from the club he had moved a counter-resolution, which was defeated: "My opinion in that matter was not that Whistler had been blameless in the conduct wh[ich] led to the motion for expulsion, but that the Club had no claim to interfere in an affair wh[ich] had not occurred in the Club-premises, nor even in the United Kingdom."

38. W. M. Rossetti to Rose, postmarked 22 November [1878], PWC 4.

39. *Reminiscences of Rossetti,* 1:179.

40. Appendix to *Time and Tide,* in *Works of Ruskin,* 17:478. Rossetti inquired of the critic whether he had adequate evidence on which to base his opinion; Ruskin replied on 27 May 1867 that during their last discussion of "Japan art" he observed that William had allowed his brother to "cram his crotchets down his throat" and reflected that he "would have kept him straighter." In fact, Whistler had introduced both William and Gabriel Rossetti to Japanese woodblock prints, and of the two brothers, William insisted he was "the more decided 'Japoniseur'" (*Rossetti Papers,* 263–64; and memorandum to Joseph Pennell, 19 November 1906, PWC 298).

41. W. M. Rossetti to Rose, postmarked 22 November 1878, PWC 4; *Reminiscences of Rossetti,* 1:182–83. Rossetti's subpoena was prepared on 16 November and served on 22 November.

42. *Reminiscences of Rossetti,* 1:183.

43. Pennell and Pennell, *Life of Whistler* (1908), 1:231.

44. Whistler to Rose, received 21 November 1878, R 128, GUL.

45. Harper Pennington, "James Abbott McNeill Whistler," typescript of an unpublished essay, PWC 297.

46. Quoted in Pennell and Pennell, *Life of Whistler* (1908), 1:231.

47. Whistler provides Keene's Chelsea address in a letter to Rose, received 21 November 1878, R 128, GUL.

48. C. Keene to Mr. Stewart, 24 November 1878, in George Somes Layard, *The Life and Letters of Charles Samuel Keene* (London: Sampson Low, Marston and Co., 1892), 343.

49. Nesfield apparently was not served with a subpoena. Matthew Elden's subpoena was prepared on 22 November 1878 and served the following day. He was not called to testify but seems to have been considered an important witness, since Rose met with Elden on 23 and 24 November 1878. T. R. Way said of "Eldon": "What he did exactly, or even how he lived, I do not know, but he was entertaining, and seemed generally to make himself useful to Whistler" (*Memories of James McNeill Whistler* [New York: John Lane, 1912], 12). After the trial, when Whistler was in Venice, Elden kept the artist informed about events in London, particularly the activities of the trustees of Whistler's bankrupt estate; see M. Elden to Whistler, [November 1879] and 12 April [1880], E 37 and E 36, GUL. These letters also suggest that Elden was Charles Howell's friend and landlord. According to Rennell Rodd, "Eldon" was a designer for Minton and Company, the English pottery firm; by the early 1880s, when Elden was visiting Whistler in his Tite Street studio, he had entirely lost his sanity but continued to "draw innumerable sketches on scraps of brown paper . . . often full of talent but always mad" (Rodd to Joseph Pennell, 3 June 1901, PWC 298). See also Young et al., *Paintings of Whistler,* nos. 243–44.

50. A subpoena was prepared for Josey on 16 November and served on 23 November 1878.

51. One of Godwin's sketchbooks preserved at the Victoria and Albert Museum (E.248–1963) contains a rough sketch of the back of Whistler's head, apparently

drawn in the courtroom. Godwin's pencil notations on the testimony of Moore, Burne-Jones, and Frith suggest that he was present on both days of the trial.

52. E. J. Poynter to Whistler, 10 October 1871, P 651, GUL.

53. Thomas Armstrong, "Whistler v. Ruskin," memorandum to Elizabeth Pennell, 14 April 1907, PWC 278 (also recounted in Pennell and Pennell, *Life of Whistler* [1908], 1:243; and Thomas Armstrong, "Reminiscences of Whistler," in *Thomas Armstrong, C.B.: A Memoir, 1832–1911,* ed. L. M. Lamont [London: Martin Secker, 1912], 208).

54. Rose, bill of costs, 23 November 1878, PWC 26. Burton's reasons for declining to testify are not known, but Poynter's refusal may have something to do with the fact that he was the brother-in-law of Burne-Jones, chief witness for the defense.

55. Alan Cole, diary extracts, 16 November 1875, PWC 281.

56. *Fors* 79 (July 1877), in *Works of Ruskin,* 29:161.

57. Whistler to J. J. Tissot, draft, n.d. [before 24 November 1878], T 191, GUL. Tissot's letters to Whistler have apparently not survived.

58. Ibid., draft, [24 November 1878], PWC 3 (typescript in PWC 19): "J'ai expliqué que je m'étais trompé en supposant que Tissot avrait été fier de se dire l'ami de Whistler—Inutile mon cher!—et je remplie mon dernier devoir d'amitié en vous evidant la prison!" (See also T 190, GUL.)

That letter is in a stamped, addressed envelope that was apparently never posted. Two closely related drafts of a similar letter in GUL (T 188, dated "Mardi. Nov. 26," and T 189, undated, evidently written the same day) suggest that Whistler waited until the second day of the trial to remind Tissot, who apparently had not been present on the first, that he was obligated by law to appear in court. In those drafts Whistler adds that he had appealed to his lawyer to save them "le spectacle fatal d'un ami 'malgré lui'" (the fatal spectacle of a friend "in spite of himself") and that Tissot would be incapable of testifying even to the virtues of the very paintings to which he had so freely served himself.

Tissot, who was often considered a plagiarist by his contemporaries, frequently borrowed devices from Whistler's paintings: Tissot's *Lex Deux Soeurs: portrait* (1863; Musée d'Orsay, Paris), for example, shows a marked similarity to Whistler's *White Girl* (fig. 10), painted the previous year; *Jeune Femme tenant des objets japonais* (1865; Sayn-Wittgenstein Fine Art) to *La Princesse du pays de la porcelain* (1864; FGA), and *The Captain's Daughter*

(1873; Southampton Art Gallery and Museums) and *The Last Evening* (1873; Guildhall Art Gallery, London) to *Wapping* (1861; National Gallery of Art, Washington, D.C.). See Michael Wentworth, "James Tissot: 'Cet être complexe,'" and Malcom Warner, "Comic and Aesthetic: James Tissot in the Context of British Art and Taste," in *James Tissot,* ed. Krystyna Matyjaszkiewicz (New York: Abbeville, 1985), 17, 34; and Christopher Wood, *Tissot: The Life and Work of Jacques Joseph Tissot, 1836–1902* (London: Weidenfeld and Nicolson, 1986), 21–22, 37–38, 62–64.

59. Whistler to George Lucas, postmarked 3 May 1869, BMA.

60. [Tom Taylor], "Grosvenor Gallery," 10. Thomas Way bought Boehm's terracotta bust at the liquidation sale on 12 February 1880 for six guineas (Pennell and Pennell, *Life of Whistler* [1908], 1:260; and T. R. Way to Elizabeth R. Pennell, 29 October 1906, PWC 302). Coincidentally, Boehm was preparing to sculpt a portrait bust of Ruskin at the time of the trial (Ruskin to Frances Graham, 12 November 1878, quoted in Frances Horner, *Time Remembered* [London: Heinemann, 1933], 56).

61. J. Edgar Boehm to Whistler, 19 October 1878, B 95, GUL.

62. Whistler to J. Edgar Boehm ("Mac"), 20 November [1878], B 98, GUL. Boehm's subpoena was prepared on 30 October and served on 22 November 1878.

63. Whistler to Rose, received 21 November 1878, R 128, GUL; Rose, bill of costs, 23 November 1878, PWC 26. Boehm, who was served on 22 November, was the first of the artists to be subpoenaed.

64. *Academy Notes 1875,* in *Works of Ruskin,* 14:272–73.

65. Alfred Lys Baldry, *Albert Moore: His Life and Works* (London: George Bell and Sons, 1894), 89.

66. Albert Moore, suggestions for proofs, [24 November 1878], PWC 27.

67. Robertson, *Time Was,* 59–60; Albert Moore to Whistler, 30 January 1885, M 438, GUL. Moore owned one painting by Whistler, *Nocturne: Trafalgar Square—Snow* (ca. 1875–77; FGA), which he may have bought to alleviate the artist's financial distress or accepted as a token of friendship. According to Graham Robertson, Moore hung the nocturne in a corner, face to the wall (*Time Was,* 195). He sold it in 1892, writing to the dealer Alexander Reid, "Of course Whistler's pictures will before long realise prices

more in accordance with their merit" (10 November 1892, Charles Lang Freer Papers, FGA/Arthur M. Sackler Gallery Archives).

68. Whistler to Albert Moore, 22 November 1878, M 437, GUL.

69. *Grosvenor Gallery* (1877), 25. The third painting was *Marigolds,* present location unknown.

70. J. Comyns Carr, *Some Eminent Victorians,* 138.

71. Albert Moore, suggestions for proofs, [24 November 1878], PWC 27. Moore's subpoena was prepared on 16 November and served on 23 November 1878.

72. Richard Ellmann, *Oscar Wilde* (New York: Knopf, 1988), 16. Wilde's full name was Oscar Fingal O'Flahertie Wills Wilde.

73. Freeman Wills, *W. G. Wills: Dramatist and Painter* (New York: Longmans, Green, and Co., 1898), 66. Princess Louise was one of the artist's pupils.

74. Jopling, *Twenty Years,* 69. *The Marchioness of Bute* was exhibited at the Royal Academy in 1872, *Ophelia and Laertes* in 1874. Neither painting has been located.

75. Wills, *W. G. Wills,* 75. According to Wills's obituary notice in the *Illustrated London News,* "it was a real ambition with him to shine as an artist as well as a writer of plays" (19 December 1891, 794).

76. Obituary notice, W. G. Wills, *Illustrated London News,* 794.

77. *Olivia* would be judged "one of the most perfect adaptations of a novel that the stage possesses" (obituary notice, W. G. Wills, *The Times,* 15 December 1891, 6). It was Ellen Terry's performance in *Olivia* that convinced Henry Irving to make her his leading lady at the Lyceum (Roger Manvell, *Ellen Terry* [London: Heinemann, 1968], 98).

78. *Ellen Terry's Memoirs,* 110; Jopling, *Twenty Years,* 69; Lawrence Irving, *Henry Irving: The Actor and His World* (New York: Macmillan, 1952), 209. For more on Wills, see Walter G. Strickland, *A Dictionary of Irish Artists* (Dublin: Maunsel, 1913), s.v. "Wills, William Gorman."

79. "English Plays and Actors," *New York Times,* 15 April 1878, 5; *Dictionary of National Biography,* s.v. "Wills, William Gorman." Louise Jopling recounts a popular anecdote about Wills: "It was believed that some one had pointed out to him that there were the remains of some egg on his beard. 'Impossible,

my dear fellow. I haven't eaten an egg these last three days'" (*Twenty Years,* 69).

80. Whistler to Rose, received 10 August 1878, PWC 4.

81. Wills, *W. G. Wills,* 53–54.

82. A subpoena ad testificandum was prepared for Wills on 16 November and served 23 November 1878. Rose met with Wills to review his evidence on 24 November 1878, the evening before he testified in court.

THE DEFENSE

1. Birkenhead, *Illustrious Friends,* 276.

2. See, for example, Cook, *Life of Ruskin,* 2:428; Birkenhead, *Illustrious Friends,* 274; and John Dixon Hunt, *The Wider Sea: A Life of John Ruskin* (New York: Viking, 1982), 373.

3. Georgiana Burne-Jones, *Memorials of Edward Burne-Jones,* 2 vols. (London: Macmillan, 1909), 2:87.

4. Severn, *The Professor,* 114.

5. Ruskin to H. G. Liddell, 18 November 1878, *Works of Ruskin,* 25:xl.

6. Ruskin to Arthur Severn, quoted in Birkenhead, *Illustrious Friends,* 274.

7. Ruskin to J. A., 24 January 1880, *Works of Ruskin,* 34:544.

8. Plaintiff's brief, PWC 26.

9. See Whistler to Rose, [19 November 1878], PWC 4: "How about Ruskin himself after all? Are you not going to subpoena him—had you not better subpoena him instantly or have you already done so?"

10. Comyns Carr, *Some Eminent Victorians,* 54–55; obituary notice, Sir John Holker, *The Times,* 25 May 1882, 9; *Dictionary of National Biography,* s.v. "Holker, Sir John." See also "Statesmen, No. CCLXV: Sir John Holker," *Vanity Fair,* 9 February 1878, 87.

11. Severn, *The Professor,* 115.

12. Armstrong, "Reminiscences of Whistler," 209 (also in Pennell and Pennell, *Life of Whistler* [1908], 1:243–44).

13. Henry Stewart Cunningham, *Lord Bowen: A Biographical Sketch* (London: privately printed, 1896), 145. Until 1879, when he became a judge in the

Queen's Bench Division, Bowen appeared for the government in all commercial and common-law cases.

14. "Judges, No. 36: The Right Honourable Sir Charles Synge Christopher Bowen, P.C., D.C.L., LL.D., F.R.S.," *Vanity Fair,* 12 March 1892, illustrated with a chromolithograph by Spy [Leslie Ward], entitled "Judicial Politeness." Sir John Coleridge, the attorney general at the time of the Tichborne case, had relied visibly upon Bowen's acumen and industry during the trial, and had appropriated his technique of phrasing a question in such a way that the answer was not suggested—"Would you be surprised to hear that . . . ?" See Cunningham, *Lord Bowen,* 141, and H. Montgomery Hyde, *Their Good Names: Twelve Cases of Libel and Slander* (London: Hamish Hamilton, 1970), 73.

Bowen attended Rugby and Balliol College, Oxford, where he received the Arnold Prize for an undergraduate essay published in 1859 (*Delphi, Considered Locally, Morally, and Politically*), as well as the 1857 Chancellor's Prize for Latin verse for *Sebastopolis: Carmen Latinum Cancellari praemio donatum et in Theatro Sheldonian recitatum* (Oxford, 1857). He would go on to translate Virgil's *Eclogues* (Boston, 1904) and the first six books of the *Aeneid*, contribute pieces with some regularity to the *Saturday Review*, deliver to the Walsall Literary Institute a lecture called "Novel Reading" (1891), take an active and abiding interest in the Working Men's College and the Royal Academy of Art, become a member of the Athenaeum Club, the Literary Society, and the House of Lords, and compose some rather respectable verses, which must have satisfied an aesthetic impulse too often stultified by the prosaic demands of life as a law lord. Bowen was chosen to write one chapter, "Administration of the Law from 1837–87," in the ambitious *Reign of Queen Victoria,* edited by Thomas Humphrey Ward (London, 1887); one of his arguments is included in *Legal Masterpieces: Specimens of Argumentation and Position by Eminent Lawyers,* edited by V. V. Veeder (St. Paul, Minn., 1903). Bowen is also the author of *The "Alabama" Claims and Arbitration Considered from a Legal Point of View* (London, 1868), and *Report of the Commissioners Appointed to Enquire into the Truck System* (London, 1871).

15. Severn, *The Professor*, 115.

16. Fulford's affidavit in support of his motion to deliver interrogatories, executed on 5 November 1878, indicates that because of Ruskin's illness, the firm had only recently received instructions from the defendant sufficient to proceed to trial (PWC 27). According to Severn, the evidence Ruskin would

have given in court was taken on commission as soon as he announced his intention not to attend the trial (*The Professor*, 114).

17. Baron Huddleston said in the jury's instructions that even if Ruskin were ill, there was no reason that he "should not have put his views in connection with this case on paper."

18. Parry, "Whistler v. Ruskin," 27.

19. The two defenses Ruskin suggested were *justification* (the words complained of are true in substance and fact) and *qualified privilege* (the words complained of were published by someone holding a responsibility to communicate with the public). The defense of privilege is restricted, but the defense of fair comment—which was only becoming a distinct defense in the 1870s—is available to any member of the public who comments on matters of public interest (such as pictures displayed in an exhibition that is open to the public). Ruskin, and his public, may have considered that he had earned the protection of the law even for defamation, but in fact his rights were no different from those of any other British citizen. See *Halsbury's Laws of England,* 4th ed. (London: Butterworths, 1979), 28:69, para. 131.

20. Fennell suggests that Holker may not have understood the brief or had not had time to give it sufficient attention ("Verdict in Whistler v. Ruskin," 19).

21. In an action for libel, the plaintiff claims damages to compensate for injury to his reputation, and should not recover damages for a reputation he does not hold. The defense is entitled, then, to give evidence relating to the plaintiff's bad character, in mitigation of damages. See *Halsbury's Laws of England,* 28:122, para. 246.

22. "Celebrities at Home, No. XCII: Mr. James Whistler at Cheyne-walk," *The World,* 22 May 1878, 5. Whistler hung his paintings in his garden "to become seasoned by wind, sunshine, and rain," in order to remove, in his words, "that objectionable gloss which puts one in mind of a painfully new hat." A neighbor of Whistler's in Chelsea, Anna Lea Merritt, wrote the Pennells that she remembered seeing nocturnes "set out along the garden wall to bake in the sun" (12 December 1907, PWC 293; also recounted in Pennell and Pennell, *Life of Whistler* [1908], 1:165). See also Pennell and Pennell, *Whistler Journal,* 120.

23. "Notes of the Week," *The Week,* 30 November 1878, 519. One commentator claims to have asked Ruskin if he had been surprised to learn of the

technique and received the reply: "Now I should have been astonished if Whistler had hung the pictures across the line to dry the sun, or if the sun had hung the line across the pictures to dry Whistler, or if the pictures had hung Whistler across the sun to dry the line, or if the line had hung Whistler across the sun to dry the pictures, or if the line had hanged the sun, or if the pictures had hanged Whistler, or if Whistler had hanged himself" (Dagonet, "Mustard and Cress," *Referee,* 2 February 1879, 17).

24. *The Grasshopper* was translated and adapted by John Hollingshead from a French farce, *La Cigale* by Meilhac and Halevy, in which the protagonist, an "Intentionist" painter named Marignan, was a caricature of Edgar Degas: see Theodore Reff, "The Butterfly and the Old Ox," in *Degas: The Artist's Mind* (Cambridge, Mass.: Belknap Press, 1987), 19–20. The Gaiety Theatre was in the Strand, across the street from the printing establishment of Thomas Way, where Whistler was learning the art of lithography; Whistler represented the theater in a lithograph, *The Manager's Window, Gaiety Theatre* (W. 114).

25. Alan Cole, diary extracts, 7 January 1878, PWC 281.

26. John Hollingshead, *The Grasshopper: A Drama in Three Acts* (London: Woodfall and Kinder, 1877), 38–39; Hamilton, *Aesthetic Movement,* 18.

27. Armstrong, "Reminiscences of Whistler," 213; "What the World Says," *The World,* 19 December 1877, 13. Accused of "bad taste in exhibiting caricatures of living people," Hollingshead had written a defense to the *Daily News* insisting that he had meant no personal disrespect and that he had received Whistler's consent to produce the painting ("Mr. Whistler and 'The Grasshopper,'" 14 December 1878, press-cutting book 1:93, GUL). A letter from Whistler written 27 October 1877 indicates that the artist planned to meet with Pellegrini and would be pleased to do anything to assist the "general completeness" of Hollingshead's performance (quoted in John Hollingshead, *Gaiety Chronicles* [London: Archibald Constable, 1898], 377). Pellegrini was also a friend of Degas, who may have attended a performance of *The Grasshopper* in London: see Reff, "Butterfly and Old Ox," 36.

28. Albert Moore, whose response is not recorded in any of the published accounts of the trial, responded to the question of whether he knew *The Grasshopper* with "what looked like guilty knowledge of the subject," explaining that he knew the engraving, but not the picture. Moore alluded to a painting by Jules Lefebvre, utterly mystifying the attorney general, who did

not know what he was talking about ("A Contemptuous Verdict," *Mayfair,* 3 December 1878, press-cutting book 2:25, GUL).

29. Ruskin to E. Burne-Jones, 2 November [1878], in *Works of Ruskin,* 29:xxiv (also quoted in G. Burne-Jones, *Memorials of Burne-Jones,* 2:87).

30. See, for example, Marsh, *Pre-Raphaelite Sisterhood;* and Gay Daly, *Pre-Raphaelites in Love* (New York: Ticknor and Fields, 1989), 249–329.

31. Dennis Farr, *English Art 1870–1940,* The Oxford History of English Art, vol. 11 (Oxford: Clarendon Press, 1978), 14. The idea that Burne-Jones was a reluctant witness appears in practically every mention of his participation in the trial. See, for example, Henry James, "On Whistler and Ruskin," 173; William Gaunt, *The Aesthetic Adventure,* 2d ed., rev. (New York: Harcourt, Brace, and Co., 1975), 88; and Christopher Wood, *The Pre-Raphaelites* (London: Weidenfeld and Nicolson, 1981), 119. In an essay on Burne-Jones, David Cecil states the typical view that testifying on Ruskin's behalf "was the last thing Burne-Jones wanted to do. He hated rows; he hated appearing in public; and he was not at all sure that Ruskin was in the right. However, it seemed ungrateful and disloyal to refuse. Reluctantly, he went into the witness box" ("Edward Burne-Jones," in *Visionary and Dreamer: Two Poetic Painters,* Bollingen Series 35, no. 5 [Princeton: Princeton University Press, 1969], 134).

32. Lochnan, *Etchings of Whistler,* 145–46. See also M. J. H. Liversidge, "The Artist as Adversary: The Burlington Fine Arts Club Affair," in *James McNeill Whistler,* ed. Denys Sutton ([Tokyo]: The Yomiuri Shimbun, 1987), 36–40.

33. Fitzgerald, *Burne-Jones,* 110.

34. E. Burne-Jones to Joan Severn, [27 November 1878], *The Brantwood Diary of John Ruskin,* ed. Helen Gill Viljoen (New Haven: Yale University Press, 1971), 425.

35. E. Burne-Jones to Joan Severn, [early November 1878], ibid., 422–23. In a letter to Frederick Leyland apparently written in November 1878, Burne-Jones said that he "would like to see the people"—presumably Ruskin's lawyers—"and state one or two things that I know" (PWC 6A).

36. The Pennells believed that Burne-Jones had willfully confused the Peacock Room decoration with Whistler's caricature of Leyland, *The Gold Scab* (fig. 71), but this is impossible, since the painting was not produced until after the trial (*Whistler Journal,* 326).

37. According to William Graham's daughter Frances, "Burne-Jones liked very much to have his friends all to himself, and in a locked compartment of which he kept the key" (Horner, *Time Remembered,* 54).

38. Burne-Jones to F. R. Leyland, [November 1878], PWC 6A. As it happened, *Nocturne in Blue and Silver* was submitted in evidence by the plaintiff, not the defendant; presumably information about the portraits was not received, as the defendant's brief states only that Whistler "painted portraits of Mr. Leyland and all his family which we believe the latter refused to have" (PWC 26).

39. Crane, *Reminiscences,* 199–200. Others present at that remarkable gathering included J. Comyns Carr and the artists Boughton, Poynter, Armstrong, and Val Prinsep.

40. Pennell and Pennell, *Whistler Journal,* 325.

41. Ruskin to E. Burne-Jones, 2 November 1878, *Works of Ruskin,* 29:xxiv (also quoted in G. Burne-Jones, *Memorials of Burne-Jones,* 2:87).

42. His gullibility astonished the Pennells: see *Whistler Journal,* 325.

43. E. Burne-Jones to Joan Severn, [early November 1878], *Brantwood Diary of Ruskin,* 423.

44. Whistler to J. Edgar Boehm ("Mac"), 20 November [1878], B 98, GUL.

45. Whistler to Rose, received 21 November 1878, R 128, GUL.

46. "There shouldn't be *laws* against immorality," Burne-Jones is known to have said. "It shouldn't be *illegal* to prefer Frith to Mantegna" (quoted in Fitzgerald, *Burne-Jones,* 105).

47. W. W. Fenn, "Our Living Artists: William Powell Frith, R.A.," *Magazine of Art* 2 (1879): 83.

48. "The Value of a Reputation," *Referee,* 1 December 1878, press-cutting book 2:16, GUL.

49. Birkenhead, *Illustrious Friends,* 275.

50. Pennell and Pennell, *Life of Whistler* (1908), 1:240.

51. *Academy Notes 1858,* in *Works of Ruskin,* 14:161–62. See also "Notes of the Week," *The Week,* 30 November 1878, 519: "We cannot recall at this moment whether Mr. Ruskin has ever criticised Mr. Frith's pictures—if he has not, Mr. Frith may thank his lucky stars. We should ourselves much like

to hear Mr. Ruskin on Mr. Frith, and we hope he may be induced to devote a *Fors* to the subject."

Ruskin had more to say about the popularity of the subject of *Derby Day* in 1880, when he lamented that no one appreciated works by the old masters, although "every one can understand Frith's 'Derby Day'—that is to say, everybody is interested in jockeys, harlots, mountebanks and men about town; but nobody in saints, heroes, kings, or wise men—either from the east or west" (Ruskin's letter in reply to a correspondent who asked how best to found an art gallery in Leicester, published in the Leicester *Chronicle and Mercury* [31 January 1880] and *The Times* [2 February 1880], and reprinted in *Arrows of the Chace,* in *Works of Ruskin,* 34:542). Ruskin subsequently apologized to Frith, explaining that he had been obliged to explain why people liked *Derby Day* so much—"namely, not for the painting, which is good, and worthy their liking, but for the sight of the racecourse and its humours." Such a picture ought not to hang on museum walls, Ruskin said, for "in a museum people ought not to fancy themselves on a racecourse. If they want to see races, let them go to races; and if rogues, to Bridewells" ("A Museum or Picture Gallery" [1880], ibid., 258–59).

52. William Powell Frith, "Crazes in Art: 'Pre-Raphaelitism' and 'Impressionism,'" *Magazine of Art* 11 (1888): 190. See also idem, *My Autobiography and Reminiscences,* 2 vols. (New York: Harper and Brothers, 1888), 2:4—"Ruskin's works bristle with errors; one of his notable ones was his saying, on the discovery of a bit of what he took for pre-Raphaelite work in one of the worst pictures I ever painted, that I was at 'last in the right way,' or words to that effect." Frith alludes to Ruskin's critique of *Many Happy Returns of the Day* in *Academy Notes 1856,* in which Ruskin, referring to "the advancing Pre-Raphaelitism in the wreath of leaves round the child's head," remarked that the picture was far above Frith's "former standard" (*Works of Ruskin,* 14:53).

53. Frith, *Autobiography,* 1:71; Jane Ellen Frith Panton, *Leaves from a Life* (London: Eveleigh Nash, 1908), 170.

54. Frith, *Autobiography,* 2:5. Cf. Whistler, *Whistler v. Ruskin: Art & Art Critics* (London: Chatto and Windus, 1878), 7: "A life passed among pictures makes not a painter—else the policeman in the National Gallery might assert himself. Let not Mr. Ruskin flatter himself that more education makes the difference between himself and the policeman when both stand gazing in the Gallery."

55. Panton, *Leaves from a Life,* 170; Frith, *Autobiography,* 1:71.

56. For a discussion of Frith's ideology, see Shearer West, "Tom Taylor, William Powell Frith, and the British School of Art," *Victorian Studies* (Indiana University) 33 (Winter 1990): 307–26.

57. Frith, "Crazes in Art," 191.

58. Panton, *Leaves from a Life,* 328. Frith testified that he had declined to testify but had received a subpoena Monday morning, 25 November, which compelled his attendance.

59. Rose, notes for W. C. Petheram, [25 November 1878], PWC 27; Rose to Whistler, 30 November 1878 (evening), R 131, GUL. Rose's notes appear to have been made during consultation with Petheram after the first day of the trial, in preparation for cross-examining witnesses for the defense.

60. Frith, *Autobiography,* 1:346. *The Road to Ruin* is now in a private collection in Italy. See Aubrey Noakes, *William Frith: Extraordinary Victorian Painter* (London: Jupiter, 1978), 119–20.

61. Rose, notes for Petheram, [25 November 1878], PWC 27.

62. Tom Taylor, *The Railway Station, Painted by W. P. Frith, Esq., R.A.* (London: Henry Graves, 1865), 26. The text of the pamphlet is based largely on Taylor's review, "The Railway Station," *The Times,* 19 April 1862, 5.

63. Edmund Yates, *Fifty Years of London Life: Memoirs of a Man of the World* (New York: Harper and Brothers, 1885), 322.

64. *Ellen Terry's Memoirs,* 93.

65. Victor Emeljanow, "Tom Taylor," in *Victorian Britain: An Encyclopedia,* ed. Sally Mitchell (New York: Garland, 1988), 783.

66. Whistler, *Gentle Art* (1890), 18.

67. "Bundles of Rue: Lives of Artists Recently Deceased. Tom Taylor," *Magazine of Art* 4 (1881), 66.

68. Winton Tolles, *Tom Taylor and the Victorian Drama* (New York: Columbia University Press, 1940), 258–59. According to Tolles, Taylor's authority among laymen was second only to Ruskin's.

69. E. W. Godwin, "Notes on Mr. Whistler's 'Peacock Room,'" *Architect,* 24 February 1877, 188.

70. [Tom Taylor], "Royal Academy Exhibition: Fourth Notice," *The Times,* 24 May 1865, 6. See also [Tom Taylor], "The Exhibition of the Royal Acad-

emy (Second Notice)," *The Times,* 8 May 1865, 8: "Mr. Whistler is the man at once of highest genius and most daring eccentricity in this school. He is equally capable of exquisite things or of gross impertinences, and this exhibition contains instances of both; of the former, in the 'Little White Girl' (530), of the latter, in his two sketches of Japanese and Chinese fabrics and screens, accompanied by slight caricatures of maidens of the flowery land, mere plays of colour and imitation of textures, ugly in form and unfinished in execution." The "sketches" to which Taylor refers are *Caprice in Purple and Gold: The Golden Screen* (fig. 11) and *The Scarf* (whereabouts unknown; see Young et al., *Paintings of Whistler,* no. 59).

71. Tom Taylor to Whistler, 13 June 1865, LB 12/54, GUL. See also Armstrong, "Reminiscences of Whistler," 204: "Tom Taylor told du Maurier that he had written a great deal more which had been suppressed by the editor. This seemed to me very strange. . . . But Tom Taylor was a truthful person, and at that time very well-disposed."

72. [Tom Taylor], "Dudley Gallery—Cabinet Pictures in Oil," *The Times,* 14 November 1871, 4.

73. Whistler to Tom Taylor, postmarked 2 April 1872, PWC 2; [Tom Taylor], "Exhibition of the Royal Academy (Second Notice)," *The Times,* 21 May 1872, 7.

74. For a discussion of Taylor's position, see West, "Taylor, Frith, and British School."

75. Quoted in Pennell and Pennell, *Life of Whistler* (1908), 1:185. Whistler returned to the theme in 1875, during a tête-à-tête with Alan Cole about "critics and their ignorance of facts, which must be either right or wrong and not matters of opinion" (Cole, diary extracts, 2 December 1875, PWC 281).

76. "Men of the Day, No. CCXXVI: Mr. Tom Taylor," *Vanity Fair,* 11 March 1876, 149.

77. Birkenhead, *Illustrious Friends,* 275.

FINAL ARRANGEMENTS

1. Robert Fulford made his initial request on 28 October 1878, and Whistler and Rose met for three hours that evening. Whistler gave Rose information on the paintings, but insisted that the fairness and reasonableness of Ruskin's criticism, not the merit of his works, was at issue; he also objected

to the inspection of any paintings but the nocturnes because the portraits (which had not been for sale) were not the object of Ruskin's attack.

2. Whistler to Rose, received 8 November 1878, PWC 4. Rose and Fulford met on 29 October; Fulford entered his application on 5 November; the judge issued an order of inspection on 6 November; Whistler and Rose met at the Arundel Club for dinner and discussion on 8 November 1878.

3. Whistler to Rose, 10 November [1878], PWC 4.

4. James Jackson Jarves, "Art of the Whistler Sort," *New York Times,* 12 January 1879, 10.

5. Severn, *The Professor,* 115; Whistler, *Gentle Art* (1890), 7.

6. *The Last of Old Westminster* (1862; Museum of Fine Arts, Boston). Arthur Severn to Joseph Pennell, 30 [November] 1906, PWC 299. Arthur shared the flat, in Manchester Buildings on the river, with his brother, the artist Walter Severn.

7. Severn, *The Professor,* 114–15; Arthur Severn to Joseph Pennell, 30 [November] 1906, PWC 299.

8. Severn, *The Professor,* 115; Burne-Jones to Joan Severn, [27 November 1878], *Brantwood Diary of Ruskin,* 425.

9. According to Serjeant Parry: see Parry, "Drama of the Law," 6.

10. Whistler to Albert Moore, 22 November 1878, M 437, GUL.

11. Whistler to J. Edgar Boehm ("Mac"), 20 November [1878], B 98, GUL; and to Mrs. W. G. Rawlinson, [November 1878], PWC 2. *Harmony in Grey and Green: Miss Cicely Alexander* (fig. 51) would not be exhibited at the Grosvenor Gallery until 1881.

12. Whistler to Rose, [22 November 1878], PWC 4. Whistler engaged Foord and Dickinson, the Wardour Street picture framers and restorers, to transport his paintings from his house in Chelsea to Westminster, at a cost of £2.8.9; the account is among Rose's papers in PWC 27.

13. See E. Burne-Jones to F. R. Leyland, [November 1878], PWC 6A.

14. Graves, "Whistler," 342. The *Carlyle* seems to have been in the possession of Henry Graves at the time of the trial.

15. Whistler, manuscript notes, [25 November 1878], PWC 27: "The Nocturne in Gold and Blue belonging to Mrs. Wyndham is the only one not seen by the jury." Also Whistler to Rose, [22 November 1878], PWC 4. Whistler

testified that he had received a telegram stating that the nocturne could not be lent.

16. Pennell and Pennell, *Whistler Journal,* 103; according to Frances Leyland, the decorated frame was damaged at some time after the trial and later regilded. In 1892, before the painting's exhibition at the Goupil Galleries, Whistler had the nocturne reframed (see Whistler to D. C. Thomson, 14 February 1892, PWC 16). F. R. Leyland was subpoenaed by the defense to produce the nocturne (defendant's brief, PWC 26).

17. See instructions for answers to interrogatories, [11 November 1878], PWC 27; Rose noted that *Nocturne in Black and Gold* and *Arrangement in Brown* had been "deposited with Mrs. Noseda for such advance by Mr. Charles Augustus Howell a friend of Mr. Whistler's and as between Howell and Mrs. Noseda they appear to be Howell's property." Noseda's subpoena was prepared on 22 November and served on 23 November 1878.

18. Severn, *The Professor,* 115–16 (also recounted in Pennell and Pennell, *Life of Whistler* [1908], 1:244).

19. Eddy, *Recollections of Whistler,* 144–45; Horner, *Time Remembered,* 56–57.

20. Severn, *The Professor,* 115. Birkenhead states that the Titian painting was taken to court "on Ruskin's instructions" (*Illustrious Friends,* 275).

21. Ruskin to Rawdon Brown, 2 September 1864, *Works of Ruskin,* 24:184 n. 5. Collingwood's copy of the painting remains in the dining room at Brantwood.

22. "The Flamboyant Architecture of the Valley of the Somme" (1869), ibid., 19:250.

23. Pennell and Pennell, *Life of Whistler* (1908), 1:243. According to Rose, Ruskin's witness (presumably Burne-Jones) saw the portrait "and began to abuse it thinking it was one of Whistler's" (notes on the back of a manuscript menu by Whistler, dated 3 December [1878], PWC 4).

24. Leslie Baily, *Gilbert and Sullivan: Their Lives and Times* (New York: Viking, 1973), 67.

25. Ruskin to C. E. Norton, dated 26 November, [25 November 1878], *Correspondence of Ruskin and Norton,* 417 (also in *Works of Ruskin,* 37:266).

26. Reay, "London," Hartford (Conn.) *Courant,* 14 December 1878, presscutting book 2:25, GUL.

27. "A Contemptuous Verdict," *Mayfair,* 3 December 1878, press-cutting book 2:25, GUL.

28. Jehu Junior [Thomas Gibson Bowles], "Statesmen, No. CLXIII: Mr. John Walter Huddleston, Q.C., M.P.," *Vanity Fair,* 28 February 1874, 105, illustrated with a chromolithograph by Ape [Carlo Pellegrini] entitled "A Future Judge."

29. Panton, *Leaves from a Life,* 341, 338–39; G. A. S. [George Augustus Sala], "Echoes of the Week," *Illustrated London News,* 30 November 1878, 510.

30. *Dictionary of National Biography,* s.v. "Huddleston, Sir John Walter." The Judicature Acts made the exchequer court a division of the high court of justice.

31. "Death of Mr. Baron Huddleston," *The Times,* 6 December 1890, 9.

32. Ibid.

33. Graves, "Whistler," 342; Horner, *Time Remembered,* 57; "A Contemptuous Verdict," *Mayfair,* 3 December 1878, press-cutting book 2:25, GUL.

PART TWO: THE TRIAL

INTRODUCTION

1. The trial was held before a *nisi prius* court, one held for the trial of issues of fact before a judge and jury.

2. The square brackets in this passage are original to the text; hereafter, brackets indicate editorial insertions.

PLAINTIFF'S CASE

1. The South Kensington Museum is now the Victoria and Albert Museum.

2. John Phillip, R.A. (1817–67), famous for his paintings of Spanish life, purchased Whistler's *At the Piano* (fig. 9) in 1860.

3. The Dudley Gallery, originally intended only to exhibit drawings, opened in London in 1864 and soon became a sort of *salon des refusés.* Whistler participated in the exhibitions of 1871, 1872, 1873, and 1875.

4. The extent of a publication's circulation and the nature of its readership can affect the amount of damages. See *Halsbury's Laws of England,* 4th ed. (London: Butterworths, 1979), 28:118, para. 237.

5. *Fors* 79 (July 1877), in *The Works of John* Ruskin, ed. E. T. Cook and Alexander Wedderburn, 39 vols., Library Edition (London: George Allen, 1903–12), 29:157. Ruskin had complimented Sir Coutts by saying that he had founded the Grosvenor Gallery "in the true desire to help the artists and better the art of his country:—not as a commercial speculation."

6. Ibid., 160.

7. It is defamatory to impute fraud or dishonorable motives. See *Halsbury's Laws,* 28:25, para. 49.

8. Whistler was born in Lowell, Massachusetts; the statement that he had been born in Russia flagrantly contradicts Parry's earlier assertion that the plaintiff was American by birth. Shortly after Whistler's death, an old friend of the Whistler family, Kate Livermore, wrote to *The Times* that "the dear artist could hardly have said that he was born in St. Petersburg. Someone else, perhaps, made the statement, and he did not deny it" (K. L., "Mr. Whistler's Birthplace: To the Editor of *The Times,*" 28 August 1903, 8).

9. Whistler went to England in the summer of 1848 and spent the following year there; after Major Whistler's death, the family returned to America. Whistler was enrolled in the United States Military Academy at West Point, New York, from July 1851 until June 1854, when he was discharged for a deficiency in chemistry.

10. Whistler visited London briefly in the autumn of 1856 and went on to Paris in November. In June he entered the studio of the Swiss artist Charles-Gabriel Gleyre, in company with the English art students Thomas Armstrong, Edward J. Poynter, and George Du Maurier.

11. Whistler moved to London in May 1859. He exhibited his first painting at the Royal Academy, *At the Piano* (fig. 9), in May 1860. According to the defendant's brief (which refers to the painting as "The Music Lesson"), *At the Piano* was acknowledged to be the "truest picture in color and tone of any in that year's exhibition" (PWC 26).

12. *Arrangement in Grey and Black: Portrait of the Painter's Mother* (fig. 18), exhibited at the Royal Academy in 1872.

13. Whistler's reference to the Grosvenor Gallery immediately after his mention of the Royal Academy led the editor of the *Magazine of Art* to conclude that "it was the hospitality of the Grosvenor, the certainty of being well hung, and of being accorded places of honor on the handsome walls of the fashionable gallery which influenced the artist in withholding from Burlington House" ("Mr. Whistler and the Royal Academy: To the Editor of *The Times,*" 15 August 1903, 6). Harry Quilter argued that the Grosvenor Gallery did not open until five years after Whistler's *Mother* had been shown at the Royal Academy, and "unless we believe that the artist had prophetic intuition that in five years' time a fashionable gallery would be open, on the handsome walls of which he had the certainty of being well hung and accorded places of honour, we must believe him to have left off exhibiting at the Royal Academy for some other reason" ("Mr. Whistler and the Royal Academy: To the Editor of *The Times,*" 18 August 1903, 8).

14. Whistler had exhibited sixteen paintings and seventeen etchings at the Royal Academy, including: *At the Piano* (fig. 9) in 1860; *La Mère Gérard* (ca. 1858–59; private collection) in 1861; *Wapping* (1861; National Gallery of Art, Washington) in 1864; *Alone with the Tide,* later titled *The Coast of Brittany* (1861; Wadsworth Atheneum, Hartford, Conn.) in 1862; *Taking Down Scaffolding at Old Westminster Bridge,* later *The Last of Old Westminster* (1862; Museum of Fine Arts, Boston) in 1863; *Ships in the Ice on the Thames,* later *The Thames in Ice* (1860; FGA) in 1861; and *The Little White Girl,* later *Symphony in White, No. 2: The Little White Girl* (fig. 25) in 1864. At the salon, Whistler had shown *La Princesse du pays de la porcelaine* (see fig. 19) in 1865; and *Au Piano* (*At the Piano*) and *Sur la Tamise; l'hiver* (*The Thames in Ice*) in 1867.

15. For an exhibition of twelve etchings in The Hague in 1863, Whistler was awarded one of three gold medals given to foreigners; he told the Pennells that he never knew how the etchings had come to be there (Elizabeth R. Pennell and Joseph Pennell, *The Life of James McNeill Whistler,* 2 vols. [Philadelphia: Lippincott, 1908], 1:104).

16. The Pennells denied that Whistler ever "said anything of the sort" (ibid., 234).

17. Whistler had explained in a letter to George Lucas, "By the names of the pictures . . . I point out something of what I mean in my theory of painting" (letter postmarked 18 January 1873, bound in *A Catalogue of Blue and White*

Nankin Porcelain Forming the Collection of Sir Henry Thompson, Rare Books Collection, Walters Art Gallery, Baltimore).

18. Whistler's reputation as an etcher was well established, and the defendant's brief informed the attorney general that Whistler had been well known as an etcher for twenty years: "His etchings on copper first brought him into notice and created quite a sensation amongst artists and those who knew anything about Engraving on copper. The first set of these plates, Subjects in Paris and views on the Thames about Limehouse, placed Mr. Whistler at once in the front rank of modern etchers" (PWC 26). The brief refers to Whistler's French Set, *Douze eaux-fortes d'après Nature,* published in 1858, and the Thames Set, *A Series of Sixteen Etchings of Scenes on the Thames and Other Subjects,* published in 1871.

19. According to the defendant's brief, Whistler continued exhibiting at the Royal Academy after the success of *At the Piano,* "but with the exception of his 'Girl in White' and a Japanese picture or two became so eccentric in his work that his pictures were rejected year after year" (PWC 26).

20. The Pennells believed that *Nocturne in Black and Gold* might have been produced upside down at this point (*Life of Whistler* [1908], 1:235), but the painting was not entered as evidence until later in the trial.

21. This line of questioning is drawn from Ruskin's Instructions to Defense Counsel (App. A). To put Whistler's price in context, consider that in 1878 J. E. Millais's *Charlie Is My Darling* (16½ × 9¾ inches) sold for £199.10 and his *Joan of Arc* (34½ × 23 inches) for £735; and that Frith's *"Bed Time"* (23½ × 19 inches—almost the same size as Whistler's *Nocturne in Black and Gold)* sold for £399, his *Keeper's Daughter* (22 × 27½ inches) for £756, and his *Group in the "Derby Day,"* designated "Sketch," for £187.19 (see George Redford, *Art Sales,* 2 vols. [London, 1888], 2:38, 81).

22. See Ruskin's instructions (App. A).

23. The nocturne was in fact in court, having been produced by the defense. William Graham may have been in the courtroom as well; his daughter wrote in her memoirs that the entire family went to the trial (Frances Horner, *Time Remembered* [London: Heinemann, 1933], 56).

24. This question may have been inspired by a sentence in Tom Taylor's review of the 1877 Grosvenor Gallery exhibition, extracted in the defendant's brief (PWC 26): "One would like to know how the actor likes being reduced to mere arrangement."

25. Anderson Rose's instructions for answers to interrogatories indicate that Whistler "was willing" to sell *Arrangement in Brown* after the exhibition, though he could not remember the price he had asked for it (PWC 27).

26. Whistler stated in his answers to interrogatories that *Harmony in Amber and Black* was in his possession but had been "painted over" since the Grosvenor Gallery exhibition (16 November 1878, quoted in the plaintiff's brief, PWC 26).

27. For an elaboration on this exchange, see Whistler, *The Gentle Art of Making Enemies* (London: Heinemann, 1890), 4–5.

28. This line of questioning is drawn from the defendant's brief: "Mr. Whistler is we understand in the habit of hanging up his pictures on his garden wall exposed to the weather previous to their being framed in order to give them a mellow tone" (PWC 26). See also Whistler, *Gentle Art* (1890), 6.

29. This line of questioning is apparently drawn from Burne-Jones's Statement to Defense Counsel (Appendix B). Albert Moore wrote a note to Serjeant Parry, presumably at this point in the trial: "Pictures are not valued with respect to the time expended on them. It is said that Tintoret's large picture of the Miracle of St. Mark was executed in fifteen days—ask the artists on the other side if they have not heard of this and their opinion on the point generally" (manuscript notes, [25 November 1878], PWC 27).

30. John Dixon Hunt notes that Ruskin had made the same point in a piece about Turner's vignettes for Rogers's *Italy* that year, and suggests that Whistler, knowing Ruskin's work, "was even invoking it ironically" (*The Wider Sea: A Life of John Ruskin* [New York: Viking, 1982], 373).

31. *Mayfair* noted that after Huddleston threatened to clear the court, "there was no more applause, and for the rest of the trial the Court of Exchequer Chamber was anything but 'clear'" ("A Contemptuous Verdict," *Mayfair* 3 December 1878, press-cutting book 2:25, GUL). Louise Jopling observed that the judge "made no remark to those who indulged in laughter" (*Twenty Years of My Life, 1867 to 1887* [New York: Dodd, Mead and Co., 1925], 126).

32. Cf. Whistler, *Whistler v. Ruskin: Art & Art Critics* (London: Chatto and Windus, 1878), 6: "When cross-examined by Sir John Holker, I contented myself with the general answer, 'that one might admit criticism when emanating from a man who had passed his whole life in the science which he attacks.'"

33. The defense had subpoenaed *Nocturne in Black and Gold* as evidence.

34. Ruskin's counsel had been permitted to inspect the works in Whistler's possession that had been exhibited at the Grosvenor Gallery, although they had requested to see all the paintings that the plaintiff proposed to produce at trial.

35. According to Whistler, Arthur Severn had inspected the pictures "for the purpose of passing his final judgment upon them and settling that question for ever" (*Gentle Art* [1890], 7).

36. "It was proposed to adjourn to the Divorce Court, and to hear the matter out in that natural arena of scandal. Mr. Whistler's Counsel, however, thought that the jury, the pictures, and all concerned, should go over to the Westminster Palace Hotel; to which the Judge objected, thus depriving the Westminster populace of a curious scene, and of a new version of Sir Frederic Leighton's picture of the triumphal procession of Cimabue" ("Whistler v. Ruskin," *Spectator,* 30 November 1878, 1486).

37. Urban Noseda, whose wife was the proprietor of a print-dealing establishment in the Strand, was required to produce *Nocturne in Black and Gold, Arrangement in Black, Harmony in Amber and Black,* and *Arrangement in Brown* at the trial.

38. According to Frances Horner, the nocturne was handed to the judge upside down (*Time Remembered,* 56).

39. Cf. Whistler, *Gentle Art* (1890), 8: "I did not intend it to be a 'correct' portrait of the bridge. It is only a moonlight scene and the pier in the centre of the picture may not be like the piers at Battersea Bridge as you know them in broad daylight."

40. Whistler had explained his intentions in a letter of 1873, written to alert George Lucas to an exhibition of his work at Durand-Ruel's gallery in Paris: "You will notice and perhaps meet with opposition that my frames I have designed as carefully as my pictures—and thus they form as important a part as any of the rest of the work—carrying on the particular harmony throughout. This is of course entirely original with me and has never been done." The practice of placing color on his frames had become so characteristic of his style, Whistler said, that any artists who did the same thing would "at once be pointed out as forgers or imitators"; he wanted Lucas to understand that he was the "inventor of all this kind of decoration in color in the frames," suspecting that "a lot of clever little Frenchmen" might try to

trespass on his territory (letter postmarked 18 January 1873, bound in *Catalogue of Blue and White,* Rare Books Collection, Walters Art Gallery, Baltimore).

41. This line of questioning is drawn from the defendant's brief, which informed the attorney general that Whistler's gold frames were "generally painted too with some of the colour of the picture so that the whole thing became an impression of grey and gold or blue and gold," and that he "stuck generally to one key of color and often to a few gradations of blue" (PWC 26).

42. Probably *Harmony in Grey and Green: Miss Cicely Alexander* (fig. 51), which Whistler had invited the sculptor J. E. Boehm to see at his studio just before the trial (see Whistler to Boehm, 20 November [1878], B 98, GUL).

43. *Harmony in Blue and Yellow* may be *Harmony in Blue and Silver: Trouville* (1865; Isabella Stewart Gardner Museum, Boston), which had recently been cleaned and given a decorated frame (see Whistler to John Cavafy, [May 1879], C 50, GUL). Whistler's courtroom description of the subject as "seaside and sand" anticipates his reference to the painting some years later as "Sea & Sand" (Whistler to E. G. Kennedy, 10 June 1892, Edward Guthrie Kennedy Papers, New York Public Library).

44. The *Daily Telegraph* records that the jury went to see the pictures in the probate court ("Whistler v. Ruskin," 26 November 1878, 2).

45. Cf. Whistler, *Gentle Art* (1890), 9: "The black monogram on the frame was placed in its position with reference to the proper decorative balance of the whole." *Nocturne in Black and Gold* is no longer in its original frame.

46. See Whistler's dramatic elaboration in *Gentle Art* (1890), 9–10.

47. Whistler lived at 7 Lindsey Row from 1863 to 1866 and at 2 Lindsey Row (now 96 Cheyne Walk) until 1878. Shortly before the trial he moved into the White House, Tite Street.

48. Rossetti reviewed the Grosvenor Gallery exhibition in a two-part article in the *Academy* published 5 and 26 May 1877. Whistler's works were discussed in the second review, "The Grosvenor Gallery (Second Notice)," *Academy* 11 (26 May 1877): 467–68; Rossetti did not comment on *Nocturne in Black and Gold* except to say that at least four of the eight exhibits (it being one) had been shown before. Rossetti saw Mrs. Leyland's *Nocturne in Blue and Silver* for the first time at the Grosvenor Gallery. Graham's *Nocturne in Blue and Silver* had been exhibited in Brighton in 1875, and Rossetti could have

seen it there: together with other landscape and moonlight paintings by Whistler, it was described in a short notice in the *Academy* ("Notes and News," *Academy,* 19 February 1876, 180), which Rossetti may have written.

49. See Rossetti, "Grosvenor Gallery," 467: "The *Nocturne in Blue and Silver,* belonging to Mrs. Leyland, is new to us, and ranks among the loveliest of the painter's works of this class. The time appears to be earliest morning—the locality, the river as seen from Chelsea: a great reach and surface of water as conveyed to the eye by a sort of artistic divination, a curious power of intuition and suggestion working through means equally simple and subtle: right in front come a few flecked leaves of a shrub, which even a Japanese artist, unapproachable in such suddennesses of perfection, might be willing to acknowledge."

50. See W. M. Rossetti, "The Dudley Gallery," *Academy* 8 (30 October 1875): 462: "Another contribution of the same painter is named *Nocturne in Black and Gold: the Falling Rocket.* This also is extremely good, and in some sense even a bolder attempt than the first-named work [*Nocturne in Blue and Gold, No. 3*]; it cannot be properly called *ad captandum,* but its artificial subject matter places it at a less high level. The scene is probably Cremorne Gardens; the heavy rich darkness of the clump of trees to the left, contrasted with the opaque obscurity of the sky, is felt and realised with great truth. Straight across the trees, not high above the ground, shoots and fizzes the last and fiercest light of the expiring rocket."

51. The legal question is whether Ruskin attacked Whistler generally as an artist, or particularly as the painter of a certain picture.

52. Rossetti mentions in passing "the seated figure of *Mr. Carlyle*" in his 1877 *Academy* review ("Grosvenor Gallery," 467).

53. Because the *Carlyle* did not appear to be one of the pictures under attack, the attorney general considered it irrelevant to the testimony. Whistler wrote a note to Rose: "The very fact of the Carlyle not being alluded to is in itself *unfair*—since it . . . was also exhibited—Does Ruskin look in the catalogue or at the pictures on the walls when criticizing" (manuscript notes, [25 November 1878], PWC 27).

54. One exception was the "figure of Mr. Irving; which, exceedingly offhand and not free from crudity, we cannot but regard as a rather strong experiment upon public submissiveness" (Rossetti, "Grosvenor Gallery," 467).

55. Felix Slade, a wealthy art collector, bequeathed funds in 1868 to endow art professorships at Oxford, Cambridge, and London universities; Ruskin was unanimously elected the first Slade Professor at Oxford in 1869.

56. This line of questioning is drawn from the defendant's brief (PWC 26), which informed the attorney general that Whistler "sat for his portrait to be exhibited on the stage of the Gaiety Theatre in the course of a play recently acted there" (PWC 26). *The Grasshopper* opened in December 1877; one of the props was a portrait of Whistler by Carlo Pellegrini, painted in the sitter's characteristic style (fig. 44).

57. In his 1875 *Academy* review, Rossetti had objected to the "artificial subject matter" of *Nocturne in Black and Gold* ("Dudley Gallery," 462).

58. The *Echo,* followed by other papers, reported that Moore testified he was "an artist and art critic." Moore responded: "It has been reported in some of the newspapers that I made a statement in the witness-box to the effect that I was an art-critic, and I venture to hope that I may rely on your giving publicity to my denial of this, as nothing of the kind was mentioned, and as I have, in fact, no claim to be counted among the privileged fraternity" ("Whistler v. Ruskin [To the Editor of the *Daily News*]," 30 November 1878, 2; also "The Case of Whistler v. Ruskin: To the Editor of *The Echo,*" 29 November 1878, press-cutting book 2:31, GUL).

59. In the 1877 Grosvenor Gallery exhibition, Moore showed *Sapphires* (fig. 36), *Marigolds,* and *The End of the Story* (fig. 37) (*The Grosvenor Gallery,* exhibition catalogue [London: Wade Phoenix Printing Office, 1877], 25).

60. At the Paris Exposition Universelle in 1878, Moore exhibited *Beads* and *The Palm Fan,* described as "two very small works, delicate harmonies in blue and gold" (Henry Blackburn, "Pictures at the Paris Exhibition: The British School," *Magazine of Art* 1 [1877–78]: 128).

61. Moore and Whistler met in London in 1865.

62. Cf. "On the House-Top," *Architect,* 26 January 1878, 49: "Mr. Albert Moore is distinctly a leader; he carries a severe principle of decoration much further than any other painter we know—to the avoidance of all expression of emotion; that the art of painting deals only with what words cannot reproduce—the beauty of matter—is a canon of his school."

63. At the time of the trial, five of Wills's plays had been produced in London: *Cora* (1877; Globe Theatre), *England in the Days of Charles II* (1877;

Drury Lane), *Olivia* (1878; Court), *Nell Gwynne* (1878; Royalty), and *Vanderdecken* (1878; Lyceum).

64. *Olivia,* an adaptation for the stage of Oliver Goldsmith's *The Vicar of Wakefield*, opened to popular acclaim in April 1878.

65. See, for example, "English Plays and Actors," *New York Times,* 15 April 1878, 5: "When [Wills] 'came a cuffer' at Drury-lane with 'England in the Days of Charles II,' he was given over by friend and foe. His work was utterly bad, his construction being too silly for criticism."

66. "The Attorney-General got more and more puzzled as he learned that artists and art critics could see any merits in the pictures, and that neither the one nor the other knew anything about 'La Cigale.' . . . Even Mr. Wills, from whom, as a dramatic author, better things might have been expected, absolutely declined the Attorney-General's bait, and was much too cautious a bird to peck at 'The Grasshopper'" ("A Contemptuous Verdict," *Mayfair,* 3 December 1878, press-cutting book 2:25, GUL).

67. *Mayfair* reported that Wills, who was standing with his back to the nocturne, "resolutely declined to admit that he could see that work of art at all. Of course, as he did not see it, he could give no opinion upon it" (ibid.).

68. None of Wills's works are recorded in the 1877 catalogue (*Grosvenor Gallery* [1877]); Wills may have said, or meant to say, 1878, when *The Bell Ringers* (no. 143) was shown in the vestibule and described as "a powerful decorative picture by the well-known dramatist" (Henry Blackburn, *Grosvenor Notes,* no. 1 [London: Chatto and Windus, 1878]).

69. Sir William Erle (1793–1880), lord chief justice of the common pleas from 1859 to 1866.

70. At the close of the plaintiff's case, the defendant may ask the judge to dismiss the action on the grounds that the plaintiff has not defeated the defense of fair comment with evidence of malice. In the case of *Whistler v. Ruskin*, the judge refused to rule and thereby to take the case away from the jury. The plaintiff had presented sufficient facts to support a judgment of libel (Ruskin's critique is capable of bearing defamatory meaning), provided the facts were not contradicted or undone by the defendant's case. Even without proof that Ruskin's words had actually damaged Whistler, the defendant's publication would be judged libelous unless he could disprove the facts the plaintiff had submitted, or establish some privilege. The burden of proof shifted to the defendant, who had to show that the subject matter was

of public interest if he was to argue that the criticism was fair comment and that his remarks were made without malicious intent and were meant to express his true opinions; defense counsel would also have to demonstrate that any honest person might hold the opinion that Ruskin expressed. The question for the jury was, Did Ruskin really believe that Whistler was virtually defrauding the public, and could a reasonable person have believed that?

DEFENDANT'S CASE

1. Cf. Whistler, *Art & Art Critics,* 6: "Over and over again did the Attorney-General cry out aloud, in the agony of his cause, 'What is to become of painting if the critics withhold their lash?'"

2. See ibid., 7: "We are told that Mr. Ruskin has devoted his long life to art, and as a result—is Slade Professor at Oxford. In the same sentence, we have thus his position and its worth. It suffices not, Messieurs! a life passed among pictures makes not a painter—else the policemen in the National Gallery might assert himself. As well allege that he who lives in a library must needs die a poet. Let not Mr. Ruskin flatter himself that more education makes the difference between himself and the policeman when both stand gazing in the Gallery!"

3. The attorney general drew his statements from Ruskin's instructions (App. A).

4. See Ruskin's instructions (App. A). The attorney general argued that *Fors Clavigera* was written on a "privileged" occasion—that Ruskin had a moral duty to make the communication to the public. If the occasion is privileged, even a defamatory statement is protected by the law, as long as it was made in good faith (bona fide) and without malicious intent.

5. Ruskin's critique, a comment on a matter of public interest, is privileged, or exempt from the usual penalties of the law, unless it is judged by the jury to be outside the bounds of fair comment. The defense must prove that the critique is one that any person, however prejudiced, could have made based on the facts, in this case the pictures.

6. There was a restaurant on the ground floor of the Grosvenor Gallery, which Sir Coutts Lindsay hoped would indemnify the expense of the enterprise.

7. *Mayfair* remarked, "Sir John apparently neither likes his ladies nor his chops to be artistically dressed" ("A Contemptuous Verdict," *Mayfair,* 3 December 1878, press-cutting book 2:25, GUL).

8. Probably drawn from Ruskin's instructions, which mention "a study in chiaroscuro for four voices, or a prismatic piece of color in four flats" (App. A).

9. The attorney general refers to the Britannia Bridge (built 1845–50), which connects Anglesey Island with the mainland of north Wales.

10. Holker did not quite remember the words of stanza 32 of "Beppo," by George Gordon, Lord Byron:

> His "bravo" was decisive, for that sound
> Hush'd "Academie" sigh'd in silent awe;
> The fiddlers trembled as he look'd around,
> For fear of some false note's detected flaw.
> The "prima donna's" tuneful heart wound bound,
> Dreading the deep damnation of his "bah!"
> Soprano, basso, even the contra-alto,
> Wish'd him five fathom under the Rialto.

11. This remark may have been suggested by Pygmalion Flippit, the "artist of the future" in *The Grasshopper,* who said: "Like my great master, Whistler, I see things in a peculiar way, and I paint them as I see them" (John Hollingshead, *The Grasshopper: A Drama in Three Acts* [London: Woodfall and Kinder, 1877], 27).

12. Drawn from Ruskin's instructions (App. A).

13. From Ruskin's instructions (App. A). For Ruskin's praise of Millais, see *Fors Clavigera* 79 (July 1877), in *Works of Ruskin,* 29:158.

14. See *Fors Clavigera* 79 (July 1877), in *Works of Ruskin,* 29:160. Ruskin refers in this paragraph to the work not of Whistler, but of Burne-Jones.

15. Holker alludes to Ruskin's critique in *Fors Clavigera* (and the insult implied by flinging a pot of paint), although in these paragraphs Ruskin apparently was not referring to *Nocturne in Blue and Silver,* which had not been priced for sale.

16. Holker uses the word "stick" in the nineteenth-century sense of a person lacking in capacity for his work.

17. Holker uses the word "daub" in the sense of a coarsely executed, inartistic painting.

18. From Ruskin's instructions (App. A).

19. Whistler quotes this sentence as the epigraph to *Nocturnes, Marines, and Chevalet Pieces,* the catalogue of a Goupil Gallery exhibition in London, 1892; the text is reprinted in Whistler, *The Gentle Art of Making Enemies,* new ed. (London: Heinemann, 1892), 297.

20. This is probably a deliberate misquotation of a Whistler title, perhaps from Ruskin's reference to "a symphony in green and yellow" (App. A).

21. The older, more precise meaning of "coxcomb" is "a superficial pretender to knowledge or accomplishments," and Ruskin alleged that Whistler "nearly approached the aspect of wilful imposture." See Ruskin's instructions (App. A).

22. From Ruskin's instructions (App. A).

23. After addressing the jury, the attorney general departed, leaving his junior to conduct the case for the defense. According to Whistler, "Mr. Bowen, by way of presenting [Burne-Jones] properly to the consideration of the Court, proceeded to read extracts of eulogistic appreciation of this artist from the defendant's own writings" (*Gentle Art* [1890], 13–14).

24. The artist's wife considered these words "a fair type of the modesty" with which Burne-Jones testified (Georgiana Burne-Jones, *Memorials of Edward Burne-Jones,* 2 vols. [London: Macmillan, 1909], 2:87).

25. In addition to the paintings named, Burne-Jones exhibited *The Beguiling of Merlin* (fig. 6) at the Grosvenor Gallery in 1877, as well as at the Paris Exposition Universelle, 1878. The picture, alternately titled *Merlin and Vivien* and *Merlin and Nimuë,* had been commissioned by F. R. Leyland in 1872 for the "Italian" drawing room of Leyland's London home. At the Grosvenor Gallery in 1878, Burne-Jones exhibited eleven paintings.

26. See G. Burne-Jones, *Memorials of Burne-Jones,* 2:188: "The words which he had uttered publicly in 1878—'I think that nothing short of perfect finish ought to be allowed by artists'—did not express an opinion of the time merely, but a sure conviction to which the great art of the world bore witness; and the fulfilment of his warning 'if unfinished pictures become com-

mon we shall arrive at a stage of mere manufacture, and the art of the country will be degraded,' seemed at hand."

27. Quoted by Whistler in *Nocturnes, Marines, and Chevalet Pieces,* (attributed to "Mr. Jones, R.A."), in *Gentle Art* (1892), 299–300.

28. See Burne-Jones's statement (App. B).

29. Quoted by Whistler in *Nocturnes, Marines, and Chevalet Pieces,* in *Gentle Art* (1892), 305.

30. See Burne-Jones's statement (App. B). Whistler includes this exchange in *Nocturnes, Marines, and Chevalet Pieces,* in *Gentle Art* (1892), 303. After the trial Burne-Jones wrote to George Howard, "My average pay for a day's work is from £5 to £7 and I was justified in saying £200 was too much—prices like that will go near to discrediting the value of the work of every one of us" (n.d., Castle Howard Archives, *Burne-Jones Talking: His Conversations 1895–1898,* ed. Mary Lago [London: John Murray, 1982], 70 n. 3).

31. Between 1798 and 1800, twenty-seven reputed Titian paintings were sold into England from the Royal Collection of France; two-thirds of those "Orleans Titians" had questionable attributions, and thorough cleaning of the works often revealed forgery (Gerald Reitlinger, *The Economics of Taste: The Rise and Fall of Picture Prices 1760–1960* [London: Barrie and Rockliff, 1961], 118). A satire of the trial in *Punch* focuses on the efforts of the judge to work his joke into the proceedings. Upon the production of the "Andrew Gatti" by Titian, Baron Puzzleton says: "I don't want to make anyone laugh—(*Everyone prepares for a grin*)—but I remember a story of some one who bought a picture as a genuine Titian (*grin on all features becoming more and more marked*), and when he came to examine it through his glasses—I must tell you he was an Op-*titian*—(*shouts—Ushers in fits*)—he found out that only half of it was by Titian; so he stuck it up as a screen, and made it into a *Part-titian!* (*Roars. Jurymen in ecstasies, punching one another in the ribs. Ushers rolling on the ground. Policeman runs out of Court into Westminster Hall, to tell it to a friend outside. . . .)* ("Une Cause Célèbre," *Punch,* 7 December 1878, 257.)

32. Cf. Burne-Jones's statement (App. B).

33. Quoted by Whistler in "Résumé," *Nocturnes, Marines, and Chevalet Pieces,* in *Gentle Art* (1892), 330: "I think Mr. Whistler had great powers at first, which he has not since justified."

34. See Burne-Jones's statement (App. B). Joan Abse points out that this is a reiteration of Tintoretto's remark, frequently quoted by Ruskin, "Sempre si fa

il mare maggiore" (Always the sea gets larger) (*John Ruskin: The Passionate Moralist* [New York: Knopf, 1981], 288).

35. In 1876, *Man in a Red Cap* by Titian had sold for £94.10, and in 1878, the year of the trial, an oil sketch, *Diana and Actaeon,* sold for £63; *Venus and Cupid* for £99.15; *Adoration of the Magi* for £199.10; and *Repose of the Holy Family* for £367.10 (Redford, *Art Sales,* 2:258).

36. Ruskin had purchased the *Andrea Gritti* for £1000 in September 1864 from the Reverend Gilbert Elliott, Dean of Bristol.

37. Whistler and Burne-Jones met through Algernon Swinburne in July 1862 and must have seen each other frequently in subsequent years. Their mutual friend D. G. Rossetti introduced both artists to F. R. Leyland. Frances Horner recollected that the judge had said to Burne-Jones, "You are a friend of Mr. Whistler, Mr. Burne-Jones, I believe," to which the witness reportedly replied, "I *was*: I don't suppose he will ever speak to me again after today" (*Time Remembered*, 57).

38. *A Knight* appears to be an alternate title for the painting listed in the catalogue as *Saint George;* W. M. Rossetti refers to *A Knight* in his review ("Grosvenor Gallery," 467). *Saint George* and *A Sibyl* were both designated "unfinished" in the catalogue (*Grosvenor Gallery* [1877], 27).

39. Frith was a Royal Academician, a Chevalier of the Legion of Honor, a Chevalier of the Order of Leopold, and a member of the Royal Academy of Belgium and the Academies of Stockholm, Vienna, and Antwerp.

40. In almost every press report, *The Road to Ruin* is called *The Rake's Progress,* the title of a series of paintings by William Hogarth executed around 1733, now in the Soane Museum, London; the prevalence of that error confirms Frith's reputation as a latter-day Hogarth.

41. Quoted by Whistler in *Nocturnes, Marines, and Chevalet Pieces,* in *Gentle Art* (1892), 304. *The Week* remarked: "Mr. Whistler, we think, may hear with patience Mr. Frith's disdain. The hand which has produced some of the most exquisite etchings of modern times need not envy any painter of sign-boards and tea-trays" ("Notes of the Week," 30 November 1878, 519).

42. Illustrated in *Judy* (fig. 62).

43. Frith is the only one of the artist witnesses who had never exhibited works at the Grosvenor Gallery. Arthur Jerome Eddy remarked, "He confessed he had not been invited to exhibit at the Grosvenor Gallery, and, as

every one knows, what is considered art in one exhibition may not be so considered in another" (*Recollections and Impressions of James A. McNeill Whistler* [Philadelphia: Lippincott, 1903], 146).

44. Frith later stated that "Ruskin's works bristle with errors" (*My Autobiography and Reminiscences,* 2 vols. [New York: Harper and Brothers, 1888], 2:4).

45. Ruskin relates the anecdote in *Notes on the Turner Gallery at Marlborough House* (1856), in *Works of Ruskin,* 13:161–62: "It was characterized by some of the critics of the day as a mass of 'soapsuds and whitewash.' Turner was passing the evening at my father's house on the day this criticism came out: and after dinner, sitting in his arm-chair by the fire, I heard him muttering low to himself at intervals, 'Soapsuds and whitewash!' again, and again, and again. At last I went to him, asking 'why he minded what they said?' Then he burst out;—'Soapsuds and whitewash! What would they have? I wonder what they think the sea's like? I wish they had been in it.'"

46. Edward M. Beloe wrote to *The Times* to correct what he had understood to be Frith's statement that *Snow Storm* had been described by Ruskin as "soapsuds and whitewash," quoting from Ruskin's *Notes on the Turner Gallery* to prove his point ("Mr. Ruskin: To the Editor of *The Times,*" 30 November 1878, 8). Frith wrote in response that the correspondent had been "incorrect in his statement in *The Times* of to-day that I attributed the description of Turner's picture of the 'Snowstorm' as 'soapsuds and whitewash' to Mr. Ruskin. With my knowledge of Mr. Ruskin's opinion of Turner, I could not have been so stupid. What I said was in reply to an observation of Mr. Serjeant Parry that some critic at the time the picture was exhibited described it in those terms—that I should have agreed with him" ("Turner's 'Snowstorm': To the Editor of *The Times,*" 2 December 1878, 8).

Frith would later elaborate upon that opinion: "Turner was, without doubt, the greatest landscape-painter that ever lived; but so mysterious were some of his last productions, so utterly unlike nature, to my eyes, that I should almost be inclined to agree with Reinagle, that they would look as well the wrong way up as the right way. . . . It was, and always will be, a puzzle to me how a man whose earlier works are the wonder and admiration of all who see them, could have reconciled himself to the production of beautiful phantasmagoria, representing nothing in the 'heavens above, or on the earth beneath.' And what is still more wonderful is that people can be found to admire and buy them at such enormous prices" (*My Autobiography and Reminiscences*, 2 vols. [New York: Harper and Brothers, 1888], 1:94).

"The ridiculous prices paid for some of the later productions of Turner are strong proofs of the evils of critic-led opinion. I am convinced that if Turner's career had been commenced with the eccentric productions of his later time, his name—now and forever to be honored—would never have been heard of" (ibid., 2:6).

47. Frith tells the story in his *Autobiography:* "Strange as it may sound, it is absolutely true that I have heard Turner ridicule some of his own later works quite as skilfully as the newspapers did. For example, at a dinner when I was present, a salad was offered to Turner, who called the attention of his neighbor at the table . . . to it in the following words: 'Nice cool green that lettuce, isn't it? and the beetroot pretty red—not quite strong enough; and the mixture, delicate tint of yellow that. Add some mustard, and then you have one of my pictures'" (ibid., 1:94).

48. Bowen, evidently more alert than Parry, clarifies the witness's testimony so that Frith appears to malign a single painting by Turner, rather than the artist's work in general.

49. Taylor had been art critic for *The Times* since 1857.

50. *The Life and Times of Sir Joshua Reynolds,* begun by C. R. Leslie and published in 1865; and *The Life of Benjamin Robert Haydon, Historical Painter* in 27 volumes, compiled from Haydon's journals and autobiography, published in 1853.

51. See [Tom Taylor], "The Grosvenor Gallery," *The Times,* 1 May 1877, 10: "It is a well-known fantasy of the painter to carry the nomenclature of music into painting, thereby giving us to understand that he holds the arts to occupy common ground, and that colour and tone are as important in the one as harmony in the other."

52. Quoted by Whistler in *Nocturnes, Marines, and Chevalet Pieces* (attributed to "The Art Critic of the 'Times'"), in *Gentle Art* (1892), 305.

53. According to Whistler, "The witness here took from the pockets of his overcoat copies of the *Times,* and with the permission of the Court, read again with unction his own criticism, to every word of which he said he still adhered" (*Gentle Art* [1890], 18). The extract is from [Tom Taylor], "Winter Exhibitions: The Dudley," *The Times,* 2 December 1875, 4. Whistler quotes a slightly altered, abbreviated version of the critique (attributed to the *Daily Telegraph*) in *Nocturnes, Marines, and Chevalet Pieces,* in *Gentle Art* (1892), 309.

54. From Taylor, "Grosvenor Gallery."

55. Quoted by Whistler in *Nocturnes, Marines, and Chevalet Pieces,* in *Gentle Art* (1892), 326.

56. Ibid., 319.

SUMMATIONS

1. In assessing damages, the jury may consider the conduct of the defendant's legal representative. Parry attempted to increase the amount of damages to which Whistler was entitled by suggesting that the attorney general had conducted Ruskin's case in an insulting and—particularly to women artists—offensive manner (see *Halsbury's Laws,* 28:120, para. 242).

2. The *Examiner* remarked, "If this be Mr. Serjeant Parry's idea of a struggling young man, it would be interesting to know what kind of people he admits to be tolerably well off, and how far the Rothschilds fall short of possessing a moderate income" ("A Symphony in Bronze," *Examiner,* 30 November 1878, 1516).

3. Serjeant Parry could have asked the witnesses this himself, but would have risked receiving an answer he did not want to hear.

4. See "Celebrities at Home, No. XCII: Mr. James Whistler at Cheyne-walk," *The World,* 22 May 1878, 4: "He insists that as music is the poetry of sound, so is painting the poetry of sight, and that the subject-matter has nothing to do with harmony of sound or of colour." See also "The Red Rag" in Whistler, *Gentle Art* (1890), 127.

5. From the plaintiff's brief: "An artist lives in an atmosphere of opinion, he finds his bread slips away from him, his position as an artist changes speedily from competence, not to say affluence, into indigence and poverty—a result which might be entirely brought about by the malignant abuse of Mr. Ruskin and the certain following which Mr. Ruskin's known powers of vituperation as well as criticism will be sure to have from the envious and from all the cowardly part of mankind" (PWC 26).

6. Parry chose to disregard the plaintiff's brief, which advised him that "the other libels scattered through *Fors* on other persons cannot be made any use of. In fact would probably rather weaken this case than otherwise as tending to disprove any malice against plaintiff and showing that the criticism in question was only part of defendant's usual style of comment" (PWC 26).

7. *Fors* 79 (July 1877), in *Works of Ruskin,* 29:146. The author of that sentence, whom Ruskin described as "an extremely foolish, and altogether insignificant, person," remained anonymous.

8. Ibid., 152 and 153. Goldwin Smith (1823–1910) was a central figure in the revival of radicalism in the 1860s.

9. Ibid., 154. Sir Henry Cole (1808–82) was an early and influential reformer who had been a major force behind the Great Exhibition of 1851; he became the first director of the South Kensington Museum and the Art Schools (now the Victoria and Albert Museum and the Royal College of Art). Cole responded to Ruskin's criticism, which he may have known only through reports of the trial, in a speech delivered to the Portsmouth School of Science and Art, reported in the *Daily Chronicle:* "In spite of the imputation upon him, [Cole] ventured to say art was in a comparatively wholesome state. As their schools were in error, they had better get hold of Mr. Ruskin, tie his leg to the table, and not let him move till he had told them in a dry, practical way how to get rid of their abominable heresy and abortive falsehoods" ("Sir Henry and Mr. Ruskin," *Daily Chronicle,* 29 November 1878, 6).

10. *Fors* 79 (July 1877), in *Works of Ruskin,* 29:154: "The Professorships also of Messrs. Agnew at Manchester have covered the walls of the metropolis with 'exchangeable property' on the exchanges of which the dealer always made his commission, and of which perhaps one canvas in a hundred is of some intrinsic value, and may be hereafter put to good and permanent use."

11. The defense of fair comment will be defeated and the critique judged libelous if the plaintiff proves that the defendant published his criticism maliciously, even though a comment on a picture publicly exhibited is prima facie fair.

12. Strictly speaking, "cockney" means one born within the sound of the peal of the bells of St. Mary-le-Bow, Cheapside; but the word is used contemptuously or banteringly to connote characteristics in which the born Londoner is supposed to be inferior to other Englishmen. According to Johnson, "cockney" may refer to any ignorant, low, mean, or despicable citizen.

13. "The Court itself, during lunch, had rather the appearance of a conversazione at some Artistic Society's rooms, with a few pictures thrown in just to give a topic for general remarks" ("A Contemptuous Verdict," *Mayfair,* 3 December 1878, press-cutting book 2:25, GUL).

JURY INSTRUCTIONS

1. The judge's summation, addressed to the jury, is meant to be an impartial explanation of the law applicable to the case, often including a brief recapitulation of the evidence, with directions on the form the verdict should take.

2. Libel Act 1792 ("An Act to Remove Doubts Respecting the Functions of Juries in Cases of Libel"), known as Fox's Act, gave the jury the privilege of deciding whether or not an alleged libel was defamatory to the plaintiff (see *Halsbury's Statutes of England and Wales,* 4th ed. [London: Butterworths, 1986], 24:88–89). The judge, before submitting the question to the jury, must rule whether the words complained of are capable of bearing defamatory meaning in the minds of reasonable people; if they are, the jury must decide whether or not they did, in fact, defame the plaintiff.

3. Benjamin Disraeli in *Lothair* (1870), chapter 35: "You know who the critics are? The men who have failed in literature and art."

4. Huddleston cites a libel trial of 1808, *Sir John Carr, Knt. v. Hood and Another,* in which the presiding judge was Edward Law, first Baron Ellenborough (1750–1818), lord chief justice of England from 1802 to 1818: "Ridicule is often the fittest weapon that can be employed for such purpose [exposing the follies and errors of another]. . . . Reflection on personal character is another thing. Shew me an attack on the moral character of this plaintiff, or any attack upon his character unconnected with his authorship, and I shall be as ready as any Judge who ever sate here to protect him; but I cannot hear of malice on account of turning his works into ridicule" (*Campbell's Reports, Nisi Prius,* in *The English Reports* [London: W. Green, 1927], 170:983–85n).

5. Charles Abbott, first Lord Tenterden (1762–1832) succeeded Lord Ellenborough as lord chief justice of England in 1818. One of Lord Tenterden's most important judgments, in *Rex v. Harvey,* dealt with libel.

6. Huddleston is unaware that Ruskin had in fact committed his position to paper; defense counsel apparently decided not to make his memorandum of instruction (App. A) known to the court.

7. Francis L. Fennell points out that Huddleston here encouraged the jury to assess the value of Whistler's works, even after Bowen's insistence that the question of fair comment was one of law rather than taste ("The Verdict in

Whistler v. Ruskin," *Victorian Newsletter* [New York, Fall 1971]: 20). It is not for the jury to agree or disagree with the defendant's comment or, as Bowen suggested, to substitute its own opinion of the merits of the work in question; but if the jury decides that the defendant's imputations were not warranted by the facts, then the plea of fair comment would be defeated (see *Halsbury's Laws,* 28:114, para. 228). By stressing the need to consider the artist's intentions, Huddleston appeared to lead the jury toward the plaintiff's point of view.

8. *Fors* 79 (July 1877), in *Works of Ruskin,* 29:161: "Most of [Tissot's works] are, unhappily, mere coloured photographs of vulgar society; but the 'Strength of Will,' though sorely injured by the two subordinate figures, makes one think the painter capable, if he would obey his graver thoughts, of doing much that would, with real benefit, occupy the attention of that part of the French and English public whose fancy is at present caught only by Gustave Doré. The rock landscape by Millais [*The Sound of Many Waters*] has also been carefully wrought, but with exaggeration of the ligneous look of the rocks. Its colour as a picture, and the sense it conveys of the real beauty of the scene, are both grievously weakened by the white sky; already noticed as one of the characteristic errors of recent landscape." Tissot exhibited ten works at the Grosvenor Gallery exhibition (see *Grosvenor Gallery* [1877], 8–9). The Millais landscape was shown in 1877 at the Royal Academy.

9. *Fors* 79 (July 1877), in *Works of Ruskin,* 29:162.

10. Excessive language may be evidence of malice if the words of the criticism are so extreme that they suggest that the publication was actuated by improper motives; in most cases, if the language of the comment is that strong, it cannot reasonably be considered fair (see *Halsbury's Laws,* 28:77, para. 147).

11. From the fool's speech in *King Lear* (2.4): "Cry to it, nuncle, as the cockney did to the eels when she put 'em i' th' paste alive; she knapp'd 'em o' th' coxcombs with a stick, and cried, 'Down, wantons, down!'" In Shakespeare, the word "cockney" bears the now-obsolete meaning of a squeamish, over-nice, wanton, or affected woman.

12. In general, the defense of fair comment succeeds if the imputation is an expression of the defendant's opinion and, in the jury's opinion, is warranted by the facts, or could have been held in good faith by any fair-minded person (see *Halsbury's Laws,* 28:74, para. 143).

VERDICT

1. Normally, under the English system, the successful party in an action is entitled to have his costs paid by his opponent; but with the award of contemptuous damages, no costs are given.

PART THREE: THE VERDICT

CAUSE CÉLÈBRE

1. Reay, "London," Hartford (Conn.) *Courant,* 14 December 1878, press-cutting book 3:9, GUL.

2. Arthur Severn to Joseph Pennell, 30 [November] 1906, PWC 299.

3. "Whistler v. Ruskin," *London Express,* 30 November 1878, 342.

4. *Halsbury's Laws of England,* 4th ed. (London: Butterworths, 1979), 28:74, para. 141.

5. Anderson Rose, notes on the back of a manuscript menu by Whistler dated 3 December [1878], PWC 4: "Huddleston drunk—asked the policeman his name."

6. Rose to Whistler, 30 November 1878 (morning), R 130, GUL. Fair comment is the honest expression of an opinion, warranted by facts, that any fair-minded person might hold; this defense can be defeated by evidence of malice, which is assumed if the defendant did not honestly hold the opinion he expressed. The jury's belief that Ruskin's opinion was honest implies that he had not been actuated by malice, which made his comment fair.

7. Arthur Severn to Joseph Pennell, 30 [November] 1906, PWC 299.

8. Because damages are meant to compensate the plaintiff for injury to his reputation and hurt to his feelings, to vindicate him to the public, and to console him for the wrong the defendant has done, nominal damages often indicate that the jury has made a compromise (*Halsbury's Laws,* 28:117 and 126, paras. 235 and 255). In this case, because the judge had so clearly instructed the jury on the question of damages, it seems unlikely that the farthing was meant as a compromise; for a different interpretation and an extended discussion of the verdict, see Francis L. Fennell, "The Verdict in Whistler v. Ruskin," *Victorian Newsletter* (New York) (Fall 1971): 17–21.

9. George W. Smalley, "Whistler: A Tribute from One of His Old Friends," New York *Tribune,* 19 August 1903, 10.

10. The rumor may have originated with G. A. Sala, who wrote of Whistler's "'arrangement in monotone'—the farthing which I am told he wears at his watch-chain" ("Echoes of the Week," *Illustrated London News,* 14 December 1878, 559); see also *The Professor: Arthur Severn's "Memoir of John Ruskin,"* ed. James S. Dearden (London: George Allen and Unwin, 1967), 116. The Pennells, who had never seen either the farthing or Whistler wearing a watch chain, denied the story (Elizabeth R. Pennell and Joseph Pennell, *The Life of James McNeill Whistler,* 2 vols. [Philadelphia: Lippincott, 1908], 1:243). Another version of the story is that Whistler kept the farthing "nailed over his studio door, like the horseshoes, to keep the evil eye of the critics away" (Tondo, "Whistler on Critics," *Truth* 5 [9 January 1879]: 38).

11. Whistler to Rose, received 30 November 1878, PWC 4.

12. Whistler to Lasenby Liberty, [November 1878], L 147, GUL.

13. See Algernon Graves to Whistler, 26 November 1878, G 164, GUL.

14. Whistler to Rose, received 30 November 1878, PWC 4; Whistler to Lasenby Liberty, [November 1878], L 147, GUL.

15. J. P. Heseltine to Whistler, 27 November 1878, PWC 27; Whistler to Rose, received 30 November 1878, PWC 4; Whistler to Lasenby Liberty, [November 1878], L 147, GUL. According to the Pennells, Whistler sent Heseltine a pastel in return for his contribution (*Life of Whistler* [1908], 1:245). Among the strangers who wrote Whistler were Charles Egg, who praised Whistler's "manipulation of color" and condemned Ruskin's attack (27 November 1878, E 34–35, GUL); and W. Macdonald of Manchester, a house painter who specialized in marbling and graining—skills that Ruskin abhorred—and hoped to enlist Whistler's aid in giving the "bullying art demagogue . . . a proper dressing" (undated letter to Whistler; letter to the editor of the *Manchester City News,* 1 February 1878; and proposed text of a letter to Ruskin, M 46–47, GUL). Whistler also received a letter from P. A. de L'Auboniere, director of the French journal *L'Art,* who expressed his willingness as an artist, art critic, and expert, to testify that Whistler was an artist in every sense of the word (26 November 1878, L 17, GUL).

16. J. H. Johnston to Whistler, 8 December 1878, J 31, GUL; G. A. Smalley to Whistler, 27 November 1878, S 105, GUL; E. Lewis to Whistler, 26 November [1878], L 55, GUL.

17. Whistler to Rose, received 30 November 1878, PWC 4; Whistler to Lasenby Liberty, [November 1878], L 147, GUL.

18. "The Oyster-shell Verdict," *Figaro,* 30 November 1878, 3.

19. Whistler to Rose, received 30 November 1878, PWC 4. The nominal verdict could easily be construed as grounds for appeal, since a new trial can be granted in cases "where the smallness of damages shows that the jury has made a compromise, and instead of deciding the issue of liability has agreed to find for the plaintiff for nominal damages only" (*Halsbury's Laws,* 28:126, para. 255). But because the judge's instructions had specifically defined the meaning of nominal damages, it would have been difficult to prove that the jury granted Whistler the farthing in the spirit of compromise; and unless it could be shown that the judge had erred, it seems unlikely that the plaintiff would have been granted a new trial.

20. Rose to Whistler, 30 November 1878 (morning), R 130, GUL.

21. Rose to Whistler, 30 November 1878 (evening), R 131, GUL.

22. "Art Chronicle," *Portfolio* 10 (January 1879), 22.

23. "The Value of a Reputation," *Referee,* 1 December 1878, press-cutting book 2:16, GUL.

24. "The Action," in Whistler, *The Gentle Art of Making Enemies* (London: Heinemann, 1890), 17. The Pennells noted that Whistler's "personal opinion of Frith for testifying against him did not extend to all of Frith's art": Whistler had admired *Derby Day* (fig. 48), commenting that it was "as good as Manet." The compliment reportedly paralyzed Frith with amazement when it was conveyed to him by the Pennells, who speculated that Frith had not known who Manet was (Elizabeth R. Pennell and Joseph Pennell, *The Whistler Journal* [Philadelphia: Lippincott, 1921], 78).

25. Rose to Whistler, 30 November 1878 (evening), R 131, GUL.

26. "Latest of London Topics," *New York Times,* 15 December 1878, 4.

27. Samuel P. Avery to Whistler, 2 January [1879], A218, GUL, reprinted in Madeleine Beaufort, "The Art of Letters: Whistling at One's Ruskin," *Confrontation: A Literary Journal of Long Island University* 18 (Spring/Summer 1979): 62–63.

THE LOSING SIDE

1. Sheila Birkenhead, *Illustrious Friends: The Story of Joseph Severn and His Son Arthur* (London: Hamish Hamilton, 1965), 275.

2. Ruskin to George Allen, 28 November 1878, *The Works of John Ruskin,* ed. E. T. Cook and Alexander Wedderburn, 39 vols., Library Edition (London: George Allen, 1903–12), 37:268.

3. "My Own Article on Whistler," in *Works of Ruskin,* 29:585.

4. Ruskin to H. G. Liddell, 18 November 1878, *Works of Ruskin,* 25:xl.

5. Ruskin to H. G. Liddell, 28 November 1878, ibid., 29:xxv.

6. John Dixon Hunt, *The Wider Sea: A Life of John Ruskin* (New York: Viking, 1982), 489 n. 112.

7. Ruskin to H. G. Liddell, [1878], *Works of Ruskin,* 29:xxv.

8. Ruskin to J.A., 24 January 1880, published in the *Glasgow Herald,* 27 January 1900, and reprinted in *Arrows of the Chace, Works of Ruskin,* 34:544. *Symphony in Blue and White,* still unidentified, was advertised in the *Glasgow Herald,* 22–23 January 1880; see Andrew McLaren Young et al., *The Paintings of James McNeill Whistler,* 2 vols. (New Haven: Yale University Press, 1980), no. 146a.

9. R. W. Dixon to G. M. Hopkins, 21 June 1886, *The Correspondence of Gerard Manley Hopkins and Richard Watson Dixon,* ed. Claude Colleer Abbott (London: Oxford University Press, 1935), 131: "Ruskin is publishing a sort of penitential edition of Modern Painters. He should take the opportunity of repenting about Whistler."

10. "Mythic Schools of Painting: E. Burne-Jones and G. F. Watts" (1883), *The Art of England* (1884), in *Works of Ruskin,* 33:287–305.

11. Burne-Jones to Ruskin ("my dear oldie"), [26 November 1878], *The Brantwood Diary of John Ruskin,* ed. Helen Gill Viljoen (New Haven: Yale University Press, 1971), 424; Burne-Jones to Ruskin ("dearest St. C."), ibid., 426.

12. Burne-Jones to J. Severn, [27 November 1878], ibid., 424.

13. Ibid., 425. Burne-Jones does seem to have occasionally regarded Whistler's works with sincere admiration: he often remarked to his studio assistant, Thomas Rooke, that Whistler's "technique is so perfect, and through the whole of it there's not one bit of bad colour—that's saying much,"

although he could not abide Whistler's "conception of a woman" (*Burne-Jones Talking: His Conversations 1895–1898,* ed. Mary Lago [London: John Murray, 1982], 69). In 1892, Burne-Jones attended Whistler's exhibition at the Goupil Gallery, London, and D. C. Thomson, the gallery's director, wrote to Whistler in Paris that Burne-Jones had paid the price of admission, stayed a long time, examined every painting, and appeared pleased with what he saw, proving himself to be "a bigger minded man than one would have thought": "A small-minded man would not have come at all. A mean-minded man would have come and pretended he was of the same opinion [as formerly]." The exhibition catalogue, *Nocturnes, Marines, and Chevalet Pieces,* included quotations from Burne-Jones's testimony in *Whistler v. Ruskin.* Thomson said, "*On dit* for he did not say so openly that he is much vexed to see his old opinions come to daylight again!" (23 and 26 March 1892, typescripts, PWC 17).

14. Burne-Jones to Joan Severn, [27 November 1878], *Brantwood Diary of Ruskin,* 425.

15. Burne-Jones to Ruskin ("my dear oldie"), [26 November 1878], ibid., 424; Burne-Jones to Ruskin ("dearest St. C."), [November 1878], ibid., 426. Georgiana Burne-Jones later wrote that because the *Fors Clavigera* paragraph containing the libel was "practically a comparison between Mr. Whistler's work and Edward's own," Burne-Jones's position was particularly "annoying" (*Memorials of Edward Burne-Jones,* 2 vols. [London: Macmillan, 1909], 2:87).

16. Anderson Rose did, however, suggest the inevitable bias of Burne-Jones's testimony in his notes for W. C. Petheram: "Mr. Burne Jones is the artist who has for a long time been persistently and fulsomely flattered by Mr. Ruskin. He is Mr. Ruskin's most intimate friend" ([25 November 1878], PWC 27). Edward A. Parry later observed that "under the circumstances friendship and good taste ought to have prevented Ruskin from inviting Burne-Jones to appear for him as a witness" ("Whistler v. Ruskin," *Cornhill Magazine* 50 [January 1921]: 27).

17. "Whistler v. Ruskin," *Pall Mall Gazette,* 27 November 1878, 11.

18. Burne-Jones to Ruskin ("dearest St. C."), *Brantwood Diary of Ruskin,* 426; Burne-Jones to Joan Severn, [27 November 1878], ibid., 424.

19. Quoted in G. Burne-Jones, *Memorials of Burne-Jones,* 2:88.

20. Burne-Jones to George Howard, n.d., Castle Howard Archives, *Burne-Jones Talking,* 70 n. 3; Frances Horner, *Time Remembered* (London: Heinemann,

1933), 57. Had Burne-Jones been truly reluctant, agreeing to testify only under subpoena, defense counsel would undoubtedly have asked him, as they did Frith, whether he appeared in court against his will.

21. Burne-Jones to Ruskin ("my dear oldie"), [26 November 1878], *Brantwood Diary of Ruskin,* 424; Burne-Jones to Joan Severn, [27 November 1878], ibid. It is telling that Burne-Jones identified with Mr. Winkle, of whom Dickens says: "Lawyers hold that there are two kinds of particularly bad witnesses: a reluctant witness, and a too-willing witness; it was Mr. Winkle's fate to figure in both characters" (Charles Dickens, *The Posthumous Papers of the Pickwick Club* [1836–37; reprint, New York: Viking Penguin, 1987], 569). Evidently, Georgiana Burne-Jones had read from chapter 34 of *The Pickwick Papers,* "a full and faithful Report of the memorable Trial of Bardell against Pickwick." Burne-Jones, in his letter to Ruskin, also confessed to feeling like Tracy Tupman, another friend of Mr. Pickwick who was "driven to the verge of desperation by excessive badgering," since counsel "wouldnt give me a chance to stand up for you."

22. Ruskin to Burne-Jones, 28 November [1878], *Works of Ruskin,* 29:xxiv; Burne-Jones to Ruskin ("dearest St. C."), [November 1878], *Brantwood Diary of Ruskin,* 425.

23. Ruskin to Burne-Jones, 28 November [1878], *Works of Ruskin,* 29:xxiv.

24. Henry James, "London Pictures, 1882" (originally published as part of "London Pictures and London Plays," *Atlantic Monthly,* August 1882), in *The Painter's Eye: Notes and Essays on the Pictorial Arts by Henry James,* ed. John L. Sweeney (1956; reprint, Madison: University of Wisconsin Press, 1989), 205.

25. Whistler to "Atlas" [Edmund Yates], dated 26 March 1892, published in "What the World Says," *The World,* 30 March 1892, 22, and reprinted by Whistler as "Final Acknowledgements" in *The Gentle Art of Making Enemies,* new ed. (London: Heinemann, 1892), 333.

THE VALUE OF A NOCTURNE

1. "A Symphony in Bronze," *Examiner,* 30 November 1878, 1516. Roger B. Stein suggests that the American response to the trial was even less conclusive: "In the English court, Whistler had won a Pyrrhic victory; the American jury was hung" (*John Ruskin and Aesthetic Thought in America, 1840–1900* [Cambridge: Harvard University Press, 1967], 198).

2. "Minor Topics," *Art Journal* 18 (1879):18.

3. Whistler, *Whistler v. Ruskin: Art & Art Critics* (London: Chatto and Windus, 1878), 5; E. Wolferstan to Whistler, 27 November 1878, PWC 27; Smalley to Whistler, 27 November 1878, S 105, GUL.

4. "Whistler v. Ruskin," *Saturday Review,* 30 November 1878, 688. See also the leading article in the *Daily News,* 27 November 1878: "The critic contemplated Mr. Whistler's works, not merely as works of art, which he had a perfect right to do, but as wares exhibited for sale, which he had a less distinct right to do. . . . The business of the critic is to judge of the quality of a performance, not to appraise its pecuniary value."

5. Ruskin, *Academy Notes 1859* in *Works of Ruskin,* 14:257.

6. Codlin, "The Showman," *Penny Illustrated Paper,* 7 December 1878, 365.

7. "A Symphony in Bronze," *Examiner,* 30 November 1878, 1516.

8. Burne-Jones to George Howard, n.d., Castle Howard Archives, *Burne-Jones Talking,* 70 n.

9. Whistler's draft of a letter to "Atlas" [Edmund Yates] of *The World* ([March 1892], W 1102, GUL) recalled Burne-Jones's testimony: "Wherefore will we always remember the courage of Mr. Jones when, before a British Jury, in company with a Times Critic and a quasi Royal Auctioneer, he minutely appraized the work of a discussed confrère, and unrestrained by various and conventional deference to 'cloth' or etiquette, unflinchingly testified that the figure was high—'when you consider the amount of earnest work done for a smaller price.'"

10. Marcel Proust, an admirer of both Whistler and Ruskin, later remarked that even as Whistler was uttering his knowledge-of-a-lifetime speech in court, Ruskin was commending D. G. Rossetti on his rough sketches, "the expression of years of dreams, of love, and of experience," insisting that a drawing delivered "at one swoop" was more precious to him than one produced over six months' time. "On this level," Proust wrote, "the two stars strike the same point with a ray perhaps hostile, but identical. There is astronomical coincidence" (Proust to Marie Nordlinger, January 1904, *Letters of Marcel Proust,* trans. Mina Curtiss [New York: Random House, 1949], 93).

11. G. M. Hopkins to R. W. Dixon, 30 June 1886, *Correspondence of Hopkins and Dixon,* 135.

12. Of that "school of incapacity" (Whistler and his "impressionist" followers), Burne-Jones said on another occasion: "They do make atmosphere but they don't make anything else. They don't make beauty, they don't make design, they don't make idea, they don't make anything else but atmosphere and I don't think that's enough—I don't think it's very much" (16 December 1896, *Burne-Jones Talking,* 122; also quoted in G. Burne-Jones, *Memorials of Burne-Jones,* 2:188).

13. G. Burne-Jones, *Memorials of Burne-Jones,* 2:187–88.

14. "Whistler versus Ruskin," *Illustrated London News,* 30 November 1878, 518.

15. *Modern Painters,* vol. 5, in *Works of Ruskin,* 7:239.

16. Cf. W. M. Rossetti, "The Royal Academy Exhibition," *Fraser's Magazine* 71 (June 1865): 747: "That other painters encounter and conquer difficulties which Mr. Whistler eludes is true, and their credit mounts up accordingly; but we cannot exact, in one artist, conformity to the ways and means of another, while a contrary method is exuding, as it were, by instinct, from his very finger-ends."

17. Whistler, "Propositions—No. 2," in *Gentle Art* (1890), 115. The "Propositions" were originally the preface ("L'Envoie") to *"Notes"—"Harmonies"—"Nocturnes,"* the catalogue of an exhibition of Whistler's works at the Dowdeswell gallery in London, May 1884.

18. C., "Mr. Whistler's Painting: To the Editor of *The Times,*" 3 December 1878, 6.

19. *Modern Painters,* vol. 5, in *Works of Ruskin,* 7:236. Among the first to observe the virtue of incompleteness in Whistler's works had been Trovey Blackmore: "It is trivial, if it is not also idle and impertinent, to remark, as some observers have remarked, that these are merely studies, or rather exercises, in the treatment of certain elements which, combined with others, make up a picture. It is true, but what then? These works profess to be no more; nevertheless, they are examples of high and precious art, and they illustrate in a sublimated fashion certain peculiarly pictorial qualities of inestimable importance, but of which the English school is prodigiously ignorant" ("The Winter Exhibition: Dudley Gallery," *Athenaeum,* 30 October 1875, 581).

20. *Fors* 79 (July 1877), in *Works of Ruskin,* 29:160.

21. *Modern Painters,* vol. 5, ibid., 7:236.

22. A. Moore, "The Case of Whistler v. Ruskin: To the Editor of *The Echo,*" 29 November 1878, press-cutting book 2:31, GUL. Moore's letter was also published as "The Ruskin Libel Case: To the Editor of the *Standard,*" 30 November 1878, 5, and "Whistler v. Ruskin: To the Editor of the *Daily News,*" 30 November 1878, 2. Whistler reprinted part of Moore's letter in *Gentle Art* (1890), 16-17.

23. *Modern Painters,* vol. 5, in *Works of Ruskin,* 7:358n; vol. 1, 3:120n; vol. 5, 7:357n; vol. 3, 5:155, 168.

24. Ibid., vol. 3, 5:151–52.

25. "The Action for Libel Against Mr. Ruskin," *Daily News,* 27 November 1878, 2.

26. Leading article, *The Times,* 27 November 1878, 9; "The Value of a Reputation," *Referee,* 1 December 1878, press-cutting book 2:16, GUL.

FIGURES OF SPEECH

1. William Powell Frith, "Crazes in Art: 'Pre-Raphaelitism' and 'Impressionism,'" *Magazine of Art* 11 (1888): 191. *Referee* referred to Frith as the "apotheosis of matter-of-fact" ("The Value of a Reputation," 1 December 1878, press-cutting book 2:16, GUL).

2. Tom Taylor, *"The Railway Station," Painted by W. P. Frith, Esq., R.A.* (London: Henry Graves, 1865); Taylor's pamphlet could be purchased for sixpence in the exhibition room.

3. Cf. J. B. Yeats to his son, W. B. Yeats, 30 June 1921: "Whistler was a fine artist, but as a portrait painter a failure. His Carlyle is ridiculous, a mere conventional coat of a prophet, the picture merely a good decorative arrangement. . . . Whistler was too arrogant or rather too insolent. . . . So he had not the patience to become the student and lover of life itself. Carlyle the man was to him nothing except an occasion for an artistic picture" (*J. B. Yeats: Letters to His Son W. B. Yeats and Others, 1869–1922,* ed. Joseph Hone [London: Secker and Warburg, 1983], 281).

4. Albert Moore, suggestions for proofs, [24 November 1878], PWC 27.

5. W. M. Rossetti, "The Grosvenor Gallery (Second Notice)," *Academy,* 11 (26 May 1877): 467.

6. Leading article, *Morning Advertiser,* 27 November 1878, 4.

7. "The Grosvenor Gallery (Second Notice)," *Examiner,* 11 May 1878, 601.

8. "Flinging Paint in the Public's Face," *New York Times,* 15 December 1878, 6; "Whistler: A Fantasia in Criticism," *London,* 18 August 1877, 63, press-cutting book 2:10, GUL.

9. *Modern Painters,* vol. 3, in *Works of Ruskin,* 5:61.

10. Burne-Jones to George Howard, n.d., Castle Howard Archives, *Burne-Jones Talking,* 70 n. 3; Wills to Rose, received 29 November 1878, PWC 27.

11. W. M. Rossetti, "The Dudley Gallery," *Academy* 8 (30 October 1875): 462.

12. *Modern Painters,* vol. 3, in *Works of Ruskin,* 5:55n.

13. "The Royal Academy," *Saturday Review,* 12 May 1877, 580.

14. Oscar Wilde, "The Grosvenor Gallery," *Dublin University Magazine* 90 (July 1877): 124.

15. Walter Hamilton, *The Aesthetic Movement in England* (1882; reprint, New York: AMS Press, 1971), 28.

16. "Whistler: A Fantasia in Criticism," *London,* 18 August 1877, 63, press-cutting book 2:10, GUL; "A Symphony in Bronze," *Examiner,* 30 November 1878, 1516; leading article, *Standard,* 27 November 1878.

17. Paul Mantz, "Salon de 1863," *Gazette des Beaux-arts* (1863), 61: "Mais l'artiste américain a eu tort peut-être de semer de tons bleus le tapis sur lequel marche son charmant fantôme; il est là en dehors de son principe, et presque de son sujet, qui n'est pas autre chose que la symphonie du blanc."

18. "Celebrities at Home, No. XCII: Mr. James Whistler at Cheyne-walk," *The World,* 22 May 1878, 4.

19. "Passing Notes," *Echo,* 27 November 1878, 1.

20. J. J. Jarves, "Art of the Whistler Sort," *New York Times,* 12 January 1879, 10.

OBJETS D'ART

1. *Modern Painters,* vol. 3, in *Works of Ruskin,* 5:66.

2. Henry James, "The Picture Season in London, 1877," in *Painter's Eye,* 143; originally published in the *Galaxy,* August 1877.

3. "Celebrities at Home, No. XCII: Mr. James Whistler at Cheyne-walk," 4.

4. Leading article, *Daily News,* 27 November 1878, 4.

5. Henry James, "The Grosvenor Gallery, 1878," in *Painter's Eye,* 165; originally published as unsigned notes in the *Nation,* 23 May 1878.

6. Leading article, *Daily Telegraph,* 27 November 1878, 5; [Tom Taylor], "Winter Exhibitions: The Dudley," *The Times,* 2 December 1875, 4.

7. "History of the Week," *John Bull,* 30 November 1878, 773.

8. "High Art for Hire," *Fun,* 11 December 1878, 235.

9. Whistler to J. E. Boehm ("Mac"), 20 November [1878], B 98, GUL.

10. Burne-Jones to George Howard, n.d., Castle Howard Archives, *Burne-Jones Talking,* 70 n. 3: "I said all the good of it I could think of—but I believe Frith who put the powerful mind of our friend [William] Morris into words was nearest the truth."

11. "Whistler versus Ruskin," *Court Circular and Court News,* 30 November 1878, 461–62.

12. "Whistler v. Ruskin," *Pall Mall Gazette,* 27 November 1878, 11.

13. Whistler to Rose, received 21 November 1878, R 128, GUL. Whistler explained in an 1873 letter to George Lucas that the butterfly mark on his pictures and frames "does as a monogram for J.W." and was "characteristic I dare say you will say in more ways than one!" (postmarked 18 January 1873, bound in *A Catalogue of Blue and White Nankin Porcelain Forming the Collection of Sir Henry Thompson,* Rare Books Collection, Walters Art Gallery, Baltimore).

14. "General," *London,* 30 November 1878, 514, press-cutting book 2:18, GUL.

15. Henry James, "London Pictures," 208. See also F. R. Leyland to Whistler, 24 July 1877, L 129, GUL: "There is one consideration, indeed, which should have led you to form a more modest estimate of yourself, and that is your total failure to produce any serious work for so many years."

16. Henry James, "On Whistler and Ruskin, 1878," in *Painter's Eye,* 173; originally published as unsigned notes in the *Nation,* 19 December 1878.

17. "Latest of London Topics," *New York Times,* 15 December 1878, 4.

18. "A Symphony in Bronze," *Examiner,* 30 November 1878, 1516; "Paint-pot v. Ink-pot," *Truth* 4 (5 December 1878): 649.

19. "Paint-pot v. Ink-pot," 649. See also "Whistler v. Ruskin," *London Express,* 30 November 1878, 344: "It is the fashion to adore bric-a-brac in any form, from a china dish only fit for a kitchen dresser, to a 'nocturne' in blue or black, or anything else, so long as it is unintelligible. . . . Whistler, then, is the fashion just now."

20. "Whistler v. Ruskin," *London Express,* 30 November, 344.

21. "Celebrities at Home, No. XCII: Mr. James Whistler at Cheyne-walk," 4.

22. Leading article, *Morning Advertiser,* 27 November 1878, 4.

23. *Fors* 79 (July 1877), in *Works of Ruskin,* 29:160.

24. Leading article, *Coming Events & Weekly Remembrancer,* 30 November 1878, 11.

25. Leading article, *Standard,* 27 November 1878; "Whistler versus Ruskin," *Illustrated London News,* 30 November 1878, 518; leading article, *The Times,* 27 November 1878, 9.

26. Leading article, *Morning Advertiser,* 27 November 1878, 4.

ART AND ART CRITICS

1. Whistler to Rose, received 17 February 1879, PWC 4.

2. Linley Sambourne to Whistler, 1 December 1878, S 11, GUL.

3. Whistler to Linley Sambourne, dated 3 December 1878, published in "What the World Says," *The World,* 11 December 1878, 14. Manuscript drafts of the letter are in GUL (S 12 and S 13), together with a copy of the final version (S 14); there is also a copy of the letter (undated) in PWC 2. The letter is reprinted by Whistler as "Professor Ruskin's Group," in *Gentle Art* (1890), 20.

4. Alan Cole, typescript of diary extracts, 22 December 1878, PWC 281. Whistler's longhand copy of the text is dated 1 December (W 750, GUL).

5. T. R. Way, *Memories of James McNeill Whistler* (New York: John Lane, 1912), 33. After the publication of *The Gentle Art* in 1890, Whistler read aloud the text of *Art & Art Critics,* together with his rendition of the trial, to a company that included Sidney Starr and Albert Moore (Sidney Starr, "Personal Recollections of Whistler," *Atlantic Monthly* [Boston] 101 [April 1908]: 535).

6. Henry James, "On Art-criticism and Whistler, 1879" in *Painter's Eye,* 175, originally published as an unsigned note in the *Nation,* 13 February 1879; Whistler to Rose, received 7 January 1879, and 15 January 1879, PWC 4.

7. Whistler to [Dr. Harold Bird], [late December 1878/early January 1879], B 79, GUL; Whistler to Rose, received 7 January 1879, and 15 January 1879, PWC 4. The fourth edition was out by 17 January: see "Notes on Current Events" in *British Architect,* 17 January 1879, 24; and G. A. S[ala], "Echoes of the Week," *Illustrated London News,* 18 January 1879, 58. Henry James mentioned in his review of 13 February 1879 that the pamphlet was in its sixth edition.

8. Way, *Memories of Whistler,* 33; "A 'Bravura' in Brown Paper," *Examiner,* 11 January 1879, 44. A writer for the *Academy* described it as "a small pamphlet of scarcely thirteen pages, in a brown paper wrapper with a strange device, probably designed by the author" ("*Whistler v. Ruskin: Art and Art Critics," Academy* 15 [25 January 1879]: 85).

9. Whistler to Rose, received 30 November 1878, PWC 4.

10. Albert Moore to Whistler, 30 January 1885, M 438, GUL.

11. Whistler to J. E. Boehm ("Mac"), 20 November [1878], B 98, GUL.

12. Whistler to Rose, received 30 November 1878, PWC 4; Whistler, *Art & Art Critics,* 5.

13. Whistler, *Art & Art Critics,* 6.

14. [Harry Quilter], "Mr. Whistler's Revenge," *Spectator,* 52 (25 January 1879): 120.

15. Whistler, *Art & Art Critics,* 7–8.

16. Rasper, "Balaam's Ass," *Vanity Fair,* 11 January 1879, 26-27, reprinted by Whistler in *Gentle Art* (1890), 41–42; Whistler to *Vanity Fair,* 11 January [1879], V 20, GUL, published in *Vanity Fair,* 18 January 1879, and reprinted by Whistler as "The Point Acknowledged," in *Gentle Art* (1890), 43.

17. Whistler to George A. Lucas, 11 January 1879, typescript, PWC 13.

18. "A 'Bravura' in Brown Paper," 445. See also "'Whistler v. Ruskin' Again," *Builder,* 18 January 1879, 68: "The writer has largely indulged in that very fault of personality and strong language for the use of which he brought his action against Mr. Ruskin; so that the whole thing is a scolding match on both sides."

19. [Quilter], "Mr. Whistler's Revenge," 119; Whistler, *Art & Art Critics,* 15 and 8.

20. "Mr. Whistler's Last Word," *Architect* 21 (11 January 1879): 21.

21. "Mr. Whistler's Appeal to the Public," *Art Journal* 98 (1879): 64. On Ruskin's talents as an artist, see, for example, [Quilter], "Mr. Whistler's Revenge," 120: "This is not the place to enter upon a detailed description of the merits of Mr. Ruskin's works [in drawing and watercolor] in general; suffice it to say, that even at the early period . . . it was of an almost matchless delicacy and skill, and erred almost entirely on the side of over-refinement and labour. That the artist confined his work to that which helped him to illustrate the work of others, rather than to create an artistic reputation for himself, does not in the least detract from his skill, and the last person to blame him for doing so should be one of that profession to whose help he has devoted his life."

22. Fresco, "Art Sayings and Doings," *Echo,* 17 January 1879, 4.

23. Henry James, "On Art-criticism and Whistler," 175; "Mr. Whistler's Last Word," *Architect* 21 (11 January 1879): 21.

24. "A 'Bravura' in Brown Paper," 44.

25. Whistler to George Lucas, 11 January 1879, typescript, PWC 13.

26. Whistler, *Art & Art Critics,* 10, 12–13. Whistler cites Taylor's article as having been published 6 June 1874, but there is no review by Taylor in that issue of *The Times;* as he confessed in court, Whistler was not good with dates.

27. Tom Taylor to Whistler, 6 January 1879, published in *The World,* 15 January 1879, and reprinted by Whistler as "The Art Critic of the 'Times'" in *Gentle Art* (1890), 35–36. The original letter is in GUL (T 5).

28. Whistler to George Lucas, [ca. 15 January 1879], bound in *Catalogue of Blue and White,* Rare Books Collection, Walters Art Gallery, Baltimore. Although the letter is bound with an envelope postmarked 30 December 1878, references to the published Taylor correspondence suggest a later date.

29. Whistler to Tom Taylor, 8 January 1879, published in *The World,* 15 January 1879, and reprinted by Whistler as "The Position" in *Gentle Art* (1890), 37. A draft of the letter signed with a barb-tailed butterfly is in GUL (T 7).

30. Tom Taylor to Whistler, 9 January 1879, published in *The World,* 15 January 1879, and reprinted by Whistler as "Serious Sarcasm" in *Gentle Art*

(1890), 38 (the original letter is in GUL [T 6]); Whistler to Tom Taylor, 10 January 1879, published in *The World,* 15 January 1879, and reprinted as "Final," *Gentle Art* (1890), 39 (a draft of the letter signed with a barb-tailed butterfly is in GUL [T 9]).

31. Whistler to George Lucas, ca. 15 January 1879, bound in *Catalogue of Blue and White,* Rare Books Collection, Walters Art Gallery, Baltimore.

MATTERS OF OPINION

1. Whistler, *Art & Art Critics,* 14.

2. Henry James, "On Art-criticism and Whistler," 175.

3. Whistler, *Art & Art Critics,* 11.

4. Whistler to J. E. Boehm ("Mac"), 20 November [1878], B 98, GUL.

5. Whistler, *Art & Art Critics,* 12.

6. Ibid., 16–17. Ruskin was in fact able to perform what he preached, if not entirely to his satisfaction: he was a proficient draftsman and his works in watercolor, which Moore mentioned in cross-examination, were well known. According to Arthur Severn, Ruskin also executed some paintings in oil (*The Professor,* 117–18 and 118–19nn), but none are extant. Concerning Ruskin's aversion to painting in oils, see Kristine Ottesen Garrigan, *Ruskin on Architecture: His Thought and Influence* (Madison: University of Wisconsin Press, 1973), 178.

7. Albert Moore, suggestions for proof, [24 November 1878], PWC 27: "Mr. R. has himself pointed out the superiority of a late picture by Turner to his early & more carefully detailed sea pieces, in that the former suggested wetness in the water, which impression was wanting in the latter—a benighted critic of the day described this picture as soapsuds & whitewash." Moore alludes to Ruskin's remarks on Turner's *Snow Storm* in *Modern Painters,* vol. 1: "Suppose the effect of the first sunbeam sent from above to show this annihilation to itself, and you have the sea picture of the Academy, 1842, the Snowstorm, one of the very grandest statements of sea-motion, mist, and light, that has ever been put on canvas, even by Turner" (*Works of Ruskin,* 3:570–71); Moore also refers to an anecdote recounted in Ruskin's *Notes on the Turner Gallery at Marlborough House, 1856* regarding the criticism of the painting as "soapsuds and whitewash" (ibid., 13:161). The idea of mentioning Turner could also have come from Algernon Graves, who suggested that

he be asked whether "Turner ever painted anything of the Nocturne class" (suggestions for proof [18 November 1878], PWC 27).

8. See Anderson Rose, draft for Parry's closing argument, [25 November 1878], PWC 27: "It has been attempted to hold up Mr. Whistler's pictures as absurdities, and to fasten on him the contemptuous epithet of 'eccentric.' Now it is well known that the idol of Mr. Ruskin's worship is Turner, many of whose pictures are almost incomprehensible to the general public, and who is looked upon by the artists and critics of the Continent, as more than eccentric—almost as insane. Nevertheless Turner is undoubtedly a good artist, only he does not please those who are not familiar with his manner of painting, and to many people who cannot appreciate his technical merits, some of his pictures appear nothing more than a meaningless confusion of colour. Mr. Ruskin has presented to the Fitzwilliam Museum at Cambridge twenty of Turner's watercolours which he looks upon as priceless treasures. Many of these are mere puzzles in which no subject can be distinguished, till the spectator places himself at a considerable distance when some faint intention may be guessed at. Yet to many art lovers these . . . afford the greatest delight."

9. Reay, "London," Hartford (Conn.) *Courant,* 14 December 1878, press-cutting book 3:9, GUL.

10. "Whistler v. Ruskin," *Saturday Review,* 30 November 1878, 687.

11. "Passing Notes," *Echo,* 27 November 1878, 1.

12. Whistler, *Art & Art Critics,* 10–11.

13. "'Whistler v. Ruskin' Again," *Builder,* 18 January 1879, 68; *Sketch: An Illustrated Miscellany of Art, Music, the Drama, Society and the Belles Lettres,* 25 January 1879, press-cutting book 3:23, GUL.

14. Severn, *The Professor,* 115. The confusion may have been occasioned by the gold cap and embroidery on the doge's cloak, which, in the dark courtroom, might have appeared similar to the golden cascade of fireworks in Whistler's *Nocturne in Black and Gold.* According to "Atlas" [Edmund Yates] of *The World,* "Some art-critics (not professional) were standing in the gangway when the great Titian was brought to be produced before the jury. 'Faugh!' said they, with a strong air of disdain; 'here is another of those rubbishy Whistlers!'" ("What the World Says," *The World,* 4 December 1878, 11). The Pennells also relate that the jury mistook the Titian for a Whistler and "would have none of it" (*Life of Whistler* [1908], 1:241); Rose makes the

implausible suggestion that the mistake had been Burne-Jones's: "Ruskin's witness saw the Titian and began to abuse it thinking it was one of Whistler's" (notes on the back of a manuscript menu by Whistler dated 3 December [1878], PWC 4).

15. A. Moore, "Whistler v. Ruskin."

16. W. Hamilton, *Aesthetic Movement,* 29.

17. Arnold Hauser, *The Philosophy of Art History* (New York: Knopf, 1959), 336.

18. Algernon Graves to Whistler, 26 November 1878, G 164, GUL. Whistler also heard from Samuel P. Avery, the New York dealer, who said that he wasn't sure he could sell a nocturne for two hundred guineas, but that an exhibition would certainly draw a number of shillings. He added that there had been two separate applications for Whistler's self-portrait—*Portrait of Whistler with a Hat* (1857-58; FGA), which Avery had purchased in 1871—"while no one has asked for Ruskin's hat, or even his head!" (2 January [1879], A 218, GUL).

19. Whistler to Rose, received 6 December 1878, PWC 4.

CONSEQUENCES AND COSTS

1. One indication that Whistler freely distributed the pamphlets is that he sent a copy to George Lucas in Paris, informing Lucas in a letter of 7 January 1879 that it was in the mail; having evidently forgotten that he had, Whistler sent another a few days later (letter, 7 January [1879], and letter postmarked 11 January 1879, BMA). Whistler also sent a copy of the pamphlet, with enclosures of press cuttings relating to the lawsuit, to the U. S. Military Academy, inscribed, "From an old cadet whose pride is to remember his West Point days" (E. W. Holden, Librarian, to Colonel C. W. Larned, n.d., PWC 303).

2. W. M. Rossetti to Whistler, 27 January [1879], R 144, GUL.

3. W. M. Rossetti, "Mr. Palgrave and Unprofessional Criticisms on Art," in *Fine Art, Chiefly Contemporary: Notices Re-printed, with Revisions* (London: Macmillan, 1867), 326, 330. Rossetti conceded that after "well-qualified professionals" (practicing artists), the best critics are those possessed of "some vividness of personal perception, or fervour of mind, or brilliancy or discursiveness of illustrative power"—of whom the greatest example was Ruskin:

"The time may come when Mr. Ruskin's opinions shall have been forgotten, and many of his theories exploded; but, long after that, his influence will be vital and beneficial, and his name sonorous in those mouths which ratify praise" (327). The essay is a review of Francis Turner Palgrave's *Essays on Art* (London: Macmillan, 1866), a collection of previously published art reviews, many from the *Saturday Review;* Palgrave's book appears to have provided the model for Rossetti's *Fine Art.*

In "Style, Subject-matter, and Successes in Art," an article originally published in *Fraser's Magazine,* 1864, and reprinted in *Fine Art,* Rossetti made the same argument: "We are the first to concede to any objector that, whether an unprofessional opinion is in fact right or wrong, there is no reason why the reader or public should yield any prompt or implicit credence to it: that is a deference due only to a professional opinion—the witness of a man who can *do* the sort of thing he is talking about, and do it well. The answer therefore is that professional people, as a class,—and some unprofessional people as well,—are qualified to apply the test [of the merits of a work of art]: but that the professional are always to be believed in preference, when the verdicts differ; though it is just consistent with possibility that the unprofessional are in fact right, and will be so proved in the long run" (38–39).

4. W. M. Rossetti to Whistler, 27 January [1879], R 144, GUL. Roger Peattie provides an account of Rossetti's severance from the *Academy* in "William Michael Rossetti's Contributions to the *Athenaeum,*" *Victorian Periodicals Review* 23 (Winter 1990): 148–55.

5. J. Comyns Carr to Whistler, 27 November 1878, PWC 4.

6. J. Comyns Carr to Whistler, [January 1879], C 43, GUL.

7. Sidney Colvin, "Art and Criticism," *Fortnightly Review,* 1 August 1879, 210.

8. Whistler to J. Comyns Carr, [January 1879], C 44, GUL; *"Whistler v. Ruskin: Art and Art Critics," Academy* 15 (25 January 1879): 85. The critique continues: "Whatever may be Mr. Whistler's talents and capabilities as an artist, he seems unable to write plain English and generally ignorant of the subjects of which he treats or to which he alludes. He has evidently managed to pick up at all events a certain smattering of French while frequenting the Parisian *ateliers;* but we do not think that a Frenchman would talk of journals winking at a *fin mot;* and we are certain that mathematics in France as

elsewhere ranks among the Sciences and not, as Mr. Whistler seems to think, among the Arts."

9. J. Comyns Carr to Whistler, 27 November 1878, PWC 4; "Stray Leaves," *Examiner,* 11 January 1879, 60.

10. G. A. S[ala], "Echoes of the Week," *Illustrated London News,* 14 December 1878, 559.

11. Burne-Jones to Ruskin ("dearest St. C."), [November 1878], *Brantwood Diary of Ruskin,* 425; Pennell and Pennell, *Life of Whistler* (1908), 1:244–45.

12. The article quoted in the circular had been published in the *Evening Standard,* 30 November 1878, 4.

13. Pennell and Pennell, *Life of Whistler* (1908), 1:245; "Mr. Ruskin's Costs in the Late Action of Whistler v. Ruskin," *Athenaeum,* 14 December 1878, 1. The total bill was £386.12.4.

14. Marcus B. Huish to Ruskin, 28 April 1879, *Brantwood Diary of Ruskin,* 462.

15. "The Guild of St. George: Master's Report, 1885," in *Works of Ruskin,* 30:95–96.

16. D. G. Rossetti to William Davis, 27 November 1878, *Letters of Dante Gabriel Rossetti,* ed. Oswald Doughty and John Robert Wahl, 4 vols. (Oxford: Clarendon Press, 1967), 4:1613–14.

17. Whistler to William Graham, [after 23 July 1877], G 150, GUL.

18. According to Gustav Kobbé, "the first effect of Ruskin's onslaught was to decrease the sales, none too large, of Whistler's pictures" ("An Epoch Making Picture," *Lotus* [Babylon, N.Y.] [April 1910]: 8). James Dearden asserts that the diminution of Whistler's business was due to Ruskin: "Whistler, who had been 'knocking off Nocturnes' at 200 guineas each, suddenly found his market vastly diminished. The picture-buying public had heard Ruskin's words—and within six months, Whistler was bankrupt" (Severn, *The Professor,* 114n). On the other hand, a contemporary commentator, William C. Brownell, argued that "the general opinion of Mr. Whistler's work cannot be said to have been affected by" Ruskin's criticism ("Whistler in Painting and Etching," *Scribner's Monthly* [New York] 18 [August 1879]: 482).

19. The letter from Whistler to George Lucas that initiates the elaborate deception is undated but probably arrived in the envelope postmarked 30

December 1878, which in bound with a letter to which it obviously does not belong in Lucas's copy of *Catalogue of Blue and White,* Rare Books Division, Walters Art Gallery, Baltimore. The correspondence continues with letters from Whistler dated 7 January and postmarked 11 and 14 January, 1879, BMA. The final letter, apparently written on or about January 15, is the one in the *Catalogue of Blue and White.* See also *The Diary of George A. Lucas: An American Art Agent in Paris,* 1857–1909, 2 vols., ed. Lilian M. C. Randall (Princeton: Princeton University Press, 1979), entries for 2–14 January 1879. Maud gave birth to a daughter she named Maud McNeill Whistler Franklin on 13 February: see Margaret F. McDonald, "Maud Franklin," in *James McNeill Whistler: A Reexamination,* ed. Ruth E. Fine, Studies in the History of Art, vol. 19 (Washington, D.C.: National Gallery of Art, 1987), 23.

20. Whistler to Rose, received 7 January 1879, PWC 4.

21. Whistler to Rose, [ca. 15 January 1879], PWC 4; folder of outstanding accounts leading to Whistler's bankruptcy, PWC 27.

22. J. Comyns Carr to Whistler, 27 November 1878, PWC 4.

23. Burne-Jones to Ruskin ("dearest St. C."), [November 1878], *Brantwood Diary of Ruskin,* 426. T. R. Way also believed that Rose, Whistler's "staunch friend and supporter," had met the expenses of the trial (*Memories of Whistler,* 33). It should be noted that when Messrs. Dodson and Fogg failed to procure costs from Mr. Pickwick, they sent the plaintiff, Mrs. Bardell, to debtor's prison.

24. By a writ served 21 March 1879, Rose claimed from Whistler £261.10.2 "for fees for work done and money expended as a Solicitor between the 28th July 1877 and the 30th November 1878 both inclusive"; because Whistler failed to appear in court, Rose was given a "Judgment in Default of Appearance in case of Liquidated Demand" on March 31, which compelled Whistler to pay Rose the full amount he owed, plus costs. A second writ was served April 10, claiming £206.10.7 for further legal fees and unpaid loans made between February 1863 and April 1879, with the same result (judgment given 18 April 1879). The papers pertaining to *Rose v. Whistler* are in PWC 26.

25. Whistler to Rose, received 30 November 1878, PWC 4; Whistler enclosed the letter from J. Comyns Carr dated 27 November 1878.

26. "Latest of London Topics," *New York Times,* 15 December 1878, 4. Joseph Middleton Jopling wrote his wife, Louise, that he had not heard of a movement to defray Whistler's costs like the one initiated by the Fine Art Society for Ruskin (Louise Jopling, *Twenty Years of My Life, 1867 to 1897* [New York: Dodd, Mead and Co., 1925], 127).

27. G. A. S[ala], "Echoes of the Week," *Illustrated London News,* 14 December 1878, 559; Pennell and Pennell, *Life of Whistler* (1908), 1:245; *Some Reminiscences of William Michael Rossetti,* 2 vols. (New York: Scribner's, 1906), 2:320. The Pennells suggest that J. P. Heseltine opened the fund, but he appears to have made his contribution to Whistler privately. *L'Art; revue hebdomadaire illustrée* was published in Paris beginning in 1875; J. Comyns Carr was the London editor.

28. Anderson Rose, manuscript draft of a circular, PWC 27.

29. Ibid.

30. Robert H. Getscher, *Whistler and Venice,* Ph.D. diss., Western Reserve University, 1971, 18. Marcus B. Huish, the director, had nevertheless placed an order on 2 December 1877, on behalf of the society, for two sets of Whistler's proposed Venetian etchings; Getscher includes a list of subscribers (8 n. 5).

31. Rose to Whistler, 29 November 1878, R 129, GUL.

32. *Exhibition: The Memoirs of Oliver Brown* (London: Evelyn, Adams and Mackay, 1968), 2.

33. Katharine A. Lochnan, *The Etchings of James McNeill Whistler* (New Haven: Yale University Press, 1984), 178–79.

34. Whistler to Anna McNeill Whistler, [ca. 26 September 1878], typescript, PWC 19.

35. Ibid. Whistler mentioned his plans to go to Venice in an undated letter to Frances Leyland, apparently written in the summer of 1876, in which he expressed the fear that Lionel Robinson would grow impatient and leave without him (PWC 2); on 29 July, the *Academy* announced that Whistler proposed to go to Venice to produce a set of twenty etchings, and in a letter of 17 August that mentioned Whistler's preliminary decorations in what would soon become the Peacock Room, F. R. Leyland referred to Whistler's planned journey (L 105, GUL); at the beginning of September, Whistler sent out prospectuses for "Venice—by Whistler," and the venture was again an-

nounced in the *Academy* on 2 September 1876. See Getscher, *Whistler and Venice,* 5–12, and Lochnan, *Etchings of Whistler,* 181, 298 n. 1.

36. *Diary of Lucas,* entries for 18–27 April 1879.

37. "The Bankruptcy Act 1869 re. James A. McN. Whistler," petition filed 9 May 1879 enclosed in H. H. Hammond to Freer Gallery of Art, 1 August 1953, Whistler 291, FGA/Arthur M. Sackler Gallery Archives. Hammond (b. 1869), who had admired Whistler during his lifetime and been among the mourners at his funeral, sent the Freer Gallery a manuscript copy of Whistler's bankruptcy papers; he had made the copy while working for the Bankruptcy Court in London and thought it would disprove the "unkind, in fact, baseless statement . . . that Leyland was the cause of Whistler's Bankruptcy and had bought up the debts in order to ruin him."

38. Maud Franklin to George Lucas, [3 May 1879], BMA; *Academy,* 18 July 1879, quoted in Getscher 1970, 28.

39. Whistler to Marcus B. Huish, 13 August 1879, quoted in Getscher, *Whistler and Venice,* 25; *Exhibition: Memoirs of Brown,* 2; Lochnan, *Etchings of Whistler,* 182. Whistler wrote George Lucas that he was going to Italy "to do the long promised set of etchings and have engaged to finish them by the 20th Dec" (ca. 13 September 1879, BMA).

40. Alan Cole, typescript of diary extracts, 7 September 1879, PWC 281. The liquidation sale, conducted by Sotheby, Wilkinson & Hodge, was held on 12 and 13 February 1880: see *Catalogue of Porcelain and Other Works of Art and Objects of Antiquity, the Property of J. A. M. Whistler (Sold in Liquidation by Order of the Trustees* (London: Sotheby, Wilkinson and Hodge, 1880).

41. *The Gold Scab,* listed as no. 88 in the liquidation catalogue, was described as "a satirical painting of a gentleman, styled 'The Creditor,' by Whistler," and was purchased by Walter Dowdeswell for £12.12. Alan Cole saw the "painting of a demoniacal Leyland playing piano—Ye gold scab—with an irruption of *Frilthy* Lucre—forcible piece of weird decoration—hideous—displaying bitter animus" on 8 September 1879 (diary extracts). Kirk Savage gives an account of the painting in "'A forcible piece of weird decoration': Whistler and *The Gold Scab,*" *Smithsonian Studies in American Art* 4 (Spring 1990): 41–53.

42. Whistler left Paris 18 September; Maud Franklin remained until 18 October, arriving in Venice by 23 October, when she wrote Lucas, "Oh isnt this a lovely place, and such a lovely day too" (BMA).

EPILOGUE

1. *Modern Painters,* vol. 2, rearranged edition (1883), in *Works of Ruskin,* 4:35n.

2. "Mr. Whistler's 'Ten O'Clock'" (1885), in *Gentle Art* (1890), 131–59.

SELECT BIBLIOGRAPHY

Because nearly every published work related to either Whistler or Ruskin includes some reference to the trial, this bibliography is limited to publications specifically related to Whistler v. Ruskin. *Citations for other sources consulted may be found in the notes. Unless otherwise stated, all periodicals are published in London.*

For an annotated Whistler bibliography, see Robert H. Getscher and Paul G. Marks, James McNeill Whistler and John Singer Sargent: Two Annotated Bibliographies *(New York: Garland, 1986). For a more complete listing of newspaper and periodical articles relevant to* Whistler v. Ruskin, *see Catherine Carter Goebel,* Arrangement in Black and White: The Making of a Whistler Legend, *2 vols., Ph.D. diss., Northwestern University, 1988.*

MANUSCRIPT COLLECTIONS

Baltimore Museum of Art, Maryland: The George A. Lucas Collection of the Maryland Institute, College of Art, on indefinite loan to the Baltimore Museum of Art.

Freer Gallery of Art, Washington, D.C.: Charles Lang Freer Papers, Freer Gallery of Art/Arthur M. Sackler Gallery Archives, Smithsonian Institution.

Glasgow University Library, Scotland: The James McNeill Whistler Papers, comprising the Rosalind Birnie Philip Papers and the Joseph W. Revillon Papers.

Library of Congress, Manuscripts Division, Washington, D.C.: The Pennell-Whistler Collection of the Papers of Joseph Pennell, Elizabeth Robins Pennell, and James A. McNeill Whistler.

PUBLISHED MATERIAL

Adams, Laurie. "The Brush or the Pen?" In *Art on Trial: From Whistler to Rothko.* New York: Walker and Co., 1976.

Beatty, Michael. "A Pot of Paint in the Public's Face: Ruskin's Censure of Whistler Reconsidered." *English Studies in Africa: A Journal of the Humanities* 30 (1987): 27–41.

Beaufort, Madeleine. "The Art of Letters: Whistling at One's Ruskin." *Confrontation: A Literary Journal of Long Island University* 18 (Spring/Summer 1979): 58–63.

Boughton, George H. "A Few of the Various Whistlers I Have Known." *International Studio* (New York) 21 (January 1904): 208–18. First published in *Studio* 30 (December 1903): 208–18.

Craven, David. "Ruskin vs. Whistler: The Case Against Capitalist Art." *Art Journal* (New York) 37 (Winter 1977–78): 139–43.

Earland, Ada. "Whistler and His Lawsuit." In *Ruskin and His Circle.* 1910. Reprint, New York: AMS Press, 1971.

Fennell, Francis L. "The Verdict in Whistler v. Ruskin." *Victorian Newsletter* (New York) (Fall 1971): 17–21.

Fine Art Society. *Whistler v. Ruskin: Mr. Ruskin's Costs.* [London]: Fine Art Society, 1878.

Frith, William Powell. "Turner's 'Snowstorm': To the Editor of The Times." *The Times,* 2 December 1878, 8.

Hyde, H. Montgomery. "An Artist's Reputation (Whistler v. Ruskin)." In *Their Good Names: Twelve Cases of Libel and Slander.* London: Hamish Hamilton, 1970.

James, Henry. "On Whistler and Ruskin, 1878." In *The Painter's Eye: Notes and Essays on the Pictorial Arts by Henry James.* Edited by John L. Sweeney. 1956. Reprint, Madison: University of Wisconsin Press, 1989. First published as an unsigned note in *The Nation* (New York), 19 December 1878. Reprinted as "Contemporary Notes on Whistler vs. Ruskin." In *Views and Reviews.* Edited by Le Roy Phillips. Boston: Ball Publishing Co., 1908.

Kobbé, Gustav. "An Epoch-making Picture: Nocturne in Black and Gold—The Falling Rocket." *Lotus* (Babylon, N.Y.) (April 1910): 7–26.

Merrill, Linda. "The Diffusion of Aesthetic Taste: Whistler and the Popularization of Aestheticism, 1875–1885." Ph.D. diss., University of London, 1985.

Moore, Albert. "Whistler v. Ruskin: To the Editor of the Daily News." *Daily News,* 30 November 1878, 2.

Parry, His Honour Judge [Edward A.]. "Whistler v. Ruskin." *Cornhill Magazine* 50 (January 1921): 21–33. Subsequently published as "Whistler v. Ruskin: An Attorney's Story of a Famous Trial." *Living Age* (New York) 21 (February 1921): 346–53.

Pennell, Elizabeth R., and Joseph Pennell. "The Trial: The Year Eighteen Seventy-eight." In *The Life of James McNeill Whistler,* 2 vols. Philadelphia: Lippincott, 1908.

———. "Appendix III: The Papers in the Whistler v. Ruskin Action." In *The Whistler Journal.* Philadelphia: Lippincott, 1921.

Richardson, E. P. "Nocturne in Black and Gold: The Falling Rocket by Whistler." *Art Quarterly* (Detroit) 10 (Winter 1947): 3–11.

Ruskin, John. "Letter 79: Life Guards of New Life." *Fors Clavigera: Letters to the Workmen and Labourers of Great Britain* 7 (July 1877). In *The Works of John Ruskin.* Edited by E. T. Cook and Alexander Wedderburn, 29:146–69. Library Edition, 39 vols. London: George Allen, 1903–12.

———. "My Own Article on Whistler." In *The Works of John Ruskin.* Edited by E. T. Cook and Alexander Wedderburn, 29:585–97. Library Edition, 39 vols. London: George Allen, 1903–12.

Senzoku, Nobuyuki. "Hoisurā to Rasukin: Soshō Jiken to Sono Shūhen" (*Whistler v. Ruskin*: The trial and its background). In *James McNeill Whistler.* Edited by Denys Sutton, 41–48. [Tokyo]: Yomiuri Shimbun, 1987.

Sizeranne, Robert de la. "Whistler, Ruskin, et l'impressionnisme." *La Revue de l'art ancien et moderne* (Paris) 14 (December 1903): 433–50.

West, Shearer. "Tom Taylor, William Powell Frith, and the British School of Art." *Victorian Studies* (Indiana University) 33 (Winter 1990): 307–26.

Whistler, James A. McNeill. *Whistler v. Ruskin: Art and Art Critics.* London: Chatto and Windus, 1878. Subsequently reprinted by Whistler in *The Gentle Art of Making Enemies,* 21–34. London: William Heinemann, 1890.

———. "The Action." In *The Gentle Art of Making Enemies,* 1–20. London: William Heinemann, 1890.

"Whistler vs. Ruskin," *Chautauquan* (Chautauqua, N.Y.) 50 (April 1908): 289–95.

INDEX

Page numbers of illustrations are in italics.